CITY OF ECHOES

CITY OF ECHOES

A NEW HISTORY OF ROME, ITS POPES, AND ITS PEOPLE

JESSICA WÄRNBERG

PEGASUS BOOKS
NEW YORK LONDON

For KGW

CITY OF ECHOES

Pegasus Books, Ltd.
148 West 37th Street, 13th Floor
New York, NY 10018

Copyright © 2023 by Jessica Wärnberg

First Pegasus Books cloth edition September 2023

ISBN: 978-1-63936-521-0

10 9 8 7 6 5 4 3 2 1

Printed in the United States of America
Distributed by Simon & Schuster
www.pegasusbooks.com

Contents

Map vi

Prologue: City of Echoes I

PART 1: BECOMING ROME

Chapter 1   In the Footsteps of Peter 9

Chapter 2   'You have won, Galilean': The Rise of
Christian Rome 33

PART 2: TURBULENT PRIESTS

Chapter 3   Crowned on the Grave of Empire 61

Chapter 4   Holy Rome: Relics, Invaders and the
Politics of Power 85

Chapter 5   Between Avignon, Babylon and Rome 113

PART 3: THE RISE AND FALL OF THE IMPERIAL PAPACY

Chapter 6   Echoes of the Ancients: The Renaissance
of Papal Rome 141

Chapter 7   Theatre of the World 173

Chapter 8   Inquisitors, the Ghetto and Ecstatic Saints 199

PART 4: WRESTLING WITH MODERNITY

Chapter 9   From the Sublime to the Pathetic:
Eighteenth-century Rome 229

Chapter 10   *Non possumus*: Popes of Rome in the Age of
Revolutions 257

Chapter 11   A Tale of Two Cities: Rome and the Vatican 293

Notes 327

Selected Bibliography 383

Timeline 419

Papal Timeline 425

Acknowledgements 431

Index 433

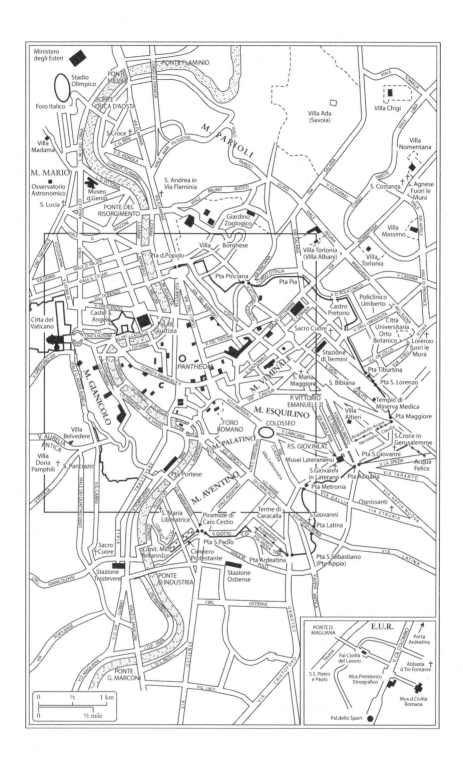

Prologue: City of Echoes

Rome is the city of echoes, the city of illusions, and the city of yearning.

Giotto di Bondone

Pacing through empty streets just after dawn, two young men slip into Santa Maria in Traspontina, a sixteenth-century church on the approach to Saint Peter's Basilica in Rome. The men are strangers in the city. Not Romans nor even Italians but Austrian Catholics, visiting Rome on a singular, grave mission. In their view, they have come to Rome to save Santa Maria in Traspontina from desecration: they have come to defend the holy Catholic faith. On a recent trip to the city, one of the men had been disturbed to discover wooden statues to a naked fertility goddess in the church, alongside altars to Saint John and the Virgin Mary, Mother of God. What's more, he could not appeal to Catholic authorities to stop what he saw as an act of sacrilege for the statues had been venerated in the Vatican Gardens in the presence of the pope himself.

Entering the silent church, the men genuflect solemnly in front of the high altar before sweeping into the side chapels to scoop up the sculptures and carry them away. Their arms full, they flee, running a few minutes to the Ponte Sant'Angelo, a bridge built by the emperor Hadrian and later adorned with angels bearing the instruments of the crucifixion of Christ. Standing beneath the angel that holds the cross itself, the men hurl the statues into the dark depths of the River Tiber. Their mission accomplished, the sun risen, they flee the scene.

Discovering the theft, the Carmelites who run the church raise the alarm. News of the incident divides Rome and Catholics across the globe. Are these men heroic champions of the Catholic faith? Or are they vandals who have disrespected the donors of the statues and stolen from a Roman church? In the ensuing investigation the chief of the Italian police dredges the river to recover the sculptures. Meanwhile, the pope is resolute. During the next papal mass, a ritual bowl of soil honouring the goddess, Pachamama, is placed on the High Altar at Saint Peter's Basilica.

——— ଔ ଡ଼ ଡ଼ ———

It was the winter of 2019 and I was leaving a restaurant in London when I heard about the theft of the Pachamama statues. A friend showed me the video on his phone as we walked through rain-washed streets. He was surprised that I had not seen it when it had emerged a few weeks before. At that time, I was living in the UK, nearly 1500 km from Rome. Despite the distance, it mattered to me what had happened in the Italian city that morning. It also mattered to me how the pope had reacted to the theft. I had encountered similar interest among friends, of various religions or no faith, who balked or rejoiced when the pope spoke on pressing questions for the modern world. For, despite appearances, Rome and the popes are not mere historic curiosities. They are ancient symbols of universal significance that survive, remarkably intact, provoking interest, affection and even bold action in the digital age.

From the time of the emperors to our own day, the deeds of the popes have reverberated beyond the walls of Rome. Within them, the fabric of the ancient capital has been transformed. In words, deeds and travertine stone, over almost twenty centuries, the city of Rome and the popes have become inextricably intertwined. Streets crowded with Baroque churches and punctuated with dimly lit shrines, the smiling face of a recent pontiff hanging behind the till of a bar – even today, the visual result of the union is so complete that it appears to be preordained. Layers of legend – whether black or golden – also cloud our view. This book illuminates its evolution over nearly 2,000 years. Tracing the history of Rome, its people and popes in conversation with one another, it tells stories with a symbolism that echoes into our own day. Ancient heiresses swap their fortunes for hair shirts. Ethiopian diplomats roar with laughter in the palaces of cardinals. The son of a hosteler rises up to rule Rome, aping emperors and popes, only to become a bloated, tyrannical disappointment. As modernity dawns, men and women from all over the globe travel to the city, shooting from behind barricades of mattresses to defend treasured ideals. Unpicking narratives familiar and strange, we can illuminate the lives of those who walked Rome's streets to reveal how the city developed its most enduring identity.

It will be a commonplace for some readers that the first Christian emperors forged the foundations of papal Rome. Lauding saints in brick, marble and paint, leaders from Constantine the Great (306–37) onwards crystallised religious belief and papal authority in monumental form. However, the story of Rome and the popes begins much earlier, with a much humbler man and a narrative that weds the city, its people and the divine. It was the mid-first century when Peter, a fisherman from the shores of the Sea of Galilee, journeyed to pagan Rome to spread the nascent Christian faith. As a younger man, he had walked the baking streets of Jerusalem. There, a man calling himself the son of God told Peter that he was the rock upon which he would build his entire Church. By the time that Peter was in Rome, that leader, Jesus of Nazareth, had been crucified. For followers such as Peter, Jesus' agony on the cross was the salvation of all of mankind. Soon enough, Peter's own blood would be spilt near a racetrack in the north of Rome. It too would become a wellspring for Christians to come. When Peter died in Rome, he imbued the city with the unique authority given to him by Jesus. On these foundations, Rome's bishops would elevate themselves as universal pastors and supreme leaders of Christ's Church on earth.

In the age of Nero (54–68), Peter's death went unnoticed by most men and women. He was killed as an anonymous criminal, compelled by a bizarre new cult. It was the feet of the earliest adherents to Christianity in Rome that marked out the first pilgrimage route in the city: a pathway to the dusty hill where they believed that the Prince of the Apostles had died. It was only some centuries later that Constantine raised a great basilica where they had long prayed. Rome became the centre of Western Christendom as the result of one unlikely visitor, whose death in the city inspired the devotion of ordinary hearts. Paradoxically, while Rome remained pagan that devotion only entrenched the city's Christian character. As men and women died for the faith in Roman circuses and streets, Christians declared that their blood steeped the city in holy prestige. Christian Rome, then, appears to emerge as an accident of history. The early popes ensured that it did not remain that way for long. Stories of the lives and deaths of the Christian martyrs, including Peter, were engraved, sculpted and painted across the city. The story of the Christian Church was written into Rome's fabric as a powerful drama that linked heaven and earth. The result has compelled countless people, from those first furtive Christians to the Ethiopians who arrived proffering jewels in exchange for salvation in the fifteenth century. Today, statues of martyrs in Rome still stand amid piles of notes scribbled with prayers. It is this continued devotion that has bolstered the Christian identity of the city down the ages, whether at the hands of Baroque artists or the guns of nineteenth-century papal Zouaves.

At the centre of this remarkable story sit the popes, totemic and enduring. Their office has survived even as monarchies, dictatorships and empires have faded into the annals of the past. 'Rome is the city of echoes', in the words of the Renaissance artist Giotto di Bondone.

The last gasps of empire certainly resonated in the foundations of the Roman Church. Nevertheless, it is the echo of Christ's words to Peter that continue to underpin the authority and significance of Christian Rome. Inside the dome of the Basilica of Saint Peter, '*Tu es Petrus …*' – those words spoken by Jesus in Jerusalem – speak out in an unbroken ring on rich gold ground. From the first centuries after Peter's death to the election of the present Pope Francis I in 2013, the Bishops of Rome, or popes, stand in a line that Peter began. The potency of this Petrine authority – a link to Jesus Christ himself – was recognised early by princes seeking legitimacy for their political power. By the early modern period, secular leaders had granted the popes so many lands in the name of Peter that the Papal States cut a swathe right across the Italian peninsula, making the pope a prince himself.

But even when the Papal State was wrested from the pontiffs in the political tumults of the nineteenth century, Rome's popes retained an inalienable authority that compelled even non-believers to seek their ear. As late as 1922, this was recognised by the fascist premier, Benito Mussolini, who knew that he could not rule Italy without Pope Pius XI (1922–39) on side. Despite the Church's waning influence in the modern West, political leaders still arrive in Rome. A century after the rise of Mussolini, Emmanuel Macron, the head of the secular French Republic, was at the Vatican imploring Pope Francis to intervene for peace in the war between Russia and Ukraine. Moreover, even as the Church becomes increasingly global, this influence is bound to the city of Rome. The idea of Rome is so powerful that it is often synonymous with Catholicism itself. When the missionary Matteo Ricci arrived in China in the sixteenth century, he adopted the dress and philosophy of Confucius to convert souls to Christianity. Now, many Chinese Catholics see proximity to Rome as the hallmark of authentic Catholic belief, in spite of (or, in some cases, because of) the political barriers that have divided them from the structure of the Church.[1]

The history of Rome and its popes is one of many narratives, which interweave not only with one another but with the history of the Christian Church and the world at large. To tell its story coherently, this book commits many sins of omission, but aspires, as far as possible, to illuminate fundamental truths. At its heart, it aims to reveal the often unlikely story of the emergence of the papacy in the city of Rome, tracing a remarkable story of mutual influence and the endurance of an institution (as well as an idea) that was born in the age of Saint Peter and lives on in our own day.

PART 1
BECOMING ROME

▷▷▷▷▷▷▷▷▷▷▷▷▷▷▷▷▷▷▷▷ ◁◁◁◁◁◁◁◁◁◁◁◁◁◁◁◁◁◁◁◁◁

A statue of Saint Anthony covered in written
prayers and requests. (Alamy)

I

In the Footsteps of Peter

'I can point out the monuments of the victorious apostles', Gaius, a
Christian in Rome, scratched in thick black ink.[1] 'If you go as far as
the Vatican or the Ostian Way, you will find the monuments of those
who founded this church.' It was around 200 AD when the now lost
papyrus bearing these words illuminated the first, shallow traces of
the Christian Church in Rome. These were the first marks of a force
that would one day shape, expand and gild the city: the monuments to
Saint Peter and Saint Paul, those early followers of Jesus of Nazareth
whom we know from biblical texts. From Jerusalem, they had taken
roads and seas westward, grazing the southern coast of Crete to
reach Reggio, Pozzuoli and then Rome. It was the mid-first century
when they had made their way down cobblestone roads into the
centre of the Roman Empire. In that pagan city, that seat of Caesar,
Paul would encounter a community of Christians: Aquila, Priscilla,
Andronicus and others. Paul's presence in Rome is well recorded. We
know less of Peter's time there. As in so many of the early chapters
of Christian and Roman history, the evidence is sparse, patchy and
often vexed. Still, the overwhelming majority of historians now agree
that both men walked among the first Christians of the city and that,
in Rome, both would eventually spill their blood.[2] The monuments
highlighted by Gaius stood on those scarlet spots. Within a few
hundred years, they would steep the city in holy prestige. Yet when
Gaius wrote, the stones that marked the memory of Peter and Paul
were humble and inauspicious, much like the Church of Rome itself.

The earliest extant Roman sources tell us that Peter chose a Roman called Linus to continue his work in the mid-first century AD.[3] After him would come Anacletus and then, around the year 96, Clement, the third Bishop of Rome. That title would one day be latched to the prestigious office of the papacy. During Clement's life, Peter and Paul were emerging legends, holy saints, but only to the humble nucleus of the Christian Church. In that day and for more than two hundred years after Clement's death, Christian Rome was invisible. As Bishop of Rome in the late first century, Clement was resident of an anonymous building, pastor of an Eastern cult and most probably a dweller of one of the lowlier quarters of Rome. Most Christians lived in one of the areas traditionally inhabited by Jews, such as the quarter of Trastevere, across the River Tiber from the legal, religious and administrative centre of the city.[4] From that deep bend of the river, he too could take you on foot to the tomb of Peter on the barren, dusty Vatican Hill. From there, snaking southwards and then crossing the Tiber, he could lead you to the lonely spot where Paul had lost his head.

By the time that Gaius wrote, the Christians of Rome had quietly begun to forge the foundations of the papal city. Rough brick after brick, footstep after footstep, in humble markers and repeated pilgrimage they began to make their belief visible in and under the streets. By 161 at the latest they had raised an *aedicula* over the bones of Peter – a small monument marking his tomb for those who wished to visit.[5] At the wayside of the via Cornelia, facing the northern walls of the Circus of Nero, the physical remains of the Prince of the Apostles lay in a ditch, shuddering as reeling chariots passed.[6] Nobody would make this a site for pilgrimage and veneration out of choice. But for many pagans and Christians alike this was an open-air graveyard, a final place to try to rest. For Christians visiting that site, one simple fact mattered: it was the location of Peter, the saint whom

Christ trusted to build his kingdom on earth and the founder of their nascent Roman Church.

The *aedicula*, too, was humble but helped Gaius and others by making the spot more visible to those who came looking. The main part of the structure comprised a simple niche covered by a stone canopy atop two columns. This was not even a distant cousin to the shelter that Gian Lorenzo Bernini raised around 1500 years later. A majestic *baldacchino* standing on barley sugar columns of swirling bronze, Bernini's monument to Peter befitted his – by then – unchallenged status as Prince of the Apostles and founder of the Church of Rome. Yet when the labourers broke the earth to dig the foundations for Bernini's canopy, they found markers of Peter's memory that were bolder yet: bodies wrapped in bandages of linen, stone chests brimming with burnt, human bones.[7] Here, the first Bishops of Rome, our proto-popes, if you will, were interred alongside the remains attributed to the apostle Peter.

For many centuries Christians knew the approximate site of Peter's tomb, but his resting place was only confidently identified in the mid-twentieth century. Reverence restrained the hand of many popes curious to dig around underneath the basilica. As late as the 1930s, Pius XI would disappoint the administrator of Saint Peter's, Monsignor Ludwig Kaas, when he asked if he might tidy up the sunken grottoes that lay beneath its floor.[8] When that pope died in 1939, the monsignor got his way, venturing down into the crypt to find his master a tomb. The walls were weak; they swiftly crumbled. Inadvertently, the monsignor inaugurated an archaeological investigation that would reveal an ancient cemetery that had laid undisturbed for hundreds of years. In 1950, Kaas led the representatives of the American magazine *LIFE* on an exclusive tour of the site. For just twenty cents, hundreds of thousands of readers could follow the monsignor on 'a journey into the unknown, whose difficulties, hardships and excitement are unforgettable to those who shared in the labours.'[9]

Even before Gaius' time, Peter's memory had spread well beyond the slopes of the Vatican Hill. Out in the far north of the city at the Cemetery of Priscilla, small, subterranean rock tombs soon bore his name, smeared in paint on the bricks facing numerous tombs.[10] The name is not Roman but Greek. It surely honours the apostle. And, like the *aedicula*, quietly commemorates Saint Peter's presence in the fabric of Rome. Travelling straight southwards from that cemetery, over the hump of the Caelian Hill, Romans would encounter another early catacomb that murmured the names of both Peter and Paul. There, on the Appian Way, that thoroughfare into the city from the south-east, rooms under the church of San Sebastiano fuori le Mura bear early pilgrims' graffitied hopes and prayers.[11] Much ink has been spilt debating the nature of this site. Was it the true grave of Peter? Or even the domestic quarters of the apostles? Was it, in fact, a hiding place for holy bones when emperors hunted the followers of Christ? What we can be sure of is that by the mid-third century, pilgrims came to this additional, humble spot of remembrance, as well as the Vatican Hill. For these Christians, the connection between Peter and Rome was undoubted well into at least the ninth century.[12]

Today some bemoan the lack of contemporary written evidence of Peter's visit to the city. For a few, the silences in the literature cry out that he was never in Rome at all. Such authors have disputed traditional literary sources such as Peter's letter to Christians in Asia Minor. In this epistle he greeted them 'from [their] sister church in Babylon' – traditionally interpreted as a greeting from Rome.[13] After it had been involved in several conflicts with Jews, the Mesopotamian city of Babylon became a byword for oppressive, worldly powers – particularly those that attacked the people of God. In turn, pagan Rome became synonymous with Babylon, a city and a power that would weigh heavily on its Christian people. Some have argued that

Rome was only identified with Babylon well after Peter's death in the mid-sixties, claiming that the apostle greeted his interlocutors from some other region where Christians were reviled.[14] Yet we know that Peter travelled from Jerusalem to Antioch, across Asia Minor to Corinth in Greece. And when Paul wrote to the Christians in Rome in the year 56, he told them that he had not yet visited, as he did not want to build 'on someone else's foundations'.[15] Rome certainly hosted a strong community of people worshipping Jesus when Paul arrived around four years later. Had Peter known that community, or even built it in the years before? Later, more missives referred to the presence of both Paul and Peter in the city. Several decades after their deaths, Ignatius, the Bishop of Antioch, assured the Roman Christians that he would not 'command' them 'as Peter and Paul' had.[16] Later writers also spoke with surety of the deaths of Peter and Paul in the city: for example, around 170, Bishop Dionysius of Corinth. In that very same period, Irenaeus of Lyon claimed that they had built the Church of Rome before delegating power to Linus, whose bones were dug up with the foundations of Bernini's Baroque *baldacchino*.[17]

The words of Gaius, Ignatius and Irenaeus punctuate silence, illuminating the very earliest days of the Christian Church in Rome. At the same time, the bricks of the catacombs, the Vatican graves and the monuments on the Appian Way and via Ostia build a quiet, fragmentary story of continued veneration and nascent tradition. The continuous worship of the followers of Jesus, their veneration of Peter and Paul in the city, is the thread that laces together the patchwork evidence of early Christian Rome. The Bishops of Rome would call upon the legacy of the apostles, particularly Peter, to assert their pre-eminence in the centuries to come. However, it is difficult to comprehend why any second-century Roman would raise a monument on the slopes of the Vatican Hill if it was not already an oft-visited and venerated spot. At that time enough Christians visited the site to warrant raising a marker in the seedy shadows of a racetrack among mainly pagan tombs. Around the year 200, Gaius would speak of these Roman monuments to the apostles as part of an established pilgrimage tradition among Christians in the city. It is known that traditions often go unwritten by their very first adherents, even if the actions of the first Christians in Rome took form in words, brick and marble.

——— ☙ ❧ ❧ ———

When we seek the faces of those early followers of Jesus in Rome we realise why shadows cloud the history of early Christianity in the city. The first Christians there were mainly low-born, Greek-speaking foreigners, arriving in the forties and fifties from the eastern provinces of the Roman Empire.[18] In Rome, the followers of Jesus worshipped within a vast, oriental crowd; they were near indistinguishable, even to keen observers, among a multilingual Roman mass. As the heart of the empire pulsated with politics, religion and the force of hundreds of cults, the first Christians appeared, were expelled and returned largely undetected. They were not hidden or hiding but merely overlooked. Over the centuries, some were brutally executed in the city, as histories and martyrologies attest. The majority of Romans saw no heroic virtue in these deaths because the majority did not see such deaths at all. In the centuries to come, the spotlight of sanctity would illuminate the executed, bathing them in the light of a Golden Legend. Yet in the first centuries after the death of Christ, they were members of a cult that was practised in lowly quarters such as the fly-filled huts on the lowlands that flanked the Appian Way.[19]

In the first century it was the traditional pagan worship of the Romans that coloured the fabric and life of the city. The very physicality of Rome was defined by its worship of many, many gods. According to tradition, the Pomerium, the very line that marked the legal limits of the city, was first ploughed on the prophecy of augury as two brothers, Romulus and Remus, debated where to found Rome. Legend tells us that Romulus saw twelve vultures on the Palatine Hill before taking yoke, cow and bull to forge a furrow defining the sacred precinct, from the Quirinal Hill in the north to the Palatine in the south.[20] With divination, plough and beast Romulus made his city. Legend this may be. Yet religion truly came to define the area of Rome within the Pomerium, where temples to gods, goddesses and deified emperors peppered the ground. From the early sixth century BC, Romans walking at the feet of the Palatine and Capitoline Hills travelled in the groove of the Pomerium and the shadow of the Temple of Jupiter Optimus Maximus. Built and rebuilt in monumental, Grecian style, this looming sanctuary for Rome's foremost god would soon be surrounded by ever denser clusters of trophies, shrines and altars. Across the city, temples to Concord, Venus and even Emperor Julius Caesar swiftly rose. Within the Pomerium, under gleaming roofs, Romans could worship gods and the first mortals to join their ranks. They also raised palaces and fora in the zone as places of business and leisure. In ancient Rome, entreaty and sacrifice to the gods was deemed essential to both.

Crossing Rome's sacred centre, men, women and children met a pagan religion that pulsated with the breath and blood of life. Oxen sauntered down the city's main streets, led for sacrifice on ice-white altars. The Roman sun blazed down on their nodding heads as they were sprinkled with grain and wine. Their assent noted, their blood was spilt for the gods.[21] Rome moved in perpetual anticipation of demands and wrath from on high. When the gods – or emperor – demanded it, everybody in the city had to make sacrifice to the higher powers. At the main sanctuaries: oxen.[22] Among ordinary people: incense and wine. Religious festivals set the meter of the year for all, leaving the city enraptured, jolly and even purified. From the Lupercalia, childless women emerged with branded backs, marked by the lashes of a thong of goat skin that promised them fecundity.[23] Participation in the Saturnalia took a more voluptuous form:

Romans shed their togas, drank heavily and gambled. Chucking down a few *sesterces* before the roll of a dice or waiting with bated breath for the wheel of a chariot to cross the finish line at the Circus Maximus, citizens, freedmen and slaves delighted in the diversions of the feast. During major religious festivals in early first-century Rome, participation was so high that Emperor Augustus (27–14 BC) sent guards to man the empty streets. Had he not, houses abandoned by their owners for the sake of religion and, often, pure amusement would have fallen 'prey to footpads because of the few people who remained at home'.[24]

It is a popular belief that the first murmurings of Christianity in Rome brought hope to the lowly: current and former slaves, foreigners and the many others marginalised in a highly stratified society. It is true that, from the very beginning, the followers of Jesus lauded a poverty and simplicity that Romans had traditionally reviled. Moreover, in Rome, the overwhelming majority lingered on the bottom rungs of a hierarchy crowned by an emperor, buoyed by patricians, equestrians and citizens of the city. Yet casting your eye around at the games or even the inner sanctums of temples of first-century Rome, you would have found many humbler figures immersed in the religious traditions of the city. Even non-citizens and slaves were obliged to take part in the revelry and sacrifices of the Roman religion, inside the temples and out on the streets. Some filled the air with the round, low tones of the twin tibia pipes, while ex-slaves could take on the work of the haruspex, leaning over marble slabs to divine prophecy from the smeared entrails of sacrificed beasts.[25] Women could become priestesses of the Great Mother Goddess, Magna Mater, whose pine tree processed through the city to her temple on the Palatine.[26] Flanking the tree, one might also find ex-slaves, wielding reeds to commemorate the death of Attis, Magna Mater's consort who lost his mind and then his life when he deliberately castrated himself on a tree.[27]

Furthermore, for all ranks of society, the Roman traditions were hardly the only religious option around, even if it was only beyond the Pomerium, in the *ager* or fields of Rome, that other cults like Christianity were permitted to live and to pray. Beliefs and traditions of all kinds were carried to Rome on the same economic and political winds that drove their foreign adherents to the city. Isis and Serapis arrived from Alexandria, Antioch and Athens.[28] By the turn of the third century, the Persian cult of Mithras had also carved out a large place in Rome. Even before the year 300, initiates had some forty places to meet.[29] In rented rooms, private homes and even military quarters, the devotees of Mithras performed rituals that raised them through ranks from Raven to Lion and Father. The bolted doors and shady rooms of Rome's Mithraea were antithetical to the city's showy temples to gods such as Jupiter. But on the Campo Marzio, a flatland flanked by the Tiber and the western ridge of the Pomerium, evidence of other Eastern cults could be seen and heard. There, sonorous chant and the metallic rattle of the sistrum rose above the walls of a sanctuary to Isis, built in fine Grecian style in the first century BC. A foreign cult it was, but its physical home in Rome was vast. With a courtyard of 70 by 140 metres, it was several times the size of the Pantheon to all of the Roman gods that stood nearby.[30] Palm trees and obelisks flanked the placid, central pool. In the apse of the sanctuary resided Isis herself, an arresting and imperious statue with figures of Sarapis and Anubis at her sides. For most Romans crossing the Campo Marzio, these tranquil scenes were concealed by lofty walls, though very occasionally devotees of the sanctuary would burst beyond its confines. With shaved heads and white robes billowing in their wake, they dashed across the plain past the ancient Theatre of Pompey.

The acolytes of Isis completed their ritual by breaking the surface of the Tiber, leaping from its banks to cleanse themselves in the murky waters of Rome. Emerging on the opposite side of the river, they would find themselves in Trastevere, where the rumble of foreign cults rang ever more strongly. Here, even further from the sacred confines of the Pomerium, immigrants from Palmyra and Syria had settled their cults in the city. Here Simios, Hadad, Sol and Atargatis were worshipped in sanctuaries etched with devotions in Latin but also Aramaic and Greek.[31] It was in this most oriental of quarters that the early third-century Emperor Antoninus (218–22), also known as Heliogabalus, would intensify the cult of El Gabal, the sun god of his homeland in the Roman province of Syria.[32] Within the Pomerium, the teenage ruler had divided Romans when he took to a bejewelled golden chariot to vaunt a black, conical stone said to represent the god. Conservative senators were scandalised when he worshipped the stone with a dance before ascending a tower to shower the crowd with presents, from cups of precious metal to living domestic pets.[33] Still, Antoninus was certainly not the first Roman emperor to embrace the rites of the East. From the dawn of the empire in the mid-first century BC, emperors had built temples to Isis, Serapis and others. Views shifted. Some cults were banned. At the turn of the first century, Emperor Tiberius (14–37) had the cultic statue of Isis taken from the Campo Marzio and sunk in the Tiber while her priests were nailed to crosses.[34] Despite such violent fluctuations in popularity, Eastern cults were a regular fixture in the religious mêlée of ancient Rome.

— ⚮ ⚮ ⚮ —

It was within this mêlée that the first Christians in the city emerged. Like the initiates of Mithras and Isis, it seems that many were not natural Romans. It seems that the first followers of Jesus in Rome were mainly Jews who worshipped at the synagogues of the city, or Gentiles who practised some elements of Judaism: the so-called 'god-fearers'.[35] Others argue that, by the fifties, just seventeen years after Jesus' death, Christian teachings in Rome had spread well beyond the Jewish community. When Paul wrote to believers in the city in the mid-fifties, he spoke of his longing to preach to them and 'other Gentiles', or non-Jews.[36] It is quite possible that men and women of other cults had thrown them off to worship the one Christian god. Some features of nascent Christianity would not be entirely alien to those caught up in the long-established religious traditions of Rome. Chastity, for example, was prized by Christians and many others, including those who lauded the Vestal Virgins who lived, veiled in white, preserving their flame at the foot of the Palatine Hill. Moreover, while the dominant Roman religion venerated a panoply of gods, like Christians the bald-headed acolytes of Isis devoted themselves to one deity, purely and totally. Members of cults were also attracted by fraternity and pragmatic benefits like group burial in Rome, which the city's Christians also soon offered.

Monotheistic and expectant of a Messiah, members of the city's Jewish community would surely have been some of the individuals most receptive to the news of his coming in Jerusalem. This was a large audience. By the Augustan period, the Jews of Rome numbered several thousand. Under the via Nomentana that stretches out of the city to the north-east, inscriptions in Jewish catacombs reveal the names of some eleven synagogues in the ancient city.[37] These do not seem to have been grand or even distinct religious buildings but rather synagogues defined by community, worship and law.[38] Some Jews may have already converted to Christianity far from Rome, during a visit or previous life in Syria or Judea, where Jesus had first inspired men to drop their tools and preach. Others might have left Rome to travel back to Jerusalem. There they would encounter apostles and acolytes, preaching of a Messiah who had come and, in just thirty-three years, left. Back in Rome, murmurings of the words and actions of this Jesus of Nazareth might have spread on the tongues of Jewish slaves brought into the city. Some masters tolerated a variety of religions under their roof. That of the Jewish community was treated with, at best, indifference or, more likely, cruel mocking.[39] When the Roman practice of manumission freed slaves from bondage, they could congregate with Jews, Gentiles and new Christians alike, believing, debating and denying the new teachings that had come from the East. Though pagan to its core – in structures and statute – the city of Rome provided a remarkably fertile ground for the growing cult of Jesus Christ.

Men and women like Aquila and Priscilla could hear of early Christian ideas in and around the synagogues of Rome, though Aquila might have become a Christian before he and his wife undertook their arduous migration to the capital. Aquila was a Jew from Pontus, a rainy Roman province on the southern shores of the Black Sea.[40] It certainly had Christians in the mid-first century; Peter addressed them from 'Babylon' in that famous letter to the persecuted faithful of Asia Minor. Perhaps Aquila and Priscilla had fled religious oppression in Pontus, a land rich in cherries, flax and vines, seeking obscurity and safety in the vast, anonymous crowds of imperial Rome. They were certainly in Rome in the mid-fifties, when Paul wrote to Christians in the city. The couple were known and addressed directly by the apostle, having met him in Corinth, a land bridge between Attica and the Peloponnese. As prominent Christians, Aquila and Priscilla might have opened their home as a house church in Rome. Leaderless for its first decades, at least, the Roman Church was not founded with a bishop, much less a pope. Rather it comprised a cumulation of disparate domestic churches, around seven by the time that Paul wrote.[41] Though far from an organised hierarchy, the nascent Church across the world was by this time a fairly extensive network. Christians such as Aquila and Priscilla in Rome were linked to brothers and sisters overseas through letters in their shared language of Greek. As we shall see, it was only in the second, third and fourth centuries that the Latin language of public life was slowly taken up by the Church, in part to accommodate new

Roman converts of higher social rank. By contrast, this early dawn of Christianity in Rome was domestic and discreet, leaving no obvious trace of exclusively ecclesiastical buildings, nor images, nor shrines, nor altars.[42] Considering these most private and humble beginnings of the Roman Church we can begin to understand the aspersions of those third-century observers who saw Christians as 'a people skulking and shunning the light, silent in public, but garrulous in corners.'[43]

For Aquila and Priscilla, home would have been a place of worship but also of work. Like Paul, they fed themselves by making tents, cutting, stretching and stitching coarse, dark goatskin into moveable shelters. As well as Trastevere, there appear to have been Christians living on the land flanking the Appian Way, far south beyond the Capena Gate where stagnant air hung between the Caelian and Aventine Hills.[44] There they might have lived in the music of clacking craftsmen's tools, hearing braying mules and women chatting as they worked wool and textile outside of their homes. The constant flow of visitors shifting in and out of Rome on this main track south-east would certainly have provided Aquila and Priscilla with plenty of customers. But Trastevere was also a hub for small craftsmen and women, a harbour quarter that packed a large bend of the River Tiber. That region also rang with the prattle and clang of work from warehouses, mills and tanneries for leather. In winding, narrow streets artisans like Aquila and Priscilla would have lived ear-to-ear with sailors, shopkeepers and haulers, who dragged cabinets and pots from ships to be hawked for coins, clothes and oil nearby. Some of their neighbours might have been forced to leave the quarter to work, taking a short stroll up the Tiber to the Vatican Hill. At its foot, not so far from the emerging shrine to Peter, men bent over fiery kilns to forge bricks of red and white clay.

Living in these lowly, often rowdy quarters, with no visible leader, distinct buildings or devotional shrines, it is not difficult to see why the first Christians in Rome left little trace in written record. In Trastevere, many lived in tenements of bricks and wood, tapering as they rose through several storeys. For so many in these poor quarters, sleeping, praying, feasting and working might take place in the same small set of gloomy rooms. In the second century, the poet Apuleius described the workshop of a textile fuller where his guests sat among downturned tools in the stench of bleaching cloth.[45] Leaving his rooms to walk the streets, the guests would not escape the implements and products of labour, passing storage facilities piled high with sacks of grain and heavy lumber for carpentry. Only atop the busy rooms of Trastevere, or in the rafters of tenements with the nesting birds, could the first Christians of Rome find the necessary peace to worship, read and pray. After downing tools, men and women like Aquila and Priscilla laid the table and said their prayers. They lit lamps and made the sign of the cross in remembrance of the crucifixion of Jesus.[46] This is an event that Christians believe saved men and women from condemnation to hell, and for them it had happened just a couple of decades before. At that time, even the flickering candlewicks at their windows would have been as unnoticed as markers of their cult, for Jews and pagans also used rituals of candlelight.

—— ઝ ৪০ ৪০ ——

The men and women who gathered to celebrate the first Christian Masses in Rome could not have dreamt of the incense-filled basilicas where their successors would soon pray. Though common for Roman Christians, the cramped quarters of Trastevere might have jarred Phoebe, a rather grand lady who met members of their community around the year 56. Phoebe had journeyed more than 1000 kilometres to get to the city, bearing that famous letter to the Romans from the apostle Paul. She had come from Cenchreae, a harbour town on the eastern side of Corinth, where she was known and respected as a patroness of Christians.[47] It is possible that Phoebe greeted Aquila and Priscilla with recognition or even warmth, for they had passed some time in Corinth around six years before. Phoebe's home, a much more capacious dwelling than the house church in which she arrived at in Rome, provided a place of worship for the Christian community of Corinth. In the letter she bore to Aquila, Priscilla, Phlegon, Hermas and others in Rome, Paul commended her as 'protector', 'sister' and even 'deaconess', a woman designated and blessed by a bishop to carry the gospel to her own sex.[48] Paul had certainly needed a protector on his travels throughout the East, where his outspoken ardour caused rancour among Christians, Jews and pagans alike. His conversion had been dramatic and imbued him with extraordinary zeal; dashed to the ground by a blinding vision of divine light on the road to Damascus, he had spent three days without sight and without eating before embracing the teachings of Jesus that he had once scorned. Now Paul preached the gospel with all of the fire with which he had once condemned it, earning himself a reputation and enemies along the way. Paul might have recommended Phoebe to the Christian Church in Rome but, in reality, it was Paul who was in need of a favourable interlocutor in the city.[49]

Paul did not come to Rome in the late fifties to found the Church, less still to act as its first pope. He came to Rome as a man unjustly accused of a crime, seeking a fair trial from the emperor himself. During the early fifties, Paul had travelled energetically: Antioch, Cyprus, Ephesus and then Corinth. By the year 56, he was in trouble, accused of causing tension and even violence at the Temple of Jerusalem.[50] To make matters worse, he had been mistaken for a malevolent Egyptian rioter, who had caused chaos in the city before fleeing and losing himself in the desert. Some deemed Paul a *loimos* or 'plague', who had wrought ill feeling and chaos in the Holy Land.[51] Paul denied this vehemently and, as a Roman citizen, requested translation to the imperial capital for his trial. By the time that he arrived in 61, Phoebe must have gone on her way. It did not matter; she had laid favourable ground. Paul was received warmly by Christians at Pozzuoli, just north of Naples, and then among the community of Rome at the Forum Appius, where the roads from the south ran together into the Appian Way. At this last stop, a day's journey from the city, Paul was greeted by two Christians near the Tre Taverne, where they could slake their thirst, consult a blacksmith and restock at a store. Together they then walked the Appian Way, through the countryside south of Rome into the heart of the city.

Paul would experience the Eternal City predominantly under house arrest. Within a few years he would be put to death, though writers from the second century onwards have disagreed on just where and just how. Such stories of detainment and violence are woven inextricably into histories of early Christian Rome. Yet like so many pages in the earliest chapters of this narrative, there are gaps and hanging threads that often prove impossible to tie up. An early episode in the story of Christian persecution comes to us from the pen of the second-century writer Suetonius, who wrote of the banishment of Jews from Rome in the year 49 by Emperor Claudius (41–54).[52] The city's Jews were cast out, he writes, after the community splintered and 'made disturbances' over a man called 'Chrestus'. Wagons packed, entire families trailed out of city. Some identify the banished as those Jews – like Aquila and Priscilla – who had embraced the teachings of Jesus and clashed with others who did not believe that Jesus was the Messiah. Writing in the same period, the historian Tacitus corroborated the story of a community divided, telling us that many had turned away from the old Jewish traditions and become known as Christians after 'Christus', a man sentenced to death by Pontius Pilate during the reign of Tiberius.[53] Other modern interpreters disagree, reading Suetonius' tale as a banishment of all Jews or even all Christians from Rome. Even the words of the original sources are far from clear cut. Suetonius' text suggests that the source of unrest, *'Chrestus'*, was present in Rome at the time of the troubles in 49 – some sixteen years after the death of Jesus Christ in Jerusalem. Moreover, we know that there were Jews who remained true to their beliefs and traditions – as well as Christians in Rome – when Phoebe, and then Paul, arrived in the next decade.

It is, therefore, not at all clear that Christians, formerly Jewish or gentile, were specifically targeted by Roman authorities in the mid-first century. Had the emperors' men burst into those first house churches in the streets of Trastevere or on the busy flatlands of the Appian Way, they would be unlikely to have been able to identify the followers of Jesus as a group distinct from Jews. And yet one of the most well-known tales of state-sponsored persecution of Christians dates to only a little later in the sixties, when that 'noxious wild beast', the anti-Christ himself, Claudius' successor – Nero (54–68) – was on the imperial throne.[54] The key year in this story is 64, when huge swathes of Rome burnt to rubble, cinder and ash. Suetonius and, later, Cassius Dio tell us that Nero watched flames devour his city from the walls, playing the cithara and reciting a poem through choking tears. When the fire died down and the emperor stepped out onto the blackened ground of Rome he found some of his people pointing the finger of blame in his direction. Writing some sixty years later, it was the Roman author Tacitus who claimed that Nero swiftly turned that finger onto the Christians of his city.[55] For was it not highly suspicious that the quarters of Trastevere and Porta Capena had been spared the flames?

Tacitus' story is a pleasingly dramatic tale but matters for us as it is often used to date the emergence of Christians as an identifiable group in Rome.[56] If Nero made Christians a scapegoat for the public they must have been a recognisable and plausible target. More importantly still, Tacitus' tale is often identified with the tradition that Saint Peter breathed his last in Rome, crucified upside down on the Vatican Hill as a victim of Nero's persecution.[57] In the heart of the Vatican complex, in the pope's own private chapel, the last ever fresco painted by the Renaissance artist Michelangelo Buonarroti depicts the tragic scene. According to one text, Peter himself specified the nature of the execution, telling Nero's henchmen: 'My cross ought to be fixed head downmost ... to direct my feet towards heaven; for I am not worthy to be crucified like my Lord.'[58] These words come to us from the Acts of Peter, a text written in the late 100s. They were echoed early in the next century when Tertullian affirmed that Peter was crucified in Rome and thus 'equalled the passion of the Lord'.[59] Later in the fourth century, the Church historian Eusebius would repeat the claim.

The earliest evidence that we have for Nero's persecution of Christians is Tacitus and Suetonius, who wrote some sixty years after the events. Yet pens contemporary to that of Tacitus fail to ratify his claim that Christians were blamed for the fire. Suetonius writes that the Christians were persecuted by Nero for practising a 'new and mischievous superstition'.[60] When he does write about the dramas of 64, he fails to mention the Christians at all. A few decades later, Cassius Dio followed suit. Pliny the Elder, who had lived through the event, suggested that Nero was to blame, with no mention of the Christian group.[61] Pliny's nephew, known as Pliny the Younger, would grow up with his uncle in Rome. When he encountered Christians as Roman governor of Bithynia in the early second century, he derided them as practitioners of a 'depraved and excessive superstition'.[62] And yet even this learned and experienced man was not sure whether he could execute Christians merely for their religion. It was the age of Trajan (98–117), a very different emperor to Nero. Yet if Pliny had lived in Rome shortly after the state had persecuted Christians as dangerous criminals, we might expect him to mention this when discussing the danger that they posed in the present day.

So what should we make of Tacitus' story? There is no reason why he should have made it up from thin air. By the time he was writing in the early second century, the followers of Jesus had begun to be recognised as a distinct sect in some places. The term 'Christians' appeared more frequently in texts and more specific attacks on the group had certainly begun to take place. Furious that his wife had become a Christian, one rankled husband divorced her before denouncing her and her teacher, Ptolemaeus, who was condemned to death.[63] Like all of us, Tacitus looked at the past through the lens of his own time, when Christians were earmarked as inciters of unrest.

We have no clear evidence from the first century that Christians were punished for their faith per se. But groups who were Christian were attacked as a threat to the equilibrium and safety of the empire. For Christians, men like Paul are martyrs for the faith, killed for refusing to refrain from teaching the gospel. However, for the Romans the gospel was neither here nor there: Paul was punished for inciting unrest in the empire. Authorities in Corinth had dismissed a conflict between Paul and some men at the temple of Achaea as a religious matter among Jews of absolutely no concern to them. It was only when Paul's preaching caused serious social unrest and violence in Jerusalem that he would have to be punished. For the Romans of Paul's day (the mid-first century), Christians might not yet have been defined by name and sect but some of them had begun to mark themselves out by their disruptive actions. In Rome, many of the Eastern cults were practised as a complement to Roman religion. Even the Jewish community made offerings for the well-being of the state, in line with their own traditions.[64] Meanwhile members of the Christian community flatly refused. In doing so, they threatened peace on earth by angering the gods in the heavens.

For Romans, these people were not Christians but dangerous atheists who recklessly endangered the safety of the empire. To make matters worse, they soon sought to spread their beliefs and practices. A silversmith named Demetrius would emerge as one of Paul's many critics, lamenting that sales for sacrificial instruments had dwindled and that the apostle's conversions were going to put him out of business.[65] For Demetrius and the Roman authorities, attacks on individuals like Paul were a way of solving pragmatic problems sparked by a troublesome new branch of the Jewish faith – not the persecution of men and women because of that faith itself. Such a discrepancy might seem trifling, for it is merely a matter of perspective. Nonetheless, it goes some way to explaining why the Christians of first-century Rome could be at once barely visible and also increasingly attacked.

For believers and many others, this does not change the sacrifice that men such as Peter and Paul made to spread and remain firm in their Christian faith. It does not matter whether Peter died in the aftermath of the fire or as a Christian punished by a dreadful Nero. He and Paul were saints and martyrs for what they believed, and what they did as a result of their beliefs. If they died in the line of duty, as named Christians or not, the Church that Jesus asked Peter to build had its foundations in their blood. For the majority of Christians in the first centuries of the religion, that blood stained the ground of the city of Rome. There, in the centre of Italy, it watered the seeds of the Church of Christ on earth.

— ⳩ ⳺ ⳺ —

The birth and growth of the Roman Church, so crucial to the Christian story, was almost entirely unpredictable. Even in its most mundane facets, the city of Rome clashed with the ways of the nascent Church. Departing from a dwelling off the Appian Way, it would not take long for a Christian to encounter the full force of pagan Rome. Nothing in that city was secular: politics, even games, involved sacrifice to the gods. Lasciviousness, excess and wanton violence were condemned by the teachings of Jesus. Yet a few minutes into their walk, Christians might hear the unbridled roar of more than 250,000 Romans watching races at the Circus Maximus.[66]

From the year 80, Romans could find a seat at the nearby Colosseum, where around 87,000 guests watched men soaked in blood grapple to the death.[67] Walking a little further into the city, Christians soon met pungent incense billowing up to the pagan gods, or the sight of a priest heading towards one of the city's temples. Sacrifices to Vulcan, Venus and Jupiter were made at political buildings and markets.[68] Christians might even find themselves working to support pagan religion: bricks fired on the Vatican Hill could build temples to the gods and frankincense sold in shops and taverns could be burnt in their honour. Christians of a better class might find themselves invited to a pagan wedding or a young man's assumption of the toga. There were, it seems, obstacles at every turn. While Jews had their law and scholarship on how to live it, the first Christians of Rome had to find a way to live their religion among the obstacles of a pagan city, interpreting the gospel as they went.

To make matters more challenging, the Roman Church, such as it existed, was fractured. A unitive, authoritative Bishop of Rome only emerged decades after the deaths of Peter and Paul. In the first century, groups met weekly, sometimes ferrying portions of their Eucharist to other Christians in the city.[69] A microcosm of the larger early Christian Church, the Church of Rome was a network of people united in belief and practice, not an organised, hierarchical institution under a monarchical head. What's more, unlike other Christian cities such as Corinth, the Church in Rome had no geographical centre, no shared place for communal worship. When Paul wrote to the Romans in the late 50s, he addressed the 'church in Rome' as particular individuals and houses, not a distinct foundation under a single leader.

The names of many of the first Roman bishops are still read at altars during the Catholic liturgy of the Mass. The seamless continuity evoked by this recital elides their struggles to guide the new, disjointed Church of Rome. Early bishops such as Clement represented congregations, showed largesse and gave support to other Christians in the empire. They also dug the administrative foundations of Christian Rome and its Church. Anacletus is said to have divided the city into twenty-five parishes, while Clement's successor, Evaristus, assigned them priests and deacons. It was not until the reign of Victor (c.189-c.199), however, that we have evidence of the Bishop of Rome acting as a monarchical and unifying force.[70] Ironically, it seems that the fractious and foreign nature of the Roman Church was the very reason that he had to assert a bold and firm authority. This was, as we have already seen, a Church of foreigners from across the empire. Victor himself was a North African Berber with a flock comprising Greeks, Egyptians, Jews and more. As the Church of Rome began to forge traditions and practices, its diverse membership wrestled over just what they should be. In these disputes, the celebration of Easter became a key node of discord. While Christians from the East urged that this crucial feast should be celebrated on the fourteenth day of the Jewish month of Nisan, no matter whether it were a Sunday or not, Romans wanted it celebrated on the Sabbath, the closest Sunday to that day.[71] Victor came down on the Romans' side, excommunicating all those who persisted in disagreement – an act that banished them from the community of the Church. Victor also made other fundamental decisions, abandoning Greek in return for greater use of Latin. With these changes, the Bishop of Rome emerged as a monarchical leader in reality, as well as by divine law.

Acting with authority, speaking the language of the Roman masses, it was now possible that the Christian Church could emerge from Rome's foreign rabble and into the city at large. The timing was fortuitous. The emperor of Victor's age, Commodus (177–192), generally left the Christians in peace. What's more, the city was facing grave economic, social and political problems. For many, a charitable Church became a welcome and even vital prospect. A century later, the seeds planted by Victor would transform the See of Rome. Rome had been the last of the early Christian bishoprics to become truly monarchical, but soon its bishop would claim supremacy over all episcopal Sees across the globe. To do this they invoked the authority of Peter: the first apostle of their city. When Victor excommunicated the Eastern Christians who insisted on their particular Easter traditions, he turned away from the more tolerant attitude of his fellow bishops in the East. Victor was able to do so as he claimed to hold authority inherited from Peter himself: Christ had made Peter head of the Church, and Peter had ministered and died in Rome.

For most Romans at the end of the second century, their city was still principally the capital of an empire. Yet, right under their noses, Christian Rome was surfacing as an increasingly clear and potent idea. For the Christians of the empire, the city's stones were already imbued with the memory and prestige of Paul and Peter. For outsiders these notions acted as an ever more intoxicating lure. The first followers of Jesus were drawn to Rome for reasons practical, political and economic: captured as trophies, working as servants or plying their trade as bakers, artisans or manual labourers. By the end of the second century, Peter, Paul and, through them, Jesus himself added to the magnetism of Rome. Christianity in the city became a fact and an inspiring idea that would draw men and women to Italy from the Holy Land itself. Rome, a pagan capital, had begun to emerge as a Christian concept. The foundations of a tradition that stretches into our own day were laid. Peter and Paul, and the monuments to their deaths illuminated by Gaius, were the keystones that bridged the old pagan city to its emerging Christian path. As the Roman Church grew, pains would be felt. Many more Christians would face brutal deaths after Peter and Paul. Yet for Christians across the globe this would not be a sad tale, nor a tragic end. Instead, their deaths were forged into an ever-expanding legend of fervour, martyrdom and glory that would shape the fabric and history of Rome for centuries to come.

2

'You have won, Galilean':
The Rise of Christian Rome

By the late fourth century, the tomb of Saint Peter was sheltered by an imposing basilica dedicated to his name. In the footsteps of Peter's early, ignoble devotees came some of the noblest persons of the city. Yet when writing to a friend from Rome in the year 384, Jerome of Stridon was far from celebratory about the increased sophistication of the Roman Church. A prominent priest and theologian, Jerome had come from the eastern shores of the Adriatic. At Saint Peter's Basilica he paced down the vast, broad nave. There he would meet some of Rome's highest born ladies. Cloaked in red linen, sat atop litters, encircled by pious eunuchs, these women could hardly be missed. According to Jerome, many of them did not want to be. Unlike the furtive, often fearful Christians of the first centuries of the Church, these noblewomen wished to be known for their faith in Jesus of Nazareth. Like peacocks of piety, they made a stately progress towards their devotions, scanning the streets for onlookers as they passed. Jerome even claimed that they would 'disfigure their faces' so that they seemed to have endured gruelling penitential fasts.[1] When they encountered an audience, they cast their faces to the ground in a flourish of feigned humility. Yet just as quickly as their gaze had shot down, one eye would stray to discover the identity of their spectator. The Christian churches of Rome, it appeared, had become the places to be seen.

As he wrote his letter, Jerome was vehement, colouring the page with remonstrances for such shows. At Saint Peter's his horror had sharpened on encountering a lady generally deemed one of 'the noblest' in all of Rome. With great ceremony, ringed by a flock of acolytes, this lady had personally distributed a gold coin to each poor soul gathered at the church. This was a great spectacle of Christian charity, but it was a charity with limits that soon became startlingly clear. When a much lowlier woman 'full of years and rags' ambled back to the litter to ask for a second coin, the grand lady struck her with such force that blood spilt from her veins. In that moment, Jesus' calls to humility and charity jarred with the human conceit now present in his Church. The basilica of Saint Peter in Rome was a monument to an apostle glorified for self-sacrifice and humility. Now some of its visitors encountered worldly hubris as they sent their entreaties heavenwards in clouds of heavy, perfumed incense.

By 384, the triumph of Christianity among the noble and ruling classes was becoming a fact. Even in the mid-second century, the philosopher who would come to be known as Justin Martyr claimed – with some credibility – that in his time 'more Christians were ex-pagans than ex-Jews'.[2] But just twenty years earlier the emperor himself had tried to turn the tide against the Church. From the moment he took the throne in 361, Julian I (361–3) – known as Julian the Apostate – worked to cleanse the powerful of Christian influence.[3] If he could only restore the traditional religion of Rome he believed that he could restore the glories of Rome itself. Julian did not have long. Ultimately, he would fail. On the night of 26 June 363, less than two years into his reign, he lay dying from a stab wound that had pierced his rib cage and liver. It is a tradition and somewhat of an irony that Julian dedicated his final laboured breath not to pray to his own gods but to that of the Christians. Addressing Jesus directly he is said to have conceded: 'You have won, Galilean.'[4]

The adoption of Christianity by the richest men and women in the empire took the Church of Rome out of the slums. But it also made the Christian faith a tool of the world. Jerome himself was not alien to this society; he had gone to meet Christian nobles the very day that he witnessed the attack on the poor beggar woman. Jerome often visited the rooms of Rome's finest palazzi, taking a seat that had likely been occupied before by another great Christian thinker of his age. To Rome came Augustine of Hippo, Ambrose of Milan and those they denounced as errant thinkers or heretics, such as Pelagius and the Spanish bishop Priscillian. Many of these men would ascend to the drawing rooms of Rome's most salubrious residents, climbing the streets of the Aventine to the Caelian Hills to speak of humility and self-denial in salons of cool, coloured marble. There, men such as Jerome sought conversions, personal patrons, as well as supporters for the Church. In counsel and conversations, he and his contemporaries played out the great theological battles of the age. Debating luxury and poverty, free will and divine aid, and the respective values of marriage and virginal chastity, they enlightened and entertained. Such society began to shape the world of the Roman Church, as donations poured in and drawing-room debates spilt out into less salubrious sites. Jerome had merely rebuked the phoney philanthropist at Saint Peter's Basilica. Yet within a year, Priscillian was executed for sorcery after the Bishop of Lusitania and others had condemned him as a pernicious heretic and idolator.[5]

In these years, the wider Christian Church was taking shape, as philosophers and theologians grappled over the true interpretation of Christ's teachings. Though theological feuds rumbled throughout the empire, Rome became an increasingly crucial node for both discussion and decision-making about the direction and teaching of the Christian Church. As the Bishops of Rome watched their flock expand into all echelons of society, they responded to queries from the lips of the erudite and lowly. In doing so, they defined the beliefs and position of the Church in Rome and beyond. Slowly, the pre-eminence of Peter in Jesus' eyes was rubbing off on the episcopal see in which he had died: the Church of Rome had begun to emerge as a leading authority in the Christian world.

The growing pre-eminence of Rome as a Christian city was founded on the rock of Peter but accelerated and intensified by powerful new adherents to the faith. It was the emperor himself, Constantine I (306–37), who had raised that mighty basilica to replace the humble markers of the apostle's tomb. He governed the western half of the Roman Empire from 306, during a period when the Roman Empire was divided in two and ruled by not one but four men. Constantine was the uncle of none other than Julian the Apostate, who would wage bitter war on Christianity during his own rule decades later. Now the story of Constantine as the first Christian emperor is enshrined in history as a moment on which the fate of the entire Church turned. Yet although the consequences were religious and, for many, divine, Constantine's support for Christianity originated in an unmistakably worldly concern. Like so many turning points in the history of Rome in this transformative period, his decision to patronise the Church was influenced by power, politics and wealth, as well as religion. The emperor would elevate the worldly presence and status of Christianity. However, his primary object was the lofty office of Caesar Augustus of Rome.

The Bishops of Rome would be elevated on the wings of the emperor's worldly power. Yet in a startling paradox they would not emphasise imperial glory when shaping the character of their growing Church. For even as the Church of Rome became more eminent in the city and the world, its bishops continued to invoke the blood and bones of martyrs who had been murdered in worldly ignominy. Constantine and the upper classes might have buoyed the rise of Christian Rome with prestige, coin and opportunity. Nonetheless, it was those Christians who had suffered and died under less favourable rulers who drove the compelling narrative that wrote Christianity into the very stones of Rome.

─── ੴ ੴ ੴ ───

It was not always clear that Constantine was destined to be 'the Great'. Since the reign of the Emperor Diocletian (284–305), rule of the vast Roman Empire had been shared out between four leaders – a pair of Caesars in the East and West and, above them, two more senior Caesar *Augusti*. In one of the first round of appointments, it was expected that Constantine would be made Caesar of the West under his father Constantius (305–6), who was already a Caesar Augustus. The entire assembly was 'struck dumb by amazement' when he was totally overlooked.[6] When Constantine heard the news, he sped to his father in York: Constantius would soon breathe his last and his son was taking no chances. Speeding across the continent with such rapidity that his horses died, Constantine arrived in York in the summer of 306.[7] By the end of July the army had acclaimed him Caesar of the West.[8] The four rulers of the empire – or tetrarchy – seemed settled. However, things turned sour when the senior emperors of the West and East proposed to withdraw the praetorian guard from Rome and remove tax exemptions long enjoyed by the Roman people.[9] Enraged at the decision, a trio of officers turned to a man as disgruntled as they were: Maxentius (306–12) who, like Constantine, was the son of a former Roman emperor.[10] Maxentius, too, had been passed over in Diocletian's imperial appointments. Now, backed by a vengeful army, he saw his opportunity to right the wrong.

It was not difficult to rile a populace facing fresh financial burdens. Rome rose and Maxentius declared himself undefeated prince of central and southern Italy, as well as the African provinces. Incumbent, immovable, Maxentius would materialise his authority in the dense walls of an enormous basilica in the Roman Forum. Flanking the north side of the via Sacra, between the Temple of the

Sacra Urbs and the temple dedicated to Venus and Rome, this was not a religious building, like the basilica of Saint Peter, but a basilica in the traditional Roman sense. Maxentius' building was a place from which to rule and to govern. Underneath its colossal arches he sat, barking out orders. It was later reported that he demanded the felling of all statues of Constantine, whom he had mocked as the son of a whore.[11] Emperors of the tetrarchy, old and new, would bargain with the self-declared prince. They colluded with Maxentius and with one another, but their endeavours to unseat the new ruler of Rome materialised and evaporated without success.

By 311 the government of the Roman Empire was in tatters. Alliances that were once much coveted lay on the scrap heap. Even Maxentius' father, former Emperor Maximian, had turned against his insubordinate son, teaming up with Constantine to plot his demise. But by the second decade of the fourth century even Maximinus was dead, hanging himself in ritual shame after betraying his latest ally. The alliances got messier still, as Constantine also lost the support of his equivalent Caesar in the East, Maximinus Daza. To make matters worse, the Caesar Augustus of the East, Severus, had turned on him to forge an alliance with Maxentius.

Surveying the city from under a heavy brow, Constantine's eyes met scenes of treachery, bloodshed and dysfunction. Yet he also saw a glimmer of opportunity – a chance to overhaul the entire system of government. In an eye-wateringly bold move, Constantine claimed power over the empire not as one of four tetrarchs but as sole emperor, all-powerful and entirely in charge. Constantine made an audacious justification for this volte-face: not only did he claim to be a descendant of Emperor Claudius II, he maintained that he had been chosen to rule by the gods Apollo and Victory themselves.[12] References to their qualities of light, truth and triumph played well in most quarters. Nevertheless, it was not these pagan deities whom Constantine invoked when he finally arrived to take the capital.

There, as he faced down Maxentius on the Milvian Bridge north of the city, he cried to the skies for approval and good fortune, beseeching the one Christian God.

In hoc signo vinces: by this sign you shall conquer. So Jesus himself was said to have told Constantine in a dream.[13] The sign was the name of Christ expressed in two Greek figures: the p-shaped *Chi* and the diagonal cross of the *Rho*. Legend tells us that Constantine even saw the figures interlocked in the fiery haze of the sun the day before he arrived in Rome. It was October 312 when Constantine and his 40,000 troops made their slow progress southwards down the via Flaminia to reach the Milvian Bridge, north of Rome. He and his men had only reached the city after weeks of draining travel – barred, battled and, increasingly, welcomed in Italian cities from Susa to Milan. Constantine was not a Christian. Growing up in Nicodemia, he had mixed with followers of Jesus, though there they were an increasingly maligned group.[14] In spite of this, Constantine took the night-time auguries of Jesus to heart. When his soldiers faced those of Maxentius on the 28 October they did so with shields emblazoned with Chi and Rho.[15]

Maxentius too turned his eyes to the heavens for wisdom, but unlike Constantine he did not keep their counsel. For the pagan gods told him to tear down most of the bridges across the Tiber and bed down safely behind the Aurelian Walls. This boundary formed a near impassable barrier of concrete and brick, three metres thick and more than four times as high. Outlandish to the last, Maxentius defied divine wisdom and marched out to meet Constantine in open battle. In haste, his men gathered wood and tools to reconstruct part of the Milvian Bridge, which they had begun to destroy when Maxentius was still heeding the gods. Fate favoured Maxentius' enemy, whether cued by Constantine's submission to Jesus or Maxentius' defiance of the pagan gods. Constantine's cavalry advanced. That of Maxentius was swiftly broken. As his men were driven back across the hastily rebuilt bridge, the wooden parts caved into the water underfoot. Constantine emerged victorious. The following year a writer evoked the dire fate of Maxentius: 'the Tiber devoured that man, sucked into a whirlpool, as he was vainly trying to escape with his horse and impressive armour up the far bank'.[16]

— ❦ ❧ ❧ —

As another contemporary Christian writer, Lactantius, would declare: 'The hand of the Lord prevailed.'[17] Constantine certainly deemed his win a gift from the Christian God. On his triumphant entrance into Rome it is claimed that he did not make the customary sacrifice of thanksgiving to Jupiter – a marked omission and rebuttal of no less than the king of the Roman gods.[18] Instead, Eusebius claims that Constantine honoured God, the one Christian deity, erecting a statue of himself wielding the cross in the busiest part of Rome, most likely the Roman Forum.[19] It was a striking decision and, according to some scholars, a colossal statue, as the seated figure measured some twelve metres tall.[20] But even this bold break with convention spoke nothing of the dramatic religious changes that he would soon bring to Rome. Under Constantine, the Christians in the city left the simple obscurity of their house churches to stride through vast, marble-clad buildings raised exclusively for their religion by an emperor who would soon become the greatest ever patron of the Roman Church.[21]

Historians have long laboured to temper and nuance accounts of Constantine, Christianity and the rise of the Church of Rome. They have questioned the time, place and sincerity of the emperor's conversion. They have emphasised his continued patronage and devotion to other cults. They have also underlined the persistence of traditional religions among the Roman people well into the 400s. Evidence suggests that they have been right to do so. Under scrutiny, the heroic story of an emperor and his empire swiftly and utterly Christianised simply does not hold up. And yet Constantine's triumph on the Milvian Bridge, under the banner of Jesus' name, did mark a symbolic and physical watershed for the presence of Christianity in Rome. For Constantine dug and filled the foundations of the city's monumental Christian architecture, making the Roman Church a visible, respectable, state-endorsed institution with a clear physical footprint in Rome. In doing so, he re-shaped the city of his predecessors, with its popular and pagan associations. Incorporating, eliding and suffocating stories of Rome past, Constantine raised new architectural, social and cultural centres in Rome, pregnant with Christian stories and ideas.

This was a pivotal change after years of persecution at the hands of some of the predecessors of Constantine, even if, paradoxically, that persecution was concrete proof of the increasing visibility and presence of the Christian cult in Rome and its empire. The followers of Jesus who lived in the city during Nero's (54–68) reign were an indistinct group, merging into the Jewish community and the Eastern cults with whom they shared Rome's lowliest quarters. In the century before the triumph of Constantine, however, the Church was a sizeable and noticeable target. It is likely that the growth of the community was what brought Christians to the attention of men such as Emperor Aurelian (270–75), who ruled a little before Constantine. According to some contemporaries, Aurelian attacked the followers of Jesus, fuelled by his piety to pagan gods such as Sol Invictus, the Unconquered Sun.[22] Like his predecessors, Aurelian was unnerved by the burgeoning number of his subjects who flatly refused to engage in traditional Roman rites. Unlike emperors of the past, such as Nero, Aurelian could certainly name the group that perturbed him: Christians. Aurelian, in turn, would be defined by them. Christian texts paint the emperor as a bitter and dangerous enemy of the faith. Constantine himself cultivated his own image in stark contrast to his predecessor. His biographer Eusebius decried Aurelian as a perse-cutor 'slain on the public highway', filling 'the furrows of the road' with his 'impious blood.'[23] Drama resonates in these words. Indeed, some have surmised that Aurelian's role as persecutor was just that: a theatrical invention of Constantine and the historians who wanted to flatter him as a benevolent patron of Christians. In other texts, Eusebius and Lactantius, another scholar who lauded Constantine, claim that Aurelian died (in an act of divine retribution) just before he could enact his anti-Christian laws.[24] Whether Aurelian's persecution was real, planned or simply invented, these tales make one fact clear. In the minds of Romans, Christians had an inferior, maligned and potentially perilous status, on the very eve of Constantine's ascent.

We know for certain that some emperors did attack Rome's Christian community. As we have seen, they were distressed about the practical effects of impiety to pagan religion. For them, it was crucial that the gods were appeased because religion could unite or rupture their empire. At the turn of the fourth century, Persia, Rome's most menacing enemy, was united by Zoroastrianism, the Persians' common faith. Diocletian, the Roman emperor at that time, saw the military strength of his nemesis as one fruit of this religious unity.[25] When he looked upon his own lands, host to the prayers, songs and ceremonies of a vast array of cults, he could not help but be filled with trepidation.[26] The emperor bristled when he heard stories of oracles made mute and priests unable to read the entrails of sacrificed animals, while Christians, standing by, made the sign of the cross. Harking back to an imagined past of religious homogeneity, Diocletian sought the chimera of a united pagan Rome and, through this, political and military strength for his empire. He would soon engage Galerius (293–311), his colleague in the East, to join him in a dogged and systematic persecution of religious minorities. First, they fixed their attention on the Manicheans, a group who had emerged in the mid-third century and esteemed Zoroaster as a prophet, along with Buddha, Jesus and the Babylonian Mani. On Diocletian's command in around 302 their leaders were burned alive, their books tossed onto the pyre beneath them.[27] Mere followers could recant. However, if they refused, they too would lose their property, face execution or be marched to a life of hard labour in the mines.

Soon, Diocletian would turn his fiery gaze towards the Christians, enflamed by the fervour of his colleague Galerius.[28] In 303, the emperors seized and destroyed the tools of the Christian religion, lighting fires across the empire to consume books, chalices and plate. Christians were entirely forbidden to meet for worship. Those who refused to conform lost their status and privileges. Even official employees of the state were enslaved, while imperial edicts dragged others to prison cells.[29] Soon the zeal of the emperors had filled the jails. Clemency was offered to all those who would recant. Still anxious to ensure complete religious conformity, in 304 Diocletian and Galerius demanded that every soul in the empire perform a sacrifice to the pagan gods. The products of a similar edict by Emperor Decius (249–51) in the mid-third century betray the trepidation that these demands stirred up in the hearts of the people. Numerous hastily drafted certificates attest utter devotion to the pagan gods, with men such as Aurelius Sarapammon, a 'servant of Appianus', assuring the authorities that he was 'always sacrificing to the gods' and 'now too ... in accordance with the orders ... sacrificed and poured the libations and tasted the offerings'.[30]

Diocletian's persecution was vehement and prolonged. Yet his inability to imprison all those who persistently adhered to Christianity illuminates the scale and strength of the Christian cult in his time. By 299, Christians fought in the Roman army.[31] Around the same time, they were working at the imperial court.[32] This presence undoubtedly increased toleration of the cult among some Roman people who lived and worked alongside Christians. While fervent vitriol against the group left a trail of ash and blood in some regions, in others the effects of Diocletian's orders were surprisingly patchy. By the end of his reign, it is likely that tens of thousands of Christians still walked the streets of Rome, as part of a population of around 800,000.[33] This was largely due to the senior Emperor of the West, Maximian (the father of Maxentius), who was far less zealous in his persecution of Christians than his co-emperors in the East. Despite their ferocity, Maximian was hesitant to enforce the harsher anti-Christian edicts in Italy, and, crucially, in Rome. In that city some books were seized, but many were squirrelled away, as Christians handed over just a portion of their scriptures and others gave state authorities books that were not scriptures at all.[34]

It seems that years of marginalisation had made the Christians of Rome cunning and tenacious in the face of trial. It is telling that the very first emperor to float the idea of toleration had done so not out of charity but sheer exasperation with the group. Sometime between mid-June and 22 July 260, Emperor Gallienus (253–68), a predecessor of Diocletian, had written a letter addressed to Dionysius, a man who was soon to become Bishop of Rome, as well as 'Pinnas, Demetrius and the other bishops'.[35] The letter told the men that they could use the document as proof that 'no one may molest' them in their Christian worship. Gallienus claimed that this was something that he had allowed 'already for a long time', in contrast to his father and co-ruler in the East, Emperor Valerian (253–60). This was not filial rebellion. Rather, it was a pragmatic acceptance of the fact that the Christian community in Rome was so resilient that further attacks appeared pointless. When Gallienus relinquished persecution altogether, the Christian group grew even stronger. In 311 in the East, Emperor Galerius was moved to promulgate a similar decree. In his declaration, the Edict of Serdica, he made it clear that persecution had not checked Christian worship. While Galerius conceded that some Christians 'were subdued by the fear of danger' and 'even suffered death' for their religion, he also conceded that most 'persevered in their determination', met anyway and simply made 'laws unto themselves'.[36]

Christians were well aware of the power of persistence. Their heroes were often defined by defiance in the face of threats. Meanwhile, Christians who complied with the demands of their persecutors could be branded with the black mark of treachery. In 303, collaboration with the state's anti-Christian edicts stained the character of Marcellinus (296-c. 304), the Bishop of Rome himself. He and his priests, Miltiades, Marcellus and Sylvester, were accused of bending to the emperors' demands that the Church of Rome hand over its holy books and burn incense for pagan gods.[37] Later Christians and, presumably, Christians of the time, decried the men as turncoats, calling for their immediate expulsion from the Christian community. The sheer force of this disapproval appears to have pushed Marcellinus from Peter's seat, depriving him of his position and forcing him to his knees at the feet of nearly 200 fellow bishops.[38]

This treatment might seem harsh, but the bar was high. Already at this time, less than 300 years since the arrival of Christianity in Rome, there was a tradition of heroic holiness that defied persecution. In the year 250, Fabian (236–50), a Roman noble and the twentieth bishop of the city, offered up his life for his faith. Fabian had rebuffed Emperor Decius' demand that all sacrifice to the gods and, like the slave Aurelius Sarapammon, produce a certificate to prove it.[39] Just three years after Fabian's martyrdom, his successor Bishop Cornelius of Rome (251–3) would refuse the same demand and die in exile with his worldly reputation in tatters. Even Emperor Valerian would be defied by a Bishop of Rome. This time it was Sixtus II (257–8) who lost his head. In contrast to these recent brave pastors who had paid the very highest price for defying imperial commands for their faith, the actions of Bishop Marcellinus would have seemed craven.

Under Constantine, such bravery would prove unnecessary. Contrary to some assumptions, Constantine did not leave Rome a Christian city. However, he did legalise and elevate the faith across the empire. Constantine's resolution to support the Christian Church formally would be made not in Rome but in Mediolanum, modern-day Milan. Moreover, it was not a decision that he would make alone. Although Constantine had fought Maxentius on the Milvian Bridge for sole power over the empire, practicalities had forced him into an alliance and, consequently, co-rule with Licinius (308–24), who would become Caesar Augustus in the East of the empire. Just four months after Constantine saw Maxentius drowned in the Tiber, he rallied with his new ally in Milan. There, the two men would discuss a marriage between Licinius and Constantine's sister, Constantia. Although this coupling and the alliance that it cemented were the focus of the meeting, history remembers it best for an agreement regarding Christianity. The so-called Edict of Milan of 313 assured that the new rulers would 'grant both to the Christians and to all men freedom to follow the religion which they choose'.[40] The decision drew together the patchwork of edicts of toleration promulgated intermittently in previous decades. It legalised Christianity across the empire and banned the persecution of Christians outright. Writing in Rome, Lactantius was jubilant about the liberation of Christians from years of persecution, as well as the just recognition of a 'Supreme Deity', by inference the one Christian God.[41] No specific edict has ever been found, despite Eusebius referring to a decree. However, the move to official, permanent toleration of Christians, addressed by both Lactantius and Eusebius, is undoubtedly true.

— ෬ ෨ ෨ —

The change brought about by Constantine did not convert the empire or even the city of Rome to the Christian faith. Pagans still dominated the aristocracy in the 380s and it was not until the mid-fifth century that the Roman élite was overwhelmingly Christian.[42] That said, the faith began to seep into the stones of the city almost immediately. Meanwhile, the status and nature of the Church was increasingly coloured by the character of empire. Soon, the Church and empire of Rome would be inextricably intertwined in a process of physical and ideological osmosis that raised the architectural cornerstones of Christian Rome that remain to this day. To survive in the city's shadier corners, the earlier Christian Church had needed simple facilities, basic – even tacit – approval and some sense of unity and direction. As a tolerated, public religion, the demands on the Church swiftly grew. Now, the Church in Rome was called to exhibit its authority and identity, while accommodating an ever-increasing number of faithful. New buildings were essential. Even if Christians could overlook the taint of past pagan worship on existing religious buildings, the structures were simply impractical for Christian ritual. Their centre of gravity was outside: a large altar used to sacrifice animals, spilling blood and innards for the gods.[43] Christianity was more like a mystery religion, the rituals of which occurred inside and undercover. The faithful witnessed the ceremony, playing their part in prayer and solemn devotion, whether in a lowly house church or the great Constantinian buildings that would soon be raised in Rome.

When Constantine drew Christianity out into the public sphere, he would give it a home not in the temple but in the basilica, the most grandiose structure of the Roman Empire. As we have already seen in Maxentius' immense project in the Roman forum, basilicas were where public meetings, ceremonies and even legal procedures took place. When he sponsored these buildings, Constantine took up another imperial tradition: patronising public architecture. In Rome, his predecessors had commissioned basilicas for the civic good and conveyed their piety by raising temples to the gods of love, war and commerce. Manifesting his faith in the Christian Church, Constantine repurposed the Romans' official state architecture for new religious ends. In doing so, he inaugurated the transformation of the term 'basilica' into a word that now rings with Christian connotations. Under rectangular roofs, these cavernous spaces had aisles at each side, defined by colonnades and appended with a raised platform at head, foot or both. Such platforms frequently appeared in the apse, a rounded space usually at the basilica's furthest extremity, but occasionally along its sides. In some Roman traditional basilicas, a judge would sit atop a formal throne, acting with authority delegated by the emperor himself.[44] In the Christian basilica, it was the bishop who would be enthroned in the seat of oversight and judgement. In Rome, imperial favour had truly elevated the once derided cult of Christ.

When Constantine built churches, he not only elevated Christianity but also wrote his own chapter in the story of Rome. In 324, the Western world's first major Christian basilica would appear on the Caelian Hill. The church that would come to be known as the Lateran Basilica, and later San Giovanni in Laterano, was built atop the ruined quarters of the praetorian guard who had sided with Maxentius. Constantine and his mother, Helena, would make this south-eastern area of Rome an important quarter for the religion of the Christians. Ten minutes' walk westward from that first basilica stood Helena's Sessorian Palace, where men, women and children would bow down to venerate a piece of wood said to be from the cross on which Jesus himself had hung.[45] In 326, Helena had set out from Rome for the Holy Land, where she used imperial funds to seek out places and objects associated with Jesus and his first followers.[46] Like Constantine she erased recent histories to build Christian monuments for a new age. In Jerusalem, she tore down a temple built by Emperor Hadrian and dedicated to either Venus or Jupiter, ploughing foundations for a new Christian building in its place. Wary of angering the Romans, Constantine took a more cautious approach. In Rome, he did not dare construct his Christian basilicas on the sites of pagan temples, or even in the central areas of the city. Yet even if the new buildings of the Roman Church were erected in the outskirts, the effects on the city's landscape were transformative, permanent and often dazzling.

Together, mother and son, Augustus and Augusta, built a new Christian cityscape. Gilded with the authority of the state, enriched with the religious treasures of the Holy Land, it grew up in an empire that was changing, gradually but dramatically and forever. On the site of Maxentius' barracks, the Lateran Basilica stretched to 100 metres in length. The creation of a triumphant ruler and religion, it was dubbed the 'Golden Basilica' after the luminous yellow marble with which it was clad.[47] At Helena's palace, the relics of the True Cross that her builders had unearthed in Jerusalem were dusted off and enshrined in the private chapel in a bejewelled casket of gold. This room was the nucleus of what is now the basilica of Santa Croce in Gerusalemme, named for that piece of the cross from Golgotha, now a permanent fixture in Rome.

Snaking across the city towards the north-west, between the Colosseum and the spot where Santa Maria Maggiore would soon stand, Romans could cross the river to reach Constantine's next major building project: the Basilica of Saint Peter on the Vatican Hill. Just as he had at the Lateran, the emperor erased the past life of the Vatican to construct his city's future. In building the Basilica of Saint Peter, he would not dismantle the barracks of his enemy, nor stones that had once honoured the pagan gods. To level the ground of the muddled, bumpy burial site where Saint Peter lay, Constantine's builders had to cover the humble monument that Christians had furtively frequented in the first centuries of the Roman Church.[48] The small *aedicula*, held up by simple marble columns, had marked and protected the site for centuries. Its surroundings were remodelled and hundreds of graves were pushed deeper and deeper into the ground as Constantine built an edifice larger even than the Lateran, stretching to some 122 metres long and sixty-six metres wide. Once the basilica was open, the vast space swelled with the faithful. Casting their glance to the end of the nave, where Mass would be celebrated, they would see Constantine's name shining out in gold letters atop a triumphal arch.[49]

—— ରଷ ଧର ଧର ——

Constantine's regime had destroyed the buildings of his enemies and erased some pagan places of piety. Now he had swept away the humble roots of the Church of Rome to dig the foundations of what would become a triumphantly Christian city. Principally, however, it was tales of martyrdom that underpinned his basilicas dedicated to Peter, John the Baptist and Christ himself. Such stories, particularly that of Peter, would remain the surest foundations for this new Christian Rome for many centuries to come.

Christian Rome, later papal Rome, would never be realised in Constantine's lifetime. Yet its institutional shape and strength were born with his decrees. This included the elevation of the Bishop of Rome, which would facilitate his emergence as pope of the entire Western Church. For Constantine established the hierarchy that still defines the Catholic Church and, at one time, shaped huge swathes of religious, political and social life across the Western world. At the top of this pyramid, beneath the emperor himself, sat the Bishop of Rome, also known as 'God's consul'.[50] It was he who would take the seat of the judge in the apse of the Lateran Basilica, and it was he who was consecrated to the office in the cavernous nave of Saint Peter's Basilica. At that time, the Bishop of Rome would be named by a cluster of priests and, acting below them, deacons.[51] The choice could then be ratified by neighbouring bishops, such as the bishop of the nearby coastal see of Ostia. As we shall see, the election of a new bishop could also be confirmed or denied formally or informally by the will of the people.[52] This was a process that had begun to emerge before Constantine. With the actions of that emperor it was cemented, as the significance of the identity and actions of the Bishop of Rome influenced the lives of an ever-growing number of Christians.

In the time of Peter and Paul, bishops had taken on a limited role in the Christian community, as the ultimate font of charity and guarantor of the safety and resources of the Church. Across the empire, they were important as administrators, but they were not yet defined as spiritual pastors of a larger flock, let alone the most powerful figures in the lives of great cities. By the second century their status had begun to change. Contemporaries urged Christians to 'follow the bishop, as Jesus Christ follows the father', undertaking nothing ecclesiastical without the bishop's say.[53] With imperial recognition and swelling coffers, the authority of fourth-century bishops grew even further. The Bishop of Rome in particular became quite rich. Imperial gifts and land gave the Lateran Basilica and its adjacent baptistery an income of around 15,000 *solidi* a year, topped up annually with around 4,000 *solidi* from the revenues at Saint Peter's. Overall, the Bishop of Rome received around 30,000 *solidi* a year.[54] This was a fraction of the income of affluent senators, who could enjoy six-figure incomes unburdened by the cost of maintaining an array of grand imperial churches. Even so, such wealth cast the bishops of Constantinian Rome in stark contrast to their predecessors. It would certainly transform the life of a bishop from a middling background, in which a family might live off just 250 *solidi* a year.[55]

Inevitably, the office was soon pursued by men hungry for position and power. Looking on, some believers lamented the effects of imperial influence on their Church. Others longed to take advantage of Christianity's new status and wealth. Even pagan aristocrats such as Vettius Agorius Praetextatus would joke to one bishop, Damasus I (366–84), 'Make me the Bishop of Rome and I will become a Christian immediately!'[56] Damasus understood the jest well. He had taken far more extreme measures to secure his own election in 366, making hard, sharp tiles rain from the roof of the Liberian Basilica on the site where the basilica of Santa Maria Maggiore now stands.[57] Those shards of stone had been hurled down by a motley gang of supporters: gravediggers, spectators from the circus and others willing to risk their lives for his cause. Their target had been the followers of Ursinus, a Roman deacon who claimed that he, and not Damasus, had been elected Bishop of Rome.[58] The city prefect fled and 137 men died. Blood stained the Esquiline Hill.[59] Yet even in this scandal, Damasus saw opportunity, commandeering the prefect's police force and turning them on his enemy. Ursinus refused to relinquish his claim, keeping his supporters armed as they regrouped a few kilometres north-east at the recently built church of Sant'Agnese.[60] That building had been raised over the tomb of a thirteen-year-old girl who had refused to relinquish her Christian faith as she was stripped, hauled through the streets of Rome and, eventually, beheaded in 304. Now, the Christian Church was so elevated that men murdered one another just to become its bishop.

And so the worldly recognition of the Roman Church brought contrasts, violent and moral, that tainted the very honour that Damasus and Ursinus sought so energetically. Witnessing such savage competition for the bishop's crook, Ammianus Marcellinus, a Roman historian and soldier, sneered, 'The contestant who wins is sure to become rich through the gifts of aristocratic ladies, to ride in comfortable carriages, to dress splendidly, and to serve feasts on a scale fit to rival the tables of kings.'[61] Damasus would relish in living up to the jibe, earning the nickname 'earpick to great ladies' after emerging victorious from his battles with Ursinus in 366. Some could not help but ask if this was appropriate for the men who held Saint Peter's See. Jerome, who would become Damasus' secretary, would decry priests who basked too eagerly in the fresh prestige of the Church of Rome. His damning descriptions reveal that many clerics emulated their aristocratic patrons, taking great labour over their own appearance and even curling their hair. For these men, it was important that their dress befit their new role in Rome's genteel society. However, other priests, such as one Macarius, would lament such show. In a Church upwardly mobile and rife with competition, he did so at the risk of a nasty backlash.

Men such as Jerome and Macarius might have been repelled by the display, but the Church needed the Roman élite. Later Romans claimed that patrician Christians had raised the very basilica where Damasus and Ursinus had fought, now known as Santa Maria Maggiore. According to tradition, construction of that church had been instigated in the 350s when a wealthy, childless couple asked God how they might leave their possessions to the Virgin Mary. As they took to their knees in prayer that hot August night, snow fell from a cloudless sky on the Esquiline Hill. That snow is said to have marked the place where the basilica now stands. This legend is not, however, the only origin story for the church. Others say it was Pope Liberius (352–66) who built the basilica after dreaming that there would be snowfall in Rome in summer. It is also argued that he made the basilica out of an existing secular building or palace owned by the Sicinini family.[62] The explanations conflict and overlap, but all suggest a Roman Church increasingly sustained by the city's wealthiest class.

—— ඥ ඔ ඔ ——

The popes, too, had become important patrons, as the story of Liberius suggests. For soon after Constantine's rise, he abandoned Rome. Though the emperor had built an alliance with Licinius, the friendship was strained and short-lived. Licinius grew to see Constantine as a power-rival and began to persecute Christians, whom he identified as the lackeys of his co-emperor.[63] By 325, Licinius would be dead, his army defeated by Constantine's and his cold corpse hanged from a rope. Constantine was finally the sole leader of the empire. However, without an ally to help him to rule the East he was plagued by worries. Warring Persians and Barbarians; the precious resources of his richer, more densely-populated eastern lands; trade on the Black and Mediterranean Seas – all kept the emperor awake at night. To maintain control, Constantine would need to move his capital from Rome, eastwards. In 324, he founded a new power centre in the ancient city of Byzantium, sitting on the crux of Asia and Europe at the centre of the rugged isthmus that separated the Marmaran and Black Seas.

Within six years Byzantium was formally re-dedicated and given the emperor's name.

The translation of imperial power to that new capital of Constantinople inevitably took imperial focus and favour away from Rome and its Church. The dilution of the city's significance was evident in the translocation of relics eastwards. Instead of arriving in Rome, like the holy treasures carried home by Helena, the remains of major apostles such as Luke and Andrew would be ferried straight to Constantinople.[64] The decision-making processes of the global Church also assumed an oriental thrust. In 325 Constantine convoked the first ever ecumenical council not in Rome but at Nicaea, around 100 km south-east of the new imperial capital.[65] Constantine invited some 1,800 Christian bishops, from Hispania to the Persian Empire, to settle disputes that had emerged between and within Christian communities. Heretics, the date of Easter and the true nature of God and Jesus were up for debate. Constantine would not have a formal vote and sat behind the bishops, yet he was clearly keen to maintain a prominent presence in Christian affairs. Eusebius tells us that the emperor made a dramatic entrance to the Council, gliding through the room in 'a purple robe ... adorned with the dazzling brilliance of gold and precious stones', glittering 'as it were with rays of light'.[66]

The transfer of imperial power eastwards perturbed some Christian leaders. But others would transform the problem into an opportunity. With Constantine gone, they could assert the supreme status of their Roman See. The Bishops of Rome further expanded and embellished his monumental blueprint for Christian Rome. Just a few weeks before Constantine died, Julius I (337–52) would be elected as bishop of the city. He would build five churches before his successor Liberius took his place. The endeavour was not without setbacks. In 381, some half a century after the migration of the capital, Damasus I would discover that Constantinople's bishop was being referred to as the bishop of 'New Rome'.[67] As the Bishop of 'Old Rome', a city that he believed held unique religious and ecclesiastical significance, Damasus was fuming. At a meeting to discuss licit and illicit scriptures in 382, he would make his feelings known by quoting Jesus himself. At the council in Rome, Damasus bolstered his own authority with the Gospel of Matthew: 'you are Peter and on this rock I will build my church'.[68] Peter had been chosen by Jesus to build the Church on earth. Peter had died in the See of Rome. Peter was the source of the Roman bishop's authority. No other bishop could trump this claim. For Damasus and others, Constantinople's title 'New Rome' only underlined the unique significance of their own Holy See, elevating the new imperial capital only by reference to the old.

It is no coincidence that Damasus I continued carving out the Christian face of Rome. Ornamenting and enlarging buildings, tombs and reliquaries, he would give many corners of the city a distinctly Christian character. Where miracles did not instigate the great building projects of the age, the stories of the Christian martyrs would. Even before Roman bishops took on the mantle of city architects, Constantine had built his churches on legends and relics of violence, blood and bone. We see a radical break with Roman culture of the past in Christian praise for men and women who had been tried and tortured as criminals. Self-sacrifice for glory was praised in pagan Rome, but Romans ultimately derided demise in defeat. Ancient Rome was the only society that entertained itself with gladiatorial fights to the death. Augustine of Hippo had described this 'bloodthirsty pleasure', lamenting the fate of his friend Alypius who became drunk on the frenzy of the Roman crowd.[69] It is no surprise, then, that the majority of non-Christian Romans ignored those who lost their lives for the teachings of Jesus Christ. They heroized those who defied death and asked blood-soaked Christians, 'enjoy your bath?'[70] The Christians' conception of death was altogether different. They belonged to a Church whose God had been publicly murdered by crucifixion, the most debasing method of execution at the time. Yet through this act, Christians believe that Jesus saved the entire human race from eternal hellfire.

Coming to Rome from Judea in the second century, Justin Martyr proudly characterised Christians as a persecuted people. For Justin, it was 'evident that no one can terrify or subdue' Christians, as 'though beheaded, crucified, thrown to wild beasts, chains and fire, and all other kinds of torture, we do not give up our confession; instead, the more such things happen, the more others – in even larger numbers – become faithful'.[71] For Justin and other Christians, the martyrs' blood had become the well-spring of the Church. The potential implications of this belief became stark in the actions of some particularly zealous believers. Before the age of Constantine, there had been men and women so heartened by the idea of martyrdom that they actively sought to die for their faith, leaving a trail of exasperated Roman officials in their wake. Emperor Marcus Aurelius (161–80) philosophised that one should approach death with 'reason and dignity' not a desire to be 'stagy ... like the Christians'.[72] One Roman prefect even told a group of would-be martyrs that he would not honour their desire for persecution and that they should look to ropes and cliffs instead.[73] Yet there were many who did attain the status of martyrs, most often, of course, unintentionally. At the foot of the Esquiline, a young man called Laurence had faced an agonising end on a flaming hot grill, after sparking the scorn of the authorities with another distinctly Christian precept. Responding to a demand that he turn over his church's valuables, Laurence had presented a group of Rome's most impoverished souls. By the fourth century, an oratory on the site of his execution celebrated his humility and suffering.

Seeking to cement Rome's position as leader in the hierarchy of holy cities, Damasus I gave its martyrs and their monuments their own poetry. Sitting in his study, he composed epithets evoking the stories of the men, women and children who had shed their blood in the streets and circuses of Rome. The bishop claimed to have learnt many of their stories first hand, growing up in the city as a little boy. As an adult, Damasus' pen did not flinch at the derision for Christians or their base and gory deaths, for these only fortified the image of a heroic Christian Rome. In an inscription dedicated to Saint Eutychius, Damasus described his 'prison's filth', the food 'denied' and the 'fragments of pottery' that pierced the saint's back.[74] The torment did not end there, Damasus' poem reveals, for the saint was thrown into a 'deep dungeon' with blood bathing his 'every wound'.[75] As ever in Christian martyrdom, the base was elevated by the miracles of God, which had revealed the location of Eutychius' body in a dream. 'Discovered, he is venerated', Damasus would beam. Now, from heaven, Eutychius could heed the prayers of all those who read Damasus' poem and invoked his saintly name.

The worldly prestige enjoyed by fourth-century bishops such as Damasus was the gift of imperial powers. Yet to crystallise the idea and status of Rome as a Christian city, the Church's leaders looked back to their recent, painful past. The binary of death and devotion epitomised in Damasus' poems would shape an ever more elevated and influential Christian Rome. At the centre, as always, was the bishop, slowly, through his ties to Peter, emerging as a pope. That once marginalised leader now sat in a palazzo, deftly employing the trappings of worldly power. Creating classical poetry, monumental basilicas and extraordinary visual art, the Bishop of Rome began to assume roles once fulfilled by the emperor. Soon the curved apses of churches such as Santa Pudenziana would glister with mosaic images of Christ and the apostles. In these representations, humble, middle-eastern men were transformed into senatorial figures clad in crisp white togas. Looking out upon the Roman people, they had real authority and gravitas. In the final line of his poem on Eutychius, Damasus could not help but underline the growing eminence of his own role. Referring to his own poem, he told the swelling Christian populace: 'Damasus has highlighted [Eutychius'] merit; you venerate his tomb.' In the coming centuries, millions would heed the command, as Rome became not only a supreme authority for the entire Christian Church but a pilgrimage centre teeming with faithful Christians from all over the world.

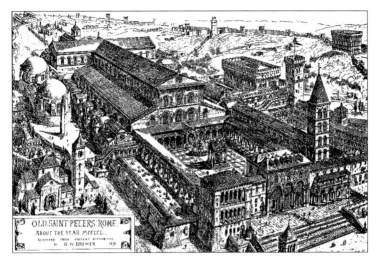

A drawing reconstructing Old St Peter's Basilica. Though the date mentioned by the artist is 1450, the structure suggests that this is how the complex may have looked at the turn of the sixteenth century. (H.W Brewer)

Early fifth-century mosaics, illustrating Christ and the apostles, at Santa Pudenziana. (Ivan Vdovin / Alamy Stock Photo)

The Meeting of Leo the Great and Attila in 452 painted by Raphael in the popes' Apostolic Palace in 1514. (Chris Hellier / Alamy Stock Photo)

A fourteenth-century manuscript illustration of pilgrims arriving in Rome for the year of jubilee. (Zuri Swimmer / Alamy Stock Photo)

A fifteenth-century manuscript copy of Lucretius' *De rerum natura*, one of the Renaissance humanists' greatest textual rediscoveries. (Svintage Archive / Alamy Stock Photo)

Pasquino, Rome's most famous 'talking statue'.

An early sixteenth-century engraving of the ancient masterpiece *Laocoön and His Sons*, which was unearthed in a Roman vineyard during the Renaissance. (UtCon Collection / Alamy Stock Photo)

The Passetto di Borgo, a covered corridor that runs above the streets, connecting the Vatican and the Castel Sant'Angelo. (RealyEasyStar/Daniele Bellucci / Alamy Stock Photo)

An eighteenth-century engraving of the Piazza Giudia by Giuseppe Vasi, showing one of the gates to Rome's ghetto. (The History Collection / Alamy Stock Photo)

The student Pomponio Algieri being executed in a pot of boiling oil in Rome. (The History Collection / Alamy Stock Photo)

A portrait of Emanuele Ne Vunda, the Congolese prince and ambassador whose untimely death in Rome secured his place in the eternal narrative of the city.
(Raffaello Schiaminossi)

Left: Anthony van Dyck's portrait of Robert Shirley, the Englishman and Catholic who acted as the ambassador of the Shah of Persia in Rome. (The Picture Art Collection / Alamy Stock Photo)

Below: A painting depicting the inquisitors of the Holy Office accusing the scientist Galileo Galilei of heresy in the seventeenth century. (CBW / Alamy Stock Photo)

MARIA ALEXANDRA CHRI STINA .SVECIÆ REGINA.

Magnus Alexandro quem soluit in Vrbe Philippus,
Froenas imperyis, Regia Virgo, tuis. D. H. Q.
Ioseph. Testan. Inv. Fecit.

At uictrix ut Regna domes maiora relictis,
Dat Tibi Alexander Nomen, et omen Equus.
Gio. Jacomo Rossi le Stampa, e le Vende in Roma alla Pace.

An engraving of Christina of Sweden, the controversial queen who
renounced her throne to convert to Catholicism and move to Rome.
(World History Archive / Alamy Stock Photo)

Bernini's sculpture of Saint Andrew, ascending into the heavens, at Sant'Andrea al Quirinale. (Alvesgaspar, (CC BY-SA 4.0))

Right: Maria Maddalena Morelli, otherwise known as Corilla Olimpica, the only female poet to be crowned with laurels on the Capitoline Hill. (The History Collection / Alamy Stock Photo)

Below: An early nineteenth-century engraving showing a female figure representing liberty tyrannised by popes. (Heritage Image Partnership Ltd / Alamy Stock Photo)

Left: Antonio Canova's sublime marble head representing 'Peace', carved in Rome as the Napoleonic Wars drew to a close. (Photograph courtesy of Sotheby's)

Below: Moritz Daniel Oppenheim's depiction of the kidnapping of Edgardo Mortara, who was taken from his Jewish parents and put under the custody of Pope Pius IX. (Art Collection 2 / Alamy Stock Photo)

A clash between the papal troops and Italian soldiers led by Garibaldi as his nationalist forces fought to seize papal Rome for the Kingdom of Italy.
(Classic Photo / Alamy Stock Photo)

A photograph staged with troops the day after Rome was captured by the nation of Italy. (ARCHIVIO GBB / Alamy Stock Photo)

The Hitler Youth in Rome during the rule of the fascist dictator Benito Mussolini. (Sueddeutsche Zeitung Photo / Alamy Stock Photo)

Right: Religious imagery used to celebrate fascist ideals at the Exhibition of the Fascist Revolution (1932–4). (ARCHIVIO GBB / Alamy Stock Photo)

Below: Adolf Hitler touring the Colosseum during his official visit to Rome in 1938. (GRANGER – Historical Picture Archive / Alamy Stock Photo)

Pope John Paul II in the moments after he was shot on St Peter's Square in 1981. (jdb collection / Alamy Stock Photo)

Pope Francis prepares to preside over an empty St Peter's Square during the Coronavirus pandemic in 2020. (Abaca Press / Alamy Stock Photo)

PART 2
TURBULENT PRIESTS

▷▷▷▷▷▷▷▷▷▷▷▷▷▷▷▷▷▷▷ ◁◁◁◁◁◁◁◁◁◁◁◁◁◁◁◁◁◁◁

A late second-century sarcophagus depicting a clash between Romans and Barbarians. (Jean-Pol GRANDMONT)

3

Crowned on the Grave of Empire

By the early fifth century Rome appeared on the brink of collapse. Shockwaves reverberate in the letter of Pelagius, who had fled the city:

> It happened only recently, and you heard it yourself. Rome, the mistress of the world, shivered, crushed with fear ... Where, then, was the nobility? Where were the certain and distinct ranks of dignity? Everyone was mingled together and shaken with fear. Slave and noble were one. The same spectre of death stalked before us all.[1]

Rome, once *caput mundi*, once a pinnacle of power and prestige, had been invaded and pillaged, over and again. For Jerome, Damasus I's secretary, it was nothing less than the end of the world.[2] Abandoned by Emperor Constantine, the city had sat in the middle of the Italian peninsula – rich, vulnerable and unprotected. In the fifth and sixth centuries it would be menaced by Barbarians, Huns and Vandals. In 410 it was the turn of the Visigoths, led by their king, Alaric (395–410). War trumpets sounded, houses were turned over, the splendid villa in the Gardens of Sallust was clubbed to stones.[3] Across the city's undulating hills, ravenous, white-hot fires were broken only by the snaking waters of the River Tiber. Yet Rome's principal Christian buildings stood unbroken, respected, undefiled.[4] For despite their brutal appearance and rugged manner, many in the Visigoth army followed the gentle teachings of Jesus Christ. They dealt the city many blows, but Rome's Christian basilicas continued defiantly to shape the skyline. Many pagan sites, on the other hand, were reduced to dust. Even in this moment of acute terror, the Romans noticed their invaders' discerning approach and sought refuge in the cavernous Christian churches built in the age of Constantine.

The stark contrasts of this architectural tableau provide an emblematic backdrop for the metamorphosis of Rome in the fifth and sixth centuries. As the remains of the city's pagan past decayed, its potency as a Christian site burgeoned. The events of this period, in Rome and beyond, also set the stage for the emergence of the papacy as we know it. When emperors no longer inspired and aided those living among Rome's ruins, the popes would emerge to occupy this gaping void. Beyond the city, Christian bishops would also turn to their colleague in Rome. As the imperial systems and authority that had supported the development and implementation of Church law broke down, they sent their queries to the successor of Peter – the Bishop of Rome. Fielding questions about the emerging theology and practice of the Church, the letters that successive popes wrote in response would soon become papal law.[5] Some 1,200 years later, Thomas Hobbes would write that the papacy was 'the ghost of the deceased Roman Empire, sitting crowned on the grave thereof'.[6] It is an evocative metaphor, but it is not the whole picture. For the popes of this period did not climb onto the tomb of the Caesars in a cynical quest for greater power. Rather they (willingly) inched ever closer to it in response to outside demands, taking on imperial tones and authority along the way.[7]

—— C3 &0 &0 ——

Rome did not get much respite in this period. After the blow of the Visigoths' attack, the old giant of a city struggled to its feet only to be knocked out with full force by yet another invader. When the Vandal Gaiseric (428–77) and his men arrived in 455, they made the attack of

Alaric's troops appear relatively restrained. The son of a king and a slave, the leader of the Vandals had vowed to repair their reputation as a fighting people. They had lost a king to the blades of the Franks while the Visigoths had dominated them in Spain. The sixth-century historian Jordanes described Gaiseric as a 'sufficient' politician: 'shrewd in winning over the barbarians and', where necessary, 'skilled in sowing the seeds of dissension to arouse enmity'.[8] Yet the Vandal leader was first and foremost a fighter. Brooding and determined, he was 'furious in his anger, [and] greedy for gain'.[9] He too was a Christian, but when Gaiseric hit Rome, neither church, nor temple, nor shrine would be spared the blow of the Vandals' sword.

Christian churches were broken into, their portals torn down. The menorah – or seven-branched candelabra – that Emperor Titus (79–81) had snatched triumphantly from the Temple of Jerusalem was now hurled with a clang onto the Vandals' cart.[10] These Vandal fighters were not the senseless iconoclasts that their name has come to imply. Their attack was a deliberate display of political and military might. Indiscriminate in their attack – striking sites pagan or Christian – they even took the glittering gilt tiles from the roof of the Temple of Jupiter on the Capitoline.[11] Across the city, merchants, patricians and servants fled their homes, sparing themselves injury and the traumatic sight of foreign invaders plundering their belongings. After fourteen days of hell on earth, the survivors looked upon a Rome ravaged beyond recognition. Drunk on glory, laden with bounty and leading away thousands of captives, the conquerors trudged south-west to their ships at Ostia, as the shell-shocked Romans timidly trailed back to their homes.

The body blows to the city in this period affected its human face as well as its material riches. While some of the élite senatorial class remained in Rome and helped to rebuild the city, many of those who had shaped its religious and intellectual life had fled.[12] In August 410, the barbarian Alaric had arrived at the gate. Some, such as the young aristocratic couple Melania and Pinian, had left the city already.[13] Setting off southwards in 408, Melania in particular was a great loss to the city. She was one of the wealthiest women in the empire and a devoted Christian to boot. Like her grandmother, Melania the Elder, the younger Melania fervently sought a humility that jarred with her senatorial class. Married off at fourteen, she had fought her family, and then her husband, to cast off the trappings of wealth, refusing luxuries like perfume and clothing herself in cheap, rough cloth. Taking little rest and even less food, she is painted by her hagiographers as a woman purging herself of the follies of her sex and youth.[14] When she and Pinian lost two babies she finally convinced him to live with her in a celibate union.[15] Frail, childless and intentionally unrefined, Melania was the anti-type of the great Roman woman. She had, nonetheless, become a powerful force in the emerging Christian city. Balking at personal wealth and bearing no heirs, Melania poured her family money upon priests and their churches. As the Church expanded in Rome, such private patronage had proven a vital lifeline. Even as Christianity had begun to truly assert its presence in the cityscape, wealthy donors such as Melania had funded the *tituli*, discreet Christian centres dotted across Rome.[16]

Anicia Faltonia Proba had escaped Alaric's attack more narrowly, fleeing to Carthage as Rome was sacked. Her departure represented a loss to both the material and spiritual riches of the city. For despite being married to one of Rome's wealthiest businessmen, she too had chosen a deliberately impoverished life.[17] In the relative safety of Carthage her friend Augustine, Bishop of Hippo, would encourage her stern abstentions from pleasures of the flesh. In zealous warnings he reminded Faltonia that no matter her material wealth she would be utterly desolate without the divine.[18] Turning heavenwards did not mean that Faltonia retreated from the world entirely. On the contrary, she was one node in a powerful network of pious Anician women who had captured the attention of some of the great Christian thinkers of her age. The Bishop of Rome, Innocent I (401–17) wrote only one unofficial letter in his life. This was not a missive to an old friend or an informal request for counsel from a trusted advisor, but a letter to one of these women: Faltonia's daughter-in-law Anicia Juliana. Innocent put pen to paper to praise her for embracing celibacy as a widow and living a pious life.[19] Juliana's daughter, Demetrias, would also receive counsel and praise from the distinguished pens of Augustine, Jerome and Pelagius. For these men, ascetic, aristocratic women combined the most elevated aspects of Roman and Christian values in elegant, female form. According to Jerome, they were 'distinguished women with the authority to command, the faith to seek and the perseverance to extract what they require'.[20] But now hardship and barbarians had chased them from the city of Rome.

In 410, Jerome posed the fall of Rome as an almost existential question. Quoting the ancient poet Lucan, he asked: 'If Rome can perish, then what can be safe?' Rome was eternal. It simply could not fall. Jerome's disbelief might have been sparked by the violent invaders, but the real problems were to be found at Rome's own political core. Alaric had not broken down the gates of the city but been let in by Romans – resident traitors to their own people. What's more, on the eve of Gaiseric's invasion in 455 Rome did not even have an emperor. That position had been vacated by Valentinian III (425–55) when he was slain by his enemies on the Campo Marzio in March of that year.[21] Descending from his horse to practise with a bow and arrow, the emperor took a blow to the back of the head before turning to face a second, fatal smack. It was a pitiful end, but the trouble had been stoked by the emperor himself. Insecure and wary of his own military, the previous year Valentinian had ambushed and murdered the general Aetius at Ravenna, the heavily fortified court near Italy's Adriatic coast where the emperor lived.[22] Ravenna had been made the capital of the Western Roman Empire in 402; during Valentinian's childhood it had been adorned with

Christian buildings of warm red brick encrusted in jewel-coloured mosaics. Back in Rome, the friends of Aetius would avenge his death with the attack on the Campo Marzio. They then raised a puppet emperor to take their victim's place.

In spite of Rome's humiliations in the early fifth century, some of the gold *solidi* that passed through the hands of the wealthy (and those who despoiled them) made a bold claim: *INVICTA ROMA AETERNA*. The motto claimed that Rome was indestructible, everlasting and unchanged. Glimpsing the portrait on the verso, Romans must have felt at least a pang of irony. For turning the *solidus*, their eyes would have met the profile of Priscus Attalus, the heavy-browed, weak-chinned usurper imposed on the city by Alaric for a few months around 410. It is not surprising that the epigram on the coin has been derided as an impudent claim from a city where dwindling wealth was consumed by ravenous invaders.[23] Honorius, the true Emperor of the West between 393 and 423, had not even dared take up a residence in Rome, making his capital in Milan. When Alaric had first entered Italy in 401, Honorius had shifted his court southwards to the relative safe haven of Ravenna.[24] From the turn of the fifth century, then, the claim that Rome was eternal and invincible could only have been made dishonestly and in some desperation. In reality, it was a conception of the city promoted by invaders and their puppets, grasping for legitimacy and continuity with a now lost past that they themselves had helped to destroy.

— ☙ ❧ ❧ —

In many quotidian ways, the old rhythm and character of Rome had endured, despite the religious change and political precariousness inaugurated in Constantine's reign. The inhabitants of the city, numbering around 800,000, jostled down streets around the foot of the Capitoline, heading to its markets and those at the Porticus of Octavia and Theatre of Marcellus.[25] There they haggled over fresh fish, bright green brassicas and radishes unearthed from the *campagna* or city farms. In the Forum, orators filled their lungs to penetrate the racket with declamations and prose. At the Circus Maximus, chariot races still set hearts pounding, while the old arches of the Colosseum overflowed with Romans heckling beasts and wrestlers alike. By the mid-fourth century the number of days given over to public games had more than doubled to 177.[26] *Ludi plebeii, ludi ceriales, ludi saeculares*: games for the people, games for grain and games just for Rome itself. Spectators looked on with pleasure as foxes ran from stadia bearing blazing torches in their tails and choruses of men dressed as satyrs sang, wearing the ears of horses.

In the continuing proliferation of traditional games we see the messy reality of Rome after Constantine. For even if that emperor had given prestige and legal protection to Christians, he had not made Rome a Christian place. In basilicas across the city, incense now billowed upwards towards a sole, Christian god, while devotion to Christian martyrs made ever-deeper impressions in the streets and traditions of Rome. Yet there was no sudden watershed in the religion of the city; beliefs old and new, Roman and foreign, monotheist and pantheist, continued to co-exist. Pagan monuments also remained, even as they fell out of use. Shrines to the gods were restored and repaired; the Temple of Vesta was renovated in 394.[27] New pagan statues were erected along the via Sacra, ornamenting the road that connected the holiest sites of the old pagan religion. Other places of worship were subsumed by new Christian structures. The basilica of San Clemente was built on top of a sanctuary to Mithras, a stone's throw from the dormitory where the gladiators of the Colosseum slept. The Irish Dominican archaeologist Father Joseph Mullooly was astonished to discover those rooms in 1867.[28] A fifth-century Roman might not have shared his surprise. For this collage of religious architecture was a fitting microcosm of a city that still cast its prayers in many different directions, even as new Christian basilicas continued to open their doors.

With Rome unconverted and the Western Empire so weak, the future might have looked ominous for the Church of Rome and her bishop. Both had been buoyed by the favour of Constantine in the preceding century and now imperial power was seriously waning. What is more, the Christians themselves had been blamed for Rome's demise. The city's resolute pagan believers saw the violence of the fifth century as the just result of Constantine's support for the Church. They argued that 'many calamities have befallen the Roman Empire through some Christian emperors'.[29] The imperial commissioner, Marcellinus, would write to Augustine for help, seeking a response to claims that Rome had only been ruined when it had forsaken its traditional pagan gods.[30] The bishops had celebrated Christian saints in gold and marble. The holy bones of Peter, Paul, Laurence, Agnes and so many others laid in the very soil. Poems around the city invoked their prayers. Yet when Rome was attacked, its many saints appeared to be asleep. The Christian God had done nothing to defend the city. When Alaric besieged Rome, the prefect made a desperate attempt to turn back the clock, celebrating pagan rituals on the Capitoline Hill with the senate in tow.[31] Later writers would also blame the rise of Christianity for the fall of the Western Empire, even if they did not see it as a supernatural failure. In the eighteenth century, the influential historian Edward Gibbon blamed the Church for eroding the Romans' sense of duty and civic pride.[32] Without these – and the help of the gods – many believed that the empire was doomed.

The Western Empire would fall, but the See of Rome would not fall with it – despite the persistence of pagan traditions and the calumny cast on the Christian Church. Emerging from the blood-stained cobbles and debris, a series of strong and assertive Roman bishops defined themselves as protectors of the city and custodians of Christians across the globe. Just as the early martyrs had shown strength in worldly weakness and death, the Bishops of Rome forged on as the secular power of their city faltered. When pagans blamed Christians for Rome's problems, Leo I (440–61) boldly turned the finger elsewhere. He had become bishop in 440 and held office through the tumults and aftermath of Gaiseric's sack. By his account, the Christian Church was the solution not the cause of recent distress. Like some modern scholars, he believed barbarian violence had merely exacerbated rot that had set in some time ago. Speaking to the emperor of the Eastern Empire, Marcian (450–57), Leo argued that God might have defended the city if proper discipline had been meted out to heretics in the past.[33] The argument was impossible to prove or disprove, of course. Still, it betrayed Leo's strength. It was this profound confidence in the pivotal role of the Church and its bishop in Rome that would secure the survival and flourishing of both during this tempestuous time.

An imposing Tuscan, a man of substance and power, Leo was known and respected far from Rome. By the time that Gaiseric appeared at that city's gates, Leo would be Rome's bishop. It would be he, not the emperor, who rode out to bargain for the people. Leo was shrewd. He knew that the Vandals had not come all the way from Carthage to leave empty-handed. Gaiseric's men were weary and hungry for booty; denied the opportunity to pillage, they would mutiny and kill. As they trudged towards the city of Rome, the Vandals had already torn down the aqueducts that channelled precious water to the city's people. Meeting Gaiseric eye-to-eye outside of the city gates, Leo was anxious to strike a deal. According to the fifth-century historian Prosper of Aquitaine, Leo demanded that Gaiseric refrain from imposing 'fire, murder and torture'.[34] In return, the bishop assured him that few within Rome's walls would rise up in defence. The two men shook hands and a systematic two-week attack ensued. Blood was spilt and Gaiseric took hostages.

Tellingly, the figures that the Vandals carried off were members of the imperial family and entourage, fallen from grace. Among the pitiful figures on the caravan train back to Carthage sat Eudoxia, Eudocia and Placidia, the wife and daughters of the recently killed Emperor Valentinian III.[35]

It was not, however, all doom and ruin. Leo had guarded the main Christian buildings of the city and, in them, sheltered the terrified Roman people. Even if Leo's negotiation had not been entirely successful, it was successful enough to mark him out as Rome's protector, even as remnants of the empire were felled and carried off as plunder. This was not the only time that Leo had acted as an influential intercessor for the state and people of Rome. On the eve of his election as bishop in 440, he had been engaged by Emperor Valentinian III to travel to Gaul as peacemaker in a bitter quarrel between that ill-fated general Aetius and Albinus, the chief magistrate in the region.[36] According to Prosper of Aquitaine, Leo 'restored friendship' between the two men. More impressive still, in the year 452 Leo would face down Attila the Hun (434–53).[37] Described as a short, stocky, fierce man whose flat nose sat amidst a stormy countenance, Attila had been preparing to march on Rome to claim the hand of Valentinian's elder sister, Honoria. By this time, Honoria was in her mid-thirties and her love life was a mess. Valentinian had planned to marry her off to the respectable but undesirable senator, Bassus Herculanus, as a punishment for sleeping with the manager of her estate.[38] In a fit of desperation, Honoria had sent out a cry for help, apparently sending Attila a ring and promising him half the Western Roman Empire. For the King of the Huns, both proposals were irresistible. Now he was on his way to claim Honoria as his wife.

With the political class divided by conflicting interests and family rivalry, it was Leo, the Bishop of Rome, who marched northwards to plead for Rome at Attila's camp in Lombardy. There Leo and his retinue of clerics encountered a man who delighted in being called the 'scourge of God', and whose army's fearful reputation rested almost entirely on his personal brutality. Writing three years after the meeting, Prosper of Aquitaine gives a remarkable account, claiming that Attila was 'so impressed by the presence of the high priest [Leo] that he ordered his army to give up ... and departed beyond the Danube', back to his homeland.[39] A later, anonymous account recounts the words of a speech that Leo apparently delivered there on the banks of the River Mincio. Valorous and pragmatic, the Bishop of Rome is said to have pleaded on behalf of 'the senate and the people of Rome, once conquerors of the world, now indeed vanquished'.[40] Attila, that restive savage, was apparently left entirely beguiled, 'looking upon [Leo's] venerable garb and aspect, silent, as if thinking deeply'.[41] By all accounts, Leo was an impressive man. Still, the latter part of this particular source suggests that Attila might have been influenced by an authority beyond Leo's individual person. It is said that after hearing Leo speak Attila shot his eyes up to the heavens where he saw brilliant images of Peter and Paul in the mitres and cloaks of bishops, stretching out heavy swords over Leo's head. Jupiter and Mars might have been abandoned but Rome was now protected by the might of Christian saints. Imbued with the authority of Peter, Leo had stepped up as protector of Rome.

There were, of course, practical arguments with which Leo could convince Attila to turn back. Scholars contend that even if Rome could not destroy the Huns' army, lack of food and plague would have seen them off before they arrived at the gates. This explanation seems likely. Leo had conversed with the Vandal Gaiseric in similarly pragmatic terms. But while the account of Prosper of Aquitaine might be peppered with heroic falsehoods, his story is emblematic of an important reality: the burgeoning significance of the Bishop of Rome. Constantine might have buoyed that office but now the leader of the Roman Church had emerged as an independently influential figure, not the mere underling of an imperial power by then waning. Instead, the office and authority of the Roman Bishop were endorsed and protected by the holy weapons of Peter and Paul themselves; those great saints of the Christian Church were also coming to be recognised as the patrons and guardians of Rome. This was not accidental. Leo saw and instrumentalised the unique power of the Petrine link. By his own request, he would be the first pope to be buried at Saint Peter's Basilica.[42] With an increasingly universal authority, rooted in the city Rome and the blood of the martyrs, the Bishop of Rome was able to transcend the political trauma of his age.

— ෨ ෨ ෨ —

As the Roman bishop became an increasingly autonomous leader in Rome, he also rose as a supreme authority in the global Christian Church. Up until the fourth and fifth centuries, each of the major Christian cities – Rome, Alexandria and Antioch – had bishops with relatively similar roles. They were patriarchs who oversaw souls from Egypt to the Italian Peninsula.[43] As the church grew, less senior bishops of smaller geographic areas would also be appointed. At this time, however, the bishops of the biggest Christian centres were the religious authorities of their own cities and guardians and voices for the lands in which they stood. More than this, together the bishops of Rome, Alexandria and Antioch worked to direct the entire Christian world.[44] In these formative years of the Christian Church as an ecclesiastical institution, discussions regarding correct belief and practice could be extremely fraught. Sparks could also fly if one bishop sought to raise his voice over those of his episcopal colleagues. This was particularly grievous if newer bishops challenged the traditional triumvirate of Rome, Alexandria and Antioch. When Constantine took his capital eastwards to Constantinople, the bishop of that new power centre jostled to stand eye-to-eye with his older, more venerable colleagues. Constantinople wanted to supplant Alexandria to become the dominant authority in the Middle East.[45] Debates and controversy could be tumultuous, though, ultimately, these were growing pains. Just as the Bishop of Rome had emerged ever stronger from the traumas facing the city and empire, bishops such as Leo would use episcopal conflicts to assert and define Rome's pre-eminent place in the global Christian Church.

Leo I was far from the only Roman bishop to flex his authority beyond the diocese of Rome. His predecessor, Sixtus III (432–40), had told the bishops of the Balkan region of Illyria that they should consider his orders as superior to those from bishops in the East.[46] Clutching an endorsement from the then long-dead Valentinian III, Leo's successor Hilarius (461–8) would also claim supremacy for Rome. Still, of all bishops in the period, it was Leo himself who did most to carve out the role of the pope in the universal Christian Church.

As we might imagine, he faced resistance. The Second Council of Ephesus in 449 saw a rejection of Roman supremacy so violent that is now known as the 'Gangster Synod'. The key protagonist in the action was the Bishop of Alexandria, Dioscorus, a man said to have so abused his influence that the brother of one of his priests died under the stress of torment.[47] The council had been convened to discuss the teachings of the church, mainly the nature of Christ. After a dispute on the matter, Dioscorus wanted Flavian, the Bishop of Constantinople, stripped of his office.[48] Leo was not present in Ephesus but sent a delegation. As they rose to deliver Rome's statement on the question, Dioscorus shut them down. The meeting descended into chaos when Dioscorus stormed the hall with a riotous band of monks and soldiers who had been waiting for his signal just outside the doors.[49] For Leo, outrage was heaped upon outrage as Dioscorus declared that he, the Bishop of Rome, was excommunicated from the Church.[50] Flavian of Constantinople would be made to suffer, too. He was beaten to a pulp and only relieved of his pains when he died from the wounds a few days later. Brazenly and violently, Dioscorus had rejected the authority of the Roman Bishop to even speak in the Church. Stupefied, a contemporary author wrote to Emperor Marcian, accusing Dioscorus of having 'barked at the apostolic see itself'.[51]

Even in this upset, Leo saw a glimmer of opportunity. He ignored the excommunication and had his statement read at another meeting, the Council of Chalcedon in 451. If Rome were to be supreme, it must act accordingly, refusing to be cowed by the demands of lesser episcopacies. This time, delegates from across Christendom heard the words from Rome. More than this, they esteemed them above those of any other living bishop. The reason was the Petrine line: the link between the Roman See and Saint Peter. Some even cried out, claiming that, at Chalcedon, Peter had 'spoken through Leo'.[52] Meanwhile, Dioscorus was damned for daring 'to hold a council without the authority of the Apostolic See'.[53] For the delegates at Chalcedon, the events of the Gangster Synod were 'something that has never happened before and should never happen' again.[54] In some ways, Constantinople – prestigious as an imperial capital – was given par with Rome, but ultimately Saint Peter's See was declared to have the 'primacy of honour'.[55] The Council of Chalcedon was by no means the only body to recognise the pre-eminent position of Rome in this period. A year earlier, Western Emperor Valentian III and Eastern Emperor Marcian had uttered the most significant imperial acknowledgement of Rome's primacy to date. Calling on Leo to take a leading role at Chalcedon, they recognised him as 'archbishop of the glorious city of Rome' but, of all bishops, 'the bishop pre-eminent in the divine faith'.[56]

Augustine of Hippo had spoken to a slightly earlier generation when he claimed that there was no need for 'dismay when earthly kingdoms passed away'.[57] Yet even well after his death in 430, the words rang true. The authority of the Roman bishop did not come from the strength of armies that could be vanquished or riches that could be spent or stolen. It came from martyrs who had already given up their life for the faith. This authority could not be undermined, debased or corrupted, like the legend of the once mighty Roman Empire. It also had the potential to compel huge swathes of people, as it was underpinned by compelling ideals such as courage, integrity and self-sacrifice. It was, therefore, an authority that was, in its essence, universal. As Leo told the Romans directly: 'thanks to Peter, you have become head of the world ... you reign over a vaster empire by virtue of divine religion than you ever did by earthly supremacy'.[58]

―― C3 ᴇᴏ ᴇᴏ ――

Back in Rome the presence and power of the papacy had already been dug into the bowels of the city, arranged in the apostolic succession – the line of bishops stretching back to Peter's age. At one time half a million bodies laid on the twenty kilometres of passageways that comprise the Catacombs of San Callisto up on the Appian Way. There, on the first stretches of that well-walked road into Rome from the East, were the bodies of bishops, from Anterus (236–250) to Cornelius (251–3), Sixtus II (257–8), Dionysius (260–8) and Felix (269–274) – pontiffs in a line that traced its roots all the way back to the apostolic age. The faithful who came to venerate these men could thank Damasus (366–84), that bishop-poet who had fought so violently for the Roman See. For he had constructed the staircase that allowed visitors to enter the graves of his predecessors.[59] Later bishops could thank the people, whose devotion to the site consolidated their arguments for the supremacy of Rome. Meanwhile, in other corners of the city, traditions that clashed with Christian beliefs were finally eroded and then erased.

By the fifth century, gladiators had all but disappeared from the Colosseum – an age-old custom now vanished forever. For centuries, politicians from the dictator Sulla to the lowliest magistrate had poured out piles of coin to stage combats between fighters. Men fighting men, men wrestling beasts, and sometimes even women, spilt blood on the sand.[60] Fights could involve thousands of combatants and hundreds of animals imported from all over the empire. In 61 BC Lucius Domitius Ahenobarbus brought in 100 Numidian bears, along with 100 Ethiopian hunters to take them on.[61] More bizarre matches saw men fight lions, lynxes and crocodiles. For staunch Christians such as the second-century writer Tertullian such events were intolerable. 'Games in honour of heathen gods and of dead men' could 'not square with true religion or with duty toward God.'[62] For Tertullian the Roman spectacles he had seen were to be condemned not only for their violence but also for their paganism: 'the dolphins spout in honour of Neptune. The columns carry images of Sessia, of Messia ... [and there were] three altars for the triple gods: the Great, the Potent, the Prevailing'.[63]

By Constantine's time, further eminent ecclesiastical voices had added to the refrain. We have already seen how Augustine lamented the fate of his friend who became intoxicated by the thrill of violent spectacle. The growth of Christianity did not obliterate the games right away. The tide turned gradually as Christian arguments against fights coalesced with secular concerns. Already in 325 Constantine had declared that 'bloody spectacles' were inimical to 'civil ease and domestic quiet'.[64] He had also stated that nobody should be coerced to fight as a gladiator against their will. Constantine's successors ordered that Christians, whatever their crime, could not be condemned to death in the arena. The beginning of the fifth century saw changes with a singularly religious motivation, as pagan festivals were banned and any remaining games were stripped of their religious trappings. It was in this period that gladiatorial fights were banned altogether. Again, this was not a wholly religious phenomenon. Such spectacles might have been sure vote-winners, but they could leave their patrons bankrupt. As the empire was attacked on all sides, military needs grew and political privileges decreased. In this climate, many former patrons of the arena found it too costly and unprofitable to go on.

Once again it seemed that the Church of Rome had been invigorated by the last gasps of the empire. Yet, as always, the self-sacrifice of ordinary Christians would intensify the Church's cause. The decision to ban gladiatorial fights altogether had come after the death of an innocent: a devout young man named Telemachus who was reduced to a lifeless, bruised pulp at the games. The occasion had begun as a grand one, as gladiators raised their weapons to celebrate the Romans' triumph over Alaric after he and his Visigoth army had forced their way into northern Italy in 404.[65] Recording the events of the day, Theodoret, a Christian historian in Syria, reported that Telemachus had travelled to Rome from the East to embrace an abstemious, ascetic life. Once there, however, he encountered the 'abominable spectacle' of the triumphal celebrations.[66] Horrified at the violence of the show, Telemachus dived between the 'men who were wielding their weapons against one another'.[67] Some say that he was stabbed by a gladiator. Theodoret writes that the crowd turned on him and 'stoned the peacemaker to death'.[68] Either way, Emperor Honorius (393–423) was appalled at the spilling of innocent blood during his own games. He banned gladiatorial combats once and for all.

To some extent, the Bishops of Rome were filling a vacuum in secular authority. When Constantine shifted his imperial capital eastwards to Constantinople, he set the tone for his successors. During the entire fourth century, the city of Rome was visited by just four of her emperors on a handful of mostly brief visits.[69] At the turn of the fifth century, Emperor Honorius made his capital in Milan before moving it southwards to Ravenna. He was nowhere near Rome when its people faced down Alaric's desperate troops. In the years after the attack, it was the assistants of the bishop, Celestine I (422–32), who had visited the beleaguered people of

Trastevere, proffering eleven kilograms of gleaming silver plate for the celebration of Mass at the church of Santa Maria in Trastevere.[70] When Rome fell under the supervision of the government of the Eastern Empire in Constantinople the emperors there sent representatives to Italy. In the late sixth century these exarchs would be based in Ravenna, and proved relatively uninterested in the city and people of Rome.[71] Within Rome itself, the senate and, at its head, the prefect of Rome, lingered on as legal and administrative powers. The names of both fall out of the sources in the 590s, reappearing – with the senate in a slightly different guise – more than 150 years later.[72] Meanwhile by the sixth century, the Bishop of Rome had emerged as a pope, a term originally used for all bishops, derived from the Greek word *páppas* or father.

As pope, the Bishops of Rome were not only a supreme voice in the Christian Church, but also the foremost leader of their city, in good times and bad. In 590, Pope Gregory I (590–604) would guide the Romans through one of their bleakest hours. A former prefect and the son of a senator, public duty was in his blood. Cometh the hour, cometh the man. Gregory was elected as the Tiber burst its banks and plague ripped through the city, killing the pope, Pelagius II (579–90), and 'wasting the people with such destruction that out of a countless multitude, barely a few remained'.[73] Peter the Deacon, the contemporary chronicler who gave us this description, also claimed that the city was visited by a 'great multitude of serpents, and a dragon of astonishing size [that] passed by the city and descended to the sea'.[74] Whatever the precise details of the events, the Romans had undoubtedly endured an *annus horribilis*. Standing on the edge of the bridge outside the mausoleum built by Emperor Hadrian, Gregory cut an impressive figure at the head of his flock. Leading a procession of thousands, their heads bowed chanting the litany, Gregory entreated heaven for respite and mercy. Together, the pope and his people walked a pilgrimage in the shadow of the mausoleum.[75]

Lifting their eyes from the sodden ground, many claimed to see a vision of the Archangel Michael, wielding a sword atop the pagan monument. In the years to come, Romans would come to know the building as the Castel Sant'Angelo. For them, reports of the vision of the conquering angel were prized evidence of divine intervention during a time of chronic duress.

Contrary to Edward Gibbon's claims in the eighteenth century, it seems that civic duty was not lost as the Western Empire crumbled. Duty was in rude health in Rome but in a new Christian guise as prominent Romans who had become Christian incorporated almsgiving into their civic persona. It was not that the wealthy of pagan Rome had ignored the needs of the masses. The *munera* were an established means of giving to the community, even if sources make it tricky to get a sense of any organised efforts.[76] Some pagan writers such as Seneca and Cicero even wrote of the importance of giving to the poor, as long as gifts were 'proportioned according to the worthiness of the recipient'.[77] Still, traditional Roman culture and society did not promote charity in the Christian sense. Sources often deride the sentiment of pity as base, and deem misfortune a just punishment from the fates.[78] As we have already seen, Saint Laurence had been grilled for preferring the poor to his duty to the Roman state. As early as the fourth century, the prominent senator Pammachius would throw a banquet for Rome's destitute in the hall of Saint Peter's basilica. As Rome became Christian, charity was elevated as a noble virtue, as patricians emulated Jesus and the pope of Rome himself.

—— ‿ ‿ ‿ ——

It is tricky to trace the feelings of ordinary Romans of late antiquity towards their pope. Vignettes such as Gregory's pilgrimage to the building now known as Castel Sant'Angelo come to us shaped by centuries of heroising legends. That said, the mere fact of the procession suggests that he was a potent and beloved pastor. More than this, despite the increased eminence of their office in the broader Christian Church, popes continued to play a central role in the spiritual life of the city. In Rome, the pope was a visible actor in the religious functions that punctuated the calendar year. Popes oversaw baptisms at Easter, ordained priests and lower clergy such as deacons in December and consecrated bread during regular Masses, with pieces distributed to smaller churches across Rome.[79] By late antiquity, parishes had spread throughout the city as the great basilicas were supplemented by around twenty-five titular churches.[80] These places of worship were thought to have been founded by the earliest patrician Christians. Now they were staffed by priests, supported by assistants, attended by acolytes, all guided by the pope.[81]

The lowlier souls of Rome would also continue to play a part in the growth of the Christian city. It was the devotion to Saint Peter among the first Roman Christians that had marked the spot of his tomb on the Vatican Hill. The basilica eventually built on that site, along with others such as the Lateran Basilica and San Paolo fuori le Mura, would form the monumental keystones that pinned Christianity into the fabric of Rome. The basilicas had a key religious function defined by the Church. Clergy were ordered to visit those of Saint Peter, Paul and Laurence weekly to absolve penitent sinners and baptise newborns and converts.[82] Yet the significance of certain sites over others would continue to be shaped by ordinary Christians, particularly at the Basilica of Saint Peter's, which would one day become emblematic of papal Rome. Despite Constantine traditionally being recorded as the patron of Saint Peter's, he appears to have ranked that church fairly low on his list of endowments, granting greater wealth to the Lateran Basilica and San Paolo.[83] Perhaps even more surprisingly, given the fact that Saint Peter underpinned the very idea and authority of the newly elevated popes, Pope Leo I's successor, Hilarius, gave greater funds to the oratory that Constantine had built for Saint Laurence. Saint Peter's was a victim of its location. It lay far from the papal palace at the Lateran in an area still haunted by drinkers and rogues. It was principally used at Christmas and for the feasts of Saint Peter and Paul.[84] Yet despite its setting and this lack of official attention, it remained a site of solid lay devotion, as Romans and foreign visitors continued to visit the tomb so venerated by the first Christians of Rome.

The popes were not yet the politicians that they would soon become. But the governing classes of the late empire recognised the importance of Saint Peter's Basilica and its popularity. This was not entirely cynical. In their devotion, politicians continued a tradition inaugurated by men such as the prefect Junius Bassus, who died in 359 and was buried in an ornately carved sarcophagus that adorned the basilica's entrance porch.[85] Soon a visit to Saint Peter's became a recognised rite of political passage. Inaugurating the triumph that saw the tragic death of Telemachus, Emperor Honorius would march into the city from his court at Ravenna and, resplendent in triumph, visit the 'memorial of the fisherman'.[86] This new itinerary marked a significant change in the world of Rome and its empire, as reverence to previous emperors and secular glory was abandoned for the Christian saints. Struck by the shift, Augustine would preach that kings and princes visiting the city had a decision to make: 'Peter is there in the tomb' and 'Hadrian is there in the temple'.[87] In the past, the choice had been easy. Arriving in Rome, any eminent political figure would have paid homage to the dead emperor. Now they passed by that monument and turned to walk through the streets flanking the Tiber towards the Vatican Hill. There 'laying down his diadem' even the emperor would 'beat his breast where the body of the fisherman lies'.[88]

In 476 the last Roman Emperor of the West, the ten-year-old Romulus Augustulus (475–6), was deposed by the barbarian soldier Odoacer, who then became de facto King of Italy. His successor would be a Goth, Theodoric the Great (493–526), a man of the same blood as the invader Alaric. When Theodoric visited Rome in the year 500, he was keen to fit in. Making a tour of the basilicas of Saint Peter and Paul, even before he met the senate, Theodoric sought out some air of Roman imperial legitimacy.[89] By that time, his itinerary had been walked by warriors, politicians and interlopers. Emulating Romans – ordinary and imperial – their visit to Peter's bones had forged a connection between them and the city. Petrine and papal identity was entrenched in Rome and used to legitimise incoming political powers. Religious prestige strengthened worldly authority as politicians bolstered their regime using the story of Peter – a man once despised by imperial powers but now vital to the character and people of the city of Rome.

— ભ ૪ ૪ —

In 410 Jerome had wept at the despoiling of Rome, evoking a city smitten with ashes, crawling with insects and littered with broken buildings. It is likely that Jerome exaggerated the devastation, but his world was certainly in flux. In Constantine's Rome, traditional Roman religion had persisted. Later, pagan politicians such as Symmachus would fail to preserve remnants of the old world such as the winged statue of Victory that had graced the Senate House. Some, including Symmachus, simply took their religion underground, reducing the scale of sacrificial ceremonies and making them in private dwellings or out in the countryside.[90] Meanwhile, the public face of Roman religion was gradually chipped away: flowers, incense and all other forms of pagan sacrifice were eventually outlawed. By 435, Romans had been told to put pagan temples, sacred groves and their adjacent precincts to better use.[91] Meanwhile, the footsteps of devoted locals and visitors trailed past ruined buildings to expand the foundations of the Christian city. By the fourth century, eminent Christians such as the prefect Junius Bassus would be buried at Saint Peter's Basilica.

As the centuries wore on, religious sites bulged with secondary chapels replete with holy objects and bodies, swelling and ornamenting the already monumental presence of the Roman Church.

The Bishops of Rome who had for so long diverged from the values and objectives of their city were now not only in concord with but directing many aspects of its life.[92] This new religious, social and political order was written into the customs and buildings of the city. In the basilica Santa Maria Maggiore, an inscription declared that Pope Sixtus III had given the great building not only to Mary, as its dedication suggests, but also to the ordinary people of Rome.[93] The pope embodied a link to Saint Peter and a divine authority, now recognised both within Christian Church and the political world. But he and his authority were also intimately tied to the city in which he lived.

As popes took on a paternal role as pastor of Christians across the globe, their city See would also become a place of refuge for their most endangered lambs. In the mid-seventh century a group of monks from Palestine, the very birthplace of Jesus, would be driven from their homeland by invaders from the Islamic world. In Rome, where Christians had once been persecuted, the pope gave these men a safe house in the shady orange groves of the Aventine Hill.[94] Here, the monks lived in a villa abandoned by a noble family who had fled the disease and dangers that had plagued Rome in recent decades. Christian refugees would soon be made custodians of sites of profound significance for the Roman Church. Across the city from the Aventine, a little outside the walls, a group of monks who had escaped southern Turkey would be given a new home on the spot where Saint Paul had been beheaded.[95] Once they were settled in their new monastery, the pope gave these monks a task that integrated them deep into the fabric of Rome. They would rear the lambs that were blessed on the feast of the teenage martyr Saint Agnes, and then shorn to clothe the new archbishops ordained at the pope's Lateran Palace. As antiquity turned into the early medieval age, outsiders were absorbed into Rome's new rhythms, still shaped and cadenced by the legends of the saints. The main authority in Rome was a pope, rather than an emperor; now Christian, rather than pagan; now poorer, but still international and eminent, and ruling through an authority with eternal claims. By late antiquity, the sun had truly set on the Western Roman Empire. But it looked like papal Rome was there to stay.

4

Holy Rome: Relics, Invaders and the Politics of Power

Along the streets of the Esquiline, doors swung open as a passing bell tolled. These were not the dour chimes of the nearby Lateran Basilica, by that time dedicated to Saint John the Baptist (or San Giovanni). This bell was swinging from the neck of a donkey, rousing local residents and workers to ritual humiliation, not solemn prayer. Emerging from nearby buildings, the murmuring crowd met a truly bizarre sight: a man mounted back-to-front on a donkey with pendulous wineskins bulging with feathers at his head and flanks.[1] He held onto the tail for dear life, as the animal bucked through the city streets. Just a short while before, he had been hanging by his hair from the equestrian statue of Marcus Aurelius (161–80), which stood outside the Lateran Palace and is now on the Capitoline Hill.

It was the year 966 when the people of Rome saw their prefect, Peter, in this degraded state. He had been their hero, leading the charge when a new pope was imposed upon them by the Holy Roman Emperor. Some centuries after the fall of the Western Roman Empire in the late fifth century, the Holy Roman Empire would grow up as the European continent's most potent political force. By the ninth century, its emperor ruled lands traversing modern-day France and Germany. According to the Roman Church, this empire would be the legitimate successor to the realm of the glorious but now long-gone ancient Caesars. Pope Leo III (795–816) legitimised this link when he crowned the Frankish King Charlemagne emperor in Saint Peter's Basilica on Christmas Day in 800. In the shadow of that church, Charlemagne founded a hospice for his subjects visiting Rome. It is now a lush garden known as the Camposanto Teutonico, lying just beyond the Vatican walls and crowded with the tombs of Germans who happened to die in the city. The hospice was hardly the only gift that the Holy Roman Emperors would give to the popes. In return for a papal blessing on their new unrivalled power, successive Holy Roman Emperors secured the authority of the pontiffs over Rome and gave them a swathe of land that stretched to Rimini and Ancona on Italy's Adriatic coast.

The King of the Franks was now Emperor of the Romans. The successor of Peter was now a papal prince. In the early ninth century, it seemed a good deal all round. By 966, however, the emperors were shaping the alliance with an ever-heavier hand. They chose pontiffs for Rome, and refused some candidates whom the people of the city favoured. They were certainly not the only ones concerned about who sat on the papal throne. The papacy was now an office with cachet in Rome, authority abroad and a decent income. The pope had considerable influence in the Church and politics far beyond his Holy See. Coveting the spiritual and worldly weight of the office, emperors, patricians and even plebeians all lobbied to get their favourite on Peter's chair. When candidates and their factions clashed, politicking, intrigue and even violence ensued. It was this hostility that led to the strange fate of Peter the prefect on the Esquiline Hill. Ultimately, it would be the popes themselves who fell foul of such bitter conflicts. They soon became victims of their own success. In 1143, the people of Rome tired of their overly political pontiff and took matters into their own hands. Overthrowing the pope, they staged a revolution, the impact of which reverberated in the city for decades.

Their exasperation was understandable. In 966 it was the pope himself who had ordered that the prefect be paraded atop a braying donkey. John XIII (965–72) was seeking vengeance after being humiliated by Peter and the people of Rome. He had been elected pope with the support of the emperor, but Roman rivals had decried him as an imperial stooge. Rising up in rebellion against the new pope, residents of the city had bundled John into a wagon and made him a prisoner in the Castel Sant'Angelo.[2] When the Holy Roman Emperor Otto I (962–73) fought back to liberate and avenge his pope, Peter the prefect was handed over to an embittered John XIII. For some, Peter's public punishment might mark a brutal end to the independence of Rome.[3] But history shows us that the tussle between the people and papal and imperial powers would rumble on. When John died, the emperor chose his successor: Benedict VI (973–4). He would end his life strangled in a cell at the Castel Sant'Angelo. The men behind the act were the aristocrat Crescentius the Elder and Cardinal Franco Ferrucci, who would later have himself crowned Pope Boniface VII (974 and 984–5). The people of Rome had a hand at almost every juncture in this saga. When Boniface VII died in 985, after a return to the papal throne, they would haul his corpse to the foot of the statue from which Peter the prefect had been hung.[4] We now know this monument as the equestrian statue of Marcus Aurelius but at that time it was thought to represent Emperor Constantine the Great (306–37). In the city of Rome it was seen as a potent symbol of just rule.

—— ☙ ☙ ☙ ——

Surprisingly, things had looked calmer when the Barbarians and Goths had returned to Rome in the late fifth century. In 476 the barbarian general, Odoacer, had deposed the final ruler of the Western Empire, the child emperor Romulus Augustulus.[5] The Western Empire, as it had been, went with the young boy. The imperial insignia were rushed to the Eastern Emperor Zeno (474–91) in Constantinople.[6] To all intents and purposes, what remained of the Roman Empire had just one emperor and he sat far away in the

Byzantine East. Zeno would make Odoacer – a tall, shabbily dressed soldier of murky origins – the first King of Italy. In Rome, however, it might have seemed that little would change. Odoacer built up his court at Ravenna, that city on the eastern Adriatic coast where the Western Emperors Honorius (395–423) and Valentinian III (423–5) had often kept theirs. Like many later non-Roman rulers in the empire, Odoacer styled himself as a traditional patrician, posturing as an authoritative figure of an old order that he had personally usurped.[7]

There was not even much change in the city in 493 when Odoacer was replaced by the Goth Theodoric the Great, who had Odoacer murdered at a banquet arranged to celebrate their collaboration. Through bearded mouth and northern twang, this next King of Italy also emphasised continuity with Rome's past, claiming that 'An able Goth wants to be like a Roman' but 'only a poor Roman would want to be like a Goth.'[8] Theodoric had learnt *romanitas* by unconventional means. The son of an important Germanic nobleman, from the age of seven or eight he had been taught by some of the finest teachers in Constantinople after he was taken prisoner by the Eastern Emperor Leo I (457–74) to secure a treaty between the Romans and Goths.[9] By the time that Theodoric became King of Italy, Roman Christianity was a key part of this culture of authority. And so, draped in deep purple garb, he visited the basilicas of Saint Peter and Paul, seeking to consolidate his authority by association with the Roman Church.

Italy's Gothic kings were Christian and could ape the Western Roman emperors, but they were in many ways fundamentally different from the men whom they had displaced. Not only did they hail from a Balkan base in the eastern stretches of Europe, they were not Roman Christians but Arians, a Christian group with its own distinct set of beliefs. They looked to Jesus Christ for guidance. However, they did not believe that he was divine, merely a human being of the absolute highest moral order. Imported to Italy in the hearts and minds of the Goths, Arianism would shape some of the peninsula's most remarkable art and architecture. This was seen above all in the Goths' capital of Ravenna. There, in the luminous mosaics of the baptistery roof, the eyes of a fresh-faced Jesus peer down on the reverent as he receives the waters of baptism from John the Baptist. This Jesus is still youthful, unchanging, from Theodoric's day to our own. In the eyes of Gothic Arians, these tiles of red, green, blue and gold reflected their belief in a wholly human Christ. This was a Jesus who could be young, age and then die, just like any man. Such teachings were particular to the Arians and heretical to the Roman Church.

Despite these differences, the Goths had a more tolerant attitude towards the Roman Christians. Theodoric allowed the popes to minister freely to souls in the city and, according to one chronicler, 'attempted nothing against the Catholics'.[10] As an old man, the king would even summon Pope John I (523–6) to Ravenna, where the two leaders devised the first ever papal visit to Constantinople. Despite Catholic misgivings about Arianism, John would voyage eastwards to entreat Emperor Justin I (518–27) to end his policies against the Arian Church.[11] When the fruits of the mission failed to satisfy Theodoric, John suffered a bitterly cruel end, starving to death slowly in one of the king's prisons. Ultimately, however, John was punished for conspiracy with Constantinople, not his Roman Christian beliefs. Away from the jails of Ravenna on the streets of Rome, the Goths' religious toleration was more obvious. The Christians of the city could kneel down at their basilica of Santa Maria Maggiore, even as Theodoric's people celebrated further along the via Merulana at their own church of San Severino.[12] Just a short walk from these two places of worship, the Arians had built a modest basilica, Sant'Agata dei Goti. The church was embedded into the Roman cityscape, defined by heavy granite columns taken from ancient imperial sites. In its decoration it was more distinctive, adorned with mosaic, pattern and picture. And in the apse that capped the broad nave, it also bore the name of its patron, the Gothic general 'FLA[VIUS] RICIMER. VI'.[13]

——— ∞ ∞ ∞ ———

Triumphant, tolerant, quietly grand, the Gothic Kings of Italy might have appeared unassailable. And yet, by the end of the sixth century, the stones bearing Ricimer's name were dashed from Sant'Agata's walls. A much more forceful authority had arrived to take Rome. The change in power was sparked by the policy of the Eastern Emperor Justinian I (527–65). Justinian had grown tired of the Gothic presence in the former Western Empire. From his capital in Constantinople, he dispatched thousands of men to drive the Goths from the Italian peninsula. Justinian's mission was far more ambitious than the annihilation of a government or a creed. Posturing as an Augustus for the late antique age, he wanted nothing less than the entire former Western Empire, conquering lands from Rome to southern Spain and the north of Africa to unite with his territories in the East. By 554 his men had a firm enough hold on Italy, even if many of his initial gains were rolled back in the decades to come.[14] The wars rocked Rome, with its ruler changing three times, but Justinian's final triumph in that city would be decisive. Eventually, Arianism was outlawed in Rome. In 592 Sant'Agata was transformed into a Catholic church.[15]

With Eastern emperors now ruling over the West, Rome would be imbued with the colours and words of Constantinople. As Justinian's weary troops laid down their weapons at the close of the Gothic war, an inscription in Greek appeared on the Porta Appia, the gate where the Aurelian Walls opened onto the Appian Way. Beseeching 'God's Grace', along with that of Saint George and another Eastern saint called Conon, it seems likely that the emperor's soldiers etched out the words to request protection against violent reprisals from their enemies.[16] The Eastern emperors adopted the Goths' capital, running their Italian territories from the city of Ravenna. But the similarities between the two regimes more or less stopped there. Whereas the Gothic kings had lived in Italy, Justinian remained in Constantinople, governing remotely through men called the exarchs. From Ravenna, these imperial delegates oversaw the various duchies that comprised the Byzantines' Italian lands. This included a new Duchy of Rome that encompassed both the centre of the city and its surrounding country-side.[17] In the early seventh century the last structure ever erected in the Roman Forum would be raised. It was the figure of the Eastern Emperor Phocas I (602–10), atop a towering column more than thirteen metres tall.[18] Phocas' sculpted image, coated in lustrous gold, stood in stark contrast to the Forum below where toppled monuments of Western emperors lay about on the ground.

The pope managed to remain authoritative in the civic, pastoral and spiritual life of Rome. To a great extent, the cityscape was still shaped by Roman Christianity. In the centuries to come, however, some of the Roman legends that had underpinned the fabric of the Christian city would be entirely supplanted by tales newly arrived from the East. At the foot of the Aventine Hill the gargling stream that ran alongside the church of San Giorgio in Velabro was associated in the minds of locals with the Roman Saint Sebastian. According to tradition, the water that flowed there was a portion of the Great Sewer into which Emperor Diocletian (284–305) had flung the corpse of the early martyr, whom he had clubbed to death after an earlier – now much illustrated – attempt to kill him with arrows. Yet by the eighth century at least the church and stream bore the name of the Eastern saint, George.[19] He was another victim of Diocletian, but one from the eastern stretches of the empire, known and beloved by the soldiers of the emperor in Constantinople. By this time, Eastern influences had also emerged a short walk away at the church of Santa Maria in Cosmedin, a few paces from the shores of the Tiber. Known as the *Schola Graeca* even in the sixth century, the church grew up from a charitable foundation on the orders of the eighth-century Pope Hadrian I (772–95). Here traditions Roman and Byzantine intertwined, as Hadrian dug out a crypt beneath the floor. Underground the bones of Roman martyrs nestled in its niches, while the decoration, congregation and name (Cosmedin) of the church upstairs rang with distinctly oriental tones.[20]

The pontiffs of Rome would also take on an Eastern flavour, as the Byzantine emperors took an ever-greater interest in who sat on Saint Peter's throne. As an elective monarchy the papacy was already an office in which Roman society had a stake and sought influence. Over centuries, methods of papal election had been revised. During some periods, the Bishops of Rome chose their own successors. At other times, a competition opened up. Under the Gothic King Athalaric (526–34) there had been some attempts to thwart corruption, with backroom deals banned and limits on the amount of money that could be spent during the election period.[21] After the Eastern imperial takeover, the Byzantine emperors often just imposed their choice, or at least demanded a right of veto over the selected candidate. Gone was Rome's independence to choose its own pontiff; popes had to secure approval from Constantinople. In 678, the election of Agatho (678–81), a Greek Sicilian, marked the beginning of a line of Greek-speaking popes, many of whom were chosen for their ability to work closely with the emperor.[22] As long as they dominated Rome, the Eastern emperors endeavoured to elevate men of whom they approved, forcing some popes to adhere to Eastern causes.

When pontiffs rebelled against Constantinople the consequences could be grave. The strong arm of Byzantium was even felt by popes endorsed by the emperor. Pope Theodore I (642–9) was a Greek and his election had been supported by the exarchs. Nevertheless, when he spoke out against an Eastern interpretation of the nature of Christ in the 640s, imperial forces hit back violently. They stormed his treasury at the Lateran, cast his associates out of Constantinople and defaced the high altar at the papal residence in the city. When

Theodore's successor Martin I (649–53) fell foul of the same debate he would die the prisoner of imperial troops, exiled on the Black Sea.[23] In 654 a new pope more favourable to the emperor took Peter's See as Eugenius I (654–7), but the conflicts did not end at his coronation.

In 708, Pope Constantine I (708–15) would be the very first pontiff to take the name of that first emperor of the eastern city. He would also be the last pope to visit Constantinople until the late 1960s. Once again, trouble emerged over the teachings of the Church. The Eastern emperor would enforce his will, even if it meant bloodshed. In 692 many in Rome had seethed when a council in Constantinople condemned practices that were the norm in their See. In Rome, Christians fasted on Saturdays in Lent and married men were banned from the priesthood unless they relinquished their wives. In 692 the so-called Trullan Decrees of the Quinisext Council censured both customs. They also condemned gambling with dice, the offering of honey, grapes and milk on the altar, as well as the transvestism that was apparently rife in the law faculty of the University of Constantinople.[24] Rome resisted the decrees. But in 710, Emperor Justinian II (685–95; 705–11) wearied of their impertinence. He summoned Pope Constantine to Constantinople to recognise the council once and for all.[25] Raised in Tyre, in modern-day Lebanon, Constantine had been formed in the thick of Eastern culture. He was, it seemed, ready to compromise with the East. To those back in Rome who persisted in their grumbling, the emperor would respond with absolute brutality. As he set out on his journey, Constantine stopped in Naples, where he crossed paths with John Rizokopos, the exarch of Ravenna. Rizokopos was on his way to Rome, on a mission from the emperor: to murder all papal officials who refused to conform to his will.[26]

— ❧ ❧ ❧ —

While these are tales of near incessant conflict and some barbarity, their most compelling thread is papal persistence. Emperors shed blood in their attempts to suppress papal independence, but even then they could not crush it for long. Just a year before Emperor Phocas' statue had been raised in the Forum, Pope Boniface III (607) had demanded that the emperor recognise Rome – not Constantinople – as the head of the Christian Church.[27] In the city of Rome itself, the popes knew that they had much more direct authority than the emperor, whatever the powers in Constantinople might publicly acknowledge. At major sites in the city, popes often asserted their supreme influence over the Church and secular sphere, even though it was officially the domain of the emperor and his exarchs. In 609, Pope Boniface IV (608–15) is said to have turned the Pantheon into the Christian church of Santa Maria ad Martyres, filling it with twenty-eight wagons of relics dug up from the catacombs.[28] It is often assumed that this conversion of the Pantheon to Roman gods symbolised the triumph of Christianity over the pagan religion. By the seventh century, however, Christianity had dominated Rome's religious sphere for some time. Indeed, at the time of its transformation, the Pantheon was no longer a pagan temple, but a secular building used by the state for legal purposes.[29] Boniface's takeover, therefore, was less a symbol of the Christian triumph over paganism and more a bold assertion of papal dominance over secular imperial power in Rome. Even if Boniface had relied on Emperor Phocas for permission (as some historical accounts suggest) it is unlikely that the emperor could have stopped him from taking the building if he had wished to do so. A couple of decades later, Pope Honorius I (625–38) would create the church of Sant'Adriano al Foro from the ruins of the Senate House built by Julius Caesar himself. Some Roman stones might have spoken the Greek of Byzantium, but others expressed the resolute voice of the Roman pontiff.

The audacity of some popes was evident in the churches of Rome. After Emperor Leo the Isaurian (717–41) sought to ban the veneration of images in 726, Pope Gregory III (731–41) risked his life to resist the command. Among the faithful of Rome and Ravenna, Emperor Leo's mandate had been explosive, condemning beautiful, holy images and vowing to take them away.[30] Thousands of ordinary men and women visited Rome's basilicas and shrines to revere images of Jesus, Mary and other saints. Amidst lives burdened by the anxieties of family and work, religious art could elevate hearts and minds towards the heavenly realm. On this matter, Pope Gregory II (715–31) had stood with his people. His successor Gregory III would go even further. Not satisfied with merely defying the imperial edict, Gregory made his rebellion brazenly public. When Eutychius, the imperial exarch of Ravenna, sent the pope six columns of striking, black onyx for the shrine of Saint Peter's Basilica, Gregory used them as stands for religious icons.[31]

Gregory III was motivated by religious conviction and solidarity with his flock. Nonetheless, he was also aware that the authority of the popes was grounded in the religious traditions and sites of Rome. By the early medieval period, the stories and remains of Peter and other martyrs had made that city into a potent spiritual centre.[32] There, the faithful sought not only icons but also the clothing, bones and severed body parts of Christian saints. For them, these objects were not mere reminders of their Church's troubled past. They were instruments of holiness, healing and even enlightenment. Faced with a maniacal imperial diplomat, John XIII – the pope who would humiliate the prefect in 966 – touched him with the chains with which Saint Peter was said to have been bound. For everybody in that room, the chains had a real, healing power in the present material world because they had grazed the skin of Peter nearly a thousand years before. From the first devotees at Peter's tomb to the Empress Helena digging for the Holy Cross of Jesus in Jerusalem, Christians believed that holiness and all of its fruits were carried in place, proximity and touch. In Rome, the relics of the holy dead that peppered the city's soil and, increasingly, inhabited its many shrines, had imbued the See of the popes with a unique spiritual power.

From the lands of the Lombards to the British Isles, people turned to Rome, its Church and its history as a means of enriching their spiritual lives. As early as the year 631 a group of men from Munster in the south of Ireland had grasped relics in their hands as they tried to resolve a dispute over the date of Easter. These were relics from Rome, which they deemed the 'chief of cities' and where they had debated the question with a Greek, a Hebrew, an Egyptian and a Scythian, all lodging in a tavern near Saint Peter's Basilica.[33] There, many foreign pilgrims gathered in the shadow of the basilica, where tiles frequently cascaded from the roof. For the Irishmen, Rome was the ultimate locus of authority. To establish the truth, they testified on those holy relics carried home with them to their windy, western isle. When the churchmen saw 'a totally blind girl opening her eyes at these relics, and a paralytic walking and many demons cast out' they knew that the relics were genuine, and, crucially, that they had established the true date of the feast of Easter.[34]

Relics, then, were a touchstone for truth. They were also believed to have a power that could sanctify and heal disease. Many considered them particularly curative for ailments thought to be caused by sin, such as the disabilities and rashes of the parishioners of Bishop Gregory of Tours who baked bread, gathered hay or mended fences on the Sabbath.[35] As Christianity spread across Europe, the faithful ventured to Rome for holy objects to place on the altars of their churches back at home. In the mid-seventh century, Wilfrid, a young nobleman from Northumbria, left his religious studies at the island abbey of Lindisfarne to travel to Rome. Venturing southwards, Wilfrid spent some time in Kent before setting sail for France and then travelling onwards to Italy.[36] Not long after his return to England, he would be made a bishop; eventually, he would become an important English saint. Yet when Wilfrid set out on his travels, he was a man in his twenties from a land where Christianity was still relatively new. It had only been in

595 that Pope Gregory I (590–604) had summoned a group of monks from the Caelian Hill and sent the reluctant men to Christianise the pagans of the island. For a little while at least, England had no known native saints. Relics, therefore, simply had to be sought in Rome. When Wilfrid arrived in the city he took full advantage, making 'daily visits to the shrines of the saints to pray ... for many months' and collecting relics.[37] Returning to Rome on business as a bishop in 680, Wilfrid made a second, similar tour, travelling 'around the holy places of the saints' and meeting 'chosen men' from whom he bought 'a great many holy relics'.[38] The excitement and significance that surrounded the exercise was evident in his approach: Wilfrid carefully labelled every purchase with 'what each of the relics was and to which saint it belonged'.[39]

For Wilfrid and other Christians, relics from Rome were powerful and important objects. Back in the weather-beaten wilds of northern England, pagan temples were made Christian through their mere presence. By the ninth century, Holy Roman Emperor Charlemagne would command that relics be housed in every altar in every church in all of Christendom.[40] In Rome, a lively market for limbs, organs, hair, teeth and nails emerged to satisfy the demand. Dispersed across Europe, the very fibre of these relics carried some of the authority in which papal Rome was steeped.[41] This was a magnetic force. For some eminent leaders nothing would do but to breathe their last on Roman soil. In 688, the thirty-year-old English King Caedwalla of Wessex left his home and renounced his throne, travelling to Italy to seek baptism from the pope and a swift death thereafter. Caedwalla's prayers were answered; he died just ten days after arriving in the city and becoming a Christian. Taking Peter's name, Caedwalla was buried in Saint Peter's basilica, his body still draped in baptismal robes.[42] Caedwalla's successor, King Ine of Wessex, would trace the very same path, shrugging off worldly power to journey to Rome for baptism and a peaceful retirement thereafter.

Rome's holiness, however, did not stop foreign powers seeking to invade the city. The popes and the emperors in this period might have quarrelled over theology but they had a common enemy: the Lombards. According to the eighth-century Lombard historian Paul the Deacon, his people had originated in the cool lands of southern Scandinavia before sweeping southwards into modern-day Germany, Austria and Slovakia.[43] By the mid-sixth century, they were further south yet. Driving into Italy, they had troubled both the Byzantines and the Goths. Those two powers continued to fight one another, but both would end up dominated by the shared foe. By 571, the Lombards had claimed a swathe of land in the north of Italy that stretched from Turin in the west across modern-day Lombardy and into Udine. They also held a vast tranche of territory from Spoleto, north of Rome, down to Bari near the very heel of Italy. In short, they had taken most of the Italian peninsula, even if the Byzantine Empire maintained its grip on peripheral lands in the far north and south, as well as Ravenna and Rome.[44]

Rome and Constantinople frequently united to protect this embattled frontier land. However, the papacy did not have the military trappings of the empire, and the powers in Constantinople and Ravenna often concentrated their focus and resources elsewhere.[45] In 728, the Eastern authorities were still reeling from the backlash over the ban on icons when the Lombards started to encroach on the city of Rome. Pope Gregory II, the pontiff who had been bold enough to defy the imperial decree, was spurred into daring action, seeking out a direct meeting with Liutprand (712–44), the Lombard king. Burnished gold coins bearing Liutprand's image showed a monarch draped and diademed, covered in a worldly glory that he was ambitious to expand. A savage fighter and a determined leader, this was not a man whom Gregory could invite into Rome: they met further north in the hill town of Sutri.

Eye-to-eye with the menace of the peninsula, the pope could rely neither on arms nor traditional diplomacy to broker a deal. He stood purely on the strength of his authority as the bishop of the See of Saint Peter and requested that Liutprand relinquish the lands from which he now threatened Rome. In a remarkable volte-face, the Lombard king agreed. He would give the conquered territory back, and to the pope rather than the emperor in Constantinople. Technically, Sutri was not part of the lands of the Church and the pope was the subject of the Byzantine emperor. Nonetheless, for Liutprand the emperor's worldly claims were irrelevant. He was willing to relinquish the territories only as 'a donation to the blessed Apostles Peter and Paul'.[46]

Liutprand's coins might have carried the portrait of a worldly conqueror on one side but on the reverse was Saint Michael the Archangel, shield and cross in hand. Here was the very figure who had roused Gregory the Great and his pilgrims from atop Hadrian's Mausoleum. In Gregory's time, the Lombards had been Arians, just like the Goths. But by Liutprand's era they were Catholic Christians, like the Church of Rome. Liutprand himself was a deeply religious man, known for beautifying churches and religious institutions across the Lombards' territories.[47] All the same, Gregory could not have been sure that the Lombards' religion would secure their acquiescence to the papacy. By taking a gamble in Sutri the pope had discovered that the unique character of his episcopal office could allow him to transcend the usual dynamics and political power-plays, making new alliances based, in large part, on his unique position as successor to Saint Peter.

—— ⚭ ⚮ ⚮ ——

It was the ever more universal significance of Rome that provided Gregory II and other popes with the leverage to negotiate with powers such as the Lombards, even where emperors and their envoys had failed to gain ground. In the late eighth century this same significance would enable popes to vanquish the Lombard armies. It was also the foundation for an alliance that would make the papacy more powerful than ever before.

Pope Stephen II (752–7) would retrace Gregory's tracks, sending out envoys to negotiate with the Lombards who had occupied Ravenna and were, once again, inching towards Rome. Negotiating with the pope, the Lombard King Aistulf quickly made his intentions clear. While he was willing to discuss the fate of Rome he would not countenance a negotiation over Ravenna. For Aistulf, as for Liutprand, Wilfrid, Caedwalla and so many others, Rome was a special case, a sacred city that he might threaten for leverage but never brazenly take. Ravenna, on the other hand, was just another place. Pope Stephen tried to bargain for his 'lost sheep' there, but ultimately to no avail.[48] He could not even rely on help from Emperor Constantine V (741–75), their official secular ruler. For the emperor was mired by more pressing problems in Constantinople, as he wrestled ongoing conflicts with the Turkic Bulgars and the Islamic Abbasid Caliphate.[49] Turning away from the troubled East, Pope Stephen looked northwards for help. His gaze settled on Francia, a kingdom that stretched across modern-day France, Germany and central Europe.

On 15 November 753, as winter set in, Stephen II made for the treacherous mountain passes through the Alps. What transpired when he reached the Kingdom of the Franks and their king, Pepin the Short (751–68), would transform the history of Rome and all of Europe. Historical sources conflict in accounts of the pivotal meeting, differing on which great man prostrated himself in front of the other first.[50] Some accounts say that Pepin sent his twelve-year-old son, Charles, 100 miles to meet the pope and escort him to their palace at Ponthion in north-eastern France.[51] Today, nothing remains of that grand palace but a single sign in an otherwise empty field, but the young man who led Stephen to that spot in December 753 is still known around the world as Charlemagne. Within less than fifty years, Charlemagne (768–814) would be the first and most famous of the Holy Roman Emperors. The seeds of his rise would be planted during Stephen's sojourn. At that time, the fate of Pepin's son was hardly the pope's most pressing concern: he faced an agonising wait for Pepin's decision at Ponthion and then, later, in the town of Saint Denis. Spring had arrived and the snows long melted when Pepin finally agreed to fight the Lombards in Italy. This time it was the Franks who would defend Rome to protect the legacy of Saint Peter. They would also grant the Holy See former Byzantine and Lombard territories that extended into Ravenna and beyond, making early medieval popes greater landowners than ever before.

With land comes authority. The popes of Rome knew this only too well. When Emperor Leo the Isaurian had wanted to punish Gregory II for his defiance in 732, he had diminished papal authority by stripping the Holy See of influence in the Italian regions of Reggio, Sicily and Sardinia, as well as Athens, Crete, Nicopolis, Patras and Thessalonica in Greece.[52] Now, just over twenty years later, Pope Stephen II had broken away from the Byzantine Empire that Leo had ruled, replacing the popes' old Eastern alliance with a new Francian deal. In the process, the popes won lands and, with them, extended authority. When Pepin finally defeated the Lombard King Aistulf after a year-long military and diplomatic tussle, the popes held the foundations of what would come to be known as the Papal States.[53] Stretching from the Roman port of Ostia to Ancona on Italy's eastern coast, these territories gave the pope clear political status. They would form the backbone of negotiations between the pope and political powers, from Pepin and Charlemagne in the eighth century, to the twentieth-century fascist dictator Benito Mussolini (1922–43).

Yet the pope also had a trump card, over and above even these men, for the authority with which he ruled his lands was not only worldly but also religious, Petrine and eternal. Pope Stephen recognised this trump card right away and deployed it to cement and gild the new alliance. In 754, before Rome and other territories had even been secured, Stephen expressed his gratitude to Pepin by anointing him with holy oil and declaring him King of the Franks and Patrician of the Romans. The second, somewhat vague, title characterised Pepin as the protector of the ancient and prestigious city. On Pepin's death in 768, Charlemagne took on the mantle and crown. On Christmas Day in the year 800, Pope Leo III would use his Petrine authority to give Charlemagne an even greater gift yet. In Saint Peter's Basilica, he took up the holy oil to make the King of the Franks the successor to the great *augusti*: the first Holy Roman Emperor. In return, he piled up yet more territory on the Italian peninsula.

Now Rome truly began to glitter with the prestige of the popes. Raised in the late eighth century on the orders of Pope Hadrian I, the church of Santa Prassede is a monument to this marked shift. As ever, the roots of the church were fed by the blood of the martyrs: the building was intended as a sanctuary for the bones of Pudentiana and Praxedes (known as Pudenziana and Prassede in Italian), two sisters who died in the second century. The young women were thought to be daughters of the Roman senator Pudens, perhaps the first convert of Saint Peter in Rome. In the seventeenth century, the church dedicated to Pudenziana (a short walk from Santa Prassede) would be decorated in marbles depicting the oozing sponges used by the sisters to mop up martyrs' blood in Rome. Pudenziana's faith had cost her her life during the reign of Antoninus Pius, while tradition holds that Prassede's body gave up under the weight of violence, service and suffering.

On 20 July 817, Pope Paschal (817–24) began a project to add the bones of other saints to those of the sisters, which rest in an ancient Roman sarcophagus in the bowels of Santa Prassede. Unearthing bishops, deacons, priests and ordinary people who had died for their Christian faith, Paschal removed some 2,300 bodies from the catacombs and interred them in the walls of the new church. Stuffed with bones, lit by candles and glistening with mosaics of gold, azure, orange and green, Santa Prassede spoke of the triumph of the Church of the martyrs, as well as the Church in Paschal's day. With the sponsorship of the Holy Roman Emperors, Christian buildings of this time reflect a period of intense artistic renewal, which would come to be known as the Carolingian Renaissance, after Charlemagne. Santa Prassede spoke of a material and cultural wealth that was lavish. It also spoke of a powerful pope. In the mosaic in the apse, Paschal stands holding a model of the church, shoulder-to-shoulder with Peter, Paul, Pudenziana and Prassede. Overhead, in the heavens, his name 'PASCAL' was written into the narrative of eternity.

— ෬ ෲ ෲ —

The alliance with the Holy Roman Emperors made the papal office more coveted than ever before. Just like the emperors of the East in times past, Holy Roman Emperors now had a stake in who sat on the papal throne in Rome. Throughout the era, they approved new pontiffs and intervened when a candidate was particularly appealing. The system was not a bad one, until fault lines appeared in the empire itself. Under Charlemagne the lands had been well-administered, wealthy and, crucially, united. Yet within a couple of generations of his death in 814, the empire would be split.[54] The Holy Roman Empire became Middle, Western and Eastern Francia, and, separate to these, a Kingdom of Italy. The crown of the Holy Roman Emperor, meanwhile, was won by election. As the Holy Roman Empire fractured and weakened, the Romans acted with ever greater autonomy when selecting a new pope. In the past, the people of Rome had been intermittently involved. Even during the period of Byzantine influence, Pope John V (685–6) was said to have been elected 'by the general population'.[55] Now powerful Romans manipulated and outright ignored imperial interventions. Before long, the contest for Peter's throne became mired in corruption and intrigue.

Even the dead were unable to escape the ambition and seediness surrounding the papal court. In 897, the corpse of Pope Formosus I (891–6), who had been dead some seven months, was exhumed, seated in a chair and put on trial at the Lateran Palace.[56] In an interrogation overseen by Pope Stephen VI (896–7), the lifeless body was accused of usurping 'the Roman See in a spirit of ambition', of taking the papal throne merely for personal gain.[57] Formosus' corpse sat stinking and mute as a deacon defended his honour. To absolutely nobody's surprise, the court found the dead pope guilty as charged. The papal vestments were torn from his body, the fingers with which he had blessed the Roman people were chopped off, and all of his actions as pope were declared null and void.

Formosus' trial and punishment were bizarre in the extreme. But he had hardly been innocent of political manoeuvring. While bishop of Porto-Santa Rufina from 864, he had sought election to the episcopate of Bulgaria after charming its king, Boris I, on a mission to the country.[58] The pope at that time, Nicholas I (858–67), also sensed Formosus' sights on the See of Rome. The accusation was grave as it implied that Formosus sought religious office cynically and, more seriously yet, was a potential papal usurper. After winning the papal tiara in 891, he had crowned Prince Lambert of Spoleto as co-ruler of the Holy Roman Empire with his father Guy.[59] Seeking to make another more favourable alliance soon afterwards, Formosus offered the very same imperial crown to a Carolingian called Arnulf of Carinthia. He encouraged his new ally to invade Italy to take his prize in 896.[60] Some believe that the so-called Cadaver Synod was meant to punish Formosus for this treachery posthumously, while reasserting the position of Lambert as the rightful emperor. Whatever its specific purpose, the macabre trial makes it clear that the political power of the popes could both aggrandise and debase the papal office. Popes – dead or alive – could be used as tools to achieve political status, both within and well beyond the hierarchy of the Roman Church.

By the tenth century, the elite families of Rome had become increasingly interested in the influence of the papacy. Clans such as the Crescenzi and Teofilatti fought bitterly over Peter's See. At the same time, the increasing secular authority of the popes meant that they mattered more than ever to ordinary people. It was for this reason that Romans often took matters into their own hands, supporting men such as Peter the prefect, whom John XIII had tied to a donkey in 966. As John's actions make clear, increased interest in the papal office could have a corrupting effect. Voices from the time decry the pernicious influence of noblewomen such as Theodora, the wife of Teofilatto, Count of Tusculum, a region near Rome. Teofilatto and Theodora were certainly political operators.[61] In the first decades of the tenth century, they adopted the ancient titles of consul and senatrix and worked with Alberico I, Duke of Spoleto, to commandeer political and ecclesiastical power in Rome. In 904, the trio manoeuvred their preferred papal candidate, Sergius III (904–11), onto Peter's seat, enforcing their will with violence during the election and aftermath.

In the toolkit of this elite, brute force was, apparently, accompanied by sex. In his account of the period, the churchman Liutprand of Cremona vilified Theodora as 'a quite shameless prostitute' who forced one pope to 'fornicate with her over and over again'.[62] Similar accusations were laid at the door of her daughter, Marozia. Liutprand charges her with seducing Sergius III and bearing him a son who would later succeed his father as Pope John XI (931–5/6).[63] It is little wonder that historians referencing Liutprand's work refer to the era as a 'Pornocracy' or 'Reign of Harlots'. His text is gripping, but not necessarily to be trusted. Like so many involved in papal politics at this time, Liutprand's motives were far from pure. He had a personal and political interest in decrying the Teofilatti, seeking the favour of the emperor whom they had rivalled.

A political shift in in Italy would see a crackdown on some papal politicking, though not before the situation had reached breaking point. In 962, Rome was, once again, threatened by an advancing military force. This time the men approaching were those of Berengar II (950–2), King of Italy and Marquess of Ivrea, a region in the mountainous north-western corner of the Italian peninsula. When the previous King of Italy had died in 950, Berengar had taken the crown for his own head, though he did not have the imperial title that so often came along with it. In 959, Berengar had set out to expand his authority by encroaching on the Papal States.[64] Pope John XII (955–64) cried out for help from inside the Leonine Walls, built around Saint Peter's in the wake of an earlier Saracen attack. According to Liutprand, John XII sent desperate pleas to Otto I, King of the Germans, begging him to 'free the pope himself and his ward, the Roman Church, from the tyrant's fangs'.[65] In February 962 Otto delivered the pope, freeing Rome from Berengar's men. After more than a century of fractured Frankish power, Otto was crowned Holy Roman Emperor in the Basilica of Saint Peter. He would rule until 973. Just like earlier emperors, Otto united territories and confirmed and expanded the pope's temporal power. In return he asked for the usual fealty and a vote of confirmation in papal elections. Nevertheless, things had changed in Rome since the Golden Age of Charlemagne. The popes of that time had been decent negotiators – now they could be ruthless politicians. Annoyed by the request, John XII refused to give the emperor any say in papal elections. Then, in an act of audacious treachery, he cut a deal with the men of Berengar II, the very foe that he had summoned Otto to crush.[66]

This time the pope had gone too far. John XII would be felled by his own greed. Otto expelled the pope from Rome and installed a new pontiff, Leo VIII (963–5), in his place.[67] Tenacious to the last, John returned to chase his successor from the city, dying soon afterwards, according to Liutprand, from injuries incurred in bed with a married woman. For the chroniclers of this period, John's inauspicious demise was unsurprising. This pope was the grandson of Marozia, the scandalous daughter of Teofilatto and Theodora who was said to have borne Pope John XI with Pope Sergius III.

More popes would emerge from this family line. Rival noble clans would also push their own candidates. As Otto and John tussled, one Roman faction had their eye on a cardinal named Benedict for Peter's throne. He was elected hastily in the wake of John's death only to be ousted so that Otto could restore his loyal ally, Leo VIII.[68] The Romans who had backed Benedict were absolutely fuming. The noble factions of Rome had become used to wielding some influence over the fate of the Church. In the end, it had been prominent voices among the laity who had demanded the nullification of the Cadaver Synod and the burial of Formosus in a dignified tomb at Saint Peter's Basilica. They had also taken care of the pope who had tried the corpse in the first place. Stephen VI was kidnapped, imprisoned and strangled during the summer of 897.[69] With the intervention of Emperor Otto in the late tenth century, it seemed that such seedy days had come to an end. But with so much at stake in each papal election, it simply could not last.

— ෬ ෨ ෨ —

The popes' copybook was not entirely blackened in the medieval period. Some pontiffs had tried to fight the corruption of the Church with real force. By the mid-eleventh century, Pope Gregory VII (1073–85) had established what would come to be known as the Reform Papacy: an effort to restore dignity and integrity to the Church at large.[70] Through councils, debates and dictates, Gregory railed against malpractice within the Church, attempting to instil it with monastic ideals through which religious houses could also be reformed.[71] Crucially, he damned the manipulation of ecclesiastical authority by secular powers: positions could not be bought, priests could not have wives and emperors could not choose popes. Imperial powers had already been marginalised in the election of pontiffs back in 1059, when the process was put in the hands of the ever more powerful cardinals.[72] Eventually, monarchs would even be banned from selecting their own bishops. Working with energy and determination, Gregory sought to sever the ties between worldly powers and the Church of Jesus Christ. Gregory's changes aimed to rid Rome of sleaze and politicking. Paradoxically, they did little to diminish the political assertiveness of popes themselves. In fact, by undermining the influence of secular leaders who might temper the actions of popes, his reform made pontiffs more powerful and autonomous than ever before.

On the feast day of Santa Prassede in 1118 it did not seem that much had changed in papal Rome. There were two popes in the city: Pope Gregory VIII, enthroned at the Lateran, and Gelasius II, celebrating Mass at Santa Prassede's church.[73] The situation was emblematic of a problem that had plagued Rome for centuries. Pope Gregory had been installed by Henry V, an elected Holy Roman Emperor, and supported by the Frangipani, a Roman family soon powerful enough to build a stronghold over two storeys of the Colosseum.[74] When Gelasius, rather than Gregory, was elected unanimously in Rome, the Frangipani turned to the force of arms. Seizing Gelasius, they huddled him into a carriage and on to captivity. On hearing the news, rival Roman nobles were incandescent and liberated Gelasius. He was their pope. But the story was far from over, for when Leone and Cencio Frangipani heard that Gelasius was celebrating Mass at Santa Prassede, a building in their territory, they picked up their swords and hurried through the narrow streets towards the church.

A sense of unity could still prevail in Rome. At Santa Prassede in 1118 it would defuse the clash over Pope Gelasius and the imperial pontiff Gregory VIII. When the Frangipani arrived, they locked swords with Gelasius' supporters, the Crescenti. In the chaos of the fight, Gelasius slipped out into the shadowy streets nearby. Realising that their man was gone, the Crescenti asked the Frangipani why they should bother with a continued fight when their prize, the pope, had fled and they were all tired from the brawl. Whether for Pope Gelasius or the imperial choice, Gregory, they were, at the end of the day, all Romans – 'relatives, if we can say so'.[75]

A few decades later, in 1143, the force of Roman unity and fatigue with papal politicking peaked. In that year, the people of Rome rose up against the pope himself in a rebellion against the arbitrary use of power. Looting the towers where nobles and some cardinals lived and storming the Capitoline Hill, the Romans had a true popular revolution. Temporal power over the city was granted to a communal government led, in the manner of the ancient Romans, by a senate of fifty-six men. Its leader would be Giordano Pierleoni, a nobleman whose family had rivalled the Frangipani. He led the charge of the revolting masses from their riverside base in Ripa and Trastevere.[76] Weary of papal corruption and intrigue among noble factions, the people asserted that the pope should have no political power. The tipping point had come when the political aims of Pope Innocent II (1130–43) had scotched the Roman people's plans to take the nearby hill town of Tivoli.[77] Anticipating defeat, the people of Tivoli had sworn fealty to the pope. In return, he had assumed control over the town himself. Pope Innocent had used his temporal and religious power to satisfy his own greed, undermining the people and secular forces of Rome in the process. When the rebels established a new senate on the Capitoline Hill, Innocent was so shocked that he took to his bed and soon died. Re-establishing the ancient Senate and People of Rome (SPQR) as a more representative governing power, Romans celebrated the revival of the ancient Republican age.

—— ⊂ꙮ ꙭ ꙭ ——

By the twelfth century, it appeared that papal ambition could only be stayed by the people of Rome – whether noble leaders or the plebeian masses who rose up behind them. After the revolution of 1143, it would take some forty-five years to restore the pontiff to Rome. For many decades, popes were elected but wandered outside of the city. After Innocent's death, the new pope, Lucius II (1144–5), attempted to storm Rome with his troops. His army was defeated, and he died when a stone struck him on the head. Lucius' successor, Eugenius III (1145–53), managed to make a deal with the Republican regime or Commune of Rome. He entered the city on Christmas Day 1145. By early spring he was gone again. He would not return for three years, and only then to excommunicate Arnold of Brescia, who had supplanted Pierleoni as leader of Rome's rebel movement.[78] Pope Hadrian IV (1154–9) – the only ever English pope – would also try to take back his city on receiving the papal tiara. As so often before, the pontiff would need the help of a secular power. In 1154, the man seeking the imperial throne was the German King Frederick Barbarossa, named for his deep red beard. Like others before him, he was willing to offer military support in return for an imperial coronation in Rome. All the same, the alliance was awkward. The medieval papacy was still tainted by the hint of sleaze. The emperor was reluctant to perform the usual custom of humbly holding the stirrups of the pope's horse. In the end, Barbarossa stepped up for Rome's apostolic legacy. He would take the stirrups not for Pope Hadrian 'but for Peter', the saint.[79] Together the pope and Barbarossa tried, convicted and burnt Arnold of Brescia, whose ashes were then slung into the waters of the River Tiber. This was a symbolic victory, but Hadrian IV had not retaken his See. As he placed the imperial crown on Barbarossa's head at Saint Peter's, the streets rocked with riots over the death of Arnold of Brescia.

Eventually, a pope would return to Rome permanently, but only on the people's terms. In the Concord Pact of 1188, the Romans reunited with their pontiff, now Clement III (1187–91). The pontiff was, once again, sovereign in his own states. His power, however, would be tempered: the pope could rule, but the senate remained, and never again could the pontiff stop the Romans from invading Tivoli.[80]

We might ask ourselves why the Romans would agree to take the pope back after all of the tumult and corruption of the previous centuries. They had pride in their republican system and its ancient Roman heritage. This was visible on the streets of the city, where great houses such as the Casa di Crescenzio were erected from a collage of capitals, sculptures and inscriptions salvaged from long-ruined ancient buildings. Yet Clement was determined and, ultimately, the people had suffered without a leader of genuine authority. A chasm of many centuries must have made it difficult to establish a truly authoritative republican state. Leaders such as Pierleoni and Arnold of Brescia could rise and fall on the strength of their own personality. As one contemporary chronicler put it, these were leaders 'whom people created on their own authority'.[81] The popes, however, were a completely different sort. Embedded in the city through the presence of Peter and bolstered by the acts and deaths of saintly men and women of the past, the papal office stood on much firmer ground, even when individual popes did not. Ultimately, the Romans recognised that the city and the papacy were now inextricably intertwined. In the next centuries, they would feel the pull of this tie even more acutely. The city faced an existential crisis when it found itself without its popes for nearly seventy years. For what were the papacy and Rome without one another?

5

Between Avignon,
Babylon and Rome

On 7 April 1378, sixteen cardinals spent a restless night at Saint Peter's. The labour of the following day was a grave matter indeed: the pope was dead and it was up to them to elect his successor. This could often prove a controversial task, but now it was more vexed than ever. Outside their quarters, Rome itself was far from peaceful. The abbot of Sistres painted a chilling image of a city where the 'axe, sword and other tools of the executioner' were publicly displayed, even outside the Basilica of Saint Peter's.[1] The symbols of capital punishment were exhibited to keep mob violence at bay. Yet at the entrance of the conclave, a menacing crowd jostled all the same, pushing against the makeshift guard of apothecaries, boatmen and carters who had been rallied to hold them back.[2] The patrol thrust back against the throng, but then faltered and broke. Unrestrained, the crowd burst free; the doors collapsed underfoot. As the mob ransacked the storerooms, meat, drink and vegetables were bagged up. Spilt wine bathed the floors. Even the cardinals' cells were not spared looting.[3] However, despite appearances, the people running through the conclave were not a senseless horde. From their cells, the petrified cardinals heard a people with a clear and specific message: 'We want a Roman, or at least an Italian, or by the keys of Saint Peter we will kill and cut to pieces these French and foreigners, starting first with the cardinals.'[4] The Romans had deposed their pontiff in 1143, but now they wanted a pope. Most of all, they wanted a pope loyal to the city of Rome.

The cries for a pope echoing through the night of 7 April 1378 might shock us, given the ire poured out on the pontiffs during the revolution of 1143. Moreover, just a few years before the conclave, some of the most eloquent tongues and pens of Italy had railed against the See of Peter, damning the popes as the ruin of Rome. The Tuscan poet Petrarch was vehement, denouncing the pontiff as a Babylonian whore. Petrarch had been made an honorary citizen of Rome in 1341 when he was crowned with laurels in the Senatorial Palace on the Capitoline Hill. He was far from alone in his biting critique. The poet Dante Alighieri had also condemned the popes' insatiable hunger for personal and political power. In the poet's *Paradiso*, he castigated the papacy through the mouth of Saint Peter himself. By Dante's pen, the founder of the Church denounced the current pontiff Boniface VIII (1294–1303) as a usurper who had made Saint Peter's 'burial ground a sewer of blood, a sewer of stench'.[5] According to Dante, Rome was now a place in which only the devil could find happiness.

There had been some efforts to repair the prestige of the papacy in the twelfth and thirteenth centuries. The concord of 1188 had smoothed over the popes' breach with the people of Rome, under-mining the pontiffs' political powers and depriving them of their ability to thwart the territorial ambitions of their people. Yet even earlier than this, Pope Gregory VII (1073–85) had failed in his attempt to stem cynical interest in the papacy. He had cleaned up the Augean Stables of corruption exemplified by figures such as Teofilatto and Marozia. But, like Hercules, Gregory would never see reward for his work, despite washing away the mess left by thousands of others. Indeed, by emphasising the papacy's authority over religious matters, over and above worldly princes, Gregory actually expanded papal power over the Church in Rome and nearly every corner of Christendom. After decades of controversy, even the Holy Roman Emperor would concede that the popes had the ultimate authority when it came to selecting leaders for the Church.

Across Europe, the effect of Gregorian Reform was deep and sweeping. Canon lawyers in monasteries and palaces would sketch out defences of papal supremacy.[6] At the continent's new universities, their ideas were elaborated in student theses. In crowded cities, papal doctrine arrived on the tongues of Dominicans and other new orders of preachers.[7] Inspired and invigorated by their sermons, men and women handed over taxes and manpower for Crusades to dislodge Islam from the lands where Jesus had walked.[8] Later popes further fortified papal supremacy over the Church, devising protocol to control papal elections and developing new systems of taxation to fund an ever more centralised papal government. Pope Innocent III (1198–1216) acknowledged his power explicitly, and in evocative metaphors. He ruled with two swords, one spiritual and one temporal. He was the blazing sun that lit the emperor's merely reflective moon. As the scope of the popes' authority grew, so did their headgear. It was in this period that their distinctive egg-shaped tiara was transformed from the mitre of a bishop to encompass two and then three crowns.[9] Encrusted with gold lace, rubies, emeralds and sapphires, the three tiers of the tiara symbolised the multiple realms over which the pope ruled.

For some people this was a red flag. Dante was among them, though he laid the blame not at Gregory's door but at that of Emperor Constantine (306–37). Dante claimed that the emperor had made the papacy monstrous by encumbering the Church with the trappings of worldly power.[10] And it was not only in Italy that hearts were troubled over papal governance. In England the philosopher and friar William of Ockham composed a tide of invective accusing popes who acted in the temporal sphere of committing 'the most blatant wrongs and iniquities'.[11] It was not as though the popes' increased authority over the Church spared them clashes with secular authorities, for the pontiffs were now compelled to intervene whenever secular powers got muddled up in matters that were now exclusively under papal jurisdiction. They also sought to shape the political world. While past popes had anointed newly chosen political leaders, Innocent III actually controlled the election of the Holy Roman Emperor.[12]

In the period preceding the conclave of 1378, it was a tussle with the French king that precipitated the power struggle that brought the Roman pontiff crashing into the fray of worldly politics. For when Petrarch, Dante and William of Ockham denounced the pope of Rome, he was not even living in the city of Saint Peter. At that time, the pontiff exercised his Petrine authority from Avignon, a city in the Kingdom of Arles, in the far south-eastern corner of modern-day France. As we shall see, the popes had been lured northwards by a desire to placate the French king, Philip the Fair (1285–1314). They would stay in Avignon for more than sixty years as return to Rome, abandoned to popular unrest and warring barons, became an ever less enticing prospect. In the meantime, the critics of the popes multiplied before their eyes, as men and women balked at the pontiffs' neglect of Rome, supposedly the centre of Christendom. When Dante's fictional princes drank the blood of the faithful, they aped the very real Roman barons who violently wrestled for power in the popes' absence. Many of the writers' barbs were directed at the general worldliness of the popes, which, as far as they could see, had only increased in Avignon. For them, the Avignon papacy was the apotheosis of the corruption of the papal office, even if it was a final destination on a much longer journey of decline.

On the eve of the conclave of 1378 the situation in Rome was desperate. The people had not suddenly become blind to the popes' faults, many shared the same perspective as the pontiffs' most vociferous critics. However, like the Romans who signed the Concord Pact in 1188, even they were convinced that only a pope could solve the problems that his papal predecessors had caused. With the papacy in Avignon, the centre of Christendom had been without its spiritual leader. The pope, meanwhile, had made himself the mere pawn of a French prince – a foreigner. When the papacy was wrested from Saint Peter's See, the distance soon corroded both the city and the papal office. Even with all of the appendages of temporal power and spiritual empire, the pope's position still turned on his role as the Bishop of Rome. The dependence was mutual. The character, economy, society and culture of that city had developed from antique foundations hand-in-hand with the emergence of the popes. Churches, businesses, streets, palaces and institutions were dedicated to and shaped by the hierarchy, trappings, dogma and devotees of the Church. When the pope was ripped from Rome's fabric, the city shook. After some sixty-nine years of papal absence, we should not be surprised that the people shouted themselves hoarse outside the conclave, crying out for the restoration of their spiritual Caesar.

—— ⃝ ⃝ ⃝ ——

It was not entirely unheard of for a pope to live outside Rome. Popular unrest, personal preference, contagious disease and 'bad air' had frequently dislodged popes from Rome, but never, ostensibly, for good. In the years between 1100 and 1303, popes spent more than half the period – some 122 years – outside of the Holy See, frequently absconding to nearby cities such as the hill town of Orvieto.[13] Sitting atop a mound of volcanic ash, this clustered conurbation of amber stone buildings had to be adapted to accommodate the grandeur of its frequent papal visitors. After 1290, Orvieto was crowned with an episcopal palace and towering Gothic cathedral, the facade of which was populated with holy figures in gold and coloured mosaic tiles. Orvieto and the other cities that hosted wandering medieval popes were in the orbit of Rome, attached by virtue of their inclusion in the Papal States. Before the fourteenth-century exile, popes had sometimes gone further afield, to Florence, Naples and even Provence. All that said, never once did it seem like the popes had left Rome forever, as it did during those long decades of exile in Avignon.

Ironically, the drama that would see the pope abandon Rome more permanently happened not in the papal city of Rome but in Anagni, one of the locations in which the popes had sought refuge during the twelfth and thirteenth centuries. In days of empire, Anagni had been a cool, placid haven for emperors such as Septimus Severus (193–211) and Caracalla (198–217).[14] This was the perfect summer escape from the hot, densely-packed streets of Rome. Anagni had its own episcopate as early as the 400s. By the ninth century, the temple that had honoured the pagan goddess of agriculture, Ceres, had been razed and replaced with a Christian cathedral. Roman nobles too enjoyed Anagni's cleaner air and calmer streets, where cobbled lanes hosted a population that was meagre in comparison to the crowds through which they elbowed at home.

By the turn of the fourteenth century it would be the Caetani family who laid claim to the town. They were a new baronial clan who had jostled with the Colonna, Capocci and Conti for palaces and influence back in Rome.[15] In 1294, the Caetani had swept past their older, more venerable rivals to stand at the peak of Rome's social and political hierarchy. In that year one of their number, Benedetto, was elected Pope Boniface VIII (1294–1303). As a ruler in Rome, Boniface was a glorious religious prince. In 1300, he inaugurated the world's first ever holy jubilee. For a year, hundreds of thousands of ordinary Christians shook off the burdens of plague and poverty, quitting towns and cities all over Europe to travel to the holy city of Rome. Journeys would be long, arduous and replete with peril. However, in the official papal announcement or bull, *Antiquorum habet,* the pope had promised an invaluable prize. No matter who they were and what they had done, pilgrims in Rome would secure 'the most full pardon of all their sins' if they received the sacrament of confession and made daily visits to the basilicas of Saint Peter and Paul for a period of fifteen days.[16]

Travelling south from Asti in the northern region of Piedmont, the pepper merchant Guglielmo Ventura was astounded by the scenes in Rome when he arrived in the chill of early December in the year of jubilee. Bodies were pushed to the ground under the crush of the masses as men and women clambered towards the basilicas, desperately seeking the pope's 'indulgence' for their sins. Some pilgrims claimed that the relics of Peter and Paul alone could liberate them from guilt and sin, provided they visited them at the turn of the century.[17] Meanwhile, Romans peddled hay and beds at astronomical prices.[18] By 1450 there would be more than a thousand inns in the city.[19] Some were merely shop rooms where locals laid down mattresses to maximise their profits.[20] Ventura and others even saw clerics using garden rakes to gather the coins thrown at the basilica of San Paolo fuori le Mura, like 'papal croupiers'.[21] Such scenes inspired cynicism in some, yet still the pilgrims came, for their hearts were full of gratitude to Boniface, the pope who had given them an opportunity to cleanse themselves of sin.

The Romans were also grateful to Pope Boniface. How could they not be when the jubilee was so lucrative? The baron Giacomo Stefaneschi admonished pilgrims that they 'should not ask questions about the price of goods when one comes in search of devotion.'[22] Boniface also gave Rome grain and scholars. He reinforced the traditional grain dole or *annona* with supplies from Rome's rural hinterland and founded the city's university, the *Studium Urbis*, in 1303.[23] This should not surprise us, for the Caetani pope was erudite, encouraging and commissioning the production and translation of a huge number of texts.[24] These vibrantly illustrated volumes swelled the papal library by nearly fifty per cent. Like his family, Boniface would feel strong ties to Anagni, where he had been born and spent much of his career. Still, in Rome he worked hard to ingratiate himself with the people and visitors of the city. It was an endeavour in which he would enjoy considerable success.

Boniface did not, however, curry favour with worldly powers beyond the city. As successor of Peter, and popes such as Innocent III, he was an intrepid defender of the sweeping papal authority that had been claimed and buttressed over the preceding centuries. Two years after becoming pope in 1294, he ordered secular princes not to appropriate ecclesiastical revenues. In 1301, they were also reminded that they could not try the pope's Catholic clergy in their own courts. In 1302, Boniface took an even bigger swipe at the realm of worldly power in the bull *Unam Sanctam*, declaring that he had an authority that superseded that of kings, whose power should be used in his service.[25] To the ambitious King of France, Philip the Fair, the bull read like nothing less than a declaration of war. Philip was a man of some personal hubris, described by one contemporary as acting like king, pope and emperor.[26] Now he was personally dressed down for subjecting priests to trial and taxation to fund his bitter wars against England.

Eager to stem the king's sweeping power, the pope threatened to excommunicate Philip the Fair. In return, Philip threatened to dislodge Boniface from Peter's chair. His agent Guillaume de Nogaret set off for Italy with audacious orders: to force the pope to retract his threat and then step down from Peter's See. Back in France a royal assembly had cooked up charges of heresy and sexual perversion to justify the removal of the pope.[27] On the road to Anagni, the Frenchman gathered support from among the Caetanis' old rivals, including the Colonna family.[28] On 7 September 1303, the men took the town, then the papal palace, and then the pope himself.[29] Just over a month later, Boniface was dead.

Nogaret and his men had not intended to kill the pope. What's more, the people of Anagni had eventually wrested Boniface from their clutches. Throughout his life, Boniface had thanked the men and women of his hometown for their affection and support. During the affair of September 1303, many of them bolted through the narrow streets of their city, crying out against the invaders and looting local shops in a confused flurry of papal loyalty and crime. It had taken three days for the *Anagniani* to liberate Boniface from his

French captors. In the end, chroniclers claim, he died 'not so much from sickness ... as from afflictions of the heart'.[30]

Boniface had ended his life burdened by the humiliation of being captured, harassed and beaten at the behest of a supposedly Christian king. In the years that followed, Rome too would find itself mortified. After Boniface's death, the new pope would not even be crowned in the city. Following the demise of Boniface in October 1303, and that of his short-lived successor Benedict XI (1303–4), Pope Clement V (1305–14) would be elected in Perugia and installed in the French city of Lyon. The new pope, previously known as Archbishop Raymond Bertrand de Got, emerged from a conclave paralysed for some eleven months by discord and indecision. He was the compromise candidate of warring cardinals, Italian and French. Neither a cardinal nor an Italian himself, and ostensibly a friend to both the former pope and the French king, Clement was the least political option on offer.[31] Even so, his victory is overshadowed by suspicions of a deal with Philip the Fair, who had so recently brought down the great papal prince Boniface VIII.

When Clement was crowned at the church of Saint Just in Lyon, Philip was just one of a sea of grandees present. The jubilant throngs at the procession were exuberant enough to topple an old city wall, killing twelve people, including Jean II, Duke of Brittany.[32] Even the crowned heads who were absent sought to express their support of the new pope. An extensive delegation proffering lavish gifts arrived from Edward I of England, who remained across the Channel otherwise engaged, earning himself the nickname 'Hammer of the Scots'.[33] Many, therefore, sought the blessing of the pope of Rome, a city that was still the head and centre of Christendom. Nonetheless, it soon became clear that Clement would not be leaving France. The reasons given were practical: he intended to negotiate a truce between France and England so that they might unite in his Crusade and to arrange a council to address the charges that Philip had levelled at Boniface

VIII.[34] Awaiting these events, Clement took up residency in Avignon, just outside of France in the lands of the Angevin Count of Provence.

Away from Rome, Clement was, ironically, in the geographical centre of Christendom, on the axis between Spain and Italy. There the pope lived in a calm, emollient climate, among a populace with whom he had neither history nor rancour. In five days a letter could be carried from Avignon to Paris; in two weeks a missive could be carried from Avignon to Rome.[35] Soon many couriers to Italy would find that their services were no longer required, as Clement relocated the entire machinery and court of the papacy to Avignon. Cardinals, diplomats, religious leaders and their families were all transplanted, as well as all those keen to remain within the economic and social orbit of papal largesse. Meanwhile, the people of Avignon looked on as their home was transformed forever. When Clement was crowned Bishop of Rome in 1305 the population was around 5,000–6,000.[36] By 1371 it was home to more than 50,000 people, many with direct links to the papal court.[37]

Avignon was not only swollen by the popes and their entourage, but also fortified and gilded. As the machinery of the papal court flowed out of the papal quarters into the streets, Avignon became host to a network of offices and libraries. Soon the more sumptuous trappings of the papacy also materialised in the south of France. As pope after pope took the throne of Saint Peter in the city, rooms were frescoed, tapestries were hung, gardens sprang up alongside cool, shadowy cloisters. It was Clement VI (1342–52), a scholar and aesthete, who would make the boldest efforts to make Avignon a permanent, new Rome. Calling upon the most talented artists, he adorned the walls of his study with colourful hunting scenes, packed with trees, deer and dogs, all painted using his predecessors' carefully preserved funds. Clement V and his successor John XXII (1316–34) had lived fairly simply at a Dominican monastery. The pope who followed them, Benedict XII (1334–42), was an austere Cistercian monk. Under his rule, gold piled high at the papal chancery. When Clement VI saw the large but restrained episcopal palace that Benedict had built around a cloister he scoffed, 'my predecessors did not know how to be popes'.[38] Expanding the building into a true papal palace, Clement stretched out the plan and elevation, building a monumental tower up into the sky. From the door of his Grand Chapel, Clement walked more than fifty metres to reach the high altar. Tellingly, an immense wing of the palace would be named 'Rome', a city, it seemed, that the popes had now left behind.

——— ☙ ❧ ❧ ———

The splendour of papal life in Avignon contrasted starkly with Roman sentiments about the city. Petrarch lambasted the popes' French enclave as a new Babylon. In the Christian world, Babylon was a byword for the 'whore' described in the biblical Book of Revelation, a wanton female figure who rode a beast with seven heads, ten horns and a scarlet hide. For his part, Petrarch knew full well that Avignon was a beautiful place. Led by his father, a Florentine notary, his family had been part of the diaspora that had drifted northwards with the pope to Provence.[39] For Petrarch, however, Avignon had been made repulsive by popes who had abandoned Rome and put 'the Church of Christ in shameful exile'.[40] Popes such as Clement VI could pay as many craftsmen, architects and artists as they liked, but they could not make this city a true papal capital. For Petrarch they only succeeded in creating a perverted, empty effigy of Rome, 'drunken with the blood of the saints, and with the blood of the martyrs of Jesus'.[41]

Petrarch's criticisms of papal Avignon were pitiless. Yet Rome without the popes was also decried. In their absence 'the queen of the cities, the seat of the empire, the citadel of the Catholic faith' had been thoroughly degraded.[42] Some even claimed that Rome's residents had declined along with the stature of their home. The former city of Augustus was now a place where criminals expected to be lauded as gods. Life for Romans had, of late, been extremely cruel. When the Black Death tore through nearby Naples in early 1348, the lack of travellers to Rome kept it safe for a breath, but by August the city was rife with pestilence.[43] The following year, survivors would suffer an earthquake that rolled in from the Apennines. According to Petrarch, the city was 'so violently shaken by the strange trembling that nothing similar to it had ever been known there in the two thousand years and more since the City's founding'.[44] The entire basilica of San Giovanni in Laterano rocked. The eastern wall of the Colosseum caved in. As the bell tower of San Paulo fell and half of the Torre delle Milizie crumbled to the ground, Romans dashed to tents from their simple dwellings of wood and stone.[45] A chronicler writing from the city painted a people 'in great distress'.[46] 'Every day there were fights and robberies. Where there was a house of virgins they were abused ... the labourers, when they are out working, are robbed ... the pilgrims ill-treated and cheated.'[47] For Romans, it must have seemed like the world that was coming to an end.

Critiques of Avignon and Rome, then, varied in their emphasis. But they agreed on the decline of both of the cities. There was another point of consensus among critics of both papal seats. It was the absence of the popes that had transformed Rome from the *caput mundi* into nothing more than a 'decaying corpse'.[48] From within Rome's walls, its people certainly noticed the decay. Having reached a peak of one and a half million in the second century, the number of people living and working in city declined and hit a nadir during the Avignon Papacy. In the fourteenth century, the population hovered somewhere between 18,000 and 30,000.[49] For those who had survived the plague and the papal exodus, life was lived out in close quarters, with Romans generally pressed into a region that would become known as the *abitato*.[50] This patch of land on the right bank of the River Tiber took up a mere four square kilometres. There, rows of houses rose up over just one or two levels, punctuated now and then with *botteghe* selling wine, oil or clothes. From the *abitato* some worked the river, earning their living fishing or in the wooden mills that bobbed on its surface.

Tenants, servants and merchants clustered around grander dwellings and baronial fortresses that pierced the skyline. Some low-ranking military men made homes in Testaccio, where tradesmen added to the mound of cracked clay vessels dumped in the region since late antiquity. Others were magnetised by the opportunities at major poles of pilgrimage: Santa Maria Maggiore, San Giovanni in Laterano and Saint Peter's. Theirs was, however, a relatively small world, in which craftsmen and lawyers might recognise one another across the market stalls at the port of Ripa and on the Capitoline.

The remaining two thirds of the city defined by Aurelian's walls was populated not by people but by fractured, stony ruins. Beyond these, the area was frequented only by cows and sheep who came to feast on the shrubs. In medieval descriptions, this *disabitato* emerges in stark contrast to the Roman countryside or *campagna*. There affluent barons and nobles dominated the land with *castelli* and *casali* from which they farmed.[51] Dotted with swamps and swarming with mosquitos, the *disabitato* was, by contrast, a rather menacing frontier.

The papacy might have flown but another governing body remained in Rome. The Commune once led by Pierleoni and Arnold of Brescia had long outlived its demagogues. Though the majority of the Commune's earliest documents have been lost to destruction or dispersal, we do know something of its history in the middle decades of the twelfth century. It was led by two senators who crowned a hierarchical system comprising men who took care of the defence, peace and physical fabric of Rome.[52] The loftiest positions in the Roman Commune were dominated, of course, by the barons; the city's nobles occupied more middling roles. Both met, butted against and engaged with the spokesmen of Rome's ordinary people, particularly those who led guilds representing merchants, craftsmen, judges and notaries. They also clashed with the *caporioni* – the powerful familial heads of Rome's regions, or *rioni*. At the bottom of the hierarchy, though weighing heavily on politics, were the Roman people. Even before the popes left for Avignon, the Roman Commune was in many respects typical of those in other city-states of Italy.[53] Though communes were born from a spirit of republicanism, a lord and leader usually emerged to rein in their power. At that time, Rome principally distinguished itself in having a religious prince.

After 1309, Rome was marked out not by the character of its leader but a power vacuum at the top. When the people bayed for a Roman pope in 1378, they expressed the longing of a city robbed of its figurehead. This tie between Rome and its popes would be evident even during Avignonian exile. John XXII, the second pope in Avignon, considered a departure shortly after being crowned in 1316. However, despite his gross military expenditure, no part of the Papal States was safe enough to retake before his death in 1334.[54] As families noble and baronial battled to push the borders of their lands into those of their rivals, the territories around the city appeared to be in a state of perpetual war. By contrast alone Avignon must have felt a safe haven. John's successor, Benedict XII, would not forget Rome entirely, sending men and 50,000 florins to make repairs to the Lateran Palace and Saint Peter's Basilica.[55] As a younger man, the pope had hunted heretics doggedly in the French village of Montaillou, but even he would not risk travel to Italy.[56] Meanwhile, his now mainly French court dug in their heels. Soon the pope followed suit. It was Benedict who transported the papal archives from Assisi to Avignon – an administrative move that seemed to prove that the popes were now gone for good.[57] Coming to the papal throne after Benedict XII, the extravagant Clement VI was practically the antitype of his predecessor. Yet on the crucial question of Avignon and Rome, it seems that the two men would have agreed. Clement stayed put at his ever more resplendent court.

—— ৫৪ ৯৩ ৯৩ ——

As he was crowned in Avignon in May 1342, Clement VI could glory in his new title as 'father of princes and kings, the ruler of the world'.

Still, a particular people, the Romans, were about to claim a special bond. In that very same month, they sent a delegation of fifteen men to Avignon to retrieve their pontiff. Wearied by baronial conflict, they had elected a populist government from their lower and middling classes, the 'Thirteen Good Men' for whom the delegation sought a papal blessing.[58] They had also come to offer the pope a deal to secure his return. Clement could have 'general lordship over the Roman government', if only he came back to Rome.[59] It was a sign of the times that this plea would be presented by Nicola 'Cola' di Rienzo. He was a twenty-nine-year-old notary and son of an innkeeper at the riverside *rione* of Regola who collected around just three to six *denarii* from his paying guests.[60] Cola might have been economically disadvantaged, but he was distinguished by his intelligence. During a youth in Anagni and Rome, he had immersed himself in the history of the eternal city, reading the works of its greatest ancient poets and scholars. He ran his fingers along the ridges of classical inscriptions to learn of great Romans past. Cola was precocious and acutely aware of his own low birth. Cloaking reality with romantic fiction, he claimed that he had been born of a remarkable love affair. According to Cola, his mother had a liaison with Henry VII, the Holy Roman Emperor, when he had hidden out at their tavern to avoid angry Roman crowds.[61] Despite his imaginative backstory, the humble administrator might have been lost amidst the eminent names of the Avignonian embassy, which included Stefano Colonna the Younger, as well as Francesco di Vico, the son of the prefect of Rome. Ahead of the trip, Petrarch himself had penned a poetic text to charm the pope back to his See.[62] Among the eminent voices of such grandees, it would be remarkable if Cola could be heard at all.

And yet when the feet of the Roman delegation sounded on the marble floors of Clement's lavish consistory hall, it was on Cola's head that the eyes of that pope would rest. The young Cola was a *rara avis*: a 'handsome man' with an 'odd smile' who was said to be utterly 'nourished in the milk of eloquence'.[63] In that cavernous room lined with knights, cardinals, monks and hermits, Cola stood at the pope's feet, apologised for the revolution and sought approval for the Thirteen Good Men. He then requested that Clement return to Rome and, echoing the now-maligned Boniface VIII, declare the second ever year of jubilee. According to a contemporary Roman chronicler, 'Pope Clement deeply admired Cola's lovely way of speaking'.[64] However, as he turned to retake his seat, the choir were prompted to intone the ancient hymn *Te Deum*.[65] As their solemn, sonorous tones filled the vast hall, they occluded all possibility of a response from the pope.

Ultimately, Clement's answer was negative. He would allow the jubilee, and, along with Bertoldo Orsini, he named Stefano Colonna the Younger a senator of Rome. Nevertheless, the pope himself would not be returning to the city.

Back in Rome, the government of the Thirteen Good Men swiftly fell. Soon the plight of the people was advertised in a shocking public display. Emblazoned on the facade of the great castellated palace of the senators atop the Capitoline, a vast panel painting met the eyes of the political class and the ordinary Romans who bought and sold at the market on the hill. The picture was harrowing, showing a fraught widow on a boat, praying, her eyes overflowing with tears. A chronicler of the time recalls that her 'hair was torn as if she had been weeping'.[66] Her black dress was torn from her body, and the rags thereof 'clad in a mourning belt'.[67] Far from a sanctuary, her boat had neither rudder nor sail and was adrift in a churned up and perilous stormy sea. Beneath her were the ships of other women, drowned, rudderless, along with their passengers. Those vessels carried the names of empires: Babylon, Carthage, Jerusalem and Troy. As if misadventure and certain death were not punishment enough, an inscription among the wrecked ships spoke words ominous and grim: 'Once you towered on high over every government. Here and now we await your collapse.'[68] These words were not for the ears of the dead women, already fallen. They were for the wailing, bare-breasted widow who still occupied a boat called Rome.

It was that articulate but as yet undistinguished notary, Cola di Rienzo, who commissioned the painting on the Capitoline Hill. He had begun to make plans for reviving the ailing city of Rome soon after leaving Avignon in the summer of 1344. In that painted panel and with loaded words, Cola echoed the laments of Romans tired of living in a city in which a single power-hungry pope had been replaced by multiple families ravenous for influence, land and wealth. The baronial clans had deep roots in the city, but their identity and ends were not fundamentally tied to those of Rome. The papacy had been blighted by the actions of individuals, but with its links to Peter, and, through Constantine, the great Roman Empire, it could still prove an authoritative and unifying force. Cola recognised this fact clearly, even as he sought to augment his own prospects. Decrying the barons and declaring himself Rome's leader in the spring of 1347, he vowed to restore the prestige and peace of the ancient Rome of his youthful studies. Like Pierleoni, he styled himself tribune, casting one eye back to the Roman Republic.[69] Tellingly, he also characterised himself as a Christian leader.[70] Before Cola ascended the Capitoline to seize power, he passed the night in the candlelit church of Sant'Angelo in Pescheria, named for the fish market nearby. There, the silence of the night was broken only by the bells and prayers of some thirty Masses.[71] When the sun rose, Cola and his men set out through the ruined ancient columns that frame the portal of the church. In their hands they carried standards bearing images of Saints Peter, Paul and George, as well as a crimson flag honouring the goddess Rome.[72] After securing his revolution, Cola went to Saint Peter's Basilica, tossing coins to the crowd as he processed resplendent in green and yellow silk.[73] Cola was speaking in the vernacular of the old Roman world – a compelling language for the people of his own troubled time.

—— ౿ ౩ ౩ ——

When Cola came to power, Rome lacked a pope but it did not lack religion. Despite the absence of the core Church hierarchy, the fourteenth-century city was still peppered with men and women who devoted their entire life to God. In the early 1300s the city hosted 413 ecclesiastical institutions, housing more than 1,100 regular and secular priests, 126 monks and some 470 nuns.[74] The previous century had seen the emergence of several major religious orders: communities of pious men and women who lived by a rule and spirit established by their founder. Those established in the 1200s were distinguished by their engagement with the ordinary people of the world. These were not monks lying prostrate in front of an altar, or tilling in the secluded herb garden of a remote cloister. These were friars, walking shoulder-to-shoulder with the masses, devoted to a region not a closed house. Preaching, itinerant, weaving across the map, they had one mission: the salvation of souls. In Cola's Rome, the friars continued to thrive, with Trinitarians and Servites, as well as Dominican preachers dwelling right behind the Pantheon at the church of Santa Maria sopra Minerva. The older order of Saint Augustine had also found a new home in the city, making its way from Santa Maria del Popolo towards the densely populated *abitato*, settling on the corner of via della Scrofa and via dei Portoghesi.

Moreover, just as in the past, the faithful continued to arrive from foreign lands. In 1348, some thirty-nine years after the popes had quit for Avignon, Bridget Birgersdotter would wander the streets of Rome. Bridget had travelled some 2,200 kilometres from her home in the Swedish city of Vadstena, south-west of Stockholm. In Rome, she met a people and climate quite different to those in Ostergötland, where nearly every undulating hill met the shores of some glittering turquoise lake. 'Kind and meek to every creature' and always with a 'laughing face', the testimonies of Bridget's Roman servants paint a picture of an active and jolly woman, ready to engage with the city in which she had arrived.[75] In Rome, Bridget lived a life of energetic

Christian devotion, tending the sick at hospitals, praying at the shrines of saints and bustling through the streets to beg for supplies and funds for her work. Even with the popes abroad, one might understand foreigners who still came to Rome to trade or work. But Bridget was driven to the city for purely spiritual and ecclesiastical reasons. She was certainly not a woman who needed to seek her fortune: Bridget was a noble, a former lady-in-waiting to her queen, Blanche of Namur.[76] Like the pious patrician women of early Christian Rome, Bridget had renounced her worldly riches after her beloved husband, Ulf, died on their return from a pilgrimage to Santiago de Compostela.[77] As Ulf took his last breath, Bridget's life had been transformed. She emerged from her grief as an important religious leader.

In Vadstena, Bridget worked with the sick in a group associated with the friars of Saint Francis. Then she turned her attention to the scorned women who had children outside of wedlock. Before long, she attracted other women keen to support her work. Except for their books, Bridget and her followers would give all of their income and belongings to the poor. Soon it seemed that Bridget had formed a religious order. In 1348, the year after Cola had taken the city, she set out for Rome to seek the official approval of the Church.

Bridget was a bright, determined woman. She knew that the popes were in Avignon. So why on earth did she still go to Rome? It seems that, like so many before her, she believed that the city had a significance and authority that could not be translated abroad because this significance came from the blood spilt there by fellow Christians. Not everybody agreed. Dante claimed that it was the classical age to which Rome should return. For him it was Augustus, the pagan emperor, who personified the values to which the Roman government should revert.[78] These ideas were potent – as Cola's evocation of ancient Rome suggests. Still, they were fundamentally remote and intangible in the fourteenth century. Who of those who longed for the revival of Rome frequented the mausoleum of Augustus – by that time a mound of earth topped with a fortress belonging to the Colonna family? How many of those who lamented Rome's demise visited the temple that was formerly dedicated to Augustus, on the grounds of his early family home? Few if any, we can conjecture. By contrast, thousands continued to visit the Roman sites, shrines and churches that commemorated the Christian martyrs, even with the popes absent and public anger at the institutional Church. It was the continuous footfall of the faithful that kept the main roads to the basilicas clear, while other thoroughfares that had once flowed with walkers became overgrown through want of traffic.[79]

Rome's Christian significance was still marked out and fortified by the actions of people, whether those first martyred Christians or those who continued to honour them in prayer. Such action might have slowed with the shift of the papacy to Avignon, but it certainly did not cease altogether. The city of Rome not only received visiting foreigners like Bridget, but also developed entirely new Christian institutions. Bridget would establish one herself, now standing on the Piazza Farnese. During her first four years in Rome, she lived in the home of Pope Clement VI's relative, the Cardinal Hugo de Beaufort.[80] His lodging, now covered by the vast Palazzo della Cancelleria, was a few minutes' walk from the Campo dei Fiori, a meadowland increasingly encroached upon by market stalls. A little further on, Bridget would found a resting place for Swedish pilgrims in Rome; a stone plaque inside the door still marks it out as the 'HOSPITALIS. S. BRIGIDE GOTHORU[M]'. In typical Roman style, practicality and enterprise often mixed with piety in hospices such as Bridget's, as those in Rome for work made their bed alongside pilgrims. Some came as mercenaries, professional fighters such as John Hawkwood, known locally as Giovanni Acuto.[81] Others would make less concerning bedfellows. Documents from the ports of Ripa and Ripetta reveal that many still came to Rome to trade, like the cloth sellers of France, Brussels and the English city of Guildford.[82]

In the absence of key figures in the Church hierarchy it was often ordinary people, such as John Shepherd and his wife, Alice, who would expand and diversify Rome's Christian centres. In Rome, John had bought and sold rosaries, beads stringed in a rhythm that allows Christians to offer devotions to the Virgin Mary. In the capital of Christendom this was very good business indeed. But one day in spring 1362, the Shepherds sat down together, set aside their rosary beads, and made a deal in something much grander than wood, glass and thread. John sold his and Alice's house, and, along with this, their services for life, all for the price of forty gold florins.[83] Their home was to become a hospice for English visitors to Rome and John and Alice were to care for them in perpetuity. Their residence was well-located for the purpose, sitting on via di Monserrato, a narrow, cobbled passage that begins near the Campo de' Fiori and runs adjacent to the Tiber towards the Basilica of Saint Peter. The thoroughfare was small but soon became a key channel for foreigners flowing through Rome. Walking for just a couple of minutes, pilgrims would reach a juncture with the via del Pellegrino, the street traditionally taken by those seeking relics and salvation at the tomb across the river. Like the street in which it lay, the Shepherds' hospice was granted ever greater significance by the footfall of ordinary Christians. Soon it took the name of Saint Thomas of Canterbury. Later it became the Venerable English College, where Catholic priests from England are trained to this very day.[84]

John and Alice were not the only couple in Rome to offer a home to their countrymen in the later fourteenth century. Their area was emerging as a key base for Rome's foreign communities. Further north, just behind the Piazza Navona, Johannes Petri and his wife Catherine set up a hospice for men and women from the German lands. Even closer to the English hospice, on the very same street, Spanish pilgrims would find the place where the Aragonese offered their kinsmen shelter and care.[85] A little further on stood Bridget's hospice for Swedes. Similar institutions had emerged in earlier periods, particularly for the jubilee of 1300.[86] Now they spread, taking on a national quality that coloured them for centuries to come.

In the absence of the pontiffs, the city's churches functioned much as before, as wealthier Romans continued to shape their form and functions. By the middle of the fourteenth century, members of the baronial and lesser nobility occupied the most prestigious positions as canons, administering the city's main basilicas, from San Paolo fuori le Mura in the south to the basilica of San Lorenzo outside the north-eastern walls. Local families would also bear an influence on the network of parish churches that now branched out across the city. On the edge of the *abitato*, the now lost parish church of San Niccolò degli Arcione even took on the name of a local noble family, adjoining it to that of Saint Nicholas of Myra.[87] The highest echelons of the Roman élite, the barons, had already managed to extend their influence into the papal court, a phenomenon that lingered long after its flight to Avignon. The Orsini, Annabaldi, Caetani and Colonna all saw their own in the scarlet mantle of the cardinalate. As we have seen, some also secured the triple tiara of the popes.

Many sought influence, but others would have it thrust upon them. In the first decade of the thirteenth century, Francis of Assisi had entered the city cloaked in a coarse, brown tunic, followed by just eleven of his closest followers. Francis had famously rejected the world, casting aside comfort for a vocation of religious mortification and poverty. And yet in fourteenth-century Rome, his followers would live on the cusp of secular power, ministering to a worldly political class. The Franciscans in the south-east of the city put down relatively humble roots on the Ripa Grande, the riverbank in Trastevere. This was where Francis himself had laid his own head when he first visited Rome. Across the river, it would be a different story altogether. There, the Franciscans found themselves at the church of Santa Maria in Ara Coeli, the vast, unornamented facade of which still looms over the edge of the Capitoline Hill. From 1291, this would be the order's main church in Rome; it would also be the church frequented by the city's government. In a cavernous nave, defined by columns taken from the ruined buildings of the ancients, rough shod Franciscans shook hands with a lustrously robed ruling class. The Franciscans were careful to protect their characteristic austerity. But soon enough, worldly concerns coloured the building itself, as the banners of Rome's rulers, including Cola's flags, swayed in blues, reds and golds from the church tower.[88]

— ෙෙ ෙ ෙ —

Papal Rome might have persisted in the absence of the popes, but it soon found itself in danger. The great tribune, Cola, would not last a year. Soon Petrarch, who had held great hope in the leader, would write to him, fumes rising from his pen. Cola had become bloated with power and, quite literally, fat. As a leader he was self-indulgent and violent, imposing new taxes and terrorising the old families of Rome.[89] The brutal murder of nobles such as Stefanuccio Colonna might have garnered cheers from some of the knights, lawyers and common people who had supported his initial tirade against corrupt power.[90] But, ultimately, for political currency, such violence was very cheap. Fearing that he had lost the plot but hopeful he might change, Petrarch begged Cola, 'consider with great zeal ... what you may be doing, shake yourself sharply, examine yourself without deceit to see who you are'.[91] Clement VI, who had been charmed by the young man he met in Avignon, had less faith, seeing him only as a 'rector', a useful administrator and ally back in the Holy See.[92] Soon enough the pope became infuriated at Cola's ever more radical plans: to unite Italy, to revive the empire and to put both in the hands of the common man. When Cola made an alliance with the King of Hungary, who planned to invade Naples, even the Romans themselves began to reject his ideas.[93] By the end of 1347, the very same year in which Cola had become *de facto* ruler of Rome, his envoys were beaten up and turned away at Avignon's gates. For Clement, this was a clear message about the state of their working relationship. For Cola it would foreshadow a demise almost as swift as his rise.

Cola rose and ruled as a symbol; he would fall in similar style. When he and his supporters had stalked Rome's streets at the dawn of Pentecost 1347, he had employed words and images with a Christian, even Petrine, flavour. When he assumed the role of tribune, he evoked the image of a glorious ancient Rome. Even after Cola was forced to abdicate and the barons returned, he remained ardent about his God-given role in the revival of Rome. Pushed from power, Cola fled to the mountainous region of Abruzzo to live among the Franciscan Spirituals. These austere, apocalyptic friars only fed his messianic pretensions. In Cola's mind, God was going to reform the earth with fire, blood and Cola himself. In 1350, his unshakeable self-belief took him all the way to the court of King Charles IV at Prague. There he told the Bohemian king that he would be the emperor in the Last Days.

In the end, the prophesy landed on deaf ears, with Cola not 'in prison but rather under guard'.[94] He was later transported to Avignon where the pope made him into a symbol once again. With the barons back in power in Rome, the pontiff, now Innocent VI (1352–62), needed to send out a clear sign of his own power. Cola became that symbol when he was released and returned to Rome as a senator. In pardoning Cola, the pope made it clear that in Rome it was he who had the power to rule, imprison and free. Cola had been a Christian lord and republican representative; then he had made himself a harbinger of apocalyptic fire. Back in Rome, he was now a walking symbol of papal supremacy. Despite these shifting masks, Cola had not changed at all. In his role as a senator, tyranny returned, as did the ire of the people. In 1354, he would be stabbed to death by a frenzy of Roman hands between the marble lions at the foot of the Capitoline Hill.[95] Cola breathed his last in a setting pregnant with every idea that he had tried and failed to manifest, dying in the shadow of the Senator's Palace and the Church of the Ara Coeli, where Emperor Augustus (27–14 BC) had been told of the coming of Christ.[96]

— ❧ ❧ ❧ —

Unlike Cola, the popes had ancient and inextricable ties to the city and people of Rome. However, these connections did not necessarily make them comfortable bedfellows. In order to return to his see, Innocent's successor, Urban V (1362–70), had to do battle, and even then he had a hard time. Urban's efforts were driven by Cardinal Gil Álvarez Carillo de Albornoz. As a nobleman, politician, lawyer and former crusader, he was one of the most eminent Spaniards of his day.[97] Like Cola, Albornoz expelled the rancorous nobility from offices of state. He also collaborated with Charles IV, by that time Holy Roman Emperor. In 1363 they began to quieten the violence in Rome. Only with this achieved could they march their forces northwards to quash the families who had encroached on papal territory. These wars were costly, and still the French prelates resisted a return to Rome. In 1367 Urban and the emperor finally achieved their aim. Sadly, Cardinal Albornoz did not live to see the day.

In October of that year, the people of Rome would gasp at the sight of a striking palfrey horse that bore the pope back into their city. The stirrups were held by the hand of the Holy Roman Emperor himself. The ceremonies were lavish. Urban would crown Charles' wife as empress at Saint Peter's basilica. After six decades, the pope was back in Rome, and it seemed just like old times. However, he had only achieved his restoration with the assent of the Roman people. They cleared the way so that the pope could return without too much conflict. Yet they also retained and augmented many of the privileges that they had exercised in his absence: representation in civic government, prestige through peace-making rituals and a participation in the patronage and life of the Church.[98] Many of these customs and privileges would persist and grow in parallel to papal power, even if responsibility for overseeing Rome in its entirety was handed back to the successor of Peter.[99]

In Rome the pope was wanted and, somehow, needed. Still the transition was rocky and soon seemed a false start. After less than two years, Urban made moves to leave Rome for Avignon once again. Catching Urban at his summer house in Montefiascone, Bridget of Sweden admonished him using words from the Virgin Mary herself. The mother of God had appeared to Bridget in a vision and revealed that any return to Avignon would cause the pope to 'be struck with a blow that will knock his teeth out … [and] tremble in every limb of his body.'[100] Bridget warned Urban in vain. A cortege of thirty-four ships soon carried the pontiff away from Italy. Arriving in Avignon in late September 1370, the pope would be dead before Christmas Day. Bridget, and the Virgin Mary, had been right about his fate.

It was Gregory XI (1370–78), Urban's determined successor, who would calmly and slowly translate the papal court back to Saint Peter's See. He, too, would be berated by a spirited saint of the age. Catherine of Siena would ask him starkly, 'What sane person doesn't see that the holiest thing is for the lord of all the world to be seated on his proper throne?'[101] To Catherine it was obvious. Papal Rome was like a puzzle. It could survive, nearly in its entirety, even without its central piece. That said, its identity and structure was fundamentally weakened without the popes. They too could not go unscathed, diminishing in prestige and significance when taken out of the context of their Holy See. For now the popes were back in Rome. In the centuries to come, the authority and fabric of papal Rome would be undermined once again. However, in those tumultuous years, the popes would bed into their Eternal City, sculpting it into an ornate and heavily fortified witness to their own supreme apostolic authority.

PART 3
THE RISE AND FALL OF THE IMPERIAL PAPACY

Rome's most famous 'talking statue', Pasquino, surrounded by notes written by the people. These often criticised popes. (The Metropolitan Museum of Art)

6

Echoes of the Ancients: The Renaissance of Papal Rome

It was the summer of 1426 and the footsteps of some 25,000 people sounded on the streets of Rome.[1] Itching to wash away the dust and slake their thirst, men and women elbowed each other at the banks of the Tiber. The only other source of refreshment was the ancient aqueduct of the Acqua Vergine, a few minutes' walk from the spot where the waters of the Trevi Fountain now rush. By the end of the fifteenth century, the Vergine's waters would flow freely, but in the summer of 1426 they were still sputtering, leaking and foul.[2] In the smothering intensity of a hot Roman summer, most would be preoccupied by the battle to keep cool and well. Yet in one quarter of the city, locals would be shaken by the cry of a small boy in mortal danger. In a simple dwelling, an old man discovered a child flailing under the body of a cat that clawed his face, crushed his body and suffocated his small, soft lungs. The man was old but he still had his wits about him; the little boy was saved by the tip of his sword. According to some Romans, other children visited by the cat were not so fortunate. For their deaths, a woman, not an animal, would pay the price.

On 8 July 1426, Finicella was tied up and burnt alive on the Capitoline Hill.[3] From the mid-sixteenth century the Roman Inquisition would oversee the prosecution of witches in Italy. Finicella was the victim of an earlier and more chaotic time. In an effort to deflect allegations that he had encouraged magical practices, the friar Bernardino of Siena stoked panic about malevolent female sorcerers in Rome.[4]

Records paint a city in alarm, telling us that 'all of Rome went to see' the woman who turned herself into a cat to kill and eat innocent children.[5] Finicella had been identified as the murderer by a wound matching the mark that the old man had made on the cat. For those watching her execution on the Capitoline, justice was done. Once again, that hill was the stable seat of the Roman Commune. The age of demagogues such as Cola di Rienzo was over and the feuds of the barons had quietened down. On that hill, where the ancient senate had sat, the senatorial court of the Curia Capitolina decided the fate of hundreds. Just as in trials, punishments and executions the world over, public justice in Rome allowed the population to see threats identified and then visibly expunged.

Still, the lived reality of Roman justice was far from clear cut.[6] As Finicella and others condemned to death met their fate, they also met every face in the human drama. From the incandescent aggrieved to Christian confraternities who urged criminals to convert, Rome's system of justice had as many faces as the crowd. By the fifteenth century, the city had eight police forces: from the men of the Governor of Rome, an intimate papal official with jurisdiction over crimes from sodomy to fortune telling, to the lower-ranking *sbirri* (or constables) abhorred for taking bribes, exposing adulterers and enforcing the law with a heavy hand.[7] There were also multiple courts. In the tribunal of the Vicar General, priests, families and individual laymen were tried for breaches of moral law.[8] On the Capitoline, civil and criminal cases were heard. The city's governor often wielded the most power. Those who fell foul of his court could find themselves in the shabby prison cells of Curia Savelli or Tor di Nona, which sat opposite Castel Sant'Angelo where grander miscreants were jailed. Yet even the governor could not seek out the high, mighty and holy who fell under his suspicion.[9] For crowning this motley hierarchy of justice, was, once again, the pope. It was he who appointed the governors and the senators and oversaw an array of powerful Church courts, the jurisdiction of which reached beyond the walls of the city, attempting to govern a whole world of souls.

In the year 1426, the pope overseeing justice, daily life and religion in the city was Martin V (1417–31). A shrewd pontiff, he had been elected in 1417. He had retaken his place in Rome only three years later, progressing from Constance, a lakeside city at the southern-most boundary of modern Germany. There, a council of the Church's bishops had decided that Martin should be pope. As the air cooled in the last days of September 1420, he arrived in Rome. It was somewhat of a homecoming, for Martin had been born Oddone Colonna in his family fief of Genazzano, just fifty kilometres south-east of the city. Entering Rome from the north, the pope would be greeted by the Porta Flaminia, that simple city gate ornamented in the Renaissance and now known as the Porta del Popolo. Weary from a journey of some 900 kilometres, Martin did not get much further that day. Alighting just inside the gate, he stopped at the church of Santa Maria del Popolo. Setting aside his pallium – the snow white neckband that marked his papal office – he took a night's rest with the friars of the church.[10] When Martin awoke it was Sunday morning and time for him to complete his journey. He took up the pallium, mounted his horse and set off for the Basilica of Saint Peter.

As Martin's steed carried him through the city he was unmistakeable. Here, under a rich purple canopy, was Rome's pontiff and temporal prince. The occasion was stately and festive: in addition to the usual retinue of guards, staff and nobles, Martin was flanked by eight jesters, travelling at the hooves of his horse.[11] Such diversion was hardly necessary. Even after the papacy returned from Avignon there had been further periods of papal absence in Rome. Now Martin's progress through the city inspired great joy. Riding through the crowds, the pope's half-moon eyes looked out over his distinctly Roman nose, surveying a people crying 'long live Pope Martin!' and sacrificing precious oil to light their pontiff's way.[12]

—— ⟨҂ ᏸᎧ ᏸᎧ ——

Rome and its new pope now looked forward to a brighter future; for both the recent past had been somewhat bleak. Though Pope Gregory XI (1370–78) had brought the papacy back from Avignon in 1377, he had done so falteringly and with much spilt blood. Attempting to reassert his power, Gregory had expanded the Papal States around Rome, provoking war and some regret at his return. In the first days of the summer of 1377, riots in Rome had pushed the pope out once again. This time he did not go so far as Avignon, but some sixty kilometres south-east to the town of Anagni. This was histori- cally dangerous territory: the city had seen the assault on Boniface VIII (1294–1303) that had catalysed the papacy's exile to Provence. Coordinating forces from this relatively safe haven, Gregory managed to quell the upheaval in Rome. By winter he was safely back in his Roman see. In one year, Gregory had achieved what had seemed, at times, impossible. The pope would not have long to enjoy his success. By spring of 1378 his exhausted body lay cold in a grave.[13] Gregory XI had died at just forty-seven years of age.

When a pope died, the see of Rome was vacant. Ceremony kicked in lest chaos and criminality take hold of the city. Men scurried up the Capitoline Hill to sound the bells at the Senator's Palace. Passing at its foot, Romans knew that the chimes signalled one of a few things: Shrove Tuesday (Carnival), the execution of a criminal, the summoning of the council or the demise of their pope.[14] Across the Tiber, on the Vatican Hill, the air rang with a more distinctive sound. In the Vatican palace, shards of broken lead ricocheted on the floor, splintered from the dead pope's seal and *annulis pescatoris*. This 'fisherman's ring' was worn by each pontiff, a symbol linking them to Saint Peter, a fisherman and their most important predecessor. When the pope died, his time in Peter's See came to an end and his ring was ceremonially hammered to pieces.[15]

In a quieter corner of Saint Peter's Basilica lay the dead pope himself. Each day, the hush was broken as the faithful visited the body to confess their misdemeanours. Rubbing the grate around the cadaver with religious objects such as rosary beads, papal devotees sought the pontiff's good word in heaven. Those with a bleaker view of his prospects in the afterlife stayed in town, but even there it was the dead pope who dictated the mood. While there was no reigning pope, Romans were banned from bearing handguns and daggers and concealing their face. If these rules sought to disarm the violent, others aimed to remove causes of conflict before it began. Jews were not to be molested; prostitutes could not accompany their clients in carriages.[16] All bets – on races, fights, or the upcoming papal election – were off the table. This was a blow for the financial hub of the via dei Banchi, where the outcome of the conclave was the object of lucrative wagers.[17] With outlets for the passions corked, a febrile atmosphere hung in the air. Forces were needed 'to keep the city in peace and fear'.[18] Regional leaders or *capirioni* and conservators stalked the streets of Rome on horseback, representing a police guard of some two hundred men.

In the ceremonies of the *sede vacante* a familiar message rang out in Rome: for true stability and security, the city needed a pope. On the eve of the conclave to elect Gregory's successor in 1378, frustration over the long exile of the popes in Avignon had sparked a violent riot among the people of Rome. As the Romans bayed for a pope from their city – or at least from Italy – a monk and archbishop from Lazio, just south of Rome, was duly elected. When Bartolomeo Prignano became Pope Urban VI (1378–89) he seemed just the ticket: firm in faith, austere in habits and relatively untainted by family corruption. Even the beleaguered cardinals declared 'firm hope and confidence' in their new pontiff.[19] In his hands they hoped that 'the state of the universal Church' would 'begin to blossom again'.

Regrettably it did not. Choleric and mercurial, Urban's orders soon made for a disaffected and increasingly distant papal court. Even Urban's electors began to lose faith in their new pope. Cardinal by cardinal, the conclave that had chosen him disintegrated, trailing away from Urban's court and Rome. The first departed in a flurry of protestations about the heat and dirt of the city. As spring turned to summer, a stream of red hats continued to pass out of the city gates. These men certainly escaped a sweltering Rome, but they also left behind the fiery reprimands of their pontiff. By August 1378, thirteen of the sixteen cardinals who had elected Urban were living in Anagni, another had died, and the final two had retreated to Avignon.[20]

The conclave had abandoned the city and their pontiff. It seemed as though history might soon repeat itself. But before Urban had the opportunity to leave Saint Peter's see, he was stripped of his office by the cardinals in Anagni. They called for a recount. The rabble outside of the palace had forced their hand; Urban VI was simply not the true pope. Ire among the nobles only bolstered their cause. Urban was in debt to local aristocrats to the tune of tens of thousands of florins. When the pope failed to settle his accounts, many cardinals were only too delighted to condemn him. To make matters worse, Urban had made a powerful enemy in Onorato Caetani when he deprived him of the office of papal Count of Campagna on ascending to the Holy See.[21] It is no coincidence at all that the cardinals had flown to Anagni, a seat of the Caetani family. From there, the rebel churchmen moved, still under Caetani patronage, to Onorato's castle at Fondi, a city halfway between Naples and Rome. Ensconced in the castellated fortress, the cardinals now acted with real nerve. Denouncing Urban as an imposter, they elected a new pope to take his place.[22] Now there were two pontiffs: Robert of Geneva, who went to Avignon as Pope Clement VII, and Urban VI, still hanging on in Rome.

These parallel papacies endured for decades, with popes Boniface, Innocent and Gregory in Rome and Pope Benedict after Clement in

Avignon.[23] In 1409, a council of bishops and cardinals met to end this farce of rival popes, now known as the Great Western Schism. Rather than resolving the problem they only added to the chaos, electing a third pope, Alexander V, who would rule from Pisa. As it happened, the cries for a Roman pope in 1378 would have to wait some thirty-nine years for satisfaction. Moreover, it was not a conclave of cardinals but a council of bishops that elevated Martin V, restoring one true pope to a singular papal city: Rome. Meeting in Constance in the German lands in 1417, the council persuaded the incumbent Pope Gregory XII of Rome and Pope John XXIII of Pisa to step down quietly. However, in Avignon, Benedict XIII flatly refused to accept that he was not the pope. Even an appeal from the Holy Roman Emperor fell on deaf ears. In the end, Benedict was excommunicated, though he continued to claim that he was the true successor of Saint Peter until his death some six years later.[24]

Within a few years, the Romans had their pope back. Still the future was far from certain. If the choice was going to stick, Martin had to refill the papal coffers and restore order in the Papal States. These were not complementary endeavours, for the latter came at a very high price. Martin spent around 100,000 ducats a year on professional mercenaries to coerce the local lords who resisted his authority.[25] To assert his influence elsewhere he needed to use more diplomatic means. In the city of Rome, the republican spirit had to be tamed, but Martin knew that the desire for popular representation had outlived the likes of Cola di Rienzo. The pope accepted the organisations that made up the SPQR (*Senatus Populusque Romanus* or Senate and People of Rome) as a municipal body to be run by lay people; men from across the city's social classes would be elected for the posts. In affluent regions such as Trevi, just north-east of the Pantheon, prestigious locals such as the Mattei and Muti more or less always took charge.[26] In the bustling commercial quarters of Ripa, Ponte and Trastevere there was a rotating cast of players, with around half of the public officials elected just once.[27] Elected members monitored and fortified the walls that had protected and betrayed the city over centuries. They also stayed the hands of greedier merchants, regulating the prices at Rome's market. Overseeing the city's aqueducts and fountains, civic representatives ensured that the Romans did not thirst. And when the pope died and the laws of the *sede vacante* kicked in they enforced law and order, as we have seen.[28]

Beyond this, popular representation was relatively skin deep. Finicella and others subject to Roman justice might have been executed at the seat of the senate, the Capitoline Hill, but their sentences were carried out under the authority of a senator appointed by the pope. Papal influence also extended to the bread supply, the collection of duties and an entire administration of priests, who worked throughout the Church and in tandem with the civic system. Beyond the public sphere, in the realm of the spirit, the pope and his staff had full rein. As we have seen, this was nothing new. By the early medieval period, the popes had asserted their authority to judge on religious and ecclesiastical matters of the highest importance across the Christian West. The tribunal of the Apostolic Penitentiary pronounced on cases related to the forgiveness of serious sins, cleansing souls of irregularities caused by misdemeanours such as the denial of Catholic teaching. Alongside this court, the Roman Rota and *Segnatura Apostolica* heard appeals from other tribunals for cases related to marriage and conflicts between the many authorities within the Church.[29] Yet more administration grew around the arm of papal justice. The Apostolic Chancery handled the administration related to any decisions made, while the *Camera Apostolica* managed the stream of money into and out of the popes' hands.[30] When the papacy had resided in Avignon, Rome was emptied of this vast bureaucracy. In Provence the numbers had only grown. When the pope returned to Rome, he did so with a staff of 650 secretaries, writers, notaries, lawyers and other officials. It was the largest bureaucracy in Europe and it was only set to expand.[31]

To avoid treachery and shore up his influence, Martin V turned to members of his family network for help.[32] Loyal men were selected to work as governors, administrators and lieutenants throughout the Papal States. As we have noted, Martin was a member of the Colonna family, a venerable, old Roman clan. While local lords long abandoned to their own devices had few good reasons to surrender their authority to comply with the pope, Martin's relatives were grateful to him for their individual and collective rise.[33] Even before Martin ascended to Peter's See, his brother Giordano Colonna had experience of rising up on the wings of papal power. When papal authority had splintered at the Great Schism, Giordano had been rewarded as a supporter of the Roman pope, Boniface IX, who elevated him to the ranks of the 'princes of the sweet city' of Rome, as well as making him the role of governor and captain of (of all places) Anagni.[34] Giordano had done well alone but his star truly began to rise when he tied his fate to that of his brother. In 1411 the young Martin, still known as Oddone, was made pontifical legate to Rome and the Patrimony of Peter, as John XXIII (one of the popes) had left the city. In turn, Giordano became apostolic vicar, or representative of the pope, to Belvedere, Olevano and Passerano in Lazio. When Oddone himself got the top job, Giordano elevated himself as lord of villages, towns and territories across the Italian peninsula, riding in to subdue them under the banner of his brother, the pope.

The Colonna pope collected hefty payments from local feudal lords, many of whom were keen to have the pontiff legitimise their rule.[35] Under papal auspices but by Giordano's hands, large chunks of the patrimony of Saint Peter also became Colonna territory. During the papacies of the early medieval period, familial elevation had become a familiar phenomenon. Still Giordano's behaviour inaugurated a tradition of popes truly aggrandising their own clans, which only declined after Innocent XII's (1691–1700) ban on nepotism in the bull *Romanum decet pontificem* in 1692.[36] The papal See and individual basilicas had become substantial landholders in the thousand years since Constantine began to enrich the Church. During the years of schism, however, those lands – like papal authority – had been rent apart. When Martin consolidated his rule in Rome, he extended his reach outwards, retaking lands lost in the fray. Only this time when towns such as Frascati returned to Roman possession they did go not back to the basilicas. Rather, they were bought, taken and ruled by men like Giordano Colonna. From the basilica of San Giovanni in Laterano, he purchased Frascati for 10,000 gold florins.[37] For Marino, just south-east of that town, he paid 2,000 florins extra.

These were good prices, but after years of schism and combat most would not have looked upon these towns as assets at all. Today the name of Frascati might evoke a vision of green hills densely packed with rosy-red brick buildings, but when Giordano bought it the Florentine diplomat Rinaldo degli Albizzi described the town as a 'useless place, uninhabitable either within or without' its boundaries.[38] For Albizzi, Marino was similarly 'ruined by the recent wars'; there was simply 'no way' that anybody would be able to live there.[39] The Florentines had fought Rome in recent struggles for the former Papal States, so Albizzi might have exaggerated the desolation of the towns won by the papal side. Agriculture, Frascati's prime function, had certainly been heavily affected by the wars. Yet in Giordano's eyes the state of the towns did not matter. For him, or rather for the Colonna family, they were strategic assets: Frascati and Marino were extensions of their traditional power base in the region surrounding Martin V's birthplace at Genazzano.

Other men around the pope would raise their status too, namely the cardinals who had emerged as the pontiffs' main counsellors and electors. The figure of the cardinal has done much to shape the popular image of the Church of Rome from Martin's period right into our own day. At the turn of the fifteenth century, however, even the pope did not have a clear notion of their exact role. The cardinals' office had been named after the Latin word for hinges, *cardines*: the mechanism on which the direction of the Church turned.[40] Some popes and bishops would have heartily agreed with the definition, saying that the cardinals acted as successors to the first apostles. Like Peter, Philip and others who had surrounded Christ, they encircled and followed Christ's vicar on earth, the pope. The definition was beautiful but somewhat limited, for those middle-eastern fishermen did not advise Jesus like cardinals counselled the pope. All too frequently, the definition of the cardinal as disciple jarred with their actions as power players, particularly in the early modern church. Far from humble acolytes, some ecclesiastical princes earned their place in Protestant controversy, Jacobean literature and modern thrillers, cultivating clients, channelling the wealth of the Church into their families and lobbying for their own promotion at the papal court.[41] They could also make themselves rich. By the late seventeenth century, Cardinal Francesco degli Albizzi (a cardinal from the age of thirty-one to ninety) would declare that men of his rank needed at least 7000 *scudi* to live in a fashion worthy of the dignity of their office.[42] This was 1000 *scudi* more than the funds given to sustain the entire faculty of the university in Rome.[43]

Many cardinals of Martin's time were also very powerful, having increased their influence beyond recognition during their time in Avignon. Working at the court, cardinals had latched on to almost every form of papal practice, involving themselves with the work of the pontiff at every turn. Some had even used their wealth to work as bankers to the Holy See. They lent the popes money and when their debtors could not pay happily took positions, responsibilities and influence in kind. Clement VI (1342–52), that lavish pope who had tried to make Avignon a New Rome, took out loans of more than 15,000 gold florins – enough to build a magnificent palace from scratch.[44] Such debts undermined the pope's authority and autonomy. This was only exacerbated when cardinals took great offices of the Church as repayment. The attitude of these later princes of the Church had been seen before, if on a smaller scale, particularly after 1059 when cardinals became the sole electors of the pope.[45] During the reign of Eugenius III (1145–53) in the twelfth century, the cardinals had reminded the pontiff: 'you belong not just to yourself but to us'. The cardinals were, after all, the people who had transformed him 'from a private person into the father of the universal church'.[46]

The most serious charge against the cardinals of Martin's time was that they did not fulfil their duties to the Church. When the conclave who had elected Urban VI fractured and left Rome in the late fourteenth century, they earned the scorn of Catherine of Siena, the young woman and future saint who had admonished Gregory XI to leave Avignon. With a tide of invective, she now lobbied for the cause of Urban VI, denouncing the cardinals who had abandoned him. For Catherine, these men were not princes of the Church but 'columns, worse than straw' who had 'turned their backs like wretched and cowardly knights' when they had elected a second pope.[47] In many ways, Catherine's anger was well-founded. Like Bridget of Sweden, Catherine had sought the end of the Avignon papacy fervently. Now the popes were back and the cardinals had blighted Christendom with a schism. For this, Catherine deemed them villains who had desecrated their office with sloth and ambition: they were 'a stench that has caused the whole world to reek.'[48]

With towns to dominate and a pontifical See to retake, Martin V could not tolerate such audacity. Moreover, his cardinals could not claim to have elevated him as Eugenius' had. After they had tried to reverse Urban VI's conclave, councils of bishops had taken over, excluding the cardinals from the process and electing the pope themselves. On his arrival in Rome, Pope Martin took strict measures to limit the cardinals' influence and ambition further. He elected just three cardinals in the first nine years of his papacy. Throughout his pontificate he made moves to tame their independent streak: financial, sexual and political satisfaction were out, while piety, humility and chastity were mandated. He even tried to limit their contact with external political influences, capping the tenure of foreign diplomats in Rome to a maximum of six months.[49] There is some evidence that these measures worked. Approaching the papal throne in 1429, an ambassador for the Knights of the Teutonic Order noted a distinct shift in the mood at the papal court. In backroom discussions he had been heartened by some cardinals' hearty promises of support for the knights' cause. Nodding their heads and patting his back, they had made him believe that his mission would find favour on the Vatican Hill. Yet in front of the pontiff the cardinals' turned 'red and pale' and would 'not speak before the Pope, save what he likes to hear'.[50]

—— ☙ ❧ ❧ ——

To shore up papal Rome in other areas, the pope needed not to destroy but to nurture. On Martin's arrival in 1420, the hooves of his horse had clacked over much craggy terrain. At this time, thoroughfares that had once been ennobled with imperial triumphs were often full of debris. In some areas, they were impossible to traverse. This was not a new situation, but one caused by long neglect. A decade earlier, the Greek scholar Manuel Chrysoloras had encountered mounds of rubble and broken buildings as he peered out from beneath the deep brim of his circular hat. Summoned from Constantinople by the Chancellor of Florence, Chrysoloras was in Italy to revive knowledge of Greek. Visiting Rome, he sought out the great works of the ancients but found a city 'crumbling beneath the natural forces of time', as well as 'the violence of human hands'.[51] As with the years of barbaric invasion during the fall of the Western Roman Empire, papal abandonment had reduced much of Rome to dust and cracked stone. The 'scars of human violence' had been inflicted in a more dramatic fashion. In 1413 the city had been sacked by Ladislaus of Naples (1386–1414), who had grown up stuttering after surviving a dose of poison administered to him by the Archbishop of Arles when he was a child.[52] The year after Ladislaus' attack, there had not been enough wealth in Rome to light the oil lamps at Saint Peter's.[53] To make matters worse, the bloody footsteps of Ladislaus had been followed by Braccio da Montone: one of Italy's most intrepid mercenaries and, for a little while, ruler of Rome.[54]

Rome had been refortified in places, as and when it was strictly necessary. Roman builders took an approach that was economical and sometimes ingenious, breaking apart ruins to fashion something new. Using stone and wood taken from dilapidated buildings, they made structures in a collage of parts and styles. The results disappointed some. Chrysoloras described Rome as a cannibal, using 'itself as a mine and quarry' to become 'a city that both nourishes and consumes itself'.[55] Visiting in the later fifteenth century, the Castilian historian and royal secretary Alfonso de Palencia painted an image that was more dramatic yet. He claimed to walk Roman streets among piles of rubble so high that only the very tallest parts of ancient structures poked out at the top.[56] Even Italians joined the critical refrain. Standing on the Capitoline, the scholar Flavio Biondo bewailed the sight of fifteenth-century Rome: 'It shames and pains me to report the ugliness that is beginning on the Capitoline.'[57] Boniface IX had built a 'brick house ... for the use of senators and lawyers' the mediocrity of which would have 'disgusted the Roman citizen' of the ancient city.[58]

Despite Palencia's protestations many of the buildings that were admired by Biondo and his imaginary ancient Roman citizens could still be seen, even if they were somewhat dilapidated. In the early sixteenth century, the Dutch artist Martin van Heemskerck would visit Rome and paint himself in front of a Colosseum decayed to a truncated semi-circle of tunnels, covered with a pelt of dust and weeds. On the other side of the Palatine, the Theatre of Marcellus also remained, a striking curved structure that had faced the Tiber Island since the time of Emperor Augustus. Hosting an audience of up to 20,000 ancient Romans, nestled into orderly rows, the theatre was built over three levels of arches in concrete, tuff and travertine stone. We do not know exactly how the highest levels of the building were laid out originally as, by the early modern period, it had been ruined, rebuilt and reused time and again. At one point, the theatre had been a fortress of the aristocratic Savelli clan. Earlier, in the twelfth century, it was the base of the family of the revolutionary leader Giordano Pierleoni, who made a medieval stronghold from this ancient place of pleasure.[59]

In other corners of Rome, ancient stones were reused for more poetic reasons, as architects raised fortresses from ruins to evoke ancient ideals. Unlike Boniface IX, the patrons of these buildings were praised by the likes of Biondo. They were often key members of the papal court. On the Esquiline Hill, Cardinal Prospero Colonna, the nephew of Pope Martin V, would use trees, walls and statuary to revive what he thought were the ancient gardens of Maecenas. In the age of Augustus, Maecenas had been a general and imperial advisor, walking the streets of Rome as the Theatre of Marcellus welcomed its first spectators. In the lines of his Odes, the ancient poet Horace wrote to Maecenas in his tower up in the clouds, painting his gardens as an idyll rising above the 'smoke, splendour and noise of the city below'.[60] Colonna's own career would take turbulent turns. After the death of his uncle, he became one of the very few cardinals ever to be excommunicated from the Church. In the happier period of his family's ascent, Colonna took the imagined ideals of Maecenas and used them to shape a gentlemanly estate, where his enthusiasm for the ancients would seep out of the stones and into erudite conversation. Seated around his table on warm Roman evenings, scholars such as Biondo elevated the minds of his dinner guests. Gesturing across the garden to portrait busts raised on plinths, the scholar waxed lyrical on the splendid marble sculptures that Maecenas himself might once have owned.[61]

In the balmy alfresco dinners of Cardinal Prospero Colonna we see a snapshot of Rome sitting between two worlds. Prospero was a noble and further aggrandised as a cardinal of the Church, an institution whose supreme authority in Rome (and beyond) was underpinned by Christian ideas and claims. Yet Prospero was also a man trying to live in the style of an ancient pagan general. He studied and lauded the ideals of a political and religious system that had been hostile to the first Christians, whose legacy bolstered his own ecclesiastical authority. Biondo even referred to Prospero as 'the Maecenas of our century'. He was a paradox. And, at this time, he was typical of the Roman élite. Prospero and scholars such as Biondo and Chrysoloras were part of burgeoning band of thoroughly Christian thinkers who nevertheless revered the culture and learning of the ancient pagan world. These enthusiasts have come to be known as the humanists: devotees of the *studia humanitatis* of philosophy, grammar, rhetoric and poetry, and inspired by the writers and artists of the ancient Greek and Roman worlds. Fired by individual curiosity and shared intellectual ardour, the humanists in Rome pored over classical artefacts, texts and buildings. The cultural phenomenon that they drove was later called the Renaissance or *Rinascimento* – for it was deemed nothing short of a rebirth of the learning and beauty of ancient world.

In Rome, thousands of objects were unearthed or re-examined in this wave of scholarly enthusiasm. The ground itself yielded all manner of ancient treasures. When the priests of San Silvestro in Capite urged people to rent and rebuild properties on their patch of the Campo Marzio, ancient inscriptions, coins and sculptures rose from the earth.[62] At the Roman port of Anzio in 1489, the graceful forms of the Apollo Belvedere were revealed after a hibernation of centuries. In Rome just over fifteen years later, the writhing marble bodies of Laocoön and his sons were dug up at a vineyard.[63] The atmosphere of the time is reflected in the sheer glee of the artist Giuliano Sangallo on seeing the sculpture with Pope Julius II and Michelangelo: here was the 'Laocoön, of which Pliny speaks!'[64]

Above ground, Rome was still littered with ancient buildings. Treading carefully as he wound through fractured rock, Biondo surveyed the ruins to write his *Roma Instaurata* (1444–8) and *Triumphans* (1459). These historical books were seminal, but Biondo was far from unique in his archaeological activity. Men such as the clerk and merchant Ciriaco d'Ancona were also engrossed by Roman civilisation and its wreckage.[65] At first, Ciriaco journeyed from his Adriatic home for trade and work, travelling to Rhodes, Chios and the city of Constantinople to perform clerical duties, buy and sell. However, when he came to Rome, he did so for intellectual pursuits, seeking to master classical Latin from the best teachers around. Soon Ciriaco's pen strayed from declensions to the broken lines of the city's ancient buildings. By the summer of 1433, he was describing them in detail, and for one of the most powerful men in Christendom. In that year, Ciriaco's lean dynamic figure could be seen guiding Holy Roman Emperor Sigismund of Luxembourg (1433–7) through the ruins of ancient Rome.[66] At this time, the city was both a rich mine of objects and ideas, enlivening the hearts and minds of an entire generation of scholars and amateur enthusiasts.

Men such as Biondo and Petrarch, that great critic of the Avignonian papacy, also studied the words of antique authors. By the fifteenth century, some of these had been lost, but many were just little known or ignored. For centuries, the sole audience for some ancient thinkers had been provided by neat rows of monks who transcribed manuscripts in Europe's monasteries. Hunched over animal skins, picking out words in inks of colour, black and gold, these monks had built vast libraries of classical and Christian texts. In the central

German region of Hesse, the Abbey of Fulda would be custodian of more than two thousand manuscripts.[67] These preserved Christian texts as well as the words of ancient writers such as Marcellinus and Tacitus. As humanism emerged, pages long closed were prised open. Carried northwards on a wave of enthusiasm, Italian scholars such as Poggio Bracciolini sought out rare manuscripts, reconsidering long neglected works. It was in the library of Fulda that Bracciolini brought to light Epicureanism, an entirely forgotten philosophical system described by Lucretius.[68]

The revelations of the humanists would be carried to Rome in volumes bought or painstakingly transcribed. Despite its pagan associations, this scholarship reached the heart of the papal court. Biondo was secretary to the Apostolic Chancery; a stream of pontiffs employed Bracciolini as Papal Secretary. One of the greatest of the humanist scholars, the priest Lorenzo Valla, was paid by Pope Nicholas V (1447–55) to translate the characters of ancient Greek into flowing and refined Renaissance Latin.[69] If they were careful, these men could even fuse their Christian and classical worlds. Bracciolini and others saw the culture of early Christians as a continuation of that of ancient Rome, mining the catacombs for artefacts and using classical Latin to compose elegies to saints and popes.[70] For other churchmen, humanism or a more passing interest in classical learning could remain distinct from their ecclesiastical work. The grand Neapolitan Cardinal Oliviero Carafa populated his Roman *vigna* with inscriptions of ancient sayings on rural life, as well images of the men who had first uttered them.[71]

Even popes delighted in the skills and enthusiasms of the humanists. Pius II (1458–64), for example, studied at the Universities of Siena and Florence before he ascended to Peter's See. Applying his linguistic and rhetorical learning, he wrote comedies, as well as an autobiography and an erotic novel, *The Tale of Two Lovers*. He is the only future pope, as far as we know, to write such a text. In 1475, Sixtus IV (1471–84) bolstered this activity by formally founding the Vatican Library. This was an intellectual powerhouse for an increasingly global institution. His predecessor, Pope Nicholas V, had overseen the genesis of the project, calling it 'a library of all books, both Latin and Greek ... appropriate to the worth of the Pope and the Apostolic See'.[72] Leo X (1513–21) expanded the library with all the zeal of a roving humanist scholar. The pope spared his own feet, sending out agents to do the donkey work. Dispatching scholars to the north of Europe, he charged them to obtain precious manuscripts in return for cash and even indulgences, those precious papal blessings that could alleviate penalties for sin in the afterlife.[73] After 1450, the Church had been able to add printed texts to the library collection, as the invention of the movable-type printing press meant handmade manuscripts could be reproduced in multiple copies. By 1467, these could even be made in Rome. The printers Arnold Pannartz and Conrad Sweynheym had carried their press southwards from the German lands, settling in Rome in the house of the princely Massimo family, just south of Piazza Navona.[74]

Despite this warm reception in some quarters, creative endeavours to revive the pagan past did not always run smoothly in Rome. This lesson would be learnt by Giulio Pomponio Leto, who had come to Rome from his home in the remote southern town of Teggiano in the mid-fifteenth century. For this able young mind, to arrive in Renaissance Rome was to enter an intellectual Arcadia. There he would learn at the feet of the likes of Lorenzo Valla. On the Quirinal Hill, he transformed a modest *vigna* into his very own academy. There, just a stone's throw from the Baths of Constantine, Leto and his friends celebrated Roman feasts, used Latin names and studied the words and faces of the ancients in the grooves of coins and the engravings on gems and stones. Leto was their *pontifex maximus* – an intellectual high priest for a humanist band of brothers. For a little while at least, they were having the time of their lives. To us, the pursuits of Leto and his friends might appear eccentric but, ultimately, harmless. Yet in 1468, the academy found themselves in the jail cells of the Castel Sant'Angelo.[75] During their confinement they were tortured and questioned about their excessive interest in paganism and ancient political principles; Pope Paul II (1464–71) feared the men were plotting a subversive, republican conspiracy.[76] Ultimately, the charges were dropped and the scholars were released. Even so, their once happy academy only resumed when Pope Paul was cold in his grave.

Paul's actions against Leto and the academy were oppressive. However, his fears were not entirely baseless. Around 1440, Lorenzo Valla had undertaken an exercise in Latin that had frayed and then unpicked one of the most significant ties between the earthly and spiritual authority of the popes. Studying a document through which Constantine was purported to have given the popes the Western Roman Empire, Valla found it to be fraudulent, a medieval fake.[77] Scanning the text, the scholar had winced to see Latin words coined a thousand years after Constantine's death. Flagging up character-istically medieval, anachronistic or erroneous phrases such as 'fief', Valla's criticism was biting. His treatise on the subject was peppered with insults: 'What a way to talk! ... What could be more absurd! ... May God destroy you, wickedest of mortals, for ascribing barbarous speech to an age of learning.'[78] The popes had other foundations for their extensive territory and powers, having gained lands legiti-mately from Charlemagne and his father Pepin the Short. Still the truth exposed by Valla did not leave the papacy unscathed, for Constantine's Donation had been cited, and maybe even manufac-tured, during negotiations with those Frankish emperors.

Valla's conclusions stung but his skills were precious. Eight years after his diatribe against the so-called Donation of Constantine he was made Apostolic Secretary to Pope Nicholas V.[79] Despite clashes between humanist scholarship and the institution of the Church, humanists, popes and other collectors of ancient artefacts generally worked towards the same goal. They all wanted to establish their individual and collective 'Romanness'. It seemed as though the anxiety of identity and status that had plagued Rome, its warring families and its popes during the Avignonian papacy had merged with the excitement sparked by ancient discoveries in libraries, vineyards and building sites. Emptying the city's market of weapons, sculptures, coins and jewels, even old families such as the Massimo filled their homes with ancient objects to underline their deep roots in Rome.[80] At Poggio Bracciolini's villa just north-east of Arezzo, Valla would turn his sharp tongue on those who forged – and even faked – links to the classical Roman past. Musing on the sculptures that lined the walkways of Bracciolini's garden, Valla suggested to other guests that their host had 'read about that ancient custom of adorning houses, villas, gardens, porticos and gymnasia with images and paintings and statues of ancestors to glorify their families'.[81] Unfortunately, as a member of a Tuscan line of no particular note, Bracciolini had 'no images of his ancestors' to erect, only 'little broken bits of marble'.[82] The comments were barbed but reveal an important truth about the age: in Renaissance Rome even fragments of ancient artefacts could be accorded more nobility than the bloodline of a great contemporary scholar such as Poggio Bracciolini.

— ∽ ❧ ❧ —

The ordinary people of Rome lived among the antique sites of the city, but this new Roman culture was undoubtedly elite. While Prospero Colonna's guests enjoyed the words of Horace over dinner, Rome's lowlier classes heard hawkers by day and, at night, the howls of roaming wild beasts. The Castilian scholar Palencia might have complained about Rome's antique debris, but he was more appalled by the city's lower classes. To him they seemed to be more interested in their local wine sellers than the ancient wine god Bacchus: they 'neither knew nor cared about ancient Rome'.[83] Palencia was, undoubtedly, a bit of a snob. Still the indifference of ordinary Romans was hardly surprising. Most saw out their days living hand-to-mouth along ill-kept thoroughfares, many of which could not yet be considered proper streets. While some grander areas had begun to be regenerated in the new Renaissance style, other sections of the city were positively rural. Plants, wildlife and animals had moved in to many corners when the papal court had vacated Rome. Walking in the Roman Forum, most residents did not share the hushed reverence of humanists such as Ciriaco d'Ancona. For them it was merely the *Campo Vaccino*, a cow field where their livestock trampled past ruins to graze.

Despite clear distinctions between the worlds of the elite and the masses in Rome, the actions of the pope and his court could still reverberate in the lives of ordinary people. The pope's very presence in Rome transformed the city's demographics. When Martin V had arrived in 1420, there were only around 20,000 in the city. The population then undulated and grew, reaching between 50,000 and 85,000 by the first decades of the sixteenth century.[84] The magnetism of Rome as a place to live, manufacture and trade directly correlated with its character as a papal city. Where there were pontiffs, there were opportunities, as the power plays of the cardinals made clear. This had a trickle-down effect as popes, cardinals and bishops employed professional and household staff, and artists, merchants, artisans and prostitutes trailed back to the city.[85] The close relationship between Roman society and the papacy was patent in the balance of the sexes. As an entirely male hierarchy, the papal court required almost entirely male serving staff: by the early 1600s, Rome had nearly twice as many men as women.[86]

The return of the popes also filled the city with foreign pilgrims, as well as courtiers and hangers-on. Some of these visitors anticipated a warmer welcome from the Romans, lamenting that 'the dwellers are wroth anon if men ask any questions'.[87] Romans might have bristled at requests for information and directions, but they had hosted pilgrims since late antiquity. With the first jubilees in the fourteenth century, religious tourists had become a key part of the Roman economy. When Pope Nicholas V inaugurated another Holy Year in 1450 there were already more than a thousand hostels for pilgrims in the city.[88] Many surrounded the large basilicas and others clustered around Rome's smaller devotional sites. John Capgrave, an English Augustinian friar who came for the jubilee of 1450, noted that there was even 'a tavern for the comfort of pilgrims' at the 'pretty little church' of Santa Maria in Palmis, where Peter was said to have met the resurrected Jesus and asked him *'Quo vadis?'* or 'where are you going?'[89] In taverns small and large, beds were sorely needed. During the jubilee of 1450 the population was said to swell to hundreds of thousands, with numbers doubling each day. In later years, some pilgrims would be received by Roman hosts with almost overwhelming enthusiasm, being greeted at the city gates with peals of bells and the clang, toot and twang of hired musicians who escorted them to taverns where they could get some rest.[90]

While some pilgrims noted the remains of antique, pagan Rome, most viewed the city through a purely Christian lens. Thanks to relic hunters such as Constantine's mother, Empress Helena, pilgrims to Rome could walk in the very footsteps of Christ. Visiting the Lateran, they could place their hand on slabs from the marble table-top from which Judas had snatched up the silver for which he had sold the life of Christ.[91] Without leaving the Lateran complex, they could also visit a staircase on which Jesus himself had walked. On their knees, the faithful retraced their saviour's route up to the rooms of Pontius Pilate, the Roman governor of Judaea, where Jesus had been condemned to humiliation and agonising death on the cross. Relics of that instrument of torture were just a short walk away from that *Scala Sancta*. In Rome, the divine and human drama that under-pinned Christianity was relived by pilgrims from around the world.

After nearly 1,400 years, Peter's burial place on the Vatican Hill was still an absolutely essential draw. When Agostino Dati, a diplomat from Siena, cast his eye around the crowds in 1450, he noted that men and women 'from the most distant corners of the earth' had come 'to visit the head of the universal Church and the tomb of the prince of the apostles'.[92]

Peter's successors, the popes, did their bit to add to the city's appeal, for they offered the people indulgences for their sins. Granted by the pope, but sometimes also by bishops, these indulgences took years off their recipient's time in purgatory. For Christians then and Catholic Christians now, this is where anybody who is not a saint or the gravest of sinners is almost sure to go when they die. Early Christians such as Augustine established the foundations of the doctrine of purgatory, which emerged more clearly as a word, idea and place in the late twelfth century.[93] Purgatory is described as a transitional experience in which a soul endures a period of cleansing for sins committed on earth. While living, a man or woman could confess their misdemeanours to a priest, who acted as a conduit for the forgiveness and absolution of God. In Christian theology, time in purgatory offers an opportunity to clean the slate fully, eradicating forgotten or only partially confessed sins so that men, women and children could enter heaven worthily. As part of the afterlife, the labours of purgatory are undertaken after death, but indulgences promise that some of the work can be alleviated by the living. This was the labour of the pilgrims, confessing, communing and praying across Rome. In 1450 Pope Nicholas declared that 'all, even those guilty of serious sin – if truly penitent and confessed – ... will obtain a most full pardon' by confessing to a priest and crossing 'the thresholds of the churches of Peter and Paul and the Lateran and Santa Maria Maggiore'.[94]

In Rome of the fifteenth century, traditions of pilgrimage were clearly in rude health. The sites visited by pilgrims, however, were often not. Magnetised by the great suburban churches of the Constantinian Age, visitors wound down lanes outwards from the city centre to reach sites such as San Lorenzo fuori le Mura. Since it had been built by Constantine, that church had been aggrandised with a campanile, portico and swirling, cosmatesque floors. Yet in the fifteenth century it was still situated in a rather humble field.[95] This rustic character coloured much grander churches yet; even the Lateran had been degraded from the main papal residence. Pontiffs might have patched up the damage caused by two fires there, but otherwise they largely ignored the dilapidated building. Many smaller churches were not even dignified with repairs. Having walked the streets near Santa Maria Maggiore, the Augustinian pilgrim Capgrave described the fifth-century church of San Vitale as 'full desolate ... all in ruin'.[96] Further into town, San Ciriaco was 'full desolate and never open'.[97] Most pilgrims were drawn to Rome by devotion, promises of indulgences and sincere longing for heaven, but even they could not ignore the material degradation that surrounded them at every turn.

— ⚜ ❦ ❧ —

Even Saint Peter's was partially ruined, and well into the sixteenth century. When Martin Luther, an Augustinian friar from the German lands, visited the basilica in 1510, the high altar was exposed to sun and rain and demolished parts of the structure stood alongside newly erected columns.[98] The German friar took a rather dim view of Rome, but his account is corroborated by Giorgio Vasari, an artist and biographer who knew the city well. Writing in the mid-sixteenth century, Vasari claimed that the Petrine basilica was commended only by the 'columns, bases, capitals, architraves, cornices, doors and other revetments and ornaments' taken from ancient sites.[99] Nonetheless, changes were afoot even as Luther strolled around the church. The ambitious aesthete Pope Julius II (1503–13) had revived Nicholas V's plans to rebuild the basilica, a Herculean endeavour that would result in the magnificent dome that crowns the church today. In Luther's time, the regeneration of Rome was still very much a work in progress. Looking towards the Ponte Sant'Angelo and the muddy banks of the river, Luther's heart sank: 'where the houses now stand there were once roofs, so deep lieth the rubbish'.[100]

The annals of history remember Luther for far more devastating criticisms of the Church. Less than a decade after visiting Rome, he catalysed a religious revolution that saw kings and paupers across Europe rescind their loyalty to the pope. Nonetheless, when Luther walked down the via Flaminia and into Rome for the first time in 1510, he had the earnest heart of a pilgrim. Luther was in Rome to call upon the pope's supreme authority in a dispute among the Augustinians in the German lands. He would also gain indulgences at the *Scala Sancta* for the soul of Heine Luder, his deceased grandfather. Still, Rome would play a part in Luther's transformation, as his experience in the city hardened his heart towards the Church. The physical degradation jarred him, but he was most appalled by the complacency that he saw in religious matters. For Luther, Romans attended church and then abandoned all semblance of morality: 'they think that he who has heard Mass is free from all danger, and cannot sin'.[101] At one church in Rome, Luther was scandalised when a man encountered his nemesis and, 'having just risen from before the altar ... stepped to him, stabbed him to death, and fled'.[102] The vulgarity and worldliness of some churchmen could not have improved Luther's impression of the city, or the behaviour of the laity who horrified him so much. In Rome, Luther claimed to have seen priests who treated their duties lightly and prelates who guffawed at the holiest things.

The tongues and pens of Europe had long scorned errant priests and prelates. In the eleventh and twelfth centuries, lustful, drunken and irreverent clerics had gambled and philandered their way across the pages of texts such as the *Carmina Burana*. Similar churchmen could be found in later novels such as Giovanni Boccaccio's

Decameron and in Geoffrey Chaucer's *Canterbury Tales*. They were caricatures, of course. Nonetheless, they had mirror images in real life, like the Corsican priests who kept concubines and handguns, while cats snoozed on the altars on which they should have been celebrating Mass.[103]

By Luther's time, even the pope was not beyond lambast. The popes had been begged to return to Rome, but this did not mean that people were blindly contented with the Church. Gossip coursed from street to street. Barbs were exchanged across the merchant's counter. Ancient stones bore criticisms, as well as poetry, as discontented Romans pasted their complaints to antique sculptures in the city. The most famous vehicle for mocking poems and sarcastic jibes was the statue known as 'Pasquino', an ancient Roman rendering of the Spartan King Menelaus renamed after a local tailor celebrated for pillorying inept officials.[104] Standing on a plinth on one truncated leg in a clearing in the streets near the Piazza Navona, Pasquino criticised the popes for their stingy grain dole and apparently punitive taxes.[105] Like Luther, Pasquino had a keen eye for immorality, decrying Pope Alexander VI (1492–1503) for selling ecclesiastical jobs and the very keys to heaven.[106] In 1521, Pasquino would strike when the corpse of Leo X was barely cold, scorning his rise, career and recent death. Hiding behind the statue, the discontented of Rome remained anonymous, leaving Pasquino to bear their punishment. In the 1520s, the much-maligned Pope Hadrian VI (1522–3) became so enraged with criticism pasted onto Pasquino that he ordered that the statue be tossed into the Tiber.[107] Hadrian died within two years of his election. Pasquino stands to this day. On Hadrian's death, notes on the statue would rejoice at his demise.

Elsewhere in the city it was the pontiffs who stood in cold, imperious marble. In the Hall of Conservators on the Capitoline Hill, their statues were visual signs of papal authority in the public sphere. These portraits were prime for vandalism when criticism bubbled over into collective popular outrage. When Paul IV (1555–9) died, his marble head would end up sunk in the Tiber, though not before children had kicked it around the city for a few days.[108] Popes of flesh and bone also bore the brunt of some rebellion, even if it was a comparatively stable time. As in other ages, uprisings were often sparked by the popes' exercise of worldly power. Ironically, this disaffection was now fomented by those who had most benefitted from papal authority. In 1431, the Colonna family of Martin V teamed up with the Duke of Milan to attack Martin's successor, Eugenius IV (1431–47). An outsider from Venice, Eugenius had stripped the Colonna of privileges and elevated their bitter enemies, the Orsini. He had also vigorously asserted his own authority, over and above that of the church council held in Basel between 1431 and 1439. Plotting from the serene quarters of Cardinal Prospero Colonna, the family incited a popular uprising against the new pope in the first year of his pontificate, followed by a more successful insurrection in 1434.[109] Confined to a cell by the summer of that year, Eugenius managed to escape when he slipped past his jailers disguised in the black shroud of a Benedictine monk. Exiled for a decade, he set up his court in Florence at the splendid monastery of Santa Maria Novella.

Back in Rome, Eugenius' successor, Nicholas V, would also be blighted by rebellion. This time the plotter was the humanist scholar Stefano Porcari, who had decided to live by the ideals that Pomponio Leto's academy had only ruminated upon.[110] Porcari planned a revolution and paid with his life. He failed, but still perturbed the pope. Turning to the monks who attended him in his last days, Nicholas would paint a sorry picture of his life: 'Never do I see a man cross my threshold who has spoken a true word to me. I am so perplexed by the deceptions of all those who surround me, that were it not for fear of failing in my duty I should have long ago renounced my Papal dignity.' Continuing, the pope claimed that 'Thomas of

Sarzana', as he had been known before his election, 'saw more friends in a day than I do in a whole year.'[111]

Porcari's love for antiquity might have led him to insurrection, but most humanists saw that the strength and significance of Rome was now inextricably tied to the popes. Likewise, ordinary Romans recognised that the popes generally maintained economic and political stability in the city. Some bemoaned the luxury of the Renaissance popes, but others deemed them new Solomons, pouring out gold to restore the once-great city of Rome. Pontiffs such as Nicholas V thought the people needed visual stimuli to fortify their faith; he threw himself into restoring the grandeur of Rome's architectural fabric.[112] He raised and repaired towers, gates and fountains, allowing people to live comfortably outside the *abitato*. He ordered the chaos of the Capitoline, built walls and restored the palace at Santa Maria Maggiore. He strengthened and ornamented countless churches, from Sant'Apostoli to San Lorenzo and Santo Stefano Rotondo, where Biondo had found mosaics, marble and paintwork falling from the walls. Responding to more than a thousand years of popular devotion, it was Nicholas who made the palace right next to Saint Peter's the main papal residence. In his grandest project of all, the pope had designs drawn up for a new Basilica of Saint Peter. It would be built with more than 2,000 carts of heavy stone, much of it purloined from the ruins of the Colosseum.[113]

Later popes, too, took up the great work, strengthening, colouring and gilding the city of Rome. In the 1480s, Pope Sixtus IV would hire Michelangelo Buonarroti to help. The result was a triumph, as exemplified in the awe-inspiring illusions of the ceiling at the Sistine Chapel. In painted forms – architectural, human and divine – Michelangelo, Raphael and others elevated the Vatican complex, adorning its rooms with images of popes, philosophers and even God himself. Sixtus also reshaped the more prosaic corners of the city, moving the market stalls that once rolled down the slopes of the

Capitoline deeper into the town. New markets would be clustered together on the Piazza Navona and Campo de' Fiori.[114] By 1525, two straight streets radiated from the head of the central axis of via Lata or via del Corso: the via Ripetta built by Leo X and the Babuino, constructed by Clement VII (1523–34).[115] More stalls would be erected in the shadow of the Pantheon, where candlemakers and potters congregated. There, Eugenius IV had struggled to keep purveyors of meat, vegetables and confectionery away from the portals of what was by then a church.[116]

Now buyers and sellers trundled between these new commercial nodes, ever closer to the Vatican Hill.[117] The popes did not wish to denude the Capitoline of all significance. They recognised its importance as a symbol of the great city of Rome. Sixtus IV himself bequeathed its new Palazzo dei Conservatori weighty ancient bronzes, including the famous she-wolf suckling Remus and Romulus, the founder of Rome.[118] One of his successors, Paul III, would engage Michelangelo to organise and ornament its once chaotic plan. In such acts of patronage, these popes highlighted and redefined aspects of the city's ancient past, but as one element in the cityscape of a thoroughly papal Rome.

— ∞ ∞ ∞ —

The Church would pay a price for this institutional prestige, well beyond the piles of golden *scudi* it poured into marble and paint. To survive and then thrive, the papacy and Church had become a state-like institution: organised, largely self-sufficient and recognised by political powers.[119] But with authority and wealth came careers, ambition and corruption, as well as lackadaisical clergy and an errant flock. Paradoxically, by the early sixteenth century, the strength of the Church began to degrade its moral authority. As a powerful, heavily gilt city, the Rome of the popes was, once again, laid open to attack. As Julius II rode out to fight for the Papal States, contemporary writers saw no heroism in it. In a narrative attributed to the humanist Desiderius Erasmus, Julius arrives at heaven's gate in papal regalia and blood-smeared armour. The pope, it seems, is impatient for entry. Meeting Julius, a confused Saint Peter asks him to prove that he is truly his successor. When the pontiff points to his crown, jewels and robes, the saint unleashes his scorn:

> the more I contemplate you, the less do I see any trace of an apostolic man ... how fierce are your eyes, how nasty your mouth, how baleful your expression, how haughty and arrogant your brow! I am ashamed to say, and at the same time disgusted to observe, that there is no part of your body that is not befouled by the marks of portentous and execrable lust; to say nothing of the fact that even now you are all belches and the smell of drunkenness and booze.[120]

The saint is even less convinced when Julius begins to boast of his military and financial prowess.

The text was printed and widely shared across Europe, from Paris to Antwerp. With biting wit, the learned men of the Renaissance had made Peter himself renounce the popes. Pontiffs had been pilloried in the past, but in the sixteenth century they would face a wave of criticism that shook the very foundations of papal Rome.

7

Theatre of the World

In the Palazzo Caetani laughter escaped the rooms of the three Ethiopian ambassadors. They still wore dour Franciscan habits and held crucifixes of iron but seemed less austere figures than when they had made their way into Rome.[1] Now as their interpreter read them an Italian manuscript about their 'dukes, princes and popes' back in East Africa they 'moved closer together, laughing and greatly enjoying' the account.[2] It was respite after eight months of travel, crossing deserts, cities and seas. Their mission from their emperor was simple but grave. They were to ask the pope if he had received the gifts brought by the last ambassador, and if he would give them the absolutions, indulgences and relics requested in return. Mitres wrapped in alabaster silk finished with precious stones; plush sacerdotal robes and rare, precious balms: the gifts that had accompanied the last embassy were valued at some 5000 ducats.[3] Yet still the ambassador had returned to Ethiopia with no sign of blessing from the pope. Stripped of his possessions, accused of embezzlement, that ambassador now languished in jail.[4] The three men who visited Pope Boniface IX (1389–1404) in 1404 had retraced his journey to seek gifts that only the pope could grant.

To some it might seem surprising that the emperor of Ethiopia would ask the pope of Rome for indulgences and absolutions for sins. That the ambassadors sought relics is more understandable. The Ethiopians had been Christians since the first centuries of the Church, when the bodies and belongings of numerous believers became relics as their owners died for the faith. Most Christians are not bound to venerate saints and some saints are not recognised officially by particular groups. Still, the stories of the men, women and children who embodied Christian virtues were valued by all those who shared their belief in Christ. In 1404, the Ethiopians visited many churches, 'vehemently demanding' to see particular relics like the 'cradle of the infant Jesus Christ'.[5]

Papal absolutions and indulgences, however, were a different matter. These blessings were granted by the pope in his capacity as supreme authority over the Christian Church. Like many others in the East, the Ethiopian Church had never accepted this dogma. The Ethiopians were Coptic Christians, who had already followed Jesus' teachings for centuries when the Bishop of Rome began to make claims for his supreme authority.[6] Other ancient sees such as Alexandria and Antioch recognised the Bishop of Rome as a 'first among equals' (*primus inter pares*) by virtue of his role as the successor of Saint Peter. What they did not accept was papal supremacy: that the pope had the last word on Christian practices and beliefs. Moreover, if the Ethiopian Church was particularly submissive to any bishop it would have been the Bishop of Alexandria, who also claimed a gilded lineage that could be traced back to Saint Mark the Evangelist.[7]

The See of Alexandria had a long history of rejecting Roman supremacy, as we saw in Dioscorus' brutal rebuttal of Leo I's authority at the 'Gangster Synod' of 449. After the scandal of that meeting, the relationship between Rome and the churches in the East became increasingly fraught. Blood had spilt and fresh fractures appeared after 692 when popes rejected the Trullan Decrees that arrived from Constantinople to condemn Roman positions on vexed questions such as married priests. When Rome officially changed the wording of the Nicene Creed, the Christians' official statement of belief, ties between East and West would break down entirely. Slightly varied versions of the Creed had been used in the West for some time, but the drama really began in February 1014 at Saint Peter's Basilica. As Pope Benedict VIII (1012–24) set the imperial crown on the head of Henry II of Germany, the choir sang a version of the Creed with the words *filioque* added to the Roman liturgy publicly for the very first time.[8] The change might appear small to us, but to bishops in the East it was fundamental: the words *filioque* declared that the Holy Spirit came not only from God the Father but also his son, Jesus. For the East, Rome had done nothing less than redefine the Holy Trinity. By 1054, quarrels over priestly celibacy, the bread used during Mass and that controversial *filioque* peaked. A papal delegation travelled to Constantinople and served the Patriarch with an excommunication at the altar of his church just as he was about to celebrate Mass. In a tit-for-tat of condemnation, the excommunicated Patriarch placed Rome under interdict, effectively excommunicating the entire Roman Church.[9] The charges of each side would not be nullified until 1965.

By the time that the Ethiopian ambassadors arrived at the Palazzo Caetani, the schism between the Eastern Church and the Latin Church under Rome had been entrenched by nearly 400 years of dispute, accusation and crusade. For their part, the Ethiopians remained allied with Alexandria and never recognised Rome as their authoritative leader, even if debates at the Council of Florence in the 1440s would touch upon the subject of union.[10] In 1404 this was still decades away, and yet there the Ethiopian delegation were, supplicating to the pope in Rome. Despite dogma and historic rifts, the Bishop of Rome held a special authority for Christians across the world.

In the centuries that followed Pope Martin V's (1417–31) return to Rome, the face of the city became increasingly international. Hundreds of thousands of people arrived seeking not only spiritual gifts but the pope's word on questions religious and political. By the late fifteenth century there were enough Coptic Christians in Rome for the Canons of Saint Peter's to protest that 'Indians' had invaded

Santo Stefano Maggiore, a monastery just behind their own basilica that would soon be known as Santo Stefano degli Abissini (of the Abyssinians or Ethiopians).[11] Soon Rome would emerge as a diplomatic hub for territories across the world, as representatives of lands within and without Europe travelled there to consult the pope. In 1608, Emanuel Ne Vunda of the Congo arrived in Rome as the first ever ambassador from Central Africa to Europe; he had journeyed for four years to reach the pontiff.[12] Popes would also establish their own permanent embassies or nunciatures around the world, as well as sending extraordinary envoys to Constantinople, Moscow and Alexandria.[13] Staffed by men with political powers and spiritual authority that trumped even that of local bishops, these nunciatures were a reflection of the pope's unique influence around the globe. The notion that all great matters should pass through the papal court had been asserted early in the fifteenth century. In 1438, the humanist Lapo da Castiglionchio the Younger had claimed that,

Whether it is a deliberation concerning war, peace or striking treaties, or marriages among the greatest kings and princes of the world, or even if it concerns some controversy that occurs among these great leaders, all things are deferred to the pope.[14]

Lapo would have been delighted when this frankly aspirational description became a reality in the sixteenth century, when men from all over the world followed in the footsteps of that remarkable embassy from Ethiopia to Rome.

—— ⚜ ⚜ ⚜ ——

Rome's enduring significance and expansive influence in the early modern period is all the more striking given the Reformation of the early sixteenth century. Calls for Church reform and even schisms had come and gone, but the Reformation shook the foundations and authority of the papacy more forcefully than any previous protest. With a rallying call that told men and women to rely on their own consciences to get them to heaven, the reformers characterised the popes of Rome as usurpers of holy authority. Soon they would conclude that they owed the pope no more obedience than they owed the devil himself. This astoundingly subversive message was sounded loudest by none other than Martin Luther, that Augustinian friar who had visited Rome as a faithful devotee in 1510, as we have seen. In the decades that followed his return to the German lands, Luther grew increasingly critical about the Roman Church. In the end he challenged papal authority outright, questioning practice and doctrine. Luther's rebellion sparked a chain of reform movements that splintered Christendom into groups of believers, known as religious confessions. The results of the movement that Luther catalysed were staggering. Around a decade after his death in 1546, Scotland, England, Scandinavia, large swathes of France and half of the Holy Roman Empire had cast off submission to the pope.

Luther was not an obvious religious insurgent. He grew up in the town of Mansfeld in the Holy Roman Empire, where his father made a living in the copper mining business.[15] At school and, later, the University of Erfurt, Luther underwent an education of rote learning and rigorous prayer. Some signs of rebellion emerged faintly in 1502 when he cast aside his father's ambitions for his career, dropping out of a degree in law after only a few months of study.[16] An introspective young man, Luther was perturbed by uncertainty and found no satisfaction in legal formulas. More anguish awaited Luther's parents yet. In 1505, their son joined an austere Augustinian friary. At a party on the eve of his departure for the cloister, Luther turned to his friends, declaring dramatically, 'Today you see me, and never again!'[17] The words might have sounded prophetic, but they would not be fulfilled. For, soon enough, the convictions that had guided Luther into the friary would spread his reputation far beyond its walls.

Luther chose a life of seclusion, fasting and prayer not out of a long-held sense of religious vocation but, apparently, to fulfil a promise to Saint Anne. Riding on horseback from a family event earlier in the summer of 1505, he had been terrified when an unexpected thunderstorm had struck. Casting his eyes up to the tempestuous heavens, Luther called upon Saint Anne, the mother of the Virgin Mary, for deliverance, vowing to become a monk if she interceded.[18] To utter such a prayer was, presumably, relatively common. To make good on it was rather less so. Luther acted on his words, even if nobody but the saints in heaven had heard them. After his return from Rome, he would act even more boldly in response to the words of another man.

It was in 1516 that Luther began to challenge Church teaching on indulgences, a matter that could not have been more fundamental to its central mission to save souls. We can presume that Luther had once accepted the traditional belief that time in purgatory could be shortened with indulgences earned through good works. We have seen how he had climbed the Scala Sancta during his visit to Rome, grazing his knees to gain indulgences for his grandfather.[19] Back in his homeland, Luther would begin to see purgatory from a radically different perspective when he heard that indulgences were being exchanged for donations to rebuild Saint Peter's in Rome. Opening your own pockets to help build a church was surely a good work. Still, Luther believed that the appeal made salvation a mere transaction. The air of seediness was only exacerbated by the manner of Johann Tetzel, a Dominican friar and the Grand Commissioner of Indulgences in the German lands. Granting these blessings to anybody who could pay and purportedly selling absolutions for sins not yet committed, Tetzel even had a catchy sales pitch: 'As soon as a coin in the coffer rings, a soul from purgatory springs.'[20] When Luther heard about these exchanges he was scandalised.

Luther preached on the wickedness of Tetzel's actions and wrote a proposition for a lengthy academic disputation on indulgences, now famous as his Ninety-Five Theses. Countering Tetzel's unsavoury sales pitch with biting critique, he plainly stated that 'when money clinks in the chest' only 'greed and avarice can be increased'.[21] Crucially, Luther's theses declared that the fate of the soul was 'in the hands of God alone' and not the grips of shady characters such as Johann Tetzel.[22] In this text and the early sermons, it might appear that he questioned just one teaching of the Church. However, the repercussions of this challenge were manifold. If the Church did not have the power to intercede and help people to heaven, what was the purpose of confessing sins to a priest? Did the pope and his delegates have any special authority at all? These fundamental themes were touched upon in Luther's early works. Luther also questioned the character of the papal office, its relationship to the Church and to the city of Rome. He even dared to ask why 'the pope, whose wealth today is greater than the wealth of the richest Crassus', sought 'to build the basilica of Saint Peter with the money of poor believers rather than with his own'.[23]

Between 1517 and 1520, Luther studied and wrote, developing and disseminating his ideas to a wide audience in cheap illustrated pamphlets written in everyday German that anybody could understand.[24] When his ideas gained currency with princes as well as the ordinary people of the Holy Roman Empire, Pope Leo X (1513–21) took extreme measures in an attempt to tame the brazen friar. In June 1520, Leo issued *Exsurge Domine*, a papal bull that excommunicated Luther from the Catholic Church. The pope had not given up on him entirely; he gave Luther sixty days to recant. Choosing exile and damnation, Luther set the bull alight.

Soon, secular leaders would be inspired by reformed teachings, as they too threw off Rome to found their own churches. Instead of Catholic teaching they used new theologies such as Lutheranism and Calvinism, named for the men who had developed them. Not all princes embraced the reformers' teachings immediately on intellectual or spiritual grounds. However, political and personal motivations also led to further defections from Rome. In 1521, Henry VIII of England had stood shoulder-to-shoulder with the popes. With the help of his learned High Chancellor Thomas More, he had penned a passionate defence of the Church after he 'saw Luther's heresy running wild'.[25] Accompanying the text with a letter to Leo X, Henry claimed that he defended tradition out of devotion to the Apostolic See; returning his affection, Leo granted Henry and all of his successors the title Defender of the Faith. Just a decade later, the relationship between the pope and Henry had soured. When Henry wanted to end his marriage to Catherine of Aragon and Pope Clement VII (1523–34) refused him an annulment, the Lutheran ideas that Henry had once condemned enticed him as a precedent and justification for ignoring Rome and starting his own church.[26] Henry's wily lawyer, Thomas Cromwell, also invoked English law for the cause, asserting that their country was a venerable old empire, the leader of which could not appeal to any foreign authority on any matter, even the pope. The motivations, then, were personal, and the arguments political. Still, it was no coincidence that Cromwell, the architect of Henry's new Church of England, was a devout Protestant of the Lutheran school.

Inadvertently Luther had given European monarchs a justification for shaking off papal influence on their lives, states and authority. Even rulers who remained devoted to Catholicism weaponised the Reformation in disputes with Rome. Holy Roman Emperor Charles V was an ardent Catholic, retiring to pray before taking pivotal decisions and relinquishing his responsibilities to lock himself in a monastery every year during the week before Easter.[27] Yet even he used the advent of Protestantism to taunt the pope in a political squabble. When Clement VII joined an alliance against the emperor in 1526, he baited the pontiff, musing that 'some day, perhaps, Martin Luther will become a man of weight'.[28]

By the sixteenth century, the pope had become an arbiter in questions of significant political weight as diplomats and envoys milled through the Vatican Palace clutching requests and queries from their masters. Often, they sought papal sanction for matters in the Church's traditional sphere of influence, such as marriage. In lowlier spheres, such cases might be personal and familial, but in the affairs of princes and queens politics permeated all. When Pope Alexander VI (1492–1503) permitted King Louis XII of France to wed his cousin's widow he also permitted two major European territories to remain united.[29] World affairs could also turn on the refusal of such a concession. While Clement VII might have justified Henry VIII's annulment using the canon law of the Church, he could never have countenanced angering Henry's devoted wife, Catherine of Aragon. She was the aunt of Holy Roman Emperor Charles V (1519–56), who was, at that time, an essential ally for Rome.

Writing from the court of Pope Clement VIII (1592–1605) in the winter of 1595, the Venetian ambassador Paulo Paruta painted the Roman pontiff as a plainly unique authority: 'two persons' combining two roles, firstly 'the head and universal shepherd of all Christendom, and the apostolic Vicar of Christ and true successor of Peter in the Catholic and Apostolic church and, after this, that of a temporal prince who holds a state in Italy'.[30] In short, the pope had the power to wage wars and forge alliances just like any prince. Yet he also wielded a spiritual authority to bestow singular honours and concessions, which often proved impervious to quotidian politics. This was an unparalleled jurisdiction that would vex secular rulers who fell foul of papal whim.

—— ☙ ❧ ❧ ——

As rivalry over territory and influence burgeoned in the fifteenth and sixteenth centuries, so did the number of princes seeking some sort of sanction from Rome. In the spring of 1493 a letter arrived in the city from Christopher Columbus. Addressed to the King and Queen of

Spain, Ferdinand and Isabella, it was put in the hands of the German printer Stephan Plannck to be translated into Latin and printed in multiple copies. Columbus' remarks in the letter were brief but extraordinary, announcing that after five months sailing around the Caribbean Sea he had 'found many islands inhabited by men without number, all of which I took possession for our most fortunate king [of Spain]'.[31] Columbus had conquered Cuba, Santo Domingo and Haiti, apparently, with 'no one objecting'.[32] Even if this were true, resistance would come closer to home when the Portuguese King João II wrote his own, much more menacing letter to the Spanish monarchs. In his missive, João claimed that the lands Columbus had conquered were already Portuguese possessions: the Spaniards' man was a thief. The Christian monarchs turned to Pope Alexander VI for arbitration; he settled the matter in the Treaty of Tordesillas of 1494, dividing conquered lands in the Americas into Spanish and Portuguese zones.

For Spain and Portugal, the pope was a relatively impartial mediator, even if Alexander's neutrality was somewhat compromised by his Spanish heritage. For his part, Alexander would claim that matters regarding the 'Indies' fell under his religious authority, as both Spain and Portugal hoped that they might make the natives of their new territories Christian.[33] Whatever the justification or rhetoric, popes of this period were, like the Iberians, in new territory. By authorising Spain and Portugal to colonise certain areas and banning them from others, the Bishop of Rome had carved up non-Christian territories several thousand kilometres from his own city and distributed them among the crowned heads of Europe. With the encouragement of some monarchs, the popes had assumed a supra-national territorial authority based on their universal spiritual power, the extent of which was as potentially expansive as the lands that the Spanish and Portuguese sought to conquer.

The colonial ambitions of such rulers accelerated the emergence of the popes as global actors, even if the kings and queens of

Iberia would jealously guard their right to elect bishops in their new lands.[34] Alexander and his peers also involved themselves in world affairs independently. Even his predecessors had dipped their toes into international waters. In the mid-fifteenth century, Pius II (1458–64) had intervened as the Ottoman Turks stamped out pockets of resistance in the Byzantine lands that they had taken after conquering Constantinople in 1453.[35] Now that second Rome had Muslim rulers. By the summer of 1461, the Ottomans had swept into Trebizond, a land on the north-eastern fringe of Anatolia. For the Ottoman Emperor Mehmed II, his army was securing their hold on rightfully conquered territory. In the eyes of the pope, however, the Muslim Sultan was waging a brutal war on Christian lands. From Rome, Pius sent out a bold order: Mehmed must desist and abandon his Muslim faith to worship the Christian God.[36] The request was assertive but audacious, and, ultimately, ignored. By August 1462, the Ottoman forces had stormed the Greek island of Lesbos, where the local lord and leader, Niccolò Gattilusio, converted to Islam on the spot in the hope of ingratiating himself to his conquerors.[37] Sadly he hoped in vain. The Turks strangled him with a bowstring and murdered around 400 other Italians, sawing their bodies in half. They enslaved the rest of the island's population.[38]

They might not have proved successful, but Pius' actions were emblematic of the growing papal self-confidence. Early pontiffs such as Leo I (440–61) had stood eyeball-to-eyeball with invaders on Italian soil and medieval popes had assumed a universal religious supremacy. Somehow their successors in the early modern period went further, asserting themselves as global pastors with a political influence that could speak across religions, borders and seas. Sometimes this could translate into hard political power, even among Muslim leaders. When Mehmed died in 1481 and his eldest son Bayezid took the throne, his embittered third son Cem made an

uneasy alliance with the Catholic Knights of Rhodes.[39] Succession
was not always linear in the Ottoman world; like others before him
Cem intended to fight his brother for the crown. In the meantime,
he traded the knights' protection for promises of his support when
he eventually rose to power. Cem spent seven years in confinement
in French castles and prisons, planning, writing poetry and, apparently, seducing the daughter of at least one guard.[40] When he
emerged he would do so not as a political manipulator but as a
diplomatic pawn.

Pope Innocent VIII (1484–92) had identified Cem as a tantalising
prize in negotiations with the Turks and demanded that the knights
hand over their Muslim prince. Innocent had judged Cem's value
accurately: Bayezid was willing to pay up to 30,000 ducats a year to
keep his brother behind bars.[41] When Cem arrived in Rome in 1490,
he greeted the pope with a kiss and warm embrace. Ultimately,
however, he was Innocent's prisoner, detained, in some style, at the
Castel Sant'Angelo. In one move, Innocent had made Rome a lively
centre of Middle Eastern diplomacy. The envoys of Kait Bey, the
Mamluk Sultan of Cairo, rushed to the city, urging the pope to join
them in an alliance against the Ottomans. Cem's brother Bayezid
also sent men to Rome, bearing more obviously attractive offerings.
Arriving at the papal court, they handed Innocent 120,000 gold coins,
carefully selected gifts and a gushing letter promising the undying
friendship of the Ottoman sultan.[42]

As ever in the history of the papacy, the popes' actions on the
world stage reverberated in Rome. Even before blood soaked the
sands of Lesbos, Pius had manifested the plight of the Greeks on
the city's streets. Invoking the help of God and his saints against
the Turkish threat, he had ordered that the head of Saint Andrew,
the brother of Peter, be carried into Rome. Andrew had died on
an X-shaped crucifix in Achaea, a part of the Roman Empire now
in north-western Greece. In April 1462, his head was brought into

Rome in the hands of Cardinal Bessarion, an erudite man born in the now conquered city of Trebizond who worked for the reunion of the Eastern Churches and Rome. As Bessarion approached the pope in the meadowland near the Milvian Bridge, north of the city, his thick white beard would be bathed with tears. In Pius' ceremony, Andrew's head became a symbol for all Christian refugees escaping the Muslims in the East.[43] The two men played out a dialogue in which the pope played Peter and Bessarion acted as Andrew.[44] Pius himself was said to tremble with emotion, laying face down before Andrew's relic and declaring: 'Thou art here at last, O sacred head, driven from thy resting-place by the fury of the Turk.'[45]

The scene was poignant but far from private. Pius was joined by local magnates, ambassadors, cardinals and other grandees and knelt before an immense crowd of spectators. When a *Te Deum* was intoned, the procession moved down the via Flaminia, swelling with pilgrims as it went. Just inside the city gate, Andrew's head was laid to rest on the high altar of Santa Maria del Popolo. It finished its journey at the Basilica of Saint Peter. If Andrew represented all Christians persecuted by the Turk, his new home, 'Alma Roma, hallowed by [his] brother's blood', was proposed as their place of refuge and 'asylum'.[46]

The emotive effect of Pius' procession relied upon the poignancy of the ceremony. It also depended on the centuries-old tradition that defined Rome as the centre on which Christendom turned. By Pius' time, this vision of the city was so charged that Rome could become a mirror and microcosm for the broader Christian world. On 1 February 1492, a messenger ran into the city to announce that, after a decade of bloodshed, the Muslims had surrendered the Spanish territory of Granada to Christian forces. That same day in Rome, workers at the basilica of Santa Croce in Gerusalemme dislodged a brick to discover a gnarled walnut board believed to have been nailed above the head of the crucified Jesus.[47] Brought to Rome by the Empress Helena more than a thousand years earlier, the *Titulus Crucis* is one of the holiest relics in the world. As workmen scraped away the dust to reveal that hallowed inscription, the triumph of Christians across the seas found its echo in a church in Rome. Collapsing space and time, the event placed the early modern city in the foundational narrative of Western Christianity, reaffirming Rome's position at the centre of Christendom.[48]

Even visitors to Rome could find themselves cast as actors in the story. When the Congolese ambassador Prince Emanuele Ne Vunda died just two days after arriving in Rome in 1608, his demise would become a chapter in this eternal narrative. Lodged above his grave in the baptistery of Santa Maria Maggiore, Ne Vunda's ebony funerary bust is the first ever portrait of a particular black African to be made in Europe. It honoured Ne Vunda. But it also honoured the Church of Pope Paul V (1605–21) and the city of Rome, which Ne Vunda had reached after four years of travel and with just four surviving members of an embassy of twenty-five.[49] Paul ensured that Ne Vunda was buried in the basilica that held one of the city's most prized relics: the crib that had held the body of the baby Jesus.[50] The Esquiline Hill was an unlikely resting place for this young prince of the Congo but by burying his body near the *praesepio* of the nativity, Paul recast Ne Vunda as one of the wise kings who had travelled to that crib in Bethlehem from the East. Paul was not alone in this characterisation of the prince. In a letter to Cardinal Alessandro d'Este, Ne Vunda was referred to as 'a new black King ... renewing the triumph and the religious offering of the Magi'.[51] He had even died on the eve of the feast of Epiphany, which commemorates the visit of the wise kings to the manger. Once again, a pope lifted Rome out of the prison of time, placing himself and the city in a narrative that transformed Rome into Bethlehem and the papal court into the Holy Family.

— ෮ ෨ ෨ —

The increasingly global character of the early modern papacy could also have less picturesque results. In the summer of 1527, papal involvement in European politics had reduced swathes of the city to blackened rubble and broken glass. Tens of thousands of homes had been lost and mounds of acrid horse dung blocked the narrow streets. Houses, libraries and archives lay empty, their floors scattered with ash. In private libraries and the university, or Sapienza, the remains of volumes procured, transcribed and treasured by the humanists were strewn across the ground in pieces.[52] Erasmus would lament the devastation of this 'most tranquil home of the Muses'.[53] At some of the most innovative building projects of the day, the ordering hand of the Renaissance was stayed as great architects such as Antonio da Sangallo abandoned their work at churches such as San Giovanni dei Fiorentini. Instead of the dulcet chorus of polyphony or the low murmur of prayer, these buildings would be filled with the bawdy humour of the barracks as invading soldiers ate, slept and gambled beneath their roofs. Many other religious buildings, including the Basilica of Saint Peter, were used as stables for horses and shelters for piles of corpses. The starving dogs that haunted their aisles also found a feast on the banks of the Tiber, where 10,000 had been hastily buried in shallow graves.[54] Weary diggers had chucked another 2,000 bodies in the water. Estimates for the effect on Rome's population vary wildly, with suggestions that between ten and thirty per cent of the population died, and some scholars citing more.[55] After seeing the city in May 1527, the Venetian Marin Sanudo wrote that even the Turks would not have left behind such scenes: 'Hell itself was a more beautiful sight to behold.'[56]

The painful humiliation of Rome was the result of the popes' growing significance in secular politics, particularly the tumultuous affairs of the Italian peninsula. Splintered into city states rather than united as a nation, Italy was vulnerable to political exploitation and violent attack. By the early sixteenth century, the peninsula's magnetism had been intensified by wealth accrued during the period of peace that followed the violence and land-grabbing that we saw in the age of Martin V. In 1454 the Treaty of Lodi had inaugurated forty years of concord, which was ruptured by King Charles VIII of France in 1494. Capitalising on tensions between Milan and the Aragonese, he laid claim to Naples, which Innocent VIII had offered him fleetingly back in 1489.[57] The French strike set off a chain of wars that threw the Italian states into shifting but ever bellicose alliances, clustered around the great rival powers of France and Spain. Lasting peace did not return until 1559. In the meantime, the patchwork states of Italy called upon the pope as a mediator and political ally.[58] The opportunities for papal politicking were numerous. Unlike the dukes and princes who ruled the other states of Italy, each pope brought a new dynasty and set of interests to be satisfied. For European princes each conclave represented a fresh opportunity for influence.

Rome's unique importance meant that it struggled to remain neutral in the conflicts over Italy. Both France and Spain pursued favour in Rome, paying cardinals to represent their interests at the papal court.[59] Along the way, partisan popes were elected. At the same time, pontiffs such as the 'Warrior Pope' Julius II (1503–13) made alliances and war to protect and expand papal territories, earning the ire of men such as Erasmus in his literary dialogue 'Julius Excluded from Heaven'. As significant as the popes' secular concerns were, the sack of Rome of 1527 occurred as a result of the efforts of Pope Clement VII to protect his religious position when Holy Roman Emperor Charles V appeared to pose a direct threat to the pope's unique status in the Christian world. Charles V also ruled the Netherlands and Spain and, through his Spanish crowns, Naples, Sicily and Sardinia. Moreover, he was heir to the Spanish conquests in the New World. Appended with 'at all times Enlarger of Empire', even his title spoke of insatiable ambition. Still the pope's gravest concerns stemmed from Charles' belief that his role as Holy Roman

Emperor gave him a right to be involved not only in Italy but in all ecclesiastical affairs.[60] Charles V's grandfather, Maximilian (1508–19), had planned and failed to fuse the imperial and papal offices; now his grandson was acting as though he had succeeded.

For a long time, Clement thought, perhaps even dithered. Charles was a threat, but the papacy was in a vulnerable position. With no large standing army and waning influence in Protestant lands, the popes needed Charles to fight the spread of the Reformation in Europe. The emperor was also essential for stemming the growing power of the Ottoman Turks. On the other hand, if Charles undermined the supreme status of the pope as the head of Christendom, the pontiff would be left with ever less authority to protect. In 1521, events had taken over when Charles personally confronted Luther at the Diet of Worms, demanding that he respond to the bull sent by Leo X and then helping the pope to reclaim territory in northern Italy. Leo had tied his fortune to that of the emperor. However, when he died in 1523 his successor Clement became alarmed by Charles' ruthless ambition. Imperial forces had been punishing France in the Italian Wars and the emperor seemed hell-bent on dominating all of Italy. Clement VII formed a secret alliance with France, the League of Cognac, which went public in 1526.[61] As France, Venice, Florence, Milan and the pope lined up against the Holy Roman Emperor, Charles vowed to 'go into Italy and revenge myself on those who have injured me.'[62] 'Especially,' he added, 'on that poltroon the Pope.'[63]

Ultimately, the forces of Emperor Charles V were to blame for the sack of Rome, though, tragically, Clement VII had signed a truce with imperial forces in the south of Italy shortly before Rome was attacked.[64] As peace was declared, the imperial forces led by the Duke of Bourbon in the north marched southwards, starving and angry that they had not yet been paid. The men entered Lazio and, eventually, the papal city. One of their commanders was blunt in his description: 'On the sixth of May we took Rome by storm.'[65]

In 1527, the people of Rome needed their bishop more than ever, just as they had in the sackings of earlier centuries. But Clement would not ride out to meet the invader like Pope Leo I had. He would not even lead his people in penitential procession like Gregory the Great (590–604). Instead, Clement looked after himself, dashing down the *passetto*, an escape tunnel that runs above the streets from the Vatican Palace to the Castel Sant'Angelo. Eventually he retreated even further, fleeing to Orvieto on 7 December disguised as a servant and hiding out in the decrepit papal palace of the city.[66] For a moment, at least, the pope had shrugged off the trappings of his office, along with the danger and responsibility that they now brought. Behind him, he left Rome in turmoil and five cardinals who were being held as hostages.[67] Yet even the rough cloak of the layman could not conceal the papal office for long. Soon after Clement's arrival in Orvieto, envoys from the court of Henry VIII came to seek the pontiff's blessing for his divorce from Catherine of Aragon.[68] In this moment the burdens of papal office were shone into sharp relief: the pope's rule over Rome might be temporarily halted, but his role as universal head of Christendom appeared inalienable.

— ෨ ෨ ෨ —

The pope did not return to Rome until October 1528, when he rode into the city a skeletal, jaundiced and utterly broken man. Though individuals were weak, the office was strong. Remarkably, neither the humiliation of the sack of Rome nor the successes of the Reformation had significantly diminished the global significance of papal Rome. The sack heralded huge economic, political and personal losses for Rome itself and Italy at large. Moreover, nations that splintered from papal oversight during the Reformation would never again call upon the pope. Nevertheless, the enthusiastic presence of Catholic powers and even some non-Christian leaders made up for their absence. By the 1530s even Charles V would be back, as artisans, architects and masons gradually recommenced projects to rebuild and beautify Rome. Like many others, the emperor had come to court the new pope. Assertive, energetic and keen to promote his family, the Farnese, Paul III (1534–49) wanted to consolidate the popes' role in the city and the world. He would not fall foul of politicking where Clement had. Maintaining neutrality, Paul refused Charles' entreaties that he come out for the empire and Spain.[69] In the end, the emperor's ambitions in Italy were satisfied all the same. By 1559, the Peace of Cateau-Cambrésis confirmed Spanish dominion over Milan, Naples and Sicily, along with the complete exile of the French from those territories.

The emperor had won political supremacy on the peninsula, but the pope had retained his unique role and would continue to attract embassies from European territories such as France, Hungary, Poland and Denmark. As we have seen in the case of Emmanuel Ne Vunda, the presence of foreigners could be deeply symbolic in Rome, with a potency that intensified when visitors came from particularly far afield. In the late spring of 1585, Nakaura Julião, Itō Mancio, Hara Martinho and Miguel Chijiwa arrived in the city from Japan. Cutting striking figures in bright white silk kimonos under the light of the Italian sun, the unfamiliar beauty of their dress was taken as compelling proof of the popes' global appeal.[70] At the turn of the seventeenth century, the turban of Robert Shirley, crowned with a cross, brought another such symbol to papal Rome. Here was an Englishman, Catholic in spite of the Henrician Reformation, bringing the recognition of the Muslim Shah of Persia to the pontifical court.[71] In more conventional expressions of international influence, the early modern city hosted the first two fixed diplomatic residences ever founded in Europe, both of which remain tied to the same countries today. The incoming Spanish ambassador, Íñigo Vélez de Guevara, bought the Palazzo Mondaleschi that his predecessors had only rented, negotiating a price of 22,000 *scudi* through the estate agent Bernardino Barber in 1647.[72] Nearby, around the same time, the French ambassadors established themselves permanently at the Palazzo Farnese.

The foreign presence in Rome also took on less grandiose forms as the popes attracted immigrants with more quotidian concerns. When a non-Italian was elected pope, his countrymen and women were often drawn to the city, compelled by a simple desire for work.[73] The pope might be head of the world's most international court, but even he could crave the entertainment, food and typical servants of his homeland, as would the cardinals and curial officials that he elected from his own country. With the rise of Aragonese popes such as Callistus III (1455–8) and Alexander VI, a veritable colony of Spanish cardinals, writers, actors and courtesans arrived in Rome. In palatial salons and the humbler rooms of notaries and clerks, the literature, plays and music of Iberia was heard in full voice. In turn Rome inspired these strangers, as art imitated life. Francis Delicado, a Spanish clerk, wrote *La Lozana Andaluza* (1528), one of the most loved dramas of the age. It followed the life of an Andalusian prostitute working in Rome.[74]

Even if the pope was Italian, as most at this time were, the pontiff, his court, his subjects and their visitors needed bankers, merchants and cooks. Frequently in the early modern period it was foreigners who took on these roles. Inns were run by Belgians, Spaniards and the Flemish.[75] The vast majority of bread was baked by German hands, while men and women from Dalmatia and Illyria worked in trade and at the ports.[76] The various dialects of the Italian peninsula also rang through the streets of Rome, as men and women arrived from north and south, seeking refuge and good fortune. As he walked past the French church of San Luigi after playing cards at the house of a courtesan, Dario di Pietro of the Benedictine Abbey at Farfa remarked that he had heard some people 'shouting in Venetian so loud you would have thought there were fifty of them'.[77] In the winter, he might have encountered more pleasing sounds in the city when shepherds descended the freezing mountains and filled the air with music from their bagpipes. Others came to the city in dribs and drabs, repelled by war or lured by a particular promise of work. Overall, the effect on Rome was striking: a year before the sack, less than a quarter of the men who headed households in Rome were from the city, and nearly twenty per cent were from another country altogether.[78]

Of all foreign tongues, German was one of the most frequently heard. Whether working as bakers, vets, carpenters or illuminators, immigrants from the German lands helped the city to turn. Men and women often descended to Rome from the north in search of less regulated and competitive markets. In their homelands, businesses could be dominated by expensive guilds that workers were bound to join.[79] Some came in response to active solicitation from the popes, who sought to replenish and revive the city. Many Germans had come in the 1420s, for example, when Martin V was anxious to refill the empty streets and shops of the Borgo region near Saint Peter's Basilica. The area was not under the ordinary civic jurisdiction of Rome until 1586.[80] This meant that, in the early fifteenth century, the pope could lure potential movers with an enticing tax break. All new residents could live for twenty-five years tax free, if they stayed long-term.[81] Many came, including Germans such as Elissa of Cologne, Maria Grisach and Egidius, Matheus, Rex and Rubeus Superbus. On arrival, they might have been alarmed by some of their neighbours as the pope had also invited criminals along. Provided that they came permanently and were not murderers or traitors to the Holy See, convicts who repopulated the Borgo would be completely exonerated of their crimes.[82] Fortunately for the pope and his new German subjects, the criminal presence was offset by attractive business opportunities. Elissa sold herbs, spices and medicines in the streets nearby, while Maria made gloves and the Superbus brothers cobbled shoes on the steps of Saint Peter's Basilica.

Religion also offered foreign communities various centres of gravity across the city. We have already seen how national hospices emerged as Rome drew devotees from all over Europe. By 1421, the German bakers had their own chapel at Santa Maria dell'Anima, in a street that runs parallel along the length of the Piazza Navona.[83] Soon they had enough men paying dues to fund a new chapel, near a small garden where they could bury their dead. By the end of the century, they had raised Santa Elisabetta, their very own church, a little further south. As their group grew, they even added a small hospital with twelve beds reserved for the use of sick German bakers.[84] The arrangement sounds exclusive, but some professional groups mixed. Between their time at Santa Maria dell'Anima and Santa Elisabetta, the bakers of the German lands knelt down with the German shoemakers at the newly built church of Sant'Agostino.[85] That particular church also saw a mix of foreign influences; the elegant Renaissance facade had been funded by a Frenchman, Cardinal Guillaume d'Estouteville. For his part, d'Estouteville had integrated himself deeply into Roman society, bearing five children with his Italian mistress, Girolama Tosti, and tying them into local networks through advantageous marriages to old Italian families such as the Massimo and the Mattei.[86]

Even ostensibly patriotic events could unite foreigners and natives in the streets of Rome. When King Louis XIV recovered from a dangerous anal fissure in 1687, his ambassador provided music, wine and food to all passing the slopes beneath the French monastery of Trinità dei Monti.[87] On that night, lemons and oranges lit with oil hung from cedar trees, recreating the mythical Greek garden of the Hesperides in the centre of Rome. Nonetheless, relations between foreign communities could also prove far less festive, as hubs for particular nations became hotspots for conflict and international rivalries played out on the streets of Rome. One spring day in 1636, a Frenchman sparked a street war that even the pope, his police and the ambassadors would struggle to quell.[88] He had made the mistake of standing outside the church of San Giacomo on Piazza Navona, which was frequented by Castilians: Spaniards, and therefore rivals of France. Emerging from Mass, a Spanish group scorned and hit the Frenchman, who might have been begging for alms.[89] The Spaniards were cocky on their territory but they had erred, for French quarters lay only a few minutes' walk away. Soon the beggar returned with back-up that he had gathered at their church of San Luigi dei Francesi. From the windows of the priest's house at San Giacomo, the Spaniards now defended themselves from assault.[90] On the Piazza Navona, market stalls and glass shops were ambushed and looted of anything that could be used as a weapon. As the entire piazza became involved in the brawl, Rome, once again, became a microcosm for world affairs. As France and Spain fought on the bloodied battle-grounds of the Thirty Years War in Europe, their subjects came to blows on streets of the papal capital.

Ambassadors themselves were not above disturbing the peace, irking popes and the ordinary residents of Rome alike. Hauled around the city by numerous horses, laden with velvet and brocade, diplomatic carriages created nasty bottlenecks on bridges and thoroughfares.[91] In the state archive of Rome there are nearly forty surviving decrees that try to regulate these machines, which could ruin religious processions on solemn feast days.[92] Even on foot ambassadors brought disruption to some private residents. In 1640, when Portugal declared itself to be independent of Spain, they sent the Archbishop of Lamego as their first ambassador to the papal court. The prelate hardly looked like a political agitator, but he caused chaos when he took up residence on Piazza Navona. Hanging up a painting presenting João of Braganza and his wife as the King and Queen of Portugal, Lamego soon attracted the curious and the appalled. Dirk Ameyden, a Flemish poet and lawyer who lived next door, claimed that the noise made his quarters uninhabitable and the soldiers outside meant that he could 'barely leave home'.[93] These armed men were most likely in the employ of the Marquis de Los Velez, the Spanish ambassador who had vowed to drive his Portuguese counterpart from the city. One evening, he almost made good on the threat when his spies reported that Lamego was making his way home from dinner.[94] At twilight, Los Velez and his henchmen met the bishop outside the church of Santa Maria in via Lata. A street fight broke out. Shots were fired but the bishop survived, even if several servants and horses did not.[95]

A French printmaker in the city would lament that politics had led to violence 'in a place so full of sanctity, before the eyes of the great pontiff, right in the middle of Rome'.[96] That printmaker might have criticised the brawl, but this did not stop him from capitalising on it, illustrating the event and making multiple copies for sale. The pope himself had also involved himself in the dispute, even before it turned violent. When the Portuguese had announced their intention to send an ambassador to Rome, Los Velez had gone to Urban VIII (1623–44) on behalf of the Spanish king, begging the pope to deny the Portuguese ambassador the usual ceremonial welcome and procession. When Rome acted the world watched so, in Los Velez's eyes, depriving Lamego of overt papal approval would deprive independent Portugal of legitimacy. Spain was powerful; the pope had complied. During the hours of darkness, Lamego's carriage had entered Rome through the Porta del Popolo with no fanfare but its own creaking wheels – a rather shabby substitute for the music, fireworks and Swiss Guards normally laid on.[97]

—— C3 EO EO ——

The ugly reality of early modern politics jarred with the unique religious character of papal Rome. The city had become a locus of devotion and authority for Christians across the globe and yet, by this very same process, it had also become a centre of truly worldly affairs. This paradox formed a tricky line that popes like Clement VII and Urban VIII navigated with difficulty and varied success. To retain their position, the pontiffs had to assert their unique authority as supreme Christian leaders. Nonetheless, in doing so they sparked conflict and competition that could only be fought with the prestige, diplomacy and weapons of the world. Popes were also beleaguered by political authorities who sought to use their richly symbolic capital as a stage set for their own ambitions. In early plans for what would become the Spanish Steps, Louis XIV of France proposed a monument crowned with his own equestrian portrait to be made by the brilliant hand of Gian Lorenzo Bernini.[98]

These pressures on the papal prince also weighed heavily on his city. Climbing from the wreckage of the sack, dodging the gunshots from diplomatic scuffles, the people of Rome rose to their feet only to face migrants and pilgrims in their thousands. Burdened by high prices, poverty and overcrowding, the supposedly holy streets of Rome hosted theft, prostitution and sickness. This was a world away from the symbolic grandeur of papal diplomacy. Nevertheless, as we shall see, popes also concerned themselves with these baser struggles. This would be expected of the popes in their role as Bishops of Rome and leaders of the city. But this care of souls was also essential to papal claims of universal authority. If the Bishop of Rome was a Holy Father to all, he had to reach out and catch those deemed the most vulnerable, whether weary pilgrims, Roman Jews, penitent heretics or the old and sick. In many cases the popes' motives were charitable. Yet, as ever, personal and political interest also played their part. As popes oversaw hospitals, confraternities, a ghetto and an inquisition, they seized diverse and often conflicting means to protect the souls of their flock. In doing so they also sought to protect something equally significant: the ideal of Rome, in the eyes of God and the entire world.

8

Inquisitors, the
Ghetto and Ecstatic Saints

Walking onto the Piazza Giudia in the eighteenth century, Romans met a striking reminder of papal justice. It was not the wooden frame that awaited the hangman's noose at the centre of the square but the door that broke a ramshackle wall just beyond it. With its dense layers of wood studded with iron and stretching about three times the height of a grown man, the gate is shown open in an engraving made by Giuseppe Vasi in 1752, the world beyond it receding in vague crosshatch. In reality, it was often closed, bolted between sunset and sunrise. Those who lived beyond the gate would be imprisoned until daylight broke. This could prove perilous. Standing just a few minutes' walk from the banks of the Tiber, this walled quarter was frequently flooded with grimy water. Disease spread and rotten furniture floated through the streets. The city outside barely flinched. In the eyes of most Romans those who suffered behind the gate on Piazza Giudia did so in the name of justice for there lived the city's Jews, isolated and punished for the sake of Christian Rome and, crucially, in the eyes of the Church, for the sake of their own errant souls.

By the time that Vasi made his engraving, the door on Piazza Giudia was one of several to the Roman ghetto, though when it was founded in 1555 there was to be only one way in and one way out.[1] On 14 July of that year a papal bull laying out the plan was read at the basilica of San Marco on Piazza Venezia, just a short walk from the Capitoline Hill where the senate had pronounced Roman law since the eighth century BC.[2] Jews, too, had a long history in the city. They were first carried to Rome in the tumults of war in the second century BC and are the oldest Jewish community in Europe. Yet in 1555, after more than 1,700 years in the city, Pope Paul IV (1555–9) transformed the lives and status of Rome's Jews for the next three centuries.

For Paul IV, the Jews of Rome had to be corralled into an ignoble and inferior position. Punishment was one purpose, but isolation from the Christian community was also key. Jews were to be treated like a pox that could infect Christian Rome at one touch. In this endeavour it was not only the high walls of the ghetto that were instrumentalised but also restrictions that made it illegal for Jews to 'play, eat or fraternise' with Christians or for Jewish doctors to save Christian lives.[3] The hierarchy was clear, but Paul wanted it underlined: Jews could not employ Christians as servants and no Jew should be addressed as a superior, even by a Christian begging on the street. To ensure absolute separation, the pope demanded that Jews make their identity known. Glaring yellow symbols marked them out as they walked through the city: a yellow hat was worn by men, while women sewed yellow handkerchiefs into their garments to ensure that this crucial marker could not fall to the ground.[4]

The reasons for these measures were made clear in the first line of Paul's bull. As long as Jews refused to accept Jesus Christ and persist in their own faith, they threatened the purity of Rome. To Pope Paul, it was 'completely absurd and inappropriate to be in a situation where Christian piety allows the Jews access to our society and even to live among us'.[5] With his laws he hoped that Rome's Jews would not tarry in the ghetto but convert and, 'won over by the piety and kindness of this [Holy] See ... at last recognise their erroneous ways'.[6]

There was little time for reflection as around 3,000 men, women and children were walled into a trapezoidal neighbourhood of a few hectares in the *rione* of Sant'Angelo, bordered on the west by the rushing waters of the Tiber.[7] The barrier went up rapidly; within two months the Jews of Rome were enclosed. Where houses formed the barricade their windows were blocked, while any gaps between buildings were filled with new walls. Inside, two main streets were punctuated with some smaller thoroughfares. Small reliefs came over the years, but there was no real respite for those inside. In 1589, Sixtus V (1585–90) enlarged the ghetto, incorporating the Tiber's banks.[8] From 1593 it would be served by water outlets from a fountain on Piazza Guidia, giving Rome's Jews access to cleaner supplies than the river could offer.[9] In time, buildings stretched upwards to alleviate the pressure on densely overcrowded streets, while bridges between the upper floors provided an escape from the dangers and squalor that came with the floods.

Rome's ghetto was far from the first. It is even likely that the term originated elsewhere. The word is thought to have come from Venice, where Jews were enclosed near a foundry or *ghèto* in 1516.[10] The Venetians had created their ghetto after the number of Jews in the lagoon burgeoned during the Italian Wars of the early sixteenth century. On the one hand, they had to accommodate a Jewish population that had become vital to the Venetian infrastructure and economy.[11] On the other, many in Venice reviled Jews and levelled astonishing accusations at the community. Venetians claimed that Jews used Christian tabernacles as toilets and defiled the consecrated bread that Christians revere as the body of Christ. Hysteria peaked when the Jews of Venice were accused of 'murdering babies in cradles' so that they could 'dip their hands in and drink of innocent blood'.[12] Writing in his diary in the early sixteenth century, the Venetian nobleman Girolamo Priuli recorded all of these common indictments. Even he admitted that 'the Venetian people complain mightily about these Jews', even if they could not live without them.[13] In these circumstances a ghetto seemed a practical compromise: Jews could stay in the city, but they would be walled into a tightly controlled zone.

In Rome, however, the situation was different. Its sizeable community of Jews pre-dated the arrival of the city's first Christians. Their numbers had then swelled in the early modern period, particularly after 1492 when King Ferdinand and Queen Isabella, the 'Most Catholic Majesties' of Spain, expelled all Jews who refused to abandon their faith for Christianity.[14] Looking at the situation superficially, it might have seemed likely that Rome would follow suit. The popes tolerated the existence of Rome's Jewish community even if extreme antisemitism was clear in much-loved traditions such as the forced racing of naked Jews on via Lata during Carnival.[15] What is more, Alexander VI (1492–1503), the pope at that time of the expulsion, was not only Spanish but also from Ferdinand's hereditary territory of Aragon. As the pope who would bestow the titles of 'Most Catholic' on the Spanish monarchs, he might have been expected to follow their lead. Yet despite all this, Alexander made absolutely no change in his approach to Jews, and he certainly did not expel the community from Rome. The pope refrained not for love of the Jews of his city but from a desire to assert his supremacy over and autonomy from Spain.[16] It was Rome that set the universal standard for Christendom, no matter how Catholic the king and queen of Spain might be.

Unintentionally, Alexander's decision ensured that Rome and the Papal States would absorb much of the Jewish diaspora fleeing Spain. The papal city was hardly an entirely safe haven for exiled Jews. Nevertheless, Rome's deep-rooted Jewish community lived in some equilibrium with the rest of the population, even if antisemitic customs and behaviour frequently and violently imbalanced the scales. Like so many other groups in Rome, the Jews of the city had refortified their economy and community on the return of Martin V (1417–31), though this was often compromised by the excessive tithes that some popes expected them to pay.[17] Jews had even served as doctors and musicians to the pontiffs. In a cruel historical irony, Paul IV's policy towards Jews was partly driven by a rejection of Spanish secular authority, just as Alexander's toleration had been. Paul loathed the Spanish who had dominated his homeland of Naples and continued to rile him during the Italian Wars.[18] Like Alexander, he refused to follow their lead and expel Rome's Jews. Instead, he would force them into the cramped penury of the Roman ghetto.

Paul's decision to isolate Jews was emblematic of papal Rome in the mid- to late-sixteenth century. At that time, popes promoted the city as a universal Christian symbol more purposefully and energetically than ever before. Rome's holy identity now underpinned and distinguished a papal power that was recognised by an astonishingly diverse cast of political actors. Some of them believed that the papacy had renewed Rome's status as the centre of the civilised world. Others like the reformers saw the popes as a taint on the city. Echoing Petrarch's diatribe against Avignon, they characterised Rome as corruption and evil itself. Even in such bitter criticism of the popes and their city, we see that Rome was a powerful idea that mattered to a great many people. More than anybody, though, Rome mattered to the pope. He was a prince with no real army and no guaranteed wealth, whose authority did not rest on the branches of an august family tree. We have seen that the pope's authority was founded solely on his role as bishop of Saint Peter's See of Rome. To safeguard the identity of that city as wholly and purely Christian was, therefore, to safeguard his own power.

—— ☙ ❧ ❧ ——

It would take ruthless measures to protect the ideal of Rome from the reality. Paul IV was a man apparently born for the job. While heavily pregnant, his mother, the Neapolitan noblewoman Vittoria Camponeschi, was said to have looked down at her swollen belly and announced that she was about to give birth to a pope.[19] As is so often the case, Camponeschi was alone in her confidence in the brilliance of her son. Growing up as Gian Pietro Carafa, he became tall, bony and severe with a hot temper and tough moral fibre. He arrived in Rome in 1494 aged twenty and began a distinguished career as a bishop and papal nuncio to the English and Spanish courts. In 1536, Paul III elevated him to the cardinalate. In short, Carafa was a useful man. Moreover, unlike many of his peers, he was not given to indulgence: full-bodied red wine was his only vice.[20]

Carafa might have lacked self-indulgence, but he also lacked friends and charm, the tools with which many popes had won their crowns. Even in the context of the sixteenth-century Church, Carafa's views were deemed zealous. Sometimes this yielded positive results. Appalled by the laxity of priests, in 1524 he founded a strict order of clerics, called the Theatines, to better serve the laity. Yet Carafa would shock some contemporaries when he claimed, 'If my own father were a heretic, I would gather the wood to burn him.'[21] Ultimately, he was an outsider, too austere to be beloved of anybody at court. It was political pragmatism and a twist of fate that led to his shock election in 1555, when the fifty-three-year-old Marcello Cervini dropped dead after just twenty-two days on the papal throne. When the weary cardinals reassembled their conclave to elect his successor they were rent apart by agendas and factions – French, Imperial and reforming. If they were to agree on a candidate, they needed to look beyond their own favourites. Soon, all eyes settled on a man whom neither the princes nor the cardinals loved. In a conclave coloured by panic and compromise, Carafa's name was first cried out by a cardinal keen to bar the election of a rival.[22] Men eager to rile Carafa's Spanish enemies soon joined the refrain.[23] In the end, the seventy-nine-year-old Carafa was elected with complete unanimity, despite the fact that nobody had really wanted him on the papal throne.

Within four weeks, the new pope had penned the words that condemned Rome's Jews to the ghetto for three hundred years. Many would have been unsurprised that Paul had struck out so brutally in the name of religious purity in Rome. In September 1553, under his supervision, copies of the Talmud had been condemned, banned and burnt publicly on the Campo de' Fiori.[24] Moreover, as a cardinal, Paul had thrived as head of the Holy Office of the Roman Inquisition. Established on Carafa's urging in 1542, Rome's Holy Office had been founded by Paul III (1534–49) to oversee the identification, conversion and, if necessary, punishment of religious rebels across the Italian peninsula.[25] When men and women of all classes had shown support for Luther's reformed Christianity, Rome had been spooked. Most of the action was in the German lands and Scandinavia, where Protestant ideas won the backing of crowned heads. In Italy, it seemed that no prince would take the reformers' side. Still the heads of some on the peninsula had been turned.[26] In 1545, Paul III summoned a council of bishops and cardinals to discuss the direction and teachings of the Church at Trent in northern Italy. In the meantime, under Carafa's guidance, the Roman Inquisition would sniff out anybody 'sick with heretical plague'.[27]

Like its ghetto, Rome's inquisitorial system was not original. Those 'Most Catholic' Monarchs of Spain had, once again, got there first. In 1478, Ferdinand and Isabella had asked Pope Alexander VI if they could found a Spanish Inquisition to root out those same Jews and Muslims whom they would eventually banish in 1492.[28] In Spain, and in later Rome, inquisitors would rely on the cooperation of ordinary people, as they roved around cities, towns and villages pasting up edicts on public squares and church doors. Did locals know a Jew who had publicly converted to Christianity but secretly continued old practices? Did any of them own books by the heretic Martin Luther? Perhaps they had heard a slur against the Virgin Mary at the local tavern. Some exposed neighbours; others turned themselves in, encouraged by inquisitorial edicts that promised, 'our arms are always ready to welcome you, and you will always find our heart soft'.[29] Statements were taken. The accused were questioned. If found guilty, correct Catholic teaching was impressed upon them until they changed their ways. In Spain, these judicial processes culminated in a theatrical public event called an *auto da fé*, or act of faith, where heaving crowds awaited the entrance of the condemned on vast stages overlooked by grandees. Even from the back rows, spectators could deduce the fate of the accused, who wore tabards marked with coloured crosses and flames. If penitent and converted, they could be spared execution. If they fled, they would be burnt in effigy. The Black Legend of Spain's Holy Office has been intensified by romance and anti-Catholic and anti-Spanish sentiment. Still, the early modern inquisitors provided much of the raw material.

As the Church reeled at Luther's successes, fires were also lit in Rome. One hot August day in 1556, crowds on Piazza Navona surrounded a flaming pyre. There they awaited the execution of a twenty-four-year-old student who would be boiled alive in a pot of oil, pitch and turpentine. Pomponio Algieri was the young man to be executed that day, still wearing his academic cap and gown.[30] Algieri had been studying law at the University of Padua when inquisitors detected a Lutheran flavour to his religious beliefs. Now he wore his robes as a reminder of a scholar's right to discourse freely. The nature of Algieri's punishment was particularly cruel. His persistent refusal to recant may have elicited a sadistic response from the fervent Paul IV. The execution of criminals was relatively common in the Italian states, including those run by the pope. Across the peninsula, the numbers of murderers, thieves and traitors far outweighed the number of prison cells, even if it was relatively common for Romans to end up in one of its two main jails: the Tor di Nona opposite the Castel Sant'Angelo and the Curia Savelli further south in Regola.[31]

In Rome, as in many other Christian states, ecclesiastical and temporal hierarchies were intertwined. To reject the authority and teachings of the Church was treachery to the state itself.[32] Crucially, religious insubordination was also a threat to souls who might be led astray. In Catholic states, the removal of heretics was often seen as a civic good, cleansing a threat to bodies and souls. In his days as an inquisitor, Carafa energetically bolstered the inquisition, creating an institution that, at times, had more influence on Church policy than the pope.[33] In its actions and their justification (given in sentences that could take up to half an hour to read out) the Roman Inquisition presented itself as the heroic force that had saved the Italian peninsula from Lutheranism and an eternity in hell.[34]

It was for this reason that Giordano Bruno had his tongue stayed with a bridle as he was burnt alive on the Campo de' Fiori in the year 1600.[35] Through stifling leather, Bruno breathed his last on the very square where Paul IV had destroyed Rome's copies of the Talmud. Ironically, Saint Dominic had founded the religious order to which Bruno belonged to help the popes to find, convert and punish heretics in the south of France in the twelfth and thirteenth centuries. These Cathars or Albigensians were snuffed out by Dominic's earlier, medieval inquisition, aided by the future Avignon pope Benedict XII. Unlike the Cathars, Bruno's ideas did not constitute a creed. He drew inspiration from Muslim astrologers, the later followers of the Greek philosopher Plato and, through them, the teachings of Hermes Trismegistus, an arcane, mythical figure who embodied the Greek god Hermes and the baboon-faced Egyptian deity Thoth.[36] Bruno's interests were diverse and, to the Roman Inquisition, deeply suspicious. However, it was his essential religious beliefs that troubled them the most. In an effort to change his mind, they sat Bruno down with Roberto Bellarmino, one of the greatest theologians of the age. When Bruno refused to alter his views on the authority of the Holy Office and the Real Presence of Christ in the bread and wine consecrated at Mass, the inquisitors condemned him to silence by flames.[37]

In Rome there had always been men and women who refuted, questioned or joked about the teachings and authority of the Catholic Church, well before Luther had set fire to the bull of Pope Leo X (1513–21). There had also been Jews in the city before the birth of Christ. For popes, the Church hierarchy and, in many cases, ordinary Romans, these had been irksome but bearable facts. All of this changed in the sixteenth century when the growth and prominent endorsement of Protestant ideas escalated fears among all those with an ideological, personal or political stake in Catholic orthodoxy. Fear of the Jewish presence also intensified after 1541. When the Spanish extended their expulsion of Jews to their Italian territories in the Kingdom of Naples, many Jews were forced to find new homes and some came to Rome.[38] To make matters worse, in 1555, the international role of the papacy was dealt a serious blow when the Peace of Augsburg formally divided Europe into Protestant and Catholic states. In that year, Christendom was carved up not according to the will of the pope but to that of each secular prince. The decision gravely undermined the authority and identity of the pope as the supreme religious figurehead of the West.

Suffering blows on the international stage and fearing a menace within their own city, popes of this time might have watered down their claims of supremacy, accepting retreat into a marginal position that was far easier to maintain. For the successor of Peter this was not an option. There was only one definition of their role. They would define and bolster it by protecting the identity of Rome as a holy, Catholic city. For some time, Rome and its pontiffs had been publicly wedded in the ceremony of the *possesso*, in which popes processed through the city after their coronation at Saint Peter's to take official control as Bishop of Rome. Now its increasing grandeur – with strict protocol and, one year, a *baldacchino* held by Japanese envoys – reflected the starring role the city played in the assertion of universal papal power.[39] It is no coincidence that the ghetto walls were raised in the summer of 1555, just as the Peace of Augsburg was signed by the Holy Roman Emperor himself. It was also not by chance that the following summer, after a process of one year, Pomponio Algieri would be boiled alive on the orders of the Roman Inquisition. When popes feared that threats to the authority of the pope and the purity of Rome itself were growing, the Church hierarchy unearthed and exterminated them with greater fervour and severity than ever before.

—— ঙ ৺ ৺ ——

If Rome were to assert itself as the global centre of Christendom, it could not be like any other place on earth. Popes, cardinals, religious orders and nobles invested in the project, with new churches and streets stretching out from the *abitato* to the ancient basilicas.[40] Itineraries and histories detailing Rome's dense landscape of holy shrines and relics were set out painstakingly in the annotations to the newly revised *Martyrologium Romanum* (1584).[41] Now the faithful could transcend centuries to literally immerse themselves in early Christian Rome. Building on his own work in the martyrology, the historian and future cardinal Cesare Baronio wrote the *Annales ecclesiastici*, employing the tools of archaeology, history and apology to illuminate ancient sites such as the catacombs of Saint Priscilla. For Baronio, they were a 'hidden city, filled with tombs from the persecutions of the Christians'.[42] As he highlighted sites in a narrative of continuous, heroic Christian worship in Rome, proof of the city's unique apostolic character materialised beneath his feet.[43] This idea of Rome would also be manifest above ground, through the genius of artists and architects such as Carlo Maderno, Michelangelo Merisi da Caravaggio and Gian Lorenzo Bernini. Across the city they made miracles in colour, marble and concrete, pushing the boundaries of convention and possibility in church architecture and decoration. Saints, angels and God himself were invoked for the cause, as apostles were resurrected in painted and sculpted flesh that looked warm to the touch. Over the course of a century the motley architecture of the ancient, medieval and Renaissance worlds was subsumed into a triumphant Baroque cityscape that still dominates Rome's centre today.

The present familiarity of the Rome's Baroque architecture belies its astonishing novelty when it was built. For those Romans living in semi-rural conditions in the early modern city, it brought heaven itself down to earth. Walking down the via Lata, by then known as the via del Corso, in the seventeenth century, they endured the racket of construction. By 1600, the narrow thoroughfare would be flanked by Maderno's San Giacomo in Augusta, its graceful columns and pilasters stretching upwards to a swirling volute and a slim, neat pediment. By the 1680s, the twin, domed churches of Santa Maria in Montesanto and Santa Maria dei Miracoli framed the head of the street. In the intervening decades, churches were raised nearby to honour men whose feet had trodden the Corso on their path to sainthood. A short walk down the street, a deep inscription on the monumental facade of San Carlo al Corso would remind locals that the late sixteenth-century cardinal Carlo Borromeo was now in heaven. After 1614, men and women could cross the threshold of that church to kneel in front of Carlo's once-beating heart.[44] Here in Rome was a potent physical sign of the personal charity that had compelled Borromeo to surrender almost all of his belongings and so earn his sanctity.[45]

Not long after the arrival of Borromeo's heart, another late citizen of Rome would be resurrected nearby on the via Caravita, this time by a painter rather than a surgeon. The artist Andrea Pozzo was a member of the Jesuit order, though not a priest. In 1626, the Jesuits had called for masons, travertine and paint to construct their second Roman church in honour of their founder Iñigo de Loyola. A Spanish knight who forsook dancing, violence and seduction when a bomb bounced from a wall to shatter his leg in 1521, Loyola's own heart had been transformed as he endured the malaise and torments of a long convalescence. By 1539, Loyola was kneeling at the feet of Pope Paul III, after an arduous journey of penitence, pilgrimage and study had taken him from Castile to Jerusalem, then on to Paris and Rome.[46] Along the way, Loyola's fervour to be a knight for Christ rather than a monarch won him devotees and companions, as well as the suspicions of inquisitors. The Holy Office in Spain would question the orthodoxy of his religious counsel to ardent female devotees. Fortunately for Loyola, he quashed suspicions of heresy and, in the end, it was only his companions who followed him to Rome.

Doubts lingered around Loyola's radically personalised approach to ridding souls of sin. Nonetheless, Loyola also won powerful admirers in Rome and transformed his personal experiences into a religious mission that engaged men and women from Modena to Macau. Guiding souls in a process that he called the *Spiritual Exercises*, Loyola told the faithful to shake themselves from perfunctory devotion, to look in the mirror and ask 'What I have done for Christ, what I am doing for Christ, what I ought to do for Christ?'[47] From the ecstatic women of Alcalá to prominent, noble churchmen such as Cardinal Gasparo Contarini, people began to look to Loyola and his companions as the future of the Church. Despite later characterisations, the Society of Jesus or the Jesuits, as they became known, were not founded to respond to the threat of spreading Protestantism. That said, their commitment to genuinely converting souls provided an inspiring response to Luther's characterisation of a shallow and transactional Catholic spirituality. By 1540, Pope Paul III had approved the Jesuits as an official religious order, allowing them to operate with a liberality that had never been seen before. By the late seventeenth century, there were more than 11,500 Jesuits in Italy, Spain and the German lands alone, styling their outfits and their teaching methods to suit the international territories where they sought to save souls.[48]

Controversy brewed in the papal curia when news of the Society's mission to China revealed that the Jesuit Matteo Ricci had donned the conical hat and philosophy of the Chinese sage Confucius. In 1601, this son of the Papal States would be the very first European to set foot in the Forbidden City of Beijing.[49] There, Ricci recounted the miracle of the virgin birth in the linear figures of traditional Chinese and allowed his converts to continue undertaking traditional rites for their dead.[50] Across the Americas, in India and in Europe, Jesuits taught orthodox Catholicism to non-Christian peoples through means that were often alien to the Church hierarchy in Rome, accommodating local tradition when and where they could. At the same time, the Jesuits' core and character were always bound to Rome. It was there that the Jesuits would set up their headquarters in the shadow of Saint Peter's Basilica and agreed to obey popes blindly when charged with foreign missions. A reality of negotiation, compromise and even rebellion tempers the popular image of a Jesuit militia unflinchingly following the pope.[51] Still, the Jesuits were a valuable tool for the reinforced, resurgent and decidedly Roman Catholic Church.

In 1622, Pope Gregory XV (1621–3) made it clear that the Jesuits were central to his vision for the Church. In a bumper canonisation, he made saints of Loyola and three others, including another Jesuit, Francis Xavier, who had died not long ago. The ceremony had been planned to canonise Isidore the Labourer, a pious twelfth-century farm hand who was to be patron saint of Madrid. Thanks to the pope's personal intervention, however, Isidore had to share his day. The banners of five new saints were hung up inside the dome of Saint Peter's, proudly declaring their personal virtues and the pontiff's aspirations for the entire Church.[52]

According to Gregory, then, there were at least two Jesuits in heaven. In Rome, the order now had thousands of trainees. From the first decades of the seventeenth century, papal projects such as the Propaganda Fide, along with the numerous colleges founded by Gregory XIII (1572–85), made Rome the lively centre of a global Catholic mission.[53] Across the city, Jesuit colleges prepared young men for a task no less than the salvation of the entire world. At specialist training centres for Germans, Englishmen, Greeks, Scots and the near-eastern Maronites, they taught men from countries where Catholics were the minority who hoped to convert men and women back in their homelands. Despite the risk of accident and violence, the response to the Jesuit missionary call was huge.

Vocations were often sparked by the tales of fresh martyrdoms that arrived in letters to the Jesuits' Roman HQ.[54] When five Jesuit brothers were brutally murdered on arrival in India, a confrere went much further than writing a letter, composing a six-book poetic epic in their honour.[55] On the walls of the church of Santo Stefano Rotondo, Jesuit students destined for missions to Hungary and the German-speaking lands saw the murders of their early Christian predecessors depicted anew.[56] By the time of Loyola's canonisation, there were 2,000 students at the main training centre of the Collegio Romano just off the via del Corso.[57]

To fortify their spirits, the students needed a far bigger church than the small chapel of the Annunziata at the Collegio. By the end of the seventeenth century, they would have Sant'Ignazio on the via Caravita. In that enormous building, Pozzo's paintbrush conjured a ceiling full of heavenly beings, suspended in a vault that appeared to extend into the heavens. Angels, saints and the embodiments of virtues dangled nude limbs from heavy cornices overhead. Sitting on a cloud buoyed by cherubs at the centre of the scene was Loyola meeting Christ himself. The entirety of the world was present, with personifications of Europe, Africa, America and Asia sitting atop a camel in mid-air. The sheer ambition of the painting reflected the spiritual and geographic scope of the Jesuits' mission, as well as that of the Church that they served. As ever, however, the project was tied to the papal city. Over the altar are the words that Loyola claimed Jesus had spoken to him: 'I will be with you in Rome.'

——— ∽ ∾ ∾ ———

At Sant'Ignazio, Jesuit students encountered a miracle made manifest in a remarkable new fashion. Yet the miraculous had been vital to Christian worship since the apostolic age. For centuries, priests had raised bread and wine in their hands, uttering Jesus' words at the Last Supper, which they believed transformed the substances into his flesh and blood. About once a year Christians actively recognised this miracle, consuming the body of Christ during the Mass. In 1263 a congregation in the Italian town of Bolsena reported that blood had soaked their altar cloths when the priest doubted the truth of the eucharistic miracle during the Mass.[58] Taking his brush to a wall of the Vatican Palace in 1512, Raphael had painted that moment when one miracle had begotten another. Working at the behest of Pope Julius II (1503–13), he had transplanted the pope to the scene opposite the wavering priest, kneeling reverently before the miracle of the Mass. Julius was far from the first churchman to do so. In 1246, bishops in Belgium had instituted the feast of Corpus Christi on the urging of the canoness Juliana of Liège.[59] The feast became mandatory for all Christian parishes when news of the Mass at Bolsena reached Pope Urban IV (1261–4). At every single church, from Saint Peter's Basilica to the humbler parishes of Europe, the body of Christ would be held in a tabernacle where anybody, whether labourer, fishwife, cardinal or queen, could encounter Jesus as they walked through the door.

By the mid-sixteenth century, however, the eucharistic miracle had become a battleground. While papal loyalists continued to kneel before the consecrated bread, other Christians responded with mockery, even disgust. In the fiery debates that had followed the Reformation, some had decided that Jesus had spoken only symbolically when he asked his disciples to eat his flesh and blood. Many in this first generation of Protestants flatly rejected the miracle of the Mass. By the time that business or curiosity drew their sons and daughters to Rome, this once familiar belief had become quite alien to them. Loitering at the back of churches and passing eucharistic processions on the streets, they were horrified to see Catholics who claimed to eat the body of Christ. Across the continent, other Protestants reviled such Catholic practices, accusing Catholics of feasting on their saviour 'as men eat oysters' or as cannibals who approached God 'with the fangs of brutes'.[60]

We might deem these comments insensitive. For early modern Catholics they were outright heresy. In response, popes ordered that this defining aspect of their faith be celebrated with ever greater fervour. The Jesuits urged the laity to abandon annual communion and consume the body of Christ on a weekly or even daily basis.[61] Sometimes it was placed in an ornamental vessel called a monstrance for veneration. Kneeling along streets and church aisles, thousands looked up to the body of their saviour, held behind the small circular window of the monstrance, and often framed by gilt sunburst. By the late-sixteenth century, eucharistic processions were used to cleanse the city during times of danger or widespread sin. As some men and women drank, danced and gambled their way through Carnival, others fell to the ground in silent devotion. Churches remained open day and night for the *Quarant'ore* or forty hours of continuous prayer.[62] In 1592 Clement VIII (1592–1605) urged priests across the 'Mother City of Rome' to host this devotion so that, from the centre of Christendom, the 'incense of prayer shall ascend without intermission before the face of the Lord'.[63] In the 1660s, Bernini built a church entirely centred on the eucharistic miracle. Crossing the threshold of Sant'Andrea on the Quirinal Hill, visitors did not face the usual long, central aisle but found themselves standing in a perfect oval just a few strides from the tabernacle that held the body of Christ.

By the seventeenth century, Rome was a monumental witness to a specifically Catholic Christianity. Though some Lutheran churches would adopt the Baroque style, the curved forms and ecstatic bodies of Rome bore a bigger and distinctly Catholic message. Here the grandiosity and drama of the style became a means of communicating and affirming the truth and superiority of the Catholic faith. In Rome, art and architecture thrust the reality of saints and miracles upon ordinary men and women, informing and intensifying their religious experience with stories that could elicit surprise and awe.[64] At Bernini's church of Sant'Andrea, Saint Andrew himself burst out from a painting over the altar, his marble figure rupturing the stone pediment to fly into heaven. At the church of Santa Maria della Vittoria, Bernini also resurrected Saint Teresa, sculpting the sixteenth-century nun at the moment in which she claimed to feel God stab her 'very entrails' with an arrow of divine love.[65] Thrust backwards in pain, the saint's lips are parted in a moan as a serene putto draws back his arm to thrust the arrow back into her chest. Every year on Teresa's feast day the sun bounced from a small lens of glass to illuminate the drapery billowing around her swooning body.[66] In early modern Rome, Catholicism was a religion that could be seen, heard and believed.

── ❦ ❧ ❧ ──

Supremacy over other places and religions was vital to the narrative. So, therefore, were the right spectators. The popes needed non-believers, as well as faithful pilgrims, to see the truth of Catholicism manifested in Rome. While inquisitors coerced Romans to expose Protestants in their midst, other non-Catholics were welcomed with open arms. In 1603, Ali-Qoli Beg, the seventy-three-year-old representative of the Persian Shah, Abbas I, took in Rome's marvels as the guest of Pope Paul V (1605–21). As the Muslim ambassador of a Muslim leader, his awe was a worthy goal. Working his way through an extensive itinerary, Beg stood at the cavernous centre of the ancient Colosseum before taking in the nave at Constantine's Lateran Basilica.[67] In the Borgo, he visited Santo Spirito in Sassia, the great hospital rebuilt in splendour by Pope Sixtus IV (1471–84). By Beg's time, Paul V could boast of its world-leading experimentation in anatomical dissection and its provision of some 10,000 medicines and 50,000 syrups.[68] A short walk away at Saint Peter's, the ambassador saw yet more papal ambition fulfilled. Julius II's plans to rebuild the basilica in the early sixteenth century had now been realised and transformed by geniuses from Bramante to Michelangelo. Beg would not see the broad, Travertine facade added by Carlo Maderno a few years later, nor the two sweeping, rhythmic colonnades with which Bernini later encircled the piazza. He did, however, scale the cupola, which crowned the building in an immense, resplendent dome. All the while, his papal host hoped that these experiences would be relayed to the Shah back in Persia, painting an image of a Christian civilisation unmatched in 'heathen' lands.

Paul's hopes might seem far-fetched but there was precedent. In 1601, the cook of the former Persian ambassador had been so taken by Rome that he became Catholic and refused to return home.[69] Long after Paul's death, men and women continued to arrive in the city seeking conversion. The tailor Samuel Hope from Coventry travelled by sea to Livorno before going on to Rome to learn more of the faith of his Catholic master.[70] For many in his native Church of England, Rome symbolised superstition and potential treachery to the crown. English detractors of the pope identified the city with its religion as intimately as the pontiffs whom they derided. Ironically, this meant that Protestants who encountered a contrastingly virtuous image of Catholicism knew precisely where they could go if they wanted to discover more.

By 1673, the city had founded an official institution to receive and support potential converts, echoing the mission of an earlier congregation that sought to welcome those who 'came to the faith spontaneously'.[71] The Ospizio dei Convertendi was set up to support Lutherans and Calvinists who arrived in Rome with doubts about their faith. It secured a permanent location in 1686 when it moved into the imposing Palazzo dei Convertendi, a grand edifice originally located in a square adjacent to Saint Peter's but moved brick-by-brick to the via della Conciliazione when that street was constructed in the late 1930s. In the seventeenth century, the Ospizio formed one node of a network of mercy, justice and Catholic triumph, embracing its converts before sending them to the Roman Inquisition where any change of heart could be officially judged and recorded. Travelling to Rome from the Netherlands to rediscover the faith of his parents, the orphan Simon Hein found himself in front of an inquisitor 'begging to be reconciled to the Holy Roman Catholic Church'.[72] The experience sounds ominous but these 'spontaneous appearances' instigated a standardised summary process that usually ended with penitential prayers, rather than fines or jail time.

In the theatre of early modern Rome, conversion became a powerful drama, a striking vindication of the truth and supremacy of the Catholic cause. While most conversions were formalised quietly in the private rooms of the Roman Inquisition, the conversion of prominent figures was proclaimed with great fanfare. In November 1655, Rome celebrated an almighty coup when Queen Christina of Sweden renounced her throne and Lutheran faith to join the Catholic Church. She was the daughter of King Gustavus Adolphus, the scourge of many Catholic armies during the Thirty Years' War. Uncommonly learned and wilful, Christina had already offended her subjects when she refused to marry, failed to brush her hair and concealed texts by pagan writers such as Virgil inside her hymn book. Her religious volte-face left the country completely scandalised. Departing from her home in Stockholm in the midst of the biting Swedish winter, the twenty-eight-year-old Christina would be accompanied by just two of her original staff. One of the pair, her chamberlain Gustav Lilliecrona, was downcast, having 'with many tears entreated her to grant [his] dismissal'.[73]

As Christina took the long journey south, she would encounter a more clement atmosphere. In the Catholic city of Innsbruck, two Jesuits received her into the Catholic Church on behalf of Pope Alexander VII (1655–67).[74] By the time that Christina entered Italy, she progressed with all the pomp of a conqueror. The blast of fireworks and roar of cheers filled the air around her carriage. After celebrations laid on by the pope in Ferrara, Bologna, Faenza and Rimini, Christina reached Rome, her new home and, according to the popes, the mother city of all souls. As she was carried under the Porta del

Popolo on a sedan chair designed by Bernini, Christina's eyes met those of thousands of onlookers joyous at the notion of a heart and crowned head claimed back for the Catholic Church. The Porta del Popolo that welcomed Christina to Rome still bears an inscription honouring the moment that she entered the city, reading 'For a happy and blessed progress.'[75]

This perfect spectacle soon disintegrated. In Rome, the pope needed Christina to be a witness to Catholic truth but she remained a thoroughly unorthodox woman. The warning signs came early. Touring churches shortly after her arrival in Rome, Christina was cold and argumentative when presented with precious relics, disputing the authenticity of the staff of the prophet Aaron and a plank from the Ark of the Covenant that was believed to have held the Ten Commandments.[76] Even in the privacy of her new Roman quarters, Christina continued to cause alarm. Initially living at the Palazzo Farnese as the guest of the Duke of Parma and Piacenza, she hosted rowdy salons, drinking heavily and flouting norms to see men freely. Later on at her theatre (founded on the site of the Tor di Nona prison), other women broke convention to take to the stage.[77] Christina also involved herself with the Vatican's liberal-minded 'Flying Squad', a group of young cardinals who refused to heed the influence of the secular rulers who tried to put their favourites on the papal throne.[78] Soon she fell madly and openly in love with Cardinal Decio Azzolino, who did not requite her affections.[79] Even in public ceremony, Christina disappointed. When she knelt to receive Holy Communion from Pope Alexander VII himself she did so with none of the ecstasy or emotion expected by spectators. In short, Christina entirely failed to play the grateful, penitent heretic.

Only four months after her arrival, an English diplomat reported to Oliver Cromwell that 'they begin to be weary at Rom[e] of their new guest the quien of Swed[en]'.[80] In 1657, Christina had one of her Italian staff, the nobleman Gian Rinaldo Monaldeschi, executed for treachery.[81] Cutting off all contact, Alexander VII is reported to have called her 'a queen without a realm, a Christian without faith and a woman without shame'. Like many others, Alexander had been horrified at Monaldeschi's murder. More than this, he was appalled that such an important player had tainted the narrative of a pure and triumphant Catholic Rome. Christina was a remarkable woman, but in many ways her case was far from unique. In Rome, even the most well-intentioned believers failed to live up to the ideal. The suspicions and strictures faced by religious outsiders in Rome meant that many converted for purely practical reasons. Even genuinely religious motivations could intertwine with pragmatism in the hearts of non-Catholic foreigners. In an atmosphere increasingly pregnant with unease and suspicion, false conversions were both common and feared, as inquisitors – and the neighbours, innkeepers and merchants who informed them – scrutinised the religious practices, personal lives and even eating habits of new converts.

In October 1553, Didaco Perez had been plucked from the streets of Rome and taken to a jail of the inquisition.[82] Like Christina, he had converted to Catholicism, but now it seemed that he was not playing his part. Didaco had been born a Jew in Portugal and stood accused of relapsing into the tenets and practices of his old religion. The records of the inquisition do not share his age nor the details of his conversion, though it is possible that he had become Catholic as a young man in his homeland in 1497. In that year, King Manuel I had ordered all Jews to convert or leave.[83] If Didaco was a much older man, he might even have endured in his faith, suffering expulsion only to convert later in Italy. In Rome in the early 1550s, signs of coercion were far less acute: there was no threat of expulsion and, for the time being, no ghetto. Still the lingering smell of burning Talmuds on the Campo de' Fiori made it clear to all Jews that life would be safer as a Catholic. Many Iberian Jewish converts found that they could immerse themselves in life at the Spanish and Portuguese churches of Rome, worshipping with their countrymen without clashing against the strictures imposed on converted Jews (known as 'New Christians') back in their homelands.[84]

Cases like that of Didaco Perez illuminate the paradox that troubled a Catholic city bent on religious purity: the Church offered attractive social and economic privileges to those who were willing to become Catholic but harboured an intense fear of insincere conversions.[85] To understand why the Church persisted in this approach, we must remember that the key protagonists had an unshakable belief in the truth of the Catholic religion. This made them confident in their hope for sincere conversions and zealous to secure any conversions at all. That said, pragmatic conversions were certainly not exclusive to newcomers in increasingly stringent Catholic lands. In the late seventeenth century, Beatrice Michiel became Fatima as she renounced Christianity for Islam, fleeing a miserable marriage in Venice for a new life in Constantinople.[86] In that Muslim capital of the Ottoman Empire, Beatrice joined her brother, an enslaved eunuch of the sultan.[87] At the Ottoman court, her conversion would be a passport to the imperial harem where she lived as a privileged concubine, privy to political and military intelligence, all of which she relayed to the embassy of Venice.[88]

Even Roman Jews, whom popes had confined with bricks, mortar and legal statute, blurred boundaries intended to protect the Catholic identity of Rome. In the late 1570s, Pope Gregory XIII had escalated Paul IV's mission to convert the community. Every Saturday afternoon in Rome around 250 to 300 Jews were taken from the rest of their sabbath to hear Catholic preachers urge them to conversion.[89] Scanning for their name on a rota posted at the synagogue, Jews discovered when it was their turn to take the ten-minute walk to the oratory of the church of Santissima Trinità dei Pellegrini. For Catholic Romans and visitors, this drama could be relished every week, as they rained taunts on Jews processing from the ghetto. In an unconsecrated room measuring just eleven by twenty-one metres square, the spectacle would reach its dramatic apotheosis.[90] A tide of dogma and invective was unleashed on the corralled Jews from a pulpit manned by Catholic priests and Jewish converts. Visiting Rome in 1581, the French essayist Michel de Montaigne heard the official preacher whom he dubbed the 'renegade rabbi'.[91] Names were crossed off a list as men and women entered at the door. Penalties for absentees were declared, even if the Rome's Jewish community were already paying for the staff who restrained their movements with the threat of a baton.

Superficially, the domination was complete, but on closer inspection subversion was rife. Some Jews in the crowd stifled the Catholic message, stuffing their ears with wax, while disguised rabbis infiltrated the room to mock the interpretations of preachers using subtle hand signals.[92] This was nothing new. By the 1540s, dissent from the narrative of Catholic supremacy threatened to breach the walls of the Casa dei Catecumeni, a school for Jewish converts founded by Loyola near the ghetto on the via delle Botteghe Oscure. In 1553, Loyola led Didaco Perez to the Casa from the cells of the inquisition, securing his release on the promise that its Jesuit teachers could ground the convert more firmly in the Catholic faith.[93] The inquisitors at the time obviously thought this a safe option. Posters on the walls of the ghetto often told a different story. There maps marked the location of the house for converts and warned unrepentant Jews not to communicate with its residents or even dare pass its windows.[94] Threats of fines, whipping and years rowing in the galleys accompanied the admonition. Interventions from the Jewish community were clearly seen as a serious threat to the Catholic missionary enterprise, even when Church institutions had shut both converts and Jews behind closed doors.

— ଔ ଛ ଛ —

The Catholic authorities were well aware that the line between faith and errancy was blurred and often well-trod. The inquisition's willingness to let Loyola take Didaco Perez from their custody was a typical acknowledgement that, in real life, conversion was not always a dramatic, one-time event. Rome was a city in which ideals were imposed but often renegotiated or side-stepped, particularly as its status as a holy city could weigh heavily on the lives of its inhabitants. As pilgrims and economic migrants poured into the papal capital, its frequently unstable economy was increasingly burdened.[95] At the edges of streets, the thin, dirty hands of Romans, pilgrims and migrants stretched out for coins and food. Families came under pressure and fractured. At the hospital of Santo Spirito in Sassia the 'baby box' for unwanted infants was filled time and again.[96] Hastening home, some women returned to a household now able to bear the struggles of mere survival, while their babies fared better than those found in fishing nets in the Tiber nearby.[97] Other women went to the streets where they worked as prostitutes. In early modern Rome, the occupation was widespread and conspicuous, sparking rivalries and public 'scornings', in which doors were burnt or scrawled with denunciations written in ink or even faeces.[98] Popes tried to control prostitution, though to little avail. Applying the concept of the ghetto, Pius V (1566–72) confined prostitutes to an area of the Campo Marzio that became known as the *ortaccio* or 'nasty garden'.[99] Later, Sixtus V looked further south to the Colosseum, proposing to turn the abandoned amphitheatre into a wool factory where women could make a more wholesome living.

Ultimately, these plans came to nothing. By the 1620s, more than a thousand prostitutes walked the streets of Rome.[100] This was only a few hundred less than there had been in 1533 when the eighteen-year-old Filippo Neri arrived in the city.[101] In the dingy streets that lay around the Colosseum, Filippo had met the city's most desperate figures, engaging vagrants and lone women in conversation about their eternal souls. Back in his hometown of Florence, his parents were disconcerted. After an intensely religious education at the friary of San Marco they had sent Filippo to work for his Uncle Romolo in the hope that he might make their son his heir. Such aspirations were disappointed when Filippo announced that he wanted to work for God instead. Leaving his uncle in San Germano, a town in the north of the Kingdom of Naples, Filippo sought his vocation in Rome. Once there, he flouted convention once again, failing to ingratiate himself with a religious institution or order and living as an 'urban hermit'.[102] He deliberately invited the ridicule of others, shaving off half his beard vertically down the centre, wearing white shoes and putting his clothes on inside out.[103] Over time, Filippo cut an increasingly eccentric figure as he squatted down to speak to the city's most derided souls with his dog Capriccio at his side.

On 22 November 1583, a bizarre procession was seen from the prison cells at the Curia Savelli. At its head was Filippo Neri and behind him trailed men bearing spades, pots and pans. This small, practical miscellany represented the sum total of Filippo's belongings.[104] When he had arrived in Rome fifty years earlier he had sold all of his books. Now what he had was mocked by bored spectators in the jail. The scene was a world away from the Catholic triumphalism of the preachers to Rome's Jews. It is unlikely that Filippo cared. On his annual pilgrimage to the seven holiest basilicas of the city he sat with his followers during the picnic and concert that broke up the day.[105] Hearing the confessions of haughty Roman priests, he encouraged them to preach poorly to humble themselves. Despite such counter-cultural advice, Filippo swiftly won influential friends such as Iñigo Loyola, as well as disciples who followed him from the streets to his rooms where they would sing and pray. Soon the group outgrew the small chamber above the little church of San Girolamo della Carità where he slept. By the time that the adjacent rooms had also reached capacity, even the popes had got wind of this new 'Apostle of Rome'. On the urging of Pope Gregory XIII, Filippo became a priest at the age of thirty-six. Later, his following was transformed into a congregation of clerics known as the Oratorians, who are meant to follow Filippo's life of charity, joy and prayer. On that winter day in 1583, Filippo and his disciples were making their way to a brand-new home for the Oratorians, taking his shovels and kitchen equipment down the via Monserrato to the magnificent church of Santa Maria in Vallicella.

In 1622 Filippo was made a saint, along with Loyola and Teresa of Avila. Somehow, his gentle and often eccentric mission was enshrined in the narrative of a triumphalist Catholic Church. Toiling in the hospital attached to Santissima Trinità dei Pellegrini, Filippo's manner contrasted starkly with those berating Jews in the church oratory in the same complex. In the sacristy, a painting of Filippo wearing his apron still stands. Painted from life, the picture is a quiet testament to his hands-on leadership of a confraternity that cared for more than 180,000 pilgrims and sick Romans in just one year.[106] Their records suggest that they gave a warm welcome to many visiting 'heretics', as well as those who 'did not know what the Catholic faith was'.[107]

In this period, papal governance of Rome created a city full of contradictions. In one breath the popes spoke of unifying Christendom under the banner of Peter, but to do so they divided their own capital with high brick walls. The presence of so many pilgrims in Rome had ugly consequences for the poor; meanwhile the charitable, missionary spirit of the Church offered up solutions to the very problems it had sparked, with successive popes endowing confraternity hospitals such as that of Filippo Neri. In this Rome, ardent inquisitors lit pyres for the bodies of the unrepentant, but also realised that compromise was necessary if they were to have any chance of winning more malleable souls. Even Andrea Pozzo's dazzling ceiling at Sant'Ignazio belied a less satisfactory truth: by the time that he mounted the scaffolding, Roman influence had been hugely diminished in some European countries, while many missions had yielded less than heroic results in areas of Asia and Africa, even as the expansion of Islam marched on.[108]

When scrutinised, the reality of early modern Rome was a muddle of impossible standards, shifting expectations and pragmatism. However, all of these strands were unified in a common project. Even figures who appear to be outliers, such as Filippo Neri and his followers, aimed to convert every errant soul whom they encountered. At the centre of this complex situation sat the popes themselves. Despite the regime's incoherence, it seems that they had the tacit obedience of the Roman populace. Like many institutions of the Church, the people of Rome accepted Catholic ideals but also knew the reality of life in their city. In 1559, they were aghast when the Bishop of Polignano was discovered in his bedchamber with a Jewish courtesan, Porzia, who was arrested and cast out of Rome.[109] In their eyes, the bishop deserved his punishment of perpetual imprisonment for violating Catholic ideals and laws by having sex with a Jew. Porzia, on the other hand, was a public prostitute who had done what was expected of her and paid her taxes to the Curia Savelli. These were the rules, some codified and many unwritten. In the eyes of many Romans, Porzia was 'guilty of nothing'.[110]

In the coming centuries, governors espousing the principles of the Age of Enlightenment would arrive in Rome, offering to save its people from the standards enforced by papal rule. To them an absolute monarchy founded on religious principles was an anachronism tainted by bloodshed and superstition. Even before they arrived, some Romans embraced radical and increasingly secular values, engaging in scientific experimentation and new approaches to philosophy, often sponsored by the popes themselves. But when the pontiff was kidnapped and exiled by a foreign interloper, many Romans swiftly changed their minds. The old system could be coercive, cruel and rife with contradictions, but when modernity arrived in Rome it brought often uncompromising ideals that were enforced by a truly arbitrary power.

PART 4
WRESTLING WITH
MODERNITY

▷▷▷▷▷▷▷▷▷▷▷▷▷▷▷▷▷▷▷   ◁◁◁◁◁◁◁◁◁◁◁◁◁◁◁◁◁◁◁◁◁

Pope Pius XII with the people of Rome after the city was
bombed in 1943. (Alamy)

9

From the Sublime to the Pathetic: Eighteenth-century Rome

It was the summer of 1787 and the Sistine Chapel was empty. The murmuring groups of tourists that normally gathered within its high, coloured walls were nowhere to be seen. Many had taken carriages out to the hill towns outside of Rome, seeking good air and respite from the oppressive heat of the city. No such option was open to the guard at the chapel, who was facing down a very long day. The tips, like the tourists, would be thin on the ground. It was with eagerness, then, that he must have accepted the coins offered to him by a well-turned-out German in his late thirties, who handed over a sufficient tip to secure the complete aversion of the guard's eyes. His ears, however, could not be bought and would betray the men's tacit agreement as they detected the soft, grunting snores of the solitary German tourist who had settled himself down for a packed lunch followed by a 'siesta on the papal throne'.[1]

In that chapel, the great drama of Christian scripture played out in a painted sky, from those fortunate souls rescued by Noah when a deluge cleansed the sins of the earth to the creation of the first man, Adam, by a broad-chested, bearded God. Beneath them, now, was a German man, slumped and sleeping like Michelangelo's Noah, drunken after the flood. We might be shocked that anyone would have ventured to sit on the throne of the pope. That German visitor, Johann Wolfgang von Goethe, was certainly esteemed in his homeland, having earned nobility through his services in the government of the Grand Duchy of Saxe-Weimar Eisenach and some fame with *The Sorrows of Young Werther*, a tragic, semi-autobiographical novel on the agony of unrequited love. Goethe's mind and hand would go on to influence literature, political thought and philosophy across the continent of Europe. Nevertheless, such worldly acclamation could not earn him the seat at the heart of the Vatican complex that was deemed worthy of nobody but the pope.

Goethe saw things differently. For he was not Catholic nor even Lutheran, like his patron the Duke Karl August. In 1782 Goethe had declared himself 'not anti-Christian, nor un-Christian, but most decidedly non-Christian', defining his position with a radical ambiguity that would have scandalised the founders of the chapel in which he now sat.[2] Even in his own age, Goethe's beliefs placed him at the frontier of a change in which the majority of Europe was not yet involved. In Goethe's day, some men and women had begun to speak openly of religious toleration and even atheism, a term hitherto voiced only in insult and condemnation. After the Protestant Reformation, the continent had endured a century ravaged by religious wars. However, spiritual motivations gave way to territorial claims and Protestant and Catholic powers forged pragmatic alliances, marginalising the confessional divides that had initially sparked conflicts. By the mid-seventeenth century, notions of religious tribalism remained intact, but their practical and political impact was much diminished.

At first glance, Goethe's pithy revelation that he was 'non-Christian' might appear glib, but it stood on firm if relatively fresh philosophical ground laid by contemporary thinkers such as Jean-Jacques Rousseau. These philosophers of what would become known as the Age of Enlightenment unsettled the fundament on which Christianity had stood for so long, advancing interpretations of humanity that challenged key Christian doctrines such as Original Sin. Meanwhile in Europe the theories of earlier scientists such as Nicolaus Copernicus were now used to explain the material world with ever greater confidence and independence from the authorities of the Church.[3] For Goethe the past life of Christianity was nothing more than a 'hodgepodge of fallacy and violence'.[4]

The Reformation might have removed the authority of the pope from the lives of believers in some parts of Europe, but the sages of the Enlightenment posed a threat that was more fundamental yet. They threatened to discard the Christian assumptions and frameworks that had underpinned private lives and politics for centuries. Monarchs would be spooked; some lost their heads, even if large swathes of the old guard endured the challenge. In Rome, the popes survived but never fully recovered: layers of authority that had been accrued over centuries had been scrutinised and peeled away. In the eyes of many, the pontiff was exposed as an ugly obstacle on the path to a brave new world. In that world, power would be legitimised not in heaven but on the streets, and a papal throne would become a mere chair on which to take a nap.

—— ⳩ ⳨ ⳨ ——

It was not that men such as Goethe were uninterested in the pope. They visited the Sistine Chapel to see paintings that the poet Samuel Taylor Coleridge deemed the 'noblest productions of human genius' but the pontiffs themselves also held an allure.[5] On his arrival in Rome in 1786, Goethe had climbed the Quirinal Hill to see Pope Pius VI (1775–99) celebrate a public Mass at the papal palace. There, the non-believer experienced 'a strange feeling' to be 'under the same roof as the Vicar of Christ'.[6] In his account of the visit, he describes how he became 'seized by the curious wish that the Head of the Church would open his golden mouth'.[7] Superficially, Goethe's urges echoed those of a Baroque pilgrim: the notion that the pope was the mouthpiece of the divine appeared intact. In reality, however, Goethe fixated on the pontiff as a mere spectacle. Like the frescos of the Renaissance masters, the pope was a curiosity that could satisfy or disappoint. In the end, Pius' performance left Goethe cold: he left when he saw that the pontiff was 'merely moving from one side of the altar to the other and muttering just like any ordinary priest'.[8] For Goethe, Pius' claim to be Christ's representative on earth was neither here nor there. He had become an old man 'droning and tottering about'.[9]

On other occasions, the pope would deliver the experience that Goethe sought. In the spring after his nap on the papal throne, he returned to the Sistine Chapel for a 'novel spectacle'.[10] There the pope celebrated Mass with cardinals 'robed in violet' just like 'some paintings by Albrecht Dürer' that Goethe had seen the week before.[11] Unlike the dull show on the Quirinal, this Mass had value as an aesthetic experience. The religious element, however, would only unsettle Goethe, who knew 'the frescoes almost by heart' but now claimed that he 'hardly recognised the place'.[12] For Goethe a visit to the Sistine Chapel was no more religious than a tour of the British Museum.

In the preceding centuries, popes had laboured to make every corner of Rome a testament to the supreme truth and authority of the Catholic Church. Yet by Goethe's time many saw the Theatre of the World as nothing more than a stage set. In the sixteenth century, Catholic spectators such as the philosopher Michel de Montaigne had written admiringly of those preachers who decried Jewish dogma from the pulpit each Saturday. Soon, however, many in the crowd would look on the same scene with dispassionate curiosity. When the English writer John Evelyn visited Rome in 1645, he thought the preaching to Jews was pointless, and not only because the 'spitting, humming, coughing and motion' made it 'almost impossible they should hear a word'.[13] For Evelyn and other visitors to Rome, the Catholic religion and its ceremonies were little more than a diversion. By the time that William Makepeace Thackeray was writing his novel *The Newcomes* in the 1850s, he could lay out an entire itinerary of entertaining religious activities for his protagonists: 'the feast of Saint so and so' and on Wednesday 'music and vespers at the Sistine Chapel'.[14] Thursdays saw the pontiff's benediction of 'droves of donkeys', 'sheep, horses and what-not', to which 'flocks of English accordingly rush' as though they had heard the blast of 'the fireworks at Vauxhall'.[15] Thackeray claimed that in 'the ancient city of the Caesars' the 'august fanes of the popes, with their splendour and ceremony', were 'all mapped out for English diversion'.[16] Thackeray's comments were mocking, but popes would have been more horrified to discover that Evelyn placed the spectacles of the Jewish faith on a par with Catholic ceremony. His curiosity piqued by the invitation of a Jewish acquaintance, he would walk beyond Santissimà Trinita dei Pellegrini and into the ghetto, where he watched a swaddled infant being circumcised.[17]

The contemporary religions of Rome were not even the city's greatest lure, as Europeans were increasingly drawn to the city by its glorious ancient past.[18] The eighteenth century was the era that saw Edward Gibbon's *History of the Decline and Fall of the Roman Empire* (1776–89), a bold and sweeping account of Western civilisation waning from the year 98 to 1590. Gibbon heroised ancient Rome as the peak of human achievement and cited the rise of Christianity among the chief causes of its decay. Gibbon's thesis was not uncontroversial; in 1779 he was forced to defend his work with a printed 'Vindication'. Yet whether detractor or disciple, Gibbon's readership had their eyes fixed not on the papal city but on the ancient Rome of the Caesars. In the early nineteenth century, Charlotte Anne Eaton, a woman of mixed English and Scottish heritage, walked around the city noting Rome's 'awful ruins of its former greatness, the proud monuments of its early years of glory, the accumulated memorials of long ages of vicissitude'.[19] Mingling praise of ancient Rome with melancholic reflections on the present city, such descriptions recall the biting observations of Renaissance men such as Flavio Biondo. This is no coincidence. Circles such as Eaton's were steeped in the values of the 'Classical Education', a system of learning shaped by humanist principles and popular among the upper classes of the British Isles. In the chilly classrooms of England, young minds learnt the verses of Virgil and the acute, economic Latin of the Roman statesman Cicero. Arriving in the city in December 1816, Eaton saw Rome as the very embodiment of 'all that we have read, thought, admired and worshipped from our earliest years'.[20] Like the pilgrims of Baroque Rome, these students of the ancients saw the city as a uniquely powerful idea, but one that had nothing at all to do with the Catholic religion.

From the late seventeenth to the early nineteenth century, ancient Rome was deployed as a political and cultural tool, as men and women far from the city identified and borrowed its virtues for their own ends. After English nobles successfully persuaded William of Orange to invade and overthrow their loathed Catholic King James II in 1688, they sought to justify their coup with republican principles of civic duty and liberty.[21] Others drew on more specific ancient sources, calling on particular men of antiquity. In the mid-eighteenth century, the statesman and writer Lord Chesterfield penned letters to his son, imploring him to learn measure from Horace and correct speech from Cicero, and to build his character like a classical Roman building: 'a Corinthian edifice, upon a Tuscan foundation'.[22] For his own part, Chesterfield had the sculptor Joseph Wilton carve his portrait in the guise of 'an elder Cato', complete with Roman nose, short hair and a strong, bare chest.[23] That ancient Roman statesman was already a favourite in the British Isles. In 1713, the actor Barton Booth had secured his fame when he revived *Cato* on the boards of the Theatre Royal on London's Drury Lane. The play by Joseph Addison celebrated Cato's resilient civic virtue in the face of Julius Caesar's monarchical tyranny. The crowds roared; people talked. The parliamentary parties of England clamoured to identify themselves with the leading role. For many, including the political philosopher William Godwin, classical learning, personal conduct and political stability were inextricably intertwined and it was ancient Rome that offered 'the purest models of virtue' for a modern society about to 'sink into effeminacy and apathy'.[24]

Across the continent and beyond, classical learning from Rome had long been prioritised in the schools of the Jesuits, who had played a leading role in education since their foundation in 1540. Establishing the first ever free schools, Jesuit teachers admonished students that 'reading other authors one should be a critic' but 'in reading Cicero, a disciple'.[25] Their influence was sweeping. By the mid-eighteenth century, the Jesuits taught hundreds of thousands of students at more than 800 colleges, from Rome to Lima and Macao.[26] By this point, classical education had coloured public life all over Europe. In his *De l'Esprit de Lois* of 1748, the judge and political philosopher Montesquieu called upon French citizens to embody virtue as defined by the ancient Romans: 'the love of the laws and of the *patrie*'.[27] This was an endeavour that the author Louis-Sébastien Mercier endorsed. Re-shelving his volumes of Cicero, Sallust and Plutarch at the end of a day of study, he claimed that he found it 'painful to leave Rome, and to find one's self still a commoner of the rue des Noyers'.[28]

For such men, their learning could only be completed by experiencing the Eternal City first-hand. Even those who were not privileged with a classical education were carried to Rome on the waves of enthusiasm that came with new discoveries about its ancient past. In the Margraviate of Brandenburg in the early eighteenth century, a cobbler's son called Johann Winckelmann went to great pains to teach himself the ancient languages of Greek and Latin, alleviating the tedium of his impoverished existence with the words of the great philosophers and historians of the classical age. After many years of diligent study, Winckelmann's erudition – and conversion to Catholicism – won him the attention and patronage of influential figures such as Cardinal Alberico Archinto and the King of Poland, Augustus III.[29] He arrived in Rome in 1755 and dedicated the rest of his life to studying the material remains of pagan Greece and Italy. These labours culminated in the seminal *History of Ancient Art* (1764), sparked and strengthened by the discoveries of the construction workers whose spades had inadvertently hit the lost ancient city of Herculaneum and, a little later, Pompeii. Winckelmann's own work inspired others from the German lands to make the trip to Rome. Goethe himself had longed to meet Winckelmann when he returned to the north in 1768. That aspiration was frustrated by the Italian cook Francesco Arcangeli, who murdered Winckelmann at a hotel en route.

Goethe found his countryman's spirit alive and well when he arrived in Rome nearly two decades later. During the day Goethe and his companions examined antiquities across the city. After dinner, they longed for their landlady's loud '*felicissima notte!*', which heralded the arrival of the candlestick with which they illuminated the day's sketches and notes.[30] Sometimes they even brought fragments of the ancient city back up to their quarters. As Goethe recorded one day, they 'walked in the ruins of Nero's palace over fields of banked-up artichokes and could not resist the temptation to fill our pockets with tablets of granite, porphyry and marble which lay around in thousands'.[31]

— ೞ ೱ ೱ —

The more permanent residents of Rome also indulged in this mania for the city's long-lost past. In the eighteenth century, Romans such as Francesco Ficoroni studied its ruins with all of the enthusiasm of those on the Grand Tour. Digging in the Vigna Moroni, a patch of land at the start of the Appian Way, Ficoroni unearthed and documented the relics of his ancient forebears, from dice of metal and fossilised stone to the masks of tragic theatre.[32] Others in Rome sought to revive classical culture through immaterial means. On summer days from 1725, a group of men and women would gather to recite poetry in a theatre in the Bosco Parrasio, a lush garden atop the Janiculum Hill. In the winter, the group retreated to the Teatro degli Arcadi nearby at the Palazzo Salviati. Casting their minds back to the pastoral eclogues of ancient writers such as Virgil, this Academy of Arcadians aimed to purify Italian poetic literature of the ornament introduced in the age of the Baroque.

On 31 August 1776, they performed their most elaborate ceremony yet on the steps of the Capitoline Hill, crowning a poet known as Corilla Olimpica with laurels.[33] Born Maria Maddalena Morelli in 1727, Corilla was the only female poet to receive this illustrious ancient honour, bestowed on men such as Tarquato Tasso and Francesco Petrarch in previous centuries. A Florentine, by then nearly fifty, Corilla became impassioned when she performed, reeling off torrents of poetry on 'new, surprising and wondrous things' entirely improvised on the spot.[34] She dazzled the Dukes of Tuscany, the aristocrats of Rome and, in Pisa, the infamous romantic adventurer Casanova. Conjuring yet more classical imagery, he claimed that she appeared 'like Venus as painted by the ancients' and that she 'had only to fix her squinting eyes on a man and the conquest was complete'.[35] Facing the Academy of Arcadians in Rome, Corilla had endured a far more gruelling task. To secure her laurels, they demanded that she improvise poetry on themes from ancient philosophy to optics and light.[36] When the French author Germaine de Staël described the coronation of her heroine in the novel *Corinne* in 1807, some might have found its description of the event somewhat of a cliché. Lauded effusively as a woman of classical ideals, Corinne appears like a sage ancient Sybil as she is delivered to the Capitoline on a 'chariot built in the style of ancient Rome'.[37] Yet Staël merely treated her protagonist as Corilla had been when she ascended that ancient hill to receive her prize, even if the author denied that she had been directly inspired by the events of 1776.

These classicising scenes in Rome appeared picturesque, but on closer inspection less charming details emerge. The custodian general of the Academy, Gioacchino Pizzi, had organised Corilla's coronation after sundown, hoping – in vain – to spare her the taunts of those scandalised by her abandonment of her husband and child.[38] Elsewhere in the city the antiquarian ideals of Francesco Ficoroni were also touched by contemporary reality. To survive, the Roman worked as a *cicerone* (or cultured tour guide) cum art dealer, procuring souvenirs for English *milordi* on Grand Tours in Rome. As Ficoroni walked the streets with the teenager Thomas Coke (later Earl of Leicester) in the early 1770s, he pointed out possible mementos and commissioned art works on classical topics particularly suited to eighteenth-century tastes.[39] A painting of the rape of Lucretia later hung at Coke's ancestral home in Norfolk showed off his knowledge of Livy's account of the birth of republican Rome, as well as his support of the Whigs who had championed the parliamentary system in England.[40] Men such as Ficoroni also catered to tourists with less sophisticated tastes. Many wanted nothing more than a portrait of themselves looking wistful in front of a Roman ruin. Superb artists in the city, such as Pompeo Batoni, cashed in on such requests with extraordinary creative flair. When Batoni painted the Scotsman Colonel William Gordon in 1766, he draped the tartan of his regiment across his chest like a toga, placing him in front of a crumbling Colosseum and an idealised figure of Rome, complete with helmet, orb and laurels.

In portraits such as Batoni's Rome's past and present appear perfectly married, but many of Rome's visitors found it impossible to wed the two. Staël's Corinne might have represented the classical ideal of the city, yet Staël herself was full of disdain for present-day Rome. Anxious to appeal to a pro-Italian audience, her publisher had asked the author if *Corinne* (1807) was going to present a positive message about Italy or an argument against the country. He must have been mortified when Staël exclaimed: 'Against, Monsieur, against!' at the top of her voice.[41] Staël conceded that her book must show that she was 'paying due respect to Italy's beautiful sky, talking about the beautiful collections of pictures and sculpture it possesses, indicating the majestic ruins everybody has talked about'.[42] Beyond this, she claimed to be lost for what to 'say in favour of Italy', a country that she found to be 'without morals, without government, without policing' and 'where the only people with any energy are the brigands who infest the thoroughfares'.[43] For Staël the ideal of Rome was nothing more than an illusion: 'all you can see is a faded luxuriousness, where the palaces are in a progressive state of dilapidation'.[44] After just a week in the city, Goethe admitted to finding it 'a difficult and melancholy business ... separating the old Rome from the new'.[45]

For many, it was the popes who were to blame. It is somewhat ironic that it was an English Catholic priest – Father Richard Lassels – who coined the term 'Grand Tour' to describe those civilising trips into Rome's classical past. In the majority of the narratives left behind by Grand Tourists, the Church and pope of that city play a marginal and maligned part. A classicist by training, Lassels would guide several young Englishmen on trips around Italy in the late seventeenth century.[46] Despite his priestly vocation, these would not be the conversionary voyages of the Protestants who found themselves knocking at the doors of the Ospizio dei Convertendi (even if many foreigners in Rome continued to seek conversion for pious and pragmatic reasons).[47] In fact, Lassels' last charge, Lord Lumley, would go on to renounce his Catholic faith and become one of the 'Immortal Seven' who summoned William of Orange to depose the Catholic King James II in the Glorious Revolution of 1688. As an adult and a Protestant, Lumley might have joined the non-Catholic northerners who visited Rome to 'admire the past and to scorn the present'.[48]

In the eyes of many non-Catholics, the gilded, marbled Rome raised by early modern popes might as well have been entirely invisible. As Goethe put it, 'What the Barbarians left the builders of Modern Rome have destroyed.'[49] When Charlotte Eaton's carriage rattled under the Porta del Popolo and into the city, reminders of the Catholic Church swiftly dampened her excitement. Catching a glimpse of Santa Maria del Popolo, she saw a symbol of the 'existing debasement of Papal Rome.'[50] She quickly averted her gaze to the centre of the piazza and the soaring granite obelisk of Seti I, quarried for the Temple of Ra in Heliopolis, Egypt. The obelisk had been hauled to Rome by Emperor Augustus in 10 BC but it had been Pope Sixtus V (1585–90) who had ordered the architect Domenico Fontana to raise it in the square where Eaton's carriage now stood. He had done so to signal the triumph of Christianity and the papacy over the pagan rulers of both Egypt and Rome, as the inscription boasts. However, when Eaton set eyes on the obelisk this hard-won narrative evaporated. For her it remained a sign 'of the fallen greatness of Imperial Rome', an 'imperishable memorial of an older world'.[51]

Others were sharper yet in their critique of papal Rome. After dining with the Jesuits at the Venerable English College, both the philosopher Thomas Hobbes and the poet John Milton bitterly decried papal rule. Hobbes would dedicate an entire chapter of his *Leviathan* to the argument, while Milton's Pandaemonium, the home of the devil's tyrannical parliament, is hosted at a building readily identified as Saint Peter's.[52] For others, the papacy was enough to frighten them off Rome altogether. When young men from the Netherlands sought travel abroad to complete their education, they generally went to England, France and Switzerland.[53] In Protestant lands, sons who ventured to the land of the Caesars only worried their parents. Books such as *New Travels into Italy* (1691), written by the Protestant Huguenot François-Maximilien Misson, confirmed their very worst fears, painting a peninsula where pot-bellied monks sold fake relics, transforming religious buildings into nothing more than a 'lucrative bazaar'.[54] Tales of the Roman Inquisition inspired pure dread as Protestants learnt of the Englishmen whose Anglican beliefs had condemned them to backbreaking labour in the galleys at Naples. Some cheerier stories also made their way north, such as that of Fynes Morrison, who passed himself off as a French Catholic while studying in Rome for his research at Peterhouse, Cambridge.[55]

For many, then, Rome appeared as a place of clear divisions: ancient and modern, Protestant and Catholic, good and bad – one was forced to take a side. However, in the streets, taverns and homes of the city the boundaries were less distinct. Pragmatism prevailed and ideological hinterlands emerged as inquisitors met with fatigue and indifference from landlords and locals who were far too busy trying to earn a living to uncover the subterfuge of crafty travellers such as Fynes Morrison.[56] In many cases Romans were perfectly willing to overlook the particulars of tourists' religious backgrounds, as long as their services and expertise met with adequate financial reward.[57] Protestants visiting Rome also adopted more nuanced views, overlooking Catholic custodians to see religious sites as part of their own spiritual patrimony. The dividing lines between pagan and Christian Rome were also smudged. When the Anglican Fathers William Conybear and John Howson wrote about the extraordinary pyramidal mausoleum of the ancient magistrate Caius Cestius in the mid-nineteenth century, they lauded the monument as the 'only surviving witness of the martyrdom of St Paul'.[58] The land at the foot of the pyramid had been granted as a cemetery for non-Catholics in the decades after 1671, when inquisitors conceded that European lords need not be demeaned with a burial among prostitutes, thieves and suicides in the Muro Torto on the Pincian Hill. For the Holy Office, the 'quiet and sheltered nook' that would preserve the remains of John Keats and Percy Bysshe Shelley was unconsecrated ground.[59] But for those Protestant authors, the 'degenerate Italians' had erred – the land had been hallowed when Saint Paul looked upon it as he walked to his death.[60]

—— ⋘ ❧ ❧ ——

Despite the criticisms of visitors, papal hegemony in Rome remained an unrealised ideal as the absolute power of the popes butted up against conflicting jurisdictions, men keen to assert their privileges and private agreements that undermined an administration that had long been jumbled.[61] Papal rule still aimed to be absolute. The inquisitors pared down their investigations but their new remit targeted those who posed a substantial threat to the authority of the pontiff, such as the secret society of the Freemasons banned by Pope Clement XII (1730–40) in 1738.[62] By the eighteenth century, the papal regime had been shaped by measures that sought to centralise and professionalise the government of the popes. In 1692 the bull *Romanum decet pontificem* had prevented pontiffs from enriching their families, while the politicking of overly ambitious cardinals was diminished when permanent assemblies for various aspects of government were established.[63] Later pontiffs attacked factionalism by doubling the size of the college of cardinals, splintering it into far too many sects for any one to prove powerful.[64] Atop the hierarchy, standing next to the pope, was now his Secretary of State, a cardinal who acted as a sort of prime minister, governing foreign affairs, the Council of State, the armed forces and Rome's global diplomatic presence.[65] Even in the 1660s, his voice trumped that of the cardinal-nephew, a cardinal related to the pope who usually wielded supreme influence.[66] After 1646, the pope also elected the senator, figures traditionally associated with more democratic governments in Rome.[67] The governor, too, worked hand-in-glove with the pontiff as chief administrator, supreme judge and head of a police force.[68] When the governor made edicts in the pope's name they had full force in law; he effectively supplanted the magistrates of the Capitoline Hill. Beyond Rome, the *Buon Governo* administered the popes' provincial territories.[69] Within the city, the brief of the Apostolic Chamber illuminates the ubiquitous influence of the popes, handling the provision of grain, meat, oil, roads, prisons, archives and water supply, as well as the navigation and ports of Tiber.[70]

With a papal prince in charge, religion pervaded all. The popes even got themselves into the Romans' pockets, with coins graven with images of Jesus, Mary and the Church. When a hosteler received a coin inscribed with a motto, the pope could speak to him even more directly. Clutching a precious gold sequin, a merchant would be reminded that, 'being as dirt' money was 'the root of all evil'.[71] Even change of less value bore moral advice of the highest worth: 'covet not silver and gold'.[72] The popes were far from alone in their fusion of religion and public life and governance, with other absolute monarchs such as Charles I of England and Louis XVI of France famously claiming to rule by divine right bestowed upon them by God. However, the popes were exceptional in their claims to be God's vicar on earth, with dominion over souls as well as land and earthly power.

For tourists the reach of papal power could feel stifling. Digging for souvenirs, they were thwarted by pontiffs' unwillingness to share. By the early nineteenth century, the pope would not 'allow any piece of antiquity, however small, to be carried out of Rome'.[73] 'Not a leg of an old statue, nor a scrap of a *basso relievo*, nor a broken-headed bust' would be taxed abroad.[74] Such laws frustrated the romantic ambitions of grand tourists eager to fill their homes with traces of a more august age, but the city and its popes desperately needed money. On the whole, the economy of the Papal States was fragmented and largely agricultural.[75] Manufacture was limited to the hands of artisans, craftsmen and carpenters whose market was restricted by a river ill-suited to heavy trade with the outside world. Where money was present in the city it sat in government bonds, land or the treasure chests of religious institutions, awaiting maintenance bills and charitable costs. The nobility generally invested in the expansion of their bricks and mortar, while big spenders among their lower and middling ranks were thin on the ground. The city's poor, however, were abundant and in many cases could not afford the roof over their heads. A couple of rooms with a store would cost around twelve *scudi* annually, which could be earned by a low-ranking clerk or a spinner working flat out.[76] Across the city, rooms were filled with individuals who had no relation to one another: immigrants, manual labourers and widows united by onerous circumstance. Tempered by benevolence or realism, some landlords did not even bother to demand all of what they were owed, lest they end up with no tenants at all.[77]

Romans had risen up in anger in the past, so why not protest their suffering now? The population was substantial, at 149,447 in 1700 and by 1794 some 166,948.[78] In 1775 the French author and geographer Gabriel-Francois Coyer claimed that the pope's reign was secure so long as he was 'keeping bread at a constant price and holding down taxes'.[79] The latter was certainly achieved, as the poorest paid absolutely nothing. For a long time, the only direct levies fell on those who owned property or ground corn.[80] When ill-fated Italian wars hit the papal coffers in the seventeenth century, some taxes on consumption had crept in on products such as wine. Overall, however, the burden was a quarter of that on men and women in Louis XIV's France, keeping bread riots, the heralds of doom for absolute monarchs elsewhere, carefully at bay. Famine would strike in the 1760s but, generally, the poorest enjoyed a better diet under paternalistic popes than they would during periods of greater economic liberalism in the nineteenth century.[81] The streets near Piazza Colonna were pervaded by the smell of cooking cabbages, roasting coffee and tripe prepared nearby. Nasty punishments awaited sellers who did not stick to regulations on price and quality, with sentences of back-breaking galley service meted out to butchers who sold off beef liver as calves'.[82] Bakers who misled customers on bread suffered the *strappado,* their feet tied to a rope before they were dropped from some height. Papal price-fixing kept people fed but it had its drawbacks. In 1771, the author Alessandro Verri looked on Rome's markets despondently: 'Tell me something we are not short of. All prices are fixed and are now too low, so that no one wants to sell.'[83]

Dissent was abated but the toll on papal finances was high. In 1773, Clement XIV (1769–74) had to borrow one million crowns to ensure that a terrible harvest did not elevate the price of bread. Loath to tax their people, the popes used novel mechanisms to stabilise public and personal finance. Crowned with an ornate bell and clock, the sweeping cream palazzo of the Monte di Pietà on via del Pellegrino does not look like your average pawn shop, yet from 1539, it was visited by poor Romans eager to exchange clothing, jewellery and plate for cash.[84] If the owners did not return the value in two years, the objects could be sold by the papal institution. It also offered shares with attractive rates of interest that were guaranteed.[85] The model was not unique to Rome but soon became a key part of the city's economic life, completely destroying the Jewish banks there.[86]

Early in the eighteenth century, the popes adopted a more thrilling means of raising revenue: a lottery for all Romans run by the Church. Each Saturday atop the sweeping, broad staircase on the Capitoline Hill, a stage, swathed in velvet, would be erected for the grand draw. Standing proudly on immense marble limbs, the horse tamers that flank the top of the steps looked down onto a silver urn holding ninety numbered ivory balls.[87] The crowd below encompassed nobles, their servants and even cardinals. All waited in anticipation as an orphan, cloaked in white, reached into the urn to draw each ball. The Romans loved the lottery for the very same reasons that we do. When a poor old woman asked a friar to predict some winning numbers, she balked at his suggestion that she spend her money on bread and wine instead. 'Forgive me but when the bread and wine are gone hunger and thirst will soon come back; with a ticket in my pocket I am rich until Saturday.'[88] When Clement XII sanctioned the weekly draw in December 1731, he knew that he was tapping into a guaranteed stream of income.[89] This was, however, a distinct shift in papal policy. Privately run lotteries had been outlawed during the previous pontificate; the U-turn came when capital left the city along with the draws. Within six years of its return, the lottery had delivered, providing a new outlet for Catholic charity and raising nearly two million *scudi*. Its average yearly income was around two thirds of the amount that Rome collected in import tariffs annually.[90] Each week ninety of Rome's most destitute girls were given tickets for free. If they scored five winning numbers they would receive a dowry of fifty *scudi*.

The raucous crowd that gathered each Saturday night at the Capitoline during Clement XII's reign stood in stark contrast to the sombre assembly that he had faced on his election in 1730. A pious and somewhat dour administrator in his late seventies, the Tuscan noble had been greeted by just four to six cries of acclamation from the crowd of 4,000 who had gathered outside Saint Peter's to discover the identity of their new pope. If Clement had felt dejected that day, he would feel much worse by the end of his pontificate when measures such as the lottery failed to prevent a deficit of nearly eleven per cent of the total papal revenue.[91] The pontiff admitted that he had gone from being 'a wealthy *abate* [abbot], a comfortably off bishop [and] a poor cardinal' to 'a ruined pope'.[92] Even Clement's successor, Benedict XIV (1740–58), would scorn his financial legacy. Sacking servants and reducing the quality and amount of food and drink consumed at the Vatican, Benedict called for every department to tighten its belt. In a private missive to a good friend, Innocenzo Storani, in 1751, Benedict complained that such strictures would have been unnecessary had Clement shown greater restraint.[93] Frugality had hardly been evidenced in the sumptuous Neo-Classical facade that he had added to San Giovanni in Laterano, nor in his commission of the enormous and outrageously ornamental Trevi Fountain. That said, blame might have been more deservedly placed on his predecessor, Benedict XIII (1724–30), who had refused to raise taxes while blithely overlooking the financial abuses of the nefarious Cardinal Niccolò Coscia, who shrank the pontiff's healthy surplus of 277,342 *scudi* a year to a deficit of 120,000.[94]

— ෬ ෨ ෨ —

The popes' position beyond the city walls was also in peril. Over the course of the eighteenth century most of the men elected pope had never even left the Papal States.[95] The demise of the popes' global influence might surprise us, given their vigorous assertion of supremacy in the sixteenth and early seventeenth centuries. When the Reformation struck, the popes had redoubled efforts to influence those who remained loyal to Rome. In 1564, the edicts of the Council of Trent had been confirmed by Pope Pius IV (1559–65) and promulgated across Catholic lands.[96] Inaugurated by Paul III (1534–49) in 1545 in response to calls for reform from figures such as Luther, the council's discussions aimed to define and affirm orthodox Catholic doctrine and practice. By the mid-seventeenth century, however, many of its edicts remained unenforced, as bishops tried to interpret and apply decrees that proved patchy and vague.[97] They also ran up against indolent clerics, preoccupied laity and royals and nobles with vested interests in retaining the status quo. Even ostensibly devout Catholic rulers had resisted papal control when it clashed with the realpolitik. When King Philip II of Spain had ordered his regent, Margaret of Parma, to use the sword to impose the rulings of Trent in his Dutch territories he had done so to enforce his own authority more ruthlessly in his lands.[98] As the papal ambassador to France said in 1589: 'The King of Spain, as a temporal sovereign is anxious above all to safeguard and to increase his dominions … The preservation of the Catholic religion which is the principal aim of the Pope is only a pretext for His Majesty.'[99]

In the seventeenth century, shifts in political perspective had further undermined Rome's influence. Sixteenth-century leaders might have been cynical at times, but, ultimately, religious divisions had still coloured their political conflicts. As long as acceptance or rejection of Roman precepts marked out political dividing lines, the popes had a voice on the international stage. In 1648, however, Innocent X (1644–55) found himself gagged, as the great powers of Europe signed the Treaty of Westphalia without involving him. This was a peace to end the Thirty Years War, which had entangled powers from across the continent, from Sweden, Poland, France, Austria and Spain. In one reading, events unfolded along familiar lines. The spark for the conflict appeared to be religious: Protestantism in the empire had breached the boundaries agreed in the Peace of Augsburg in 1555. In reality, however, the situation was far more complex. The issue of religious difference had intertwined with concerns about political power and territorial sovereignty, igniting revolts in the Holy Roman Empire and power struggles between Catholic dynasties such as Bourbon France and the Habsburgs who ruled Austria and, at that time, Spain.[100] Political pragmatism had trumped religious purity in the past, but when the Catholic monarchs of France teamed up with the staunchly Lutheran King Gustavus Adolphus of Sweden, they cast off any premise of protecting of the faith. When peace was settled in 1648 and the pope refused to negotiate with 'heretics', the discussion simply proceeded without him.

Pope Innocent was outraged and made a vehement, legal protest. In the bull *Zelo domus Dei* he decried the Treaty of Westphalia as 'void, null, unjust' and devoid of any real legal power.[101] He declared all articles that undermined the power and possessions of the Church illegal.[102] Few, it seems, heeded his complaint. The trend was to continue in the early eighteenth century when the powers of Europe drew up battle lines in the dispute over the Polish throne. Seeing the Catholic princes as feuding sons of his Church, Clement XII offered to mediate between the Habsburgs and their enemies the Bourbons, who by then ruled both France and Spain.[103] The overture was flatly refused. With peace and sovereignty on the line, secular leaders – and even some papal diplomats – did not want interference from popes who ranked security below religious purity and the supremacy of the Catholic Church.[104]

By the mid-eighteenth century, popes such as Benedict XIV were shoring up papal power by other means. He took stricter control over the celebration of Catholic liturgy around the world, as well as the processes through which men and women were declared to be saints.[105] Yet even in matters of faith and morality, the popes were sometimes forced to dance to the princes' tune, as worldly leaders clambered for ever more authority over religious matters in their own lands. For many, to pursue sovereignty meant to corrode Roman influence; they were Catholic leaders but they would not cede an inch of authority, even to the pope. As so often in the history of Rome, the impact of global trends reverberated in the city. Every Maundy Thursday for centuries, popes had tossed a flaming torch from the loggia of Saint Peter's Basilica to herald the publication of the bull *In Coena Domini*. Dictating the decree each year, a leading cardinal would reel off an extensive list of crimes proscribed by the Church and forgiven only by the pope. The tradition ceased permanently after the election of Clement XIV in 1769, decried as an imposition of foreign law in the sovereign territories of Europe.[106]

By 1771, the Jesuits who had set out from Rome to save souls around the world had been expelled from Portugal, France, Spain and their overseas dominions.[107] A malignant storm of religious and political controversies surrounded the order, from bitter disputes with the pessimistic theologians of the Jansenist movement to their refusal to absolve the mistress of King Louis XV, Madame de Pompadour.[108] In the wake of the tempest, the Jesuits found themselves banished, while their land and property was seized by the state. The worldwide mission celebrated in the vivid paintwork of Pozzo at Sant'Ignazio was over, its agents consigned to exile, imprisonment or death on arduous journeys to find a new home. For major powers such as France and Spain even this was not enough. As many former Jesuits reached the safety of the Papal States, Clement XIV announced that the order should be outlawed entirely.[109] With the brief *Dominus ac Redemptor noster* of 1773, the pope solemnly pronounced that the 'Company of Jesus can no longer produce those abundant fruits' for which it had been founded.[110] Sitting in Rome diminished and sidelined by shifting political priorities, the pope found himself declaring that great agent of global Catholic influence 'forever extinguished and suppressed'.

——— ❦ ❧ ❧ ———

Politically weakened, financially diminished, for many, papal Rome would stand as a bastion of culture and learning alone. Here, at least, popes often judged the mood perfectly. They created institutions that enticed men and women of all political and confessional stripes. Even in the seventeenth century, Alexander VII had sought to restore Rome to her 'ancient splendour', attracting the cultivated visitor as well as the potential convert.[111] When Clement XI (1700–21) handed over five ancient Egyptian vases to the collection of antiquities on the Capitoline he believed the display could only bolster reverence for the papacy.[112] He would have been thrilled to see Clement XIV throw open the doors to the Vatican's own collections in 1771. In the next pontificate, Pius VI would enlarge this *Museum Clementinum* with the freshly excavated busts, *bassi relievi* and figures denied to Grand Tourists. By 1784, the *Museum Pium Clementinum* comprised a world-leading collection of ancient art and remains the heart of the Vatican Museums.[113] In 1794, the Spanish Grand Tourist Leandro Fernández de Moratín marvelled at the generosity with which the galleries were run: 'open to the public daily, and for the six *reales* that one pays on entering, anyone can remain inside as long as he wishes'.[114] That such efforts would enhance the reputation of the popes was not left to chance, for these popes were shoring up the symbols of an old world that was under threat.[115] Engaging great artists such as Antonio Canova to maintain the ancient monuments along the Appian Way, Pius VI ensured they were dotted with inscriptions lauding his efforts.[116]

Popes also supported learning beyond the Vatican Walls, embracing the early dawn of what would become known as the Scientific Revolution. Geographically, the phenomenon was broad. From 1666, a government-funded Academy of Sciences met in the library of the King of France, while in England Isaac Newton experimented with gravity at the University of Cambridge and Gresham College hosted innovative thinkers such as the first modern chemist Robert Boyle. Although Boyle had gone to Florence to learn of the latest experiments in astronomical science, Rome had been a hotbed of experimentation in medicine and surgery since the fifteenth century. At hospitals such as Santo Spirito in Sassia, lecturers in practical medicine were paid five times the salary of those who taught maths.[117] In 1603, the Accademia dei Lincei 'or lynx-eyed' was founded for cutting-edge observational science. Some popes supported these new developments directly. Visiting Rome for six weeks in 1624, the Pisan astronomer Galileo Galilei had enjoyed weekly audiences with Urban VIII (1623–44).[118] Galileo dedicated *The Assayer* to the pope, a work that argued that the world should be understood through scientific means rather than medieval philosophy. Urban himself believed that one risked limiting the power of God with arguments that he had only created one world.[119] When Urban had become pope in 1623, Francesco Stelluti, a member of the Lincei, had written to Galileo declaring 'we are about to have supreme patronage'.[120]

Well into the eighteenth century, pontiffs sponsored the expansion of scientific knowledge. Even the frugal Benedict XIV founded new professorships in experimental science at Rome's university, the Sapienza. The same pope personally sponsored individuals such as Laura Bassi Veratti, whose work in fields such as Newtonian mechanics made her one of the first women ever to earn a doctorate and, eventually, the first salaried female professor.[121] With such clear papal approval for experimentation, the salons of cardinals and other prelates soon followed suit. Around 1707, Cardinal Alessandro Albani threw open his lavish rooms at the Quirinal Palace in the name of science. There, a young monk swathed in the black hood and white habit of the Celestine order assembled equipment to test Newton's optical theories.[122] Scientific endeavours had become so valued in Rome that academies were established as a means of cementing social status. Monsignor Giovanni Giustino Ciampini passed his days drafting bulls and decrees at the Vatican, but when he finished work he gathered a scientific academy in his lodgings behind the church of Sant'Agnese on Piazza Navona. From 1679, this Accademia Fisico-Matematica met every weeknight except Wednesdays and Fridays. Despite this apparent enthusiasm, Ciampini was far from a dutiful son of science, having begun his studies with the archaeology of the early Christian Church. Nor was he a particularly devoted son to his parents, his elder brother Pietro accusing him of caring only about the 'acquisition of fame'.[123] At his academy in Rome, the younger Ciampini frequently diverted the discussion to carriages – his personal obsession – and appeared most excited by the fact that his home had become a 'Temple of the muses'.[124]

But scientific learning did not always inspire delight in papal Rome. Studying in his quiet cell at Sant'Eusebio, the monk who had experimented for Cardinal Albani would become perturbed. Celestino Galliani had devoted himself to evidence-based research in the scientific realm, now he wanted to pursue a rational, evidence-based approach to all his studies – including those of Holy Scripture. Here the monk sat on the shoulders of late seventeenth-century thinkers such as Baruch Spinoza, a Jewish philosopher from the Netherlands who had concluded that we should be able to understand anything that truly exists through reason and evidence, with no need to reference outside concepts or authority. In seventeenth and eighteenth-century societies this was quite radical. Spinoza's deductions only appeared to justify the scandal: he concluded that texts traditionally attributed to the prophet Moses in the Old Testament came from entirely different hands.[125] Undermining centuries of rabbinic teaching, at the tender age of twenty-three, Spinoza was labelled a pronouncer of 'abominable heresies' and expelled from the Jewish community of Amsterdam.[126] Sitting in Rome half a century later, Galliani inched ever closer to this world of rational, empirical thought. In Rome and beyond, this was new and dangerous territory, where reason and evidence took their place alongside Scripture and Church as legitimate sources of truth.

In a Church where the authority of the popes and the Bible was accepted as supreme, this was an unsettling and sometimes incendiary development. It was on these grounds that Urban VIII had ordered his old interlocutor Galileo to see out the remainder of his life under house arrest, 'vehemently suspected of heresy'.[127] Galileo believed that the movement of rushing and receding oceans over the course of a day proved that Nicolaus Copernicus had been correct to suggest that the earth moved around the sun. Copernicus had died in Poland in 1543, but in Rome in 1616 the inquisition had condemned his theory as 'foolish and absurd in philosophy, and formally heretical since it explicitly contradicts in many places the sense of Holy Scripture'.[128] Galileo was playing with fire, though the pope himself had given him a false sense of security. Even after the condemnation of Copernicus, Urban had suggested that it was perfectly possible to discuss and even test such controversial theories.[129] The problem arose when a text published by Galileo in 1632 seemed to argue for Copernicus' cause and mock the pope, proposing Urban's own ideas through the mouth of a buffoon called 'Simplicius'. Back in 1616, Cardinal Roberto Bellarmino had warned Galileo not to teach on the movement of the earth. For Bellarmino, Copernicus' theory could never be defended without tangible evidence: 'a true physical demonstration that the sun does not circle the earth'.[130]

At the time of his trial, Galileo had no such proof. His conclusion was, however, entirely correct. It is for this reason that the 'Galileo affair' is frequently cited as a salutary tale of the Catholic Church's wilful ignorance of modern science. Look a little closer, however, and there is more nuance to the picture: Galileo's fate reflects a Rome where the Church had embraced science but then recoiled at its implications, as the rise of new means of interpretation and understanding jarred with centuries-old systems for grasping and governing the known world. Bellarmino wanted tangible evidence, like a scientist. In the meantime, however, the authority and teachings of the Church were always assumed to be supreme. The Galileo case may represent an injustice, but it is also a snapshot of Papal Rome beginning to engage with a world in radical flux.

—— ଔ ଅ ଅ ——

By the end of the eighteenth century, that world had arrived in Rome demanding recognition from the popes. In France, there had been a revolution, sparked by food shortages and an unjust and inefficient economy. It had been given form and justification by Enlightenment philosophers who championed reason and utility above traditional authorities. Political unrest had begun to simmer in Paris in the spring of 1789. By summer, the decapitated head of the Minister of Finance was on a spike, his mouth filled with faeces, grass and hay. By 1793, the king and queen were also dead. France was now ruled by a National Convention. Soon, one of its ambassadors was on his way to Rome.

Facing a consistory of his cardinals, Pius VI denounced the execution of the French royals as nothing more than a wicked murder. Meanwhile, the gates of Rome flew open for terrified relatives of the king. Pius also welcomed some 5,000 French priests fleeing the increasingly violent and secular regime.[131] The Roman press recoiled at scenes in France that could only 'make humanity shudder'.[132] The papers were heavily censored, but arguments made in print were soon echoed on the streets. When the National Convention sent the former journalist Nicholas Hugou de Basseville as a representative to the Holy See, it seemed that the people would solve the problem for the pope. When Pius refused him an audience, the outlandish Basseville took his cause directly to the Romans, pronouncing himself protector of the city's 'Jacobins' and suggesting that the French might also liberate the people of Rome. He also took the lilies of old France from above the door of the embassy, supplanting them with lady liberty herself. After a banquet in January 1793, Basseville hopped into a carriage draped in the tricolour flag and took to the busy via del Corso with his wife, child and fellow Frenchman Charles de la Flotte. Basseville soon discovered that Romans who did not want liberation. In a sea of stones, fists and musket shots a barber took his razor and cut the diplomat's throat.[133] Clamouring for calm, the pope sent his personal physician to tend to the dying man. Meanwhile, the Romans were impenitent, calling out 'Long live the pope!' and 'Death to the French!' and publishing a celebratory poem called the *Bassviliade*.[134]

They did not know it at the time but, inadvertently, the Romans had ushered revolution into their city. From the north of Italy, the voice of the hubristic young general Napoleon Bonaparte cried out for vengeance. By 1797, his army had swept down to Foligno, grazing the borders of the Papal States and cornering the pope. Confident of the inevitability of the revolution, Napoleon did not even bother to conquer Rome. Instead he despoiled the city through the Treaty of Tolentino, an agreement that denuded Pius of 32,700,000 francs in addition to the millions demanded through an earlier armistice.[135] It also stripped the pope of hundreds of books, manuscripts and works of art, as well as the states of Ancona, Bologna, Ferrara and the entire region of Romagna.[136] Now Pius himself went to the Monte di Pietà for an interest-free loan.[137]

Brushing off calls from the French government (by that time two councils governed by a Directory) to depose Pius, Napoleon predicted that: 'the old machine will fall apart by itself'.[138] In the end, he would force the change, though, once again, the Roman people played their part. It began in December 1797 when a small group of Romans cried out for equality and liberty in the streets of Trastevere.[139] It had been some years since Basseville's assassination, but many in Rome were still inimical to revolution. Chased through the streets flanking the River Tiber, the would-be revolutionaries sought shelter at the Palazzo Corsini. In the humiliations of Tolentino, that vast pink pleasure palace had been transformed into a French embassy and a magnificent home for Napoleon's younger brother, Joseph Bonaparte. Roused from his dinner, Joseph now stepped out into a storm of violence. This time it was his colleague Léonard Duphot who would lose his life. The papal troops who guarded the palace would shoulder the blame. This time, the French would not leave revolution in Rome to chance.

On 15 February 1798, the pope was at Saint Peter's celebrating the twenty-third anniversary of his election. As the polyphonous voices intoning the *Te Deum* resonated in the vault of the basilica, French sympathisers were at the Roman Forum, ceremoniously erecting a

Liberty Tree. The act echoed recent events in revolutionary France and the stories of ancient Rome, recalling the fig tree where Romulus and Remus had sheltered to suckle from the She-Wolf.[140] In the months to come, French forces stormed the public buildings and churches of the city, cleansing or repurposing symbols of the old regime. At the Jesuit church of Il Gesù at the foot of the Capitoline Hill, Pierre Gros' glittering statue of Loyola was melted down like scrap. Meanwhile, other symbols of the city were lionised. French revolutionaries had already adopted the classical Roman fasces and Phrygian cap.[141] Later, the ancient architecture of city would be redeployed in Paris with grandiose monuments such as the Arc du Triomphe.

The French revolutionaries' vision of Rome shared much with that of the purists of the Grand Tour. In the city they would echo and intensify the tourists' disdain for papal Rome. Less than a week after his anniversary celebrations, Pius was a pregnant sign of the *ancien régime*, lying prostrate in front of a crucifix in his chapel as the footsteps of the French Commissioner Haller approached. Haller had come to take the pope from his See. For Pius, this was senseless: as successor of Peter, his fate was tied to that of Rome. When the pope begged to at least die in Rome, Haller's response reflected an entirely different view of the city and its pontiff. 'You can die anywhere', he apparently told the eighty-year-old Pius, before bundling him into a carriage.[142] In the face of Enlightened values, the symbolism of the pope and papal Rome disintegrated. As the carriage holding Pius sped away from the city, it might have seemed as though the Rome of the popes had come to a bleak and abrupt end. In reality, the kidnap of the pope only inaugurated a long and intense stand-off between the Holy See and the modern world.

Non possumus: *Popes of Rome in the Age of Revolutions*

It was 1870 and concerns about the Roman pontiff had reached the boulevards of Paris. For nearly twenty-five years, Pius IX (1846–78) had occupied Peter's throne as a resolute custodian of papal sovereignty. As calls for radical change hailed down on him, he would emerge as the unyielding pope of *non possumus:* 'we cannot'. Pius would be the third pontiff within a century to face down revolution and refuse to surrender an inch of Petrine authority. To some, Pius was an unassailable bastion, to others an immovable barricade. Now, word arrived in Paris that he might not have enough undergarments to maintain his personal comfort.

Perturbed by the news, a woman dispatched a package to Rome.[1] The woman was obviously a charitable soul, but she was far from the only person worried about the pope. Since 20 September 1870, Pius IX had proclaimed to the world that he was a prisoner in the Vatican. Two of his recent predecessors – Pius VI (1775–99) and Pius VII (1800–23) – had been taken as hostages of revolution. When Pius IX was cornered by the forces of Italy, he retreated into the Vatican Palace. At that time, the nation of Italy was less than a decade old. From Lombardy to Naples, almost all the Italian states had been conquered and merged into a kingdom by 1861, including the Papal States of Romagna and Le Marche.[2] Previously governed by a motley group of dukes, princes and kings, now all were ruled by the swashbuckling and audaciously moustached King Vittorio Emanuele II

(1861–78), formerly King of Sardinia-Piedmont. That state had ruled the north-western corner of Italy and the island of Sardinia before its troops stretched their reach down the boot of Italy. In 1866, the Austrian forces who occupied the Veneto finally marched into the distance. Only in Rome did the old rule persist in the papacy – a glaring anachronism for the new Italian nation.

Rome was *caput mundi,* the centre of Italy's great ancient empire. The nation might have been declared in 1861, but nationalist forces could not rest until they ruled over Rome. Without Rome, the process of unification, known as the Risorgimento or 'Rising Again', would remain incomplete.[3] For nearly a decade, the borders of the Papal States were attacked and redrawn by Italian troops bolstered by the men of Giuseppe Garibaldi, a doughty and charismatic revolutionary whose vision for a united Italy was apparently sparked by a chance meeting on a ship full of oranges destined for Russia.[4] As bombs menaced the walls of Saint Peter's Basilica on the morning of 20 September 1870, even Pius had to admit that papal fortunes had turned. Across the city, anthems, rumours and tricolour flags filled the air, while the footfall of the new Italian guard resounded in the streets. On the pope's orders, officials scuttled up more than 500 steps within the dome of the basilica. The white flag billowing over Saint Peter's must have seemed an inadequate herald for the demise of some fifteen centuries of papal rule.

Pacing into the Borgo, men and women were eager to discover what was happening beyond the walls of the palace at Saint Peter's. Some claimed that Pius was enchained like a beast. One enterprising man sold straw apparently plucked from the imprisoned pope's bed.[5] The Italian forces, meanwhile, insisted that they were only there to protect the pope.[6] Enraged at the assault on their sovereign pontiff, the city's nobles commanded their servants to bolt the front doors. The façades of the palaces of families such as the Massimo, Sacchetti and Lancelotti would remain in this mournful protest for decades to come.[7] At the pope's palace on the Quirinal Hill, a faithful guard refused to surrender the keys.[8] In some corners of the city, the strange new reality was slower to arrive. On the Capitoline, behind a barricade of mattresses, a residual cluster of the papal army of Zouaves clutched their weapons still awaiting their order to stand down.[9]

For these young soldiers, Rome was the land of the popes and the seat of their Holy Mother Church. In a matter of hours, it had been declared a foreign land. Many of the Zouaves had made long journeys from the Netherlands, the British Isles and the Americas to defend the Patrimony of Peter, and Pius himself, with their blood.[10] Well beyond these modern-day military martyrs, Pius IX was beloved as a leader, even before he was shut behind the palace walls. Across the states of Italy and beyond, his serene countenance beamed out from coloured scarves, tiepins and cigarette cases. In Turin, the shop of Signor Riccardi sold a fizzy drink named after Pius IX.[11] The advertisement delighted in the fact that, when poured, the beverage took on the pope's colours – yellow and white. Even its flavours of cinnamon and almonds would remind consumers of pope's achievements in the Papal States.[12]

In earlier centuries, Catholics around the world might have struggled to name the pontiff. News of his election, actions or death could take some months to arrive. Yet in these first decades of late modernity, photography, mass production and the rapid expansion of cheap printed media meant that the person of the pope could feel truly distinct and ubiquitous.[13] In the 1800s, the popes became icons on whom the faithful could pin their hopes, concerns and disdain. We need only look to Pasquino's barbs to see that Romans had long viewed their papal rulers as individuals. But even in the See of Peter, the first popes of modernity took on a heightened status. The spotlight had already shone more brightly on popes such as Pius VI at the turn of the century, as they paid a steep personal price for their resolute resistance to revolutionary tides. By the time that Pius IX took to the papal throne in 1846, the sea of change was an overwhelming force. In the eyes of many Romans, their entire future rested on the character and intentions of the pope. By the end of the century, all eyes were fixed on the area around Saint Peter's. For the pope, it was all that he had left. There, Pius locked the doors and embraced his role as totem of the old world, refusing to acknowledge the young nation of Italy with a single footstep on Roman soil.

— ෨ ෨ ෨ —

Less than a hundred years earlier, in the summer of 1799, Pius VI could not have felt much like an icon. As night turned to morning on 29 August, it seemed like all was lost. As his eighty-two-year-old frame lay on a bed in Valence, south-eastern France, his exhausted lungs heaved out their final laboured breaths. At 1.30am the pontiff died, still a prisoner some 900 kilometres from Rome. In the wake of his kidnapping the previous year, his Apostolic Palaces had been seized by the French, but the prefect of of those palaces, Giuseppe Maria Spina, remained at the pope's side.[14] Echoing the Roman ceremonies of the *sede vacante*, Spina now solemnly removed Pius' fisherman's ring. As Pius' body was embalmed, little evidence of his high office remained. The pope's few shabby clothes would soon be claimed as the property of the French nation, and inside a lead pipe would be secreted an inscription lauding the pope's endurance and strength that was penned by Father Joseph Marotti, the secretary Pius had hired just a few hours before he was taken from Rome.[15]

For six months Pius lay un-interred in Valence, as Spina and his entourage begged the French revolutionary government to repatriate the pope. As far as they were concerned Citizen Braschi, as they called the dead pope, could have a secular funeral in France.[16] His coffin would be accompanied by a simple epitaph: 'Body of Pius VI, Sovereign Pontiff. Pray for him'. Under no circumstances, however, would the French return him to Rome. For the enemies of the deceased pontiff, he was still a powerful symbol. Having taken the city in February 1798, French forces were working hard to recast Rome as a modern, secular republic. In this city, there would be no pope – dead or alive.

Only a political coup in Paris could break the impasse. This came in early November when the brothers Napoleon and Lucien Bonaparte misled and intimidated the French government of the Directory into extinction. By that time, Napoleon had won popular adoration and political influence with a streak of military successes on the continent. Leading a failing campaign in Egypt in 1798, a less hubristic man might have thought that his star was beginning to wane. With characteristic pomposity, Napoleon only saw opportunity. Looking westwards to a France torn apart by political division and overseen by a weak government, he left his troops behind him in Egypt and made for Paris, bent on seizing power.[17] By December, Napoleon and his allies had drawn up a new constitution, which was then re-written by Napoleon alone. As First Consul he reconstructed the government of France, placing himself at the top as the *de facto* dictator.

As he did so, the fortunes of the dead pope were also transformed. His corpse was now in the custody of a ruler who saw papal power not as something to be crushed, but rather used as a political tool. On New Year's Eve 1799, Napoleon decreed that Pius VI should be 'buried with the honours usual to persons of his rank', 'in accordance with the dignity of the French nation'.[18] For Napoleon, to honour the pope was to honour his own regime. Pius would be buried in the Catholic manner in consecrated ground in Valence. He would not rest there for long, for in 1801 Napoleon decided to dig him up and bury him in Rome. Once again, he did so not for the pope but for his own ends: Napoleon was striking a deal with the new pontiff, Pius VII, whom he would also restore to Saint Peter's See.

On 3 July 1800, Pius VII arrived in Rome and headed straight for the basilica of Saint Peter's. Standing in the warm light of its gold and marble interiors, he faced the High Altar and dropped to his knees. There, the pope adored the Blessed Sacrament as the choir sang out the motet *Tu es Petrus*, echoing the words of Jesus when he told Peter that he would be the rock on which he built his church.[19] After piety came the people; Pius mounted a carriage drawn by eight horses. Progressing to the Piazza di Monte Cavallo on the Quirinal Hill, the pope extended his pale hand over a sea of bowed heads to bless them.

The journey to that point had been gruelling, for the people and their pope. For some, the arrival of the French had marked the end of the world as they knew it. A short walk from the Forum, the young and old women of the monastery of San Domenico e Sisto had been ordered to leave.[20] Gathering up their lives in a haze of disbelief, the nuns sought refuge with religious sisters nearby. All over the city, stomachs growled as the government struggled to maintain an adequate food supply. Chronicling the Romans' hardships, the young priest Giuseppe Sala would complain in his diary, 'Especially on Fridays and Saturdays we don't know if we will eat ... eggs and dairy products are incredibly scarce, one can't find cured meats, or fish, and finding them one needs a treasure to buy some.'[21] More difficulty had come in November 1798, as Rome faced an incursion from an uninvited liberator: Ferdinand, the King of Naples (1759–1806; 1815–1816) who vowed to 'revive the Catholic Religion, put an end to anarchy, slaughter and pillaging'.[22] After twenty days of chaos the king and his army had fled Rome on the ship of Horatio Nelson, having lost both that city and Ferdinand's own capital to republican troops.[23] Things were bleak, but some Romans still managed to muster a laugh. On Ferdinand's departure a note scrawled on Pasquino declared '*veni, vidi, fuggi*' (I came, I saw, I ran away) – his quest cast in stark contrast to the triumphs of Julius Caesar.[24]

By spring of 1800 Ferdinand had quashed the Republic of Naples and returned to his throne. Pius VII, however, remained in exile from

Rome. Elected by a conclave in Venice, the new pope was a mild and moderate Benedictine monk, a fitting temperament for a pontiff crowned with a papier-mâché tiara dignified only by jewels donated by the charitable ladies of the lagoon. As Pius VII was made pope at Venice's San Giorgio Maggiore, Napoleon and his troops were tightening their grip over northern Italy. Reflecting on the fate of his predecessor, for Pius this could only be bad news. Yet when the First Consul took Milan in early June 1800, he marched down the vast nave of the duomo and, facing the clergy, declared his 'formal intention that the Christian, Catholic and Roman religion be maintained in its entirety'.[25] Napoleon had never expressed the ardent atheism of some Jacobite revolutionaries, but this proclamation was not an act of Christian devotion. Napoleon knew that the Roman religion could prove a useful political tool: 'Catholicism is the only religion,' he proudly informed the priests before him, 'which can procure true happiness for a well-ordered society, and strengthen the basis for good government.'[26]

The very next day, the ship that would bear Pius VII to the Papal States pulled away from its mooring in the murky harbour of Venice. The outlook for the new pope was brighter, but the auguries remained mixed. The ship began to sink before it had reached open waters and it would take eleven days for its incompetent crew to carry the pope southwards to Pesaro, a trip that should have taken just twenty-four hours.[27] Restored to Rome, Pius began to get the measure of Napoleon. In just over a year, the two men had brokered the restoration of the Church to revolutionary France. Pius dispatched the erudite and engaging Cardinal Ercole Consalvi to Paris, where the shrewd, urbane Talleyrand negotiated on Napoleon's side.[28] Meetings ran all night and tempers flared. Meanwhile, solemn *Te Deums* became Napoleon's favourite means of marking his achievements. In reality, religious ceremony was a fig leaf for the true spirit of Napoleonic rule, as disgruntled generals barged past clerics and the vandalised religious statues that still surrounded the portals of Notre Dame.[29]

Within a few years, the fig leaf was off and Napoleon's true intentions were patently clear. The Church was back in France, but he had colour-coded the cardinals – red or black – according to their personal loyalty to him.[30] In Rome, Pius himself would be tested constantly for his fealty to the Napoleonic regime. In 1807 a flurry of correspondence demanded that the pope take a stand against Napoleon's enemies. Pius refused, for he had the measure of his interlocutor long before the orders arrived. In 1804, when Napoleon had crowned himself Emperor of France the pope's presence was demanded at the event. Having raced to France with a retinue of more than one hundred, Pius was marginalised to a supporting role.[31] The pope waited for Napoleon at Notre Dame for more than an hour, then he was asked merely to anoint the crown that Napoleon placed on his own head.[32] Now the new emperor claimed to be heir to the ancient Caesars, the Lombard kings and Holy Roman Emperor Charlemagne. With the pope back in Rome, Napoleon demanded more than any of these men had ever dared. Abandoning the age-old relationship of mutual benefit, the French emperor insisted that Pius approve his every action with a blanket blessing. At the same time, he failed to protect the Patrimony of Peter, encroaching on the Papal States with his own troops. When Pius continued to refuse Napoleon's demands, the frustrated emperor resorted to intimidation. In February 1808, French troops returned to the city.[33] At the Quirinal Palace, Pius remained at his desk, founding the episcopal Sees of Boston, Philadelphia and New York.

By the summer of 1809, Napoleon had lost patience with the pope. If Pius would not work for him, he would take his city outright. On 10 June, a French official rushed to the flagpole atop Castel Sant'Angelo and replaced the papal banner with a billowing standard of red, white and blue.[34] Rome was declared a 'free imperial city' after 'centuries of oblivion' under papal rule.[35] The pope's riposte soon appeared on the vast wooden doors of the great basilicas of the city. 'The time for clemency is over', declared the savage bull in which Pius damned everybody who worked with the new government of Rome.[36] Top of the list of excommunications was Napoleon himself. His power asserted, Pius returned to his work at the Quirinal Palace. The pope was resolute but ill-at-ease, repeating the words of Christ as he hung on the cross: '*Consummatum est*'.[37] On the night of 5 July, footsteps sounded on the palace roof. A furore broke out below as four divisions of French soldiers stormed the state rooms. Pius was seized from his bed, forced into a carriage and sped northwards to the Napoleonic city of Savona. Soon ships would carry cardinals, heads of religious organisations and thousands of crates of art and documents to Paris.

On New Year's Day 1810, Napoleon tried to revive the imperial veto, declaring that 'the Popes shall swear allegiance to me, as they did to Charlemagne and his predecessors. They will not be inducted until after my consent, as the use was for the emperors of Constantinople.'[38] Napoleon had never failed to appreciate the significance of the popes as custodians of legitimacy. However, his brazen actions betrayed a total misunderstanding of their motivations and modus operandi. Popes had clothed Pepin and Charlemagne with legitimacy when they protected and expanded the Patrimony of Peter. Constantinople had its own prestigious pedigree and even its emperors lost papal allegiance when they failed to protect the popes' temporal power. For his part, Napoleon had totally violated the authority of Saint Peter's See. To make matters worse, he had done so in an audacious attempt to grab legitimacy to which he had no right. In the process, he destroyed the good will of the pope, the very means through which he might have secured legitimate authority. Without Pius, Napoleon could not even elect legitimate bishops to lead the French Church. When Napoleon realised that he could not force Pius to exercise papal power for his benefit, he pretended that he had not wanted it all along: 'from the present Pope I demand nothing; I ask him for no oath, not even to recognise the annexation of Rome to France; I have no need for it.'[39]

—— ෴ ෴ ෴ ——

In Rome, Napoleon's government lacked popular support. The people balked when he proffered his newborn son as a new figurehead for the city and King of Rome in 1811. As ever, Pasquino revealed the mood: 'the little bastard has been crowned'.[40] In the more rarified atmosphere of Saint Peter's Basilica, the reception was just as frosty, as the musical maestro Niccolò Antonio Zingarelli refused to contribute to a *Te Deum* to be sung for the new king. At the appointed hour, dignitaries gathered, candles were lit but the choir of the basilica stood empty.[41] The emperor's guests got more than they bargained for when they looked up to see policemen corralling Zingarelli and his choir into position by force. Whispers broke out below, but the lips of the singers remained firmly shut. Marched to the Castel Sant'Angelo, these awkward representatives of Roman resistance were swiftly consigned to prison cells.[42] High up on the Capitoline, the stale air of discontent was not so easily concealed. Of all the noblewomen in the city, just seven deigned to dress and appear at the celebratory ball.[43] At other events, it was the guard of honour who failed to turn up. At government offices, curious excuses rolled in from men claiming not to own complete uniforms to wear and one man who was simply too busy working on his farm.[44]

Napoleon had promised to restore the people of Rome to the august position of their ancient ancestors. Yet, once again, the emperor misjudged his task. The efforts began well. For the role of prefect of Rome he had selected Camille de Tournon, a sympathetic and highly attentive administrator in his early thirties. Arriving in Rome, however, the young Frenchman was plagued by the melancholic idealism of the Grand Tourist. The day after he arrived, he reeled off a letter to his mother, pledging to 'Plant some seeds of prosperity in this soil which is so poetic, but so wretched.'[45] Lauding Rome's antique past, the French regime was full of contempt for the modern city, which it deemed a turgid, decadent product of the Catholic Church.[46] Like monuments such as the Arch of Titus, the people were to be cleansed of the undignified accretions of the post-classical age. The new authorities banned Roman men from swimming nude in the Tiber; they stopped women from bathing there at all.[47] Religious orders were kicked out and forced conscription was introduced: all measures aimed to tackle the indolence that the French claimed had crept in under the popes. Tournon might have been wide-eyed when he gazed at the Roman Forum, but looking at the people of modern Rome he recognised a clear lack of enthusiasm, noting that, for the Romans, the ancient grandeur of the city was 'an idea that occupies the imagination without descending to the soul'.[48]

Despite grand designs to ameliorate life in the city, as well as excavating its prestigious past, the French regime achieved little beyond some restoration at the Forum and the ordering and ornamentation of the gardens over the Piazza del Popolo on the Pincian Hill.[49] It would not be enough to win over locals. Even early in the narrative of the French occupations, people scoffed that they were informed of their 'mortal inertia' by officials who held their first daily meetings with young Roman prostitutes.[50] Soon the emperor would also lose his grip on the military and political influence that underpinned his regime. In 1810, Tsar Alexander of Russia echoed Pius VII and refused to heed Napoleon's demands. He effectively abandoned the emperor's Continental System, relaxing trade rules to open up the Russian market to the enemies of France.[51] Soon the British were bolstering uprisings against French incursions on the people, priests and religious orders of Portugal and Spain. In 1812, Napoleon would lose thousands of men to the brutal Russian winter as he made a vain attempt to punish the rebellious tsar. Two years later, Napoleon's own brother-in-law united with his enemies in a bid to make himself King of Italy.[52]

By the summer of 1815, the powers of Europe had finally felled Napoleon. Pius VII had, once again, been returned to Rome. This time the pope's journey was not blighted by an overburdened ship or an inept crew. He entered Rome in a carriage drawn by sixty-four local girls clothed entirely in black.[53] This eccentric transport symbolised popular submission and adoration for the restored pope. It hardly seemed necessary as men, women and children ran alongside the carriage calling out for Pius' blessing. Now he was not just a pope but also a great man in Europe: he had stuck to his principles, endured exile with dignity and even mended his own cassocks. On his return to Rome Pius VII was numbered among the triumphant saints who had walked its streets: a living martyr, 'the Head of the Church and 'the greatest man of his century'.[54]

Far beyond Rome, popular acclaim, printed portraits and rhyming verse celebrated Pius, who was emerging as the first papal icon of the modern age. Ideology chimed with image in Rome and Catholic countries such as France, where thinkers engaged in an influential debate about whether the recent wars in Europe proved the necessity of a papal sovereign. For men like Joseph de Maistre, the wild, bellicose ambition of Napoleon was obviously the fruit of the 'Gallican' idea that a nation's secular ruler should be its ultimate religious authority. For him, a safer world was guaranteed by an 'Ultramontane' stance, with men and women looking towards Rome and a papal pastor with genuine universal sovereignty.[55] Another French theorist, Félicité de Lamennais, would sum up this stance with a confidence bordering on the glib: 'without the Pope, no Church; without the Church, no Christianity; without Christianity, no religion and no society; thus European national life ... has its unique source in pontifical power'.[56]

—— ⟨ﾟ ﾟ⟩ ——

On 21 November 1825, a message coursed around the streets off the via del Corso: 'Mastro Titta is crossing the bridge.' The words were a telling sign that papal power in Rome was alive and well. Mastro Titta had grown up in Senigallia, in the eastern stretches of the Papal States, yet in the pope's capital everybody knew what his movements meant. In a narrow street facing Saint Peter's, he departed the home that he shared with his wife. Theirs was a quiet life near the church of Santa Maria in Transpontina, where they were often seen standing reverently at Mass.[57] When Mastro Titta walked over the bridge known as Ponte Sant'Angelo his mood became more furtive, as he scanned the streets for insulting gestures or potential attacks. He had been born Giovanni Battista Bugatti, but Romans knew him only by his nickname, which meant 'Master of Justice' in local dialect. When he crossed the bridge an execution was imminent; people gathered to see.[58] On that November day in 1825 it was Angelo Targhini and Leonida Montanari who were to be killed.

The execution was 'ordered by the pope, without proof and without trial', their memorial on Piazza del Popolo now reads. The two men were young, in their mid-twenties, but Mastro Titta was unsympathetic. He had seen his first execution as a young man with a cool attitude evoked in a memoir attributed to his own hand. Recalling the quartering and decapitation of one Nicola Gentilucci, the memoir lauds the executioner who worked 'with frankness and precision, as the most expert butcher would have been able to do... I was seventeen years old, and I felt no emotion at all'.[59] The attribution of the text to Mastro Titta is likely to be erroneous but the tone befits a man who killed some 516 people over sixty-eight years.[60] The people gathered to see the execution of Targini and Montanari on the Piazza del Popolo appeared equally unmoved. According to reports in Parisian and American newspapers, the Romans were angered, 'filled with consternation by the sangfroid displayed by the condemned'.[61]

Like everyone who faced execution in the Papal States, they had been offered the opportunity to confess their sins and die good Christians. 'The pope, even though still very weak, passed part of the night in prayer for this pious purpose.'[62] Still, the men had refused, displaying an 'invincible incredulity unheard of in the Holy City'.[63]

In this scene, papal rule appeared to have returned entirely intact. This was certainly the presumed outcome when the Congress of Vienna had ended in 1815. At that meeting, the great European heads of state had thrashed out the fate of the continent following the fall of Napoleon and more than two decades of war. An imperialist prince, the Austrian foreign minister Klemens von Metternich, emerged as the 'coachman of Europe', eager to drive the continent 'back into its ancient political paths'.[64] Under his guidance, delegates sought a balance of power and peace by quashing the liberal ideas that sought to assert democracy and individual rights. Bargaining for Rome, once again, was the erudite Cardinal Consalvi, who had returned from exile in France as a 'black cardinal' only to be sent back to prepare for the Congress. Going on to press the pope's case in England, Consalvi had intended to avoid anti-Catholic backlash by setting aside the red robes of his office. In the end, he was cheered by crowds of Englishmen who saw him and the pope as fellow assailants of Napoleon.[65] Writing from London, Consalvi told Pius of the jovial encouragement of the Prince Regent (the future George IV) who joked that his support of the cardinal gave him visions of 'Henry VIII and his daughter Elizabeth pursuing me like avenging spirits'.[66]

Pius declined the offer to join a Holy Alliance against democracy, secularism and revolution, but still benefitted from the backlash of political conservatives. Apart from Avignon, Venaissan and a small part of Ferrara, he won back all of the territory rent from the Patrimony of Peter in recent years. Meanwhile, in many corners of Rome the city of gentler times re-emerged intact. Even before the Congress of Vienna was concluded, the celebrated sculptor Antonio

Canova was in his studio on via San Giacomo putting the finishing touches to a serene Neo-Classical bust. The marble head represented the 'Peace' now descended on Europe; a diadem crowned her spiralling ringlets. In a cruel historical irony, the full-scale model made by Canova is now in the Ukrainian capital of Kyiv. When the bust was packed up as a gift to Canova's long-time patron and friend Lord Cawdor, the act marked a quiet but potent moment in the restoration of the old status quo. The mission to restore Papal Rome in its entirety would require a greater cultural exchange yet and Canova played a crucial part, setting out for Paris after the fall of Napoleon at Waterloo in June 1815. Tracing Consalvi's footsteps from Rome, Canova lobbied France's new ruler, King Louis XVIII, not for territory but cultural riches: the marbles, paintings and books that Napoleon had stolen from Rome. Once again, the Roman party could count on the support of, among others, the British: George IV helped finance the transport, while the Duke of Wellington supported a call to arms if the French refused to return the art so beloved of foreigners in Rome.[67]

Pius VII's European allies would be less enthusiastic about other restorations to the city: the inquisition, the Jewish ghetto and the Jesuits all returned while Consalvi was still away.[68] By the time that Targhini and Montanari were executed, Rome faced harsher measures yet. Elected on Pius' death, Leo XII (1823–9) would attempt to purge the city of any infringement on his Catholic ideal. Entrenching his rule across the Papal States, Leo banned laymen from government, ordered that all schooling be undertaken in Latin and forced Jews to surrender their property and rights to own it. At the church of Sant'Angelo in Pescheria, the weekly compulsory sermon to Rome's Jewish community was revived.[69] At carnival, Romans were now banned from dancing the waltz.[70] Dressmakers were excommunicated for producing revealing clothes; men, meanwhile, were prohibited from walking too closely behind women in the street.[71]

Skinny and pale, Leo had appeared on the precipice of death at his election. To the chagrin of many, he managed to rule for six long years. His more moderate successor, Pius VIII (1829–30), would not be so lucky. Blighted by an abscess in his neck at the conclave, he died just eighteen months later.[72] Pius VIII's swift demise paved the way for the rise of the reactionary Gregory XVI (1831–46), whose portraits disguise his own physical ailment: a large facial tumour resulting from using huge quantities of snuff. Despite this affliction, Gregory was of sturdy constitution and determined to continue Leo XII's work. The day after his election in February 1831, the people of Rome seemed consigned to their course. As Gregory cruised through the streets of the city in a gilt, brocaded carriage, he peered out from the window to see a stream of clapping hands.[73]

— ଔ ଠ ଠ —

Three weeks later, a similar scene was reported among the people of Monti, a *rione* sitting between the Quirinal and Esquiline Hills. There the faithful had chased the papal carriage, acclaiming Gregory XVI in full voice as women and children seeking his blessing had dropped their knees to the ground, and men threw their hats in the air alongside the banner of Christian religion. The scene outside was jolly, but within the carriage Gregory was morose. Just a week into his papacy, the pope was facing a revolution in Bologna.[74] In this main city of the northern Papal States, rebels had raised a new tricolour flag, flatly declaring that 'the temporal power of the Pope over this province has ended in fact and forever by law'.[75] The revolutionaries ordered the pope to retreat into a purely spiritual role, while the other states of Italy should unify with them as a nation finally free of foreign rule. The residents of Monti came out for papal power, and one, Carlo Ruspi, even commemorated the event in a print. All the while, the pope was scrambling to quash an attack not only on his power but the entire status quo.

Regrettably for Gregory, the incident was neither isolated nor new. Even under Leo XII, cases like that of Targhini and Montanari had involved serious political dissent. Superficially, those two men had been condemned for the murder of a man known as Spontini, who had felt a dagger in his chest just a few minutes after entering the shadowy vicolo Sant'Andrea with Targhini.[76] Spontini's injuries had been grave, but Targhini had missed his heart. As the assailant ran off into the night, papal policemen ferried the ailing man to the Farmacia dei Peretti.[77] Remarkably, Spontini's evening was about to get worse: Montanari would be the surgeon on hand. Watching over the patient, the concern of the policemen turned to horror when they noticed Montanari digging in his instruments and deliberately worsening Spontini's wounds.[78] These were brutal crimes, but the two men would not repent, for Spontini was a traitor to their cherished political cause. As the drum beat heralded the drop of the guillotine on Piazza del Popolo, the two men had apparently cried out: 'I die a good *Carbonaro*.'

As *Carbonari,* or charcoal burners, Targhini and Montanari were liberal, nationalist dissidents. They were condemned for their brutal attack on Spontini but killed for treachery to the Papal State. To be a *Carbonaro* was to belong to an underground network of radical cells peppered across the Italian states. Their covert nature obfuscates their origins, which seem to coincide with the rule of Napoleon and link to the secret society of Freemasons condemned by Clement XII (1730–40) in 1738. Among *Carbonari* there was no united plan for reform, with divisions between grandees, who embraced extremely radical ideas, and the landowners, civil servants and soldiers who made up the core of the membership.[79] Still, like the revolutionaries in Bologna, they were agreed in their aim to unite the Italian peninsula and rid it of foreign powers such as Austria and France. They also shared a hatred for the 'fat wolf' Napoleon.[80] Ironically, the ideas that he had brought with him had sparked and nurtured their own movement in many ways. By dominating and uniting large swathes of the Italian peninsula, Napoleon had contrived a series of republics before declaring a Kingdom of Italy. Technically, it remained divided – with the Kingdom of Italy in the north and separate departments of the French Empire and Kingdom of Naples – but this had been a near-united Italy ruled over by a single regime.

Across the *rioni* of Colonna, Parione, Pigna and Campo Marzio informal clusters of dissidents emerged. At Il Caffè degli Milanesi, Il Caffè Nuovo and others, Romans debated how they might achieve Italy's destiny, swapping ideas and books with the foreign thinkers, artists and tourists who also frequented these spots.[81] Patriots even met at the barbershop on via dei Greci, where Father Carlo Bilotti read radical newspapers with the carriage maker Saverio Pediconi and grocer Agostino Guerrini.[82] At the pharmacy or Spezieria della Regina on Piazza Pollarola, just north of the Campo de' Fiori, people danced, debated reform and vented complaints about the current regime.[83] Again, the visions and plans discussed were disparate, lacking clear direction and form. In 1831, the Genoese journalist and *Carbonero* Giuseppe Mazzini would found 'Young Italy' to forge a more united movement. Determined and precociously intelligent, Mazzini had found himself at university at the age of fourteen. He was in his mid-twenties when he founded Young Italy for 'One, free, independent, republican nation'.[84] Soon Mazzini was deemed a pernicious enough threat to be exiled to Marseille, and then Switzerland and London. Though far from the Italian peninsula, he continued to inspire other exiles and coordinate revolutionary uprisings via fiery correspondence.

Popes had long tried to choke these movements, which had begun to surface in the wake of the Enlightenment. In the eighteenth century, Clement XII and Benedict XIV (1740–58) had banned secret societies. In the 1820s, Pius VII and Leo XII condemned the *Carbonari* by name. Many who had joined underground cells in the intervening years had claimed immunity from the earlier bulls, hungry for change but sheltering on the right side of the law. By 1821, they had every reason to hide as Pius decreed that the society of the *Carbonari* should be subjected to severe punishments as 'they affirm, errone-ously, that they are not included in the Bulls of Clement XII and Benedict XIV'.[85] Pius was fuming to have discovered that their rituals emulated Catholic liturgy.[86] The main aim of the ban was, however, political: to quash dissent in the Papal States. As in so many systems of justice in the *ancien regime*, brutality was a thin veil for weakness – most dissidents were never caught.[87] For those who remained at large, the pope hoped that the thudding heads of Targhini and Montanari would ring out as a compelling warning.

Looking out from Rome in the twenties and thirties, however, revolutionaries had reason to feel hopeful, as uprisings in states such as Spain and Portugal successfully demanded liberal reforms and limitations on monarchical power. In the summer of 1830, France had revolted once again, rejecting hereditary dynasties for a popular, constitutional monarchy. For the popes, this was deeply troubling. There were also worries closer to home. In the same year as Bologna revolted against Gregory XVI, an insurrection erupted in the nearby state of Modena. As dissidents cried out for a liberal nation of Italy, the leaders of the Italian states began to hedge their bets. The volatility of the situation would be exemplified in the fate of a Modenese *Carbonero* called Ciro Menotti, who was promised support by Duke Francis IV of Modena who then reneged, leaving Menotti to face the scaffold.[88] In Modena, the Austrians put down the revolt. They also had a hand in rolling back reforms in Spain, the Kingdom of Naples and Sardinia-Piedmont. As a staunch conservative, King Carlo Alberto of Sardinia-Piedmont had supported the Austrian interventions in Italy, banishing revolutionary figures such as Mazzini from his state. But by the late 1840s, even he appeared to throw his lot in with the patriots, responding to their call to drive Austria from

Lombardy in the hope that he might emerge as the leader of a future nation of Italy.[89]

Gregory XVI would not demonstrate the same foresight, calling in the Austrians to crush rebels in the Papal States. In doing so, he quashed the immediate threat to his temporal power. Nonetheless, in the long-term, he only exacerbated the menace to his rule. Not only had the pope worked with the enemies of the patriots, he had also exposed the galling fact that he could not protect his temporal power alone. The pope could only remain prince of his states as long as a foreign army defended him.

— ∞ ∞ ∞ —

In 1868, the future of Italy was clear for readers of *Lo Spirito Folletto*, a newspaper published in Milan: progress had arrived and it could not be stopped. In a cartoon printed on its pages in the late nineteenth century, this irrepressible force is emblazoned on a flag, accompanied by the concepts of 'Science' and the 'Future'.[90] Wielding the banner is a capped man, standing on the front of a hurtling train. Behind him stands a powerful female figure, representing the liberal arts. Looking down the track, the man cries out 'Go away! Clear off, for I cannot divert the train!' Before him is the figure of a pope, standing right in the way. But this pontiff is no bulwark. It is he who is in danger. A clash would be messy, but the train would drive on to its destiny. Meanwhile, the pope is resplendent in his triple tiara but, under his vestments, made out of straw. In a crash, more casualties would surround him, namely the donkey pulling his cart and the faithful sheep gathered below.

The reference to railways was pointed. Gregory XVI had deemed them 'highways to hell'. He and his advisors had even resisted the allure of a gleaming silver model railway that one railroad company had sent to tempt the pope into laying tracks. Gregory recoiled at the thought of locomotives speeding into the Papal States, carrying bourgeois ideas and inexpensive manufactured goods into its conservative communities and markets.[91] In Gregory's time, people had begun to identify the train as a symbol of modernity and progress. Gregory was long dead when the cartoon was published in 1868, but the papacy remained in a standoff with the modern world. In the summer of that year, Gregory's successor, Pope Pius IX, was in the Vatican Palace, summoning cardinals, bishops and heads of religious orders from all over the world to confront the overwhelming challenges of their age. When the First Vatican Council opened in December 1869, it would be the first such meeting since the sixteenth century, when the Council of Trent had convened to discuss the Reformation. The challenge facing the Church under Pius IX was, perhaps, even graver than that splintering of Christendom. The Vatican fathers were not addressing a cluster of reforming Christian movements, but a world flooded by ideas inimical to Christian tradition as they knew it and openly hostile to absolute religious rule.

Pius IX's Church responded with a string of condemnations: of liberalism, secularism, naturalism, modernism, materialism and pantheism. What is more, by 1870 the council fathers had doubled down on the pope's own role. Because of the 'supreme apostolic authority' that he had inherited from Peter, his official pronouncements on morality and faith were declared infallible.[92] Responding to the Archbishop of Bologna, who suggested that bishops also had a role in discerning Church tradition, Pius made the Church's official position crystal clear. Summoning every ounce of the Petrine authority distilled in his office, he declared, 'I am the tradition.'[93]

Even before 1868 many Romans had believed that liberal reforms were as inevitable as the course of a train on tracks. That the pope would stand in the way of such change was, however, far from clear. On Gregory XVI's death in June 1846, many had looked to Pius IX to lead change. Candid and emotional, he had liberated hundreds of political dissidents from papal jails less than a month after his election. As the summer sun beat down on the Corso, Romans burst from their houses crying out the pope's name.[94] The hands of artists moved almost as quickly to memorialise this great turn. For them, the symbol of change was not the train but Pius; printmakers enthroned the pope above men whose iron chains now lay broken on the ground. Other creative minds made vast coloured banners emblazoned with pictorial riddles. When solved, one medley of laurels, wings, birds and altars acclaimed the 'papa vero'. In August, celebrations continued at the church of San Pietro in Vincoli. There, in the building that held the chains that had bound Saint Peter, fifty-one of the freed convicts knelt to receive Holy Communion from the pope.[95] The poetry almost wrote itself, but soon a full commemorative sonnet appeared.[96]

As winter arrived in Rome, the celebrations continued as hundreds of men and women crammed into the Teatro d'Alimbert. In the orchestra and galleries of that theatre, near the Spanish Steps, they knocked elbows over a festive lunch accompanied by nationalist lectures as a beaming image of the pontiff overlooked them from the stage.[97] Just four days earlier, Pius had announced that there would be reform to both civil and criminal law in the Papal States and that trains were now on their way. The year after his election, he agreed to the creation of a Civic Guard, a measure that had been called for by liberal nationalists who now marked his anniversary with a new anthem known as the Roman Marseillaise.[98] As their rowdy procession marched from the Papal palace at the Quirinal to the ancient seat of civic power on the Capitoline Hill, the gulf between the pope and the people appeared almost entirely bridged.

By September 1847, the excited mood in Rome seemed to have reached the dour streets of London, where the exiled Mazzini sat in his Bloomsbury flat and penned an open letter to the pope. In fervent and rather grandiose tones, he asked Pius to back a united Italy:

'I call on you, after so many centuries of doubt and corruption, to be the apostle of the Eternally True ... Abhor being a king, a politician, a statesman ... say that Humanity is the sacred daughter of God, and that those who violate its rights to progress and free association are on the road of error ... Unite Italy, your country. We will make you rise around a Nation over whose free and popular development you, living, will preside.'[99]

The idea was not new. In 1843, the philosopher and politician Vincenzo Gioberti had written a bestseller calling for a united Italy with the pope as its king.[100] When Pius granted a constitution and asked God to bless Italy in the spring of 1848, many Italians saw him as the liberal leader of whom they had dreamt.[101]

Whatever his letter said, Mazzini was not so naive. Just a week after he sent his appeal to Pius he told a friend, 'I have sent a useless letter to the Pope' that 'will serve only to give him a headache – if he has a head'.[102] Despite popular hopes Mazzini knew that Pius would never embrace the role of a liberal nationalist king. The pope's very first encyclical had spoken vehemently of those who promoted the 'outlandish errors' of liberalism and secularism. 'Without doubt,' wrote Pius, 'nothing more insane than such a doctrine, more impious or more opposed to reason itself could be devised.'[103] In June 1847, Romans eager for political change had focused their ire on the government not the pope, crying out 'Long live Pius IX, alone!' However, it was Pius himself who had denounced their actions and called for an immediate end to protest. By 1848, Gioberti's text was on the Index of Forbidden Books.[104]

Writing to the erudite Jesuit Luigi Taparelli d'Azeglio, Pius was clear: 'I do not want to do what Mazzini wishes ... I cannot do what Gioberti wants.'[105] Pius had made liberal concessions to avert a full revolution, reforming only to preserve the status quo.

To many around him, it seemed as though his hands and mouth belonged to two different popes. On 11 February 1849 he would respond to calls for a government free of priests, saying: 'I cannot, I should not, I do not want to hear them.'[106] Yet the following day he signed off a new cabinet of which four of the nine members were laymen. Some were so fearful of his concessions that they had already abandoned their posts. Pius' Secretary of State, Cardinal Tomasso Gizzi, had resigned in 1847 when the pope sanctioned the Civic Guard. For Gizzi it was madness for a sovereign to arm a people on the brink of revolt. As pressure mounted on all sides, the pontiff considered abdication before deciding that more reform was the only way to preserve papal Rome. Looking out upon the crowds gathered outside of the Quirinal Palace his eyes were open and his heart full of resolution and fear: 'We know where they want to lead us. We shall cede as long as our conscience permits, and having arrived at the limits that we have already established, they can cut us into tiny pieces, but, with the help of God, we shall not go beyond them one step.'[107]

Pius had already arrived at his limits in the spring of 1848 when the people demanded that he go to war against Austria. As the First Italian War of Independence broke out in Lombardy, Pius announced that, as pope, 'I cannot declare war against anyone'.[108] Begging him for just one more concession, his cabinet threatened to resign en masse. The ministers pocketed their letters when the pope appeared to relent, promising them, 'I shall make you happy.'[109] They were bemused the following day when Pius' original statement was reiterated in a printed letter pasted all over Rome. The pope would concede to another letter, in which he requested that the Austrian emperor remove his troops. As the guarantor of papal power, Austria had the upper hand and absolutely no interest in relinquishing their hold on Italy. Facing down a long, hot summer of disorder in Rome, the ministers of Pius' government reshuffled once again. By autumn, Pius had chosen Count Pellegrino Rossi as Minister of the Interior. A frosty economic liberal who supported only limited suffrage, he was distrusted by both the masses and ardent nationalists who thought he lacked true patriotism.[110] On the morning of 15 November 1848, the pages of *Il Contemporaneo* accused Rossi of fuelling concerns about non-existent problems simply to swell his own power base.[111] As the Minister paced through the marble hall to the Assembly Chamber at the Palazzo della Cancellaria that day he was felled by the swipe of an umbrella and a stiletto dagger to the neck.[112]

By 3 o'clock the next afternoon a delegation representing the people walked the halls of the Quirinal Palace where the pope was held under siege by a cannon at the door.[113] His hand forced by the cries outside the palace, Pius IX agreed to yet another new cabinet. As the Swiss Guard was replaced by the Civic Guard, which he himself had sanctioned, the pope declared himself a prisoner. In less than ten days the prisoner had fled, disguised in the clothes of an ordinary priest and heavy dark glasses.[114] On the evening of Friday 24 November, Pius escaped from Rome through the Porta San Giovanni, taking a road southwards to Gaeta in the Kingdom of Naples.

—— ☙ ❧ ❧ ——

By spring 1849 the Caffè dei Crociferi was known as a *'caffè nero'* – or 'black cafe' – frequented by priests and others hostile to the revolution. For those who sat inside sipping an aperitif or playing chess, even the crashing waters of the Trevi Fountain failed to drown out the cries from outside, 'Long live the red Republic! Death to priests – arms, money, war!'[115] On the evening of 1 April, however, the sympathies of the cafe appeared transformed. Gingerly finding his feet on the small table where he had been enjoying a drink, a priest began to preach loudly about the great Roman Republic declared on 9 February 1849.[116] On that very same day in February, the Genoese agitator Mazzini had been made a citizen of Rome. By the time that the priest got down from the table, that citizen ruled the city as one third of a triumvirate.

While in Florence, Mazzini had received a short but thrilling telegram: 'Rome republic. Come.'[117] In March the republic had joined the First War of Independence against Austria. With some delight, Mazzini offered the pope a marginal role back in Rome: he could run the Catholic Church as one religious institution among many. Meanwhile, a mob sped to the seat of the inquisition at Santa Maria Sopra Minerva to burn it down.[118] Easter celebrations continued without the pope and Saint Peter's was adorned with a glowing tricolour cross.[119] Freedom of religion and press were declared, education was secularised and Church property was put in the hands of peasants. On the Capitoline Hill, the equestrian statue of Marcus Aurelius now carried the tricolour flag and branches were dragged onto the Piazza del Popolo where a Liberty Tree was illuminated with fire.

Despite appearances, however, not everybody had abandoned the pope. The priest at the Caffè dei Crociferi had been coerced to preach for the republic under threat of violence. At the end of April, a cleric in Trastevere would be murdered for denouncing the new regime.[120] Many others longed for the return of the pope, even if they still wanted reform. After Pius' flight to Gaeta in the winter of 1848, what remained of his government had ventured south in a futile mission to retrieve him. During the election in January 1849, however, the voices of many papal supporters would not be heard as, from exile, Pius had called the elections illegal and threatened to excommunicate all who took part.[121] Now a government of doctors, professors, merchants, lawyers and writers sat in the Palazzo della Cancelleria. Outside, the carriages of Roman cardinals lay in splinters, crushed together to form a barricade.[122]

For Mazzini, this was a new Rome: the city of the people. But the pope's universal significance to Catholics still held sway. At the Spanish parliament a politician declared that Pius' removal could spark nothing less than 'the collapse of European civilisation', stating that 'it is necessary that the Sovereign of Rome return to Rome, or else no stone will remain standing'.[123] On 30 March 1849, representatives of Naples, Spain, France and Austria took action, meeting the papal court-in-exile at Gaeta to discuss how they could restore Pius to Rome. At the Quirinal Palace, the French ambassador had kept the lights in Pius' room burning as he had fled. Now, President Louis-Napoleon (1848–70) agreed that it would be his men who returned the pontiff to Rome.

On 25 April, 10,000 French troops landed at Civitavecchia to break the republic. They were confident as they faced down the young Roman state. Just two days later, their prospects looked much bleaker, when men and women rushed around the city, shouting 'He has come, he has come!'[124] On a white horse, Giuseppe Garibaldi, recently elected General of the Republic, rode into the city at the centre of a legion of 'wild-looking warriors ... wearing conical-shaped hats with black, waving plumes; their gaunt, dust-soiled faces framed with shaggy beards'.[125] By 29 April, they had mobilised Rome. Now nothing was sacred but the republic. On the Janiculum Hill, the nuns were driven from the Renaissance loggia of Giuliano Romano's Villa Lante when Garibaldi seized the building as a strategic military base.[126] A look-out point was erected on the cupola of Saint Peter's; on the banks of the Tiber, the Palazzo Corsini was garrisoned.[127] The French struck a day later and met the grit of the *Trasteverini* at the bottom of the hill. In a shock outcome, the makeshift republican forces pushed the French all the way back to the coast.

Knowing that the Romans did not have the means to fight on, Mazzini struck the invaders with diplomacy. Rome would nurse the wounded and free any healthy prisoners. When the authorities proved unreceptive to this offer, Mazzini tried to tempt their forces with some 50,000 cigars, each wrapped in a note.[128] Unmoved, the French readied to renew battle. Back in Rome, republicans put their shoulder to the wheel as women sent out appeals to fellow mothers and wives, urging them to encourage their men to fight. Others stood outside of churches begging for funds for the war.[129] When the French siege began on 1 June 1849, alms were handed to Princess Trivulzio Belgiojoso, a striking heiress and disciple of Mazzini who had returned from exile in France to oversee Rome's hospitals.[130] Taxi drivers arrived at these infirmaries, ferrying the wounded from trenches dug by followers of the charismatic wine carter and *Carbonaro*, Angelo Brunetti. Lovingly nicknamed *Ciceruacchio* ('chubby piece' in Roman dialect), the corpulent Brunetti had once rallied Romans behind Pius. Now, he called them to defend the republic and delivered drinks to the fighters. Foreigners such as the American journalist Margaret Fuller also lent their help.[131] Fuller ran one of the hospitals; the sculptor William Wetmore Story occasionally brought ice creams to the staff.[132]

For a month sheer grit kept Garibaldi's men going, but even their tenacity was not a sufficient match for cannon fire. In the first days of July, they withdrew from Rome and trudged towards the safe haven of San Marino, as Garibaldi declared: 'Where we are, there will be Rome!'[133] For now, the republic was over, but a new path had emerged. In the days of the Avignon Papacy, the popes had declared something much the same: *ubi papa ibi Roma* – it had been the pontiffs who made Rome. Reassured that his status and power had been fully restored, Pius IX returned to the city on 12 April 1850. His hair now entirely grey, the pontiff retook Rome to lukewarm applause; it was a weak echo of the acclaim that had met Pius VII in 1815. The old regime had been restored, but the secularisation of the Italian state was underway. Just a week before his return, the papal nuncio to Sardinia-Piedmont had stormed out of the court as the government banned ecclesiastical tribunals.[134] Back in Rome, the Austrian diplomat, Count Moritz Esterházy, sensed profound unease. Favourable or hostile to Pius, Romans did not believe that his return could halt the course of change.[135] The pope himself was bitterly aware that his temporal authority was now only guaranteed by a foreign power. Turning to

Esterházy in exasperation, he asked: 'whose hands am I in today? The hands of the French.'[136]

——— ೞ ಐ ಐ ———

Pius IX was the last pope on whom flowers were thrown from the balconies of Rome, for whom crowds rallied at the Quirinal Palace, crying out until he emerged and spoke.[137] More than any of his predecessors, Pius had been transformed into an icon. As support for liberal nationalism grew, he became a totem for change even as he desperately tried to stem the extent of reform. Even during the exile in Gaeta, some of Pius' French allies naively believed that he might continue to liberalise Rome, planning to put him in a neutral territory where he was 'completely freed from the influence of the cardinals'.[138] For Pius, the jarring reality had already hit: modernisation could not be piecemeal, and absolute religious monarchy could not coexist with a liberal, democratic state. The marginalisation of the Catholic hierarchy into a purely religious role was equally intolerable. Pius was 'the successor of Peter, the Roman pontiff [who] holds supremacy over the whole world and is the true vicar of Christ'.[139] As such, he could be the subject of nobody but God himself.

By 1850, Pius was a symbol not of reform but intransigence. Decrying the 'spasm of revolution' and 'mania for modernisation', he ordered staff to pack up his things at the Quirinal and retreated to the Vatican Palace.[140] Responsibility for temporal government was handed over in large part to Cardinal Giacomo Antonelli, the Secretary of State, who cleansed the government of liberals, laymen and modernising priests. The old order was assured by the lingering presence of French troops. In the summer of 1854 in front of the Bocca della Verità, the twenty-eight-year-old sculptor Sante Constantini was beheaded for the murder of Minister of the Interior Pellegrino Rossi.[141] Hearing a reminiscence of days when he had been more politically engaged, Pius reacted with emotion, 'Let us not speak of times that never can come back!'[142]

Turning away from worldly matters, Pius shored up the spiritual work of the Church, ensuring that all new bishops were Ultramontane supporters of papal power.[143] No pontiff before him had made so many saints. On the morning of 8 December 1854, he declared a new dogma, as a volley of artillery from Castel Sant'Angelo shot out amidst the tolls of every bell tower in Rome.[144] In the presence of fifty cardinals and 150 bishops, Pius transformed the traditional belief that Mary was born free from sin into an official teaching to be accepted by all Catholics. Looking out across the globe, he restructured the ecclesiastical hierarchy in Ireland and appointed bishops across new dioceses in America, where immigration from Europe had rapidly swollen the Catholic population. As the number of priests in North America burgeoned from 700 to 6000, Pius would establish a college for their training in Rome. From 1859, it stood on the 'Via dell'Umiltà, just a short walk from the cafe where that priest had been forced to denounce papal rule just a decade earlier.[145] All over Rome, Pius poured funds into the restoration of the city's oldest Christian monuments in an effort to underline the longevity of the Church of Rome and preserve whatever was left of a better, bygone age.[146]

Unfortunately for Pius, his retreat from overtly political affairs did not shelter him from the scrutiny of the world. In 1846, a sonnet had given the liberated dissidents communing at San Pietro in Vincoli signs of Pius' liberalism. Just over ten years later, the fate of a small boy living in the grounds of that church would become a symbol of the pope's intolerable rigidity. Edgardo Mortara was just seven years old when he moved into the college there; he would attend a school run by the Lateran Canons Regular, an ancient religious order. Dressed in a white cassock, cape and skull cap, Mortara must have looked like a miniature pope when the French journalist, Louis

Veillot, spotted him on a school trip to Saint Peter's Basilica. On that day in 1859, Mortara was just one of a train of boys dressed in identical habits to their masters. In reality, however, he was not like any of them at all. Pointing at Mortara, the French bishop guiding Veillot exclaimed, 'Voila! There is the famous celebrity who has so much occupied all of Europe.'[147] Soon, Mortara would be immortalised in both print and on canvas. In a painting by Daniel Moritz Oppenheim he wears even simpler white clothing as he is led away from his fainting mother by papal police accompanied by a priest, friar and a nun. In reality, there had been no religious retinue when Mortara began his journey to Rome. Their presence in Oppenheim's painting symbolises the oversight of the Catholic Church, and especially of Pius IX.

While absent on the day (and in Oppenheim's painting) the pope was the figure who loomed largest in the fate of the little boy. The story had begun far from Rome in the streets of Bologna, one quiet June evening in 1858.[148] The apartment of the Jewish Mortara family was quiet, the children asleep, when the twenty-three-year-old servant, Anna, answered a knock at the front door. Her master was out, and she turned the men away. It was only when they reappeared at the back of the apartment that Anna's mistress, Marianna Mortara, came to see what was wrong. She shook with horror as the police asked her to list the names of all her children. Her husband, Momolo Mortara, would satisfy their query when he returned for the evening. Edgardo's name was highlighted and he was roused from a sofa-bed. Ushering Anna and the children out of the room, the marshal of the papal carabinieri turned to Momolo to deliver the agonising blow, 'Your son Edgardo has been baptised and I have been ordered to take him with me.'[149] It was the servant Anna, a Christian, who had performed the act when it had seemed that Edgardo was on the brink of death. Bologna was in the Papal States and it was illegal for a Christian to be raised by Jews. Through the night, two policemen guarded Edgardo, as he sat, laid down and went to the toilet. Amid tears, fainting and pleas the Mortara family made a plan to overturn the ruling. By the next evening, Momolo had secured an audience with the inquisitor, Pier Gaetano Feletti. Calmly, Father Feletti informed them that their efforts were all in vain. The Mortara family were assured that they need not worry, as all laws had been followed perfectly.[150] What is more, their son was destined for Rome where he would live under the care of the pope himself.

As the news of Edgardo's fate filtered out from the Italian peninsula, many corners of the world were utterly aghast. In Britain, the *Spectator* presumed a misreading of the law: 'Precedents and illustrations crowd upon us', so why was Pius keeping the boy?'[151] On the Iberian peninsula, the *Diario Spagnol* was less circumspect, deeming the act 'a kidnapping and a crime'.[152] In 1859, the British envoy to the Vatican, Odo Russell, appealed for a papal audience for Sir Moses Montefiore, a Jewish British peer. Montefiore had been charged to present a report that suggested Edgardo was not validly baptised, according to Catholic canon law. The report was talking the Church's language, but Antonelli replied that the case was not up for discussion.[153] In some Catholic quarters, Pius' actions would be lionised. This was 'the grandest moral spectacle which the world has seen for ages,' even if it was also a 'windfall to the enemies of the church'.[154] In Italy, the case was meat and drink to nationalists who sought to roll out secularisation. In Sardinia-Piedmont, the nationalist Prime Minister Camillo Benso, Count of Cavour, was absolutely thrilled. Now the world's eyes were fixed upon a heart-wrenching case that represented the most anachronistic elements of the pope's temporal rule. Even the ambassador of Pius' French protector talked of seizing the boy and shipping him to Cavour.[155]

In France, Louis-Napoleon (now known as Emperor Napoleon III) was incandescent. But even for him, Pius had just one answer: I cannot.

All the governments of the Old and the New World united and conspired to take away from me, from Christ and from His Church, the soul of this child … I do not feel sorry, though, for what I have done on his behalf, to save a soul that cost the blood of God. On the contrary, I ratify and confirm everything.[156]

As universal pastor, Pius refused to abandon the soul of Edgardo Mortara. Moreover, as papal sovereign he would enforce the laws of his Papal States.

For a moment the fate of Italy appeared to turn on that of the little boy. As the strongest state on the Italian peninsula, Sardinia-Piedmont now led the nationalist cause. King Vittorio Emanuele II had enjoyed some success, accompanied by the dogged nationalist Cavour. Yet even with an alliance of Italian states they were unable to liberate the peninsula from foreign powers without some external support. By 1850, Austria occupied Tuscany and the Papal Legations, while the French hung on in Rome. In the summer of 1858 the balance would finally shift, as the French agreed to take up their guns with Sardinia-Piedmont against the Austrians. While Vittorio Emanuele saw the war as a means of uniting Italy, France hoped that they might diminish their rival Austria, while radically reducing the pope's territory and, Napoleon III hoped, his opportunities to embarrass himself. In France, the war proved unpopular. Sardinia-Piedmont took Lombardy back from Austria and the French withdrew. Now the nationalist cause would be buoyed by Garibaldi, who re-emerged with his 'Hunters of the Alps'. They drove the Austrians from Varese and Como. Nationalist forces went on to subsume Tuscany, Parma, Modena, Reggio and the Papal territories in Bologna, Ferrara, Umbria, Le Marche, Benevento and Pontecorvo. By 1860, Garibaldi had handed over the southern Kingdom of the Two Sicilies as well. By 1861, Italy was a kingdom, even if the pope hung on in Rome and its environs. Vittorio Emanuele appeared to abandon Pius IX to destiny as he declared Rome his capital all the same.

— ☙ ☜ ☞ —

Turning to Cardinal Antonelli in 1868, the American poet Henry Wadsworth Longfellow spoke with sentimental tones. In Rome, he said, it was if the clock had been stopped. With some relief, Antonelli agreed, 'It is so indeed, thanks be to God.'[157] Superficially, it seemed, the papal government was confident. The decree on papal infallibility of July 1870 would speak in similar tones. Yet even some years earlier, the reality of the decline of papal power had begun to dawn. When Pius reiterated his condemnation of modern ideas in the *Syllabus of Errors* of 1864, the government of France had simply refused to publish the document.[158] Soon the guardians of the pope's temporal power would withdraw even further. The day after the bull *Pastor aeternus* made papal infallibility official, the French declared war on the German state of Prussia. In the first weeks of August 1870 their troops left Rome.[159] As Italian forces neared Rome in the autumn, Pius was protected only by the Zouaves, a force of devoted international Catholics who travelled to Rome to fight for an idea a millennium and a half old.

Cornered, Pius still refused to compromise his position. When the Italian government tried to trade diplomatic immunity and state support of the papacy for peaceful entry into Rome, Pius denounced them as a 'set of vipers, of whited sepulchres wanting in faith'.[160] Vehement, the pope told Vittorio Emanuele, 'you will never enter Rome'.[161] At 5.15am on 20 September, the Italian troops began to bombard the Aurelian Walls. In the palace at Saint Peter's, Pius IX began his day as ever before. At around 7am he walked in silence to the Capella Paolina to celebrate Holy Mass.[162] As bombs flew over Saint Peter's Basilica, the gentle ringing of the bells in that chapel could barely be heard. Retreating to his private library afterwards, the pope regaled diplomats with a long reflective monologue. As ever in his pontificate, the changing world encroached on Pius IX. Subjected to some forty shots a minute, the walls near the northern gate of Porta Pia soon crumbled. The news arrived in the library and Pius retreated to sign the surrender. Contrary to his predictions, the Patrimony of Peter had been felled.

For the nationalists it was a moment of sheer glory, as Romans wrapped their babies in the tricolour flag. 'They who a moment before ruled Rome with a rod of iron, were nearly all prisoners, or had taken refuge in the Castel of Sant'Angelo, or St Peter's square.'[163] The nationalist troops had defeated the papal city, a symbol of all that they sought to change. Declaring himself a prisoner of the Italian state, Pius maintained his totemic status at the Vatican. Refusing to acknowledge Rome as the Italian capital, he would not set foot outside. Within the confines of the Leonine Walls that surrounded Saint Peter's Basilica and palace, papal officials gathered around the pope. There Pius would continue his reign as a steadfast symbol of tradition. Beyond the walls, Romans clamoured, seizing arms from Zouaves and singing patriotic songs.

As the commotion calmed, new dilemmas would dawn on the city. Rome had to redefine itself without the hand of the popes who had shaped its life and fabric for more than 1500 years. The path was complex and replete with hazards. Even as the Italian regime forced its way into the city, it was carefully selecting symbols to celebrate or attack. Even on that morning, the walls had been broken some fifty metres away from the Porta Pia to protect parts of the gate made by Michelangelo. Returning the next day to re-stage the event for photographs, the Italian soldiers had a clearer target in mind. As the noted photographers Fratelli d'Alessandri snapped away at the sidelines, the men turned their guns on decorations erected to celebrate Pius IX's temporal power only a year before.

II

A Tale of Two Cities: Rome and the Vatican

When bombs rained on Rome in the summer of 1943, people could scarcely believe their eyes. Men hurriedly raised brick walls around the Columns of Trajan and Marcus Aurelius. The equestrian statue of Marcus Aurelius was taken from the Capitoline. The world was at war and Italy with it but, until then, Rome had been spared. Since 1870, the city had been the capital of the Italian nation. Its kings and prime ministers had spent millions of lire writing a new nationalist mythology into its monuments and streets. Yet more than seventy years later, many Romans still saw themselves as the people of a papal city. In 1943, they believed that the presence of the pope in Rome would protect them from attack.[1]

On 19 July the Romans had a brutal wake up call. In the minds of the American and British Allies, their leader was Benito Mussolini (1922–43) not Pope Pius XII (1939–58). Mussolini was a fascist who had led Italy to war shoulder-to-shoulder with Nazi Germany. In any case, the Allies would not give Rome special treatment on account of the Holy See. Even when Mussolini was arrested and King Vittorio Emanuele III (1900–46) inched towards the Allied side, appeals to protect Rome as a uniquely significant place were treated with circumspection, particularly if they came from the pope. Pius XII, himself a Roman, intervened on behalf of the city, begging President Roosevelt to 'save our beloved Rome from devastation'.[2] The president's aide, the straight-talking Iowan Harry Hopkins, was sceptical, fearing 'one hell of a row' if Americans discovered that concessions had been made under pressure from the pope.[3]

In the end, 9,125 bombs fell on Pius' beloved Rome that day. The Allies aimed for the steel factory, freight yard and airport, but their bombs could not discriminate. In that single attack, 1500 civilians would die. The working-class district of San Lorenzo was devastated. It was a cruel irony that the bombs also destroyed the ancient basilica of Saint Laurence, that deacon whom imperial authorities had cooked alive for his charity to the poor. When Pius XII heard of the tragedy on 19 July he left the safety of the Vatican to bless the survivors and their dead. His bright white cassock became speckled with blood as he climbed 'through the smoking rubble of charred houses where more than five hundred victims were strewn'.[4] Standing over a sombre-faced crowd, the pope stretched out his arms in blessing, making his body a stark white crucifix.

Within a week of Pius' visit to San Lorenzo, Mussolini was locked up in jail. He had been toppled by a vote of his own Fascist Grand Council and arrested swiftly afterwards by the king.[5] Hitler was aghast as Rome's fascists 'melted away like snow in the sun'.[6] It would fall to the Nazis to liberate Mussolini, installing him in a puppet state in Salò on the banks of Lake Garda in the northern region of Lombardy. It would also fall to the Nazis to restore fascist leadership to Rome. Like Pius, the Italian general Pietro Badoglio attempted to protect the capital, declaring Rome a demilitarised or 'open' city in August 1943. Ultimately, his efforts were vain. The Nazis were soon sweeping southwards on a mission codenamed Operation Alaric, after the Gothic king who had invaded Rome in 410. On 9 September, Badoglio abandoned the city to its fate, fleeing down the via Tiburtina with the king ahead in a green Fiat.[7] The battle for Rome took place the next day at the Porta San Paolo, where Saint Paul had departed the city to walk to his death. Junior officers and civilians fought Nazi artillery in a struggle that was heroic but futile. 'We have no more ammunition. Do what you can for yourselves, boys,' one officer reportedly said.[8] For the first time, the doors of Saint Peter's Basilica were bolted during the hours of daylight. According to the diary of an American nun, Mother Mary, 'Blood ran in the streets.'[9]

Up on via Veneto in the glamorous rooms of the Hotel Excelsior, the Nazi General Kurt Mälzer passed his days drinking, lunching and cavorting with women. Intoxicated by power, for nine months he would be 'absolute master' of Rome's 1.5 million citizens.[10] Men and women were accosted in the street. Nazis barged through apartment doors. People and supplies were seized, day and night. The cells of the Regina Coeli prison became a squalid waiting room for deportation and, for many, death. Writing from the wreckage, the journalist Paolo Monelli evoked Mälzer's rule of terror: 'he commanded, he forbade, he oppressed'.[11]

In the summer of 1943 Pope Pius XII had rushed to the people. When four bombs fell on the Vatican in November, the people ran to him. Windows had shattered into the cupola of Saint Peter's; the Vatican radio station was blown to bits. Nazi propaganda swiftly turned the finger on 'barbari anglo-americani'. The Roman people knew better than this. A crowd gathered in the square in front of Saint Peter's where Pius appeared at the window of his library to hear their cries. The Germans were still in the city the following spring when Pius emerged on the balcony to a crowd of tens of thousands. Beleaguered by bombing, starvation and Nazi raids, the people had requested an audience with their pope. According to one woman there, the pope was their only sanctuary and solace as they huddled into the curve of Bernini's colonnade: 'German soldiers [were] patrolling the borderline, almost as if to remind us of how near we were to where that area of peace ended and the afflicted city began.'[12]

The enduring significance of the pope for the Roman people might have appeared remarkable to outsiders at the time. Like the king, Pius XII and his predecessor, Pius XI (1922–39), had worked closely with Mussolini. In 1933, when Pius XII was still Secretary of State, the two men had negotiated with Hitler to secure a concordat. Yet even before the flight of King Vittorio Emanuele III, the German diplomat Ernst von Weizsäcker declared that, 'At the moment the Pope is morally King of Rome.[13] 'To create a Papal State under his rule' at that time would have been 'easy'.[14] However, it would have been hard to keep the pope in power, for although the pope was still recognised in his role as Holy Father, the expectations, priorities and principles of the world in which he lived were being transformed. When the Second World War ended, the monarchy born at the Risorgimento died: on 2 June 1946, Italy voted to become a republic with a majority of 54 per cent. For men such as the socialist politician Pietro Nenni, this was a protest against the entire *ancien regime*. He claimed that he cast his vote 'not only against the Quirinal but also against the Vatican'.[15]

Whether Nenni liked it or not, however, the papacy lived on. Its existence depended on principles that were not democratic but eternal and divine. With societies in flux, the popes were still respected and beloved by many people in their role as universal pastor. In 1870, the new Italian king had stripped Pius IX (1846–78) of his traditional political power. By 1945, the pope was the only monarch left in Rome.[16]

— ᚳ ᛒᚩ ᛒᚩ —

Even in 1870 the presence of the popes had weighed heavily on the city, particularly in the mind of King Vittorio Emanuele II (1861–78). The city's symbolic significance as the seat of empire and centre of Christendom was the reason it was chosen as the Italian capital. Musing on the choice, the king's portly Prime Minister, Cavour, described Rome as 'the only city of Italy that did not have memories that were exclusively municipal; all of the history of Rome from the time of the Caesars to today is the story of a city the importance of which extends infinitely beyond its territory'.[17] Looking out through the small, oval spectacles pushed to the top of his nose, Cavour envisaged a Rome that was 'destined to be the capital of a great state'.[18] Cavour would never actually visit the city before his death in 1861. When Vittorio Emanuele II did, the idea of Rome dwarfed the reality. Arriving to take his capital on New Year's Eve 1870, the king was said to have said: 'So, this is it?'[19] He had planned to enter with pomp and ceremony, but the Tiber had burst its banks, flooding Rome's streets with filthy water.

Despite Vittorio Emanuele's low view of the city, it soon seemed like Rome might eclipse the king himself. The bellicose minister, and later Prime Minister, Francesco Crispi complained that 'the King of Sardinia is too trifling a matter for Rome'. Longing for a leader with gravity that would befit the city, Crispi declared, 'Rome, the capital of the world, ought to be the seat of a great monarchy, or of the papacy.' Now that the heroic struggle for a united Italy was over, Vittorio Emanuele would find it difficult to make his mark in a city that was already crowded with symbols. Moreover, affection for the pontiff – who maintained that he was a prisoner in the palace at Saint Peter's – persisted in Rome. The situation was so delicate that the king did not even wish to live at the Quirinal Palace. As the main residence of the papal monarch this was the obvious royal seat, but the pope refused to hand over the keys. Through the Law of Guarantees (1871), he had been offered the palaces of the Lateran and Vatican, as well honours and freedom to act in his religious role.[20] Pius flatly refused the offer, which would make him subject to a law of the Italian state: his actions as head of Christ's Church could not be governed by the whims of a fallible temporal prince. Infuriated by the request to relinquish the Quirinal Palace, the pope mused that even the kidnappers sent by Napoleon Bonaparte had not had the temerity to ask to be let in the front door.[21] Meanwhile, the king refused to barge into the Quirinal like a conqueror. According to his Prime Minister, Giovanni Lanza, Vittorio Emanuele found 'the idea of residing in a palace contested by the pope to be truly repugnant … he would rather bring his hunting tents with him to live in'.[22]

Nationalist accounts of 20 September 1870 paint a city awash with cheering crowds and tricolour flags, but the Italian king was well aware that the capture of Rome had not taken place by popular demand. Even in the broader context of Italy there were divisions about the seizure of the papal capital. Joy rang through the house of the teenage Vittorio Scialoja – later a professor and senator. However, at the home of Filippo Crispolti, the family cried.[23] In Rome itself, foreign visitors noted scenes of fervent exultation, but also saw more cynical tableaux. The British envoy H. Clarke-Jervoise admitted that he witnessed 'many instances where [celebration] was done through terror, the inhabitants being summoned by the crowd to illuminate and hang out the Italian colours'.[24] Some scholars have stated that it is unlikely that so many Romans were ardent enough nationalists to secretly own the illegal tricolour flag. The Papal Zouave Patrick O'Clery was obviously partial, but went as far as claiming that 'the dregs of other Italian cities' were imported to Rome to celebrate.[25]

Even if this were an exaggeration, Vittorio Emanuele's worst fears were borne out in some quarters: there were Romans who considered his actions nothing more than a shameful coup. Settling down to write in his diary on the evening of 20 September, the Roman Prince Vittorio Emanuele Massimo was frothing with scorn:

Thursday 20th. A day that will be eternally memorable for Rome and ignominious for the Italian army of King Vittorio Emanuele, who, wishing to take it from the pope with the ridiculous pretext of making it capital of Italy, has given the whole world the spectacle of seeing this city – the capital not of Italy but of the world – bombed for six hours by the troops of a Catholic king, who, by waging war on religion, has violently taken [Rome] from its sovereign with whom [the king] was not [even] at war.[26]

Unable to fall back on claims of dynastic authority, let alone absolute, God-given power, Vittorio Emanuele's government sought a popular mandate for their seizure of Rome.[27] Concerned about the apathy of the city's inhabitants, Prime Minister Lanza offered free transportation for voters to come from all over Italy.[28] In the end, the Italian government secured a landslide majority with around 80 per cent of the eligible vote.[29]

With the battle for the nation finally completed, the government turned to a much graver task. When the Kingdom of Italy had been established in 1861, the much-admired statesman Massimo d'Azeglio had boldly declared: 'We have created Italy, now we must create Italians.'[30] This was no mean feat. The regions of the peninsula spoke dialects so different that some sounded like distinct tongues. The construction workers who poured into Rome spoke three languages: using a lingua franca on the job, resorting to their local Italian as they took off their boots and murmuring Latin on Sundays at church.[31] Furthermore, the Romans were all too aware of what divided them from their new government: the Piedmontese were said to strut through the city with the 'air of conquistadors'.[32] More rifts appeared when the population swelled from 226,022 inhabitants to 244,484 in just one year. The mood soured further as the city saw unbridled and often corrupt property speculation. The rapid and disjointed development of Rome was described by the poet Gabriele D'Annunzio as 'a battle for gain' fought with 'the pickaxe, the trowel and bad faith'.[33] Government bodies and staff took palazzi while Roman families were housed in disused haylofts.[34]

Poor Romans had lived in the shadow of grand residences in the past, but their new overlords could not justify their position with the blood of old Roman dynasties or Christian martyrs. The new regime needed its own hagiography to smooth over the cracks. In September 1870, a special committee was established for the 'Amplification and Embellishment of the Capital'; the following February, government ministries began to be transferred from their temporary home in Florence.[35] Before a new narrative could be imprinted on Rome, the government had to destroy symbols of papal power. Unwilling to fight the vicar of Christ head on, the governments of Vittorio Emanuele and his son, Umberto I, focused on signs of the temporal authority of the Holy See. Demolition teams would take aim on papal fortifications, such as the military tower built by Paul III on the Capitoline Hill.[36] New government bodies would find homes through the symbolic seizure of the administrative offices of the Papal State. In June 1633, the inquisitors of Pope Urban VIII had exacted justice on Galileo at Santa Maria sopra Minerva. Now it became the Ministry of Finance for an entirely secular regime.[37] Some new seats of authority were also established: the finance minister Quintino Sella founded a new region called the *Città Alta*, sitting in lofty distinction from the old city up on the Quirinal Hill. Much nearer to the Vatican, in the shadow of Castel Sant'Angelo, a vast new supreme court was built in bright white travertine. Lavishly embellished with cornices, balustrades and sculptures, the Palazzo di Giustizia used the Renaissance style beloved of the popes, only now it was employed to proclaim a bold new secular power.

In a piazza behind the court, a saint of the Risorgimento now stood: the corpulent form of Cavour immortalised in bronze. Across the river on the Janiculum, Garibaldi was memorialised atop his horse. His gaze trained on the palace at Saint Peter's, the adventurer still appeared to be working for the Risorgimento cause. Even on the Ponte Cavour, a bridge that would link the area near Saint Peter's to the rest of Rome, figures of victory raised laurels to the city and guns towards the Vatican Hill. On streets nearby, the spirits of the popes' former adversaries were summoned from beyond the grave: when the new residential region of Prati was laid out north-east of the Borgo, the names of Arnold of Brescia and Cola di Rienzo appeared on the street signs. Just as in papal Rome, men and women in the national capital became even greater heroes after their death. While Crispi might have deemed King Vittorio Emanuele 'too trifling a matter' for Rome during his lifetime, the monarch became a figurehead of some gravitas when he died in 1878. Some of Rome's most striking monuments were brought in to service this important new idea. His funeral took place at the Pantheon, once the temple to all gods and, since late antiquity, a church. Below the triangular pediment outside was emblazoned: VITTORIO EMANUELE II FATHER OF THE NATION. The ceremony's location latched the story of Italy's first modern king onto Rome's great imperial and papal pasts, making Vittorio Emanuele a new apotheosis in the grand narrative.

Vittorio Emanuele's son and heir, Umberto I, wanted to make a bolder statement yet: he suggested that his father be buried under the centre of the Pantheon's dome, echoing the position of Saint Peter's tomb at his basilica.[38] Pius IX's successor, Leo XIII (1878–1903), would win the argument on that question. Yet within two years, a similarly brazen claim for the significance of the dead king materialised on the southern slopes of the Capitoline Hill. There, mounds of earth, along with the wreckage of medieval and Renaissance buildings, were carried away to make space for an audacious monument to Vittorio Emanuele. Cutting into the ancient hillside – and the back of the church of the Ara Coeli – the Vittoriano is a sweeping, heavily embellished temple of stark white marble. Sitting atop a complex of staircases and crowned by chariots driven by winged victories, the focus of the monument is an equestrian statue of the king so large that it dominates even this great pile. The writer Primo Levi hoped that the Vittoriano would embody the identity of the nation of Italy in its capital. It would be the 'altar of the new Religion' where 'Rome will feel Italian, and Italy Roman ... This will be the temple of Jupiter, this will be St. Peter's'.[39]

Levi's prediction was poetic, but it was a destiny never to be realised. Today few esteem the Vittoriano above Saint Peter's Basilica. Even while it was under construction, some observers expressed a lack of confidence. Invited to view the monument under construction, the scholar Edoardo Soderini was more taken by the views. Looking out from the staircase, he cried, 'Just look at St. Peter's!'[40] There was a building that provided an 'eternal touchstone for comparison' and showed that 'the political ideal will never accomplish what the religious ideal has done and continues to do'.[41] For the Kingdom of Italy, the battle for the idea of Rome appeared to be lost just as it was beginning, even if symbols of the old regime were also falling away. Pope Pius IX would die, still declaring himself a prisoner, within three weeks of Vittorio Emanuele. The crowd mourning the pope at his funeral at Saint Peter's was three times the size of the group who had gathered for the king at the Pantheon.[42]

— ∽ ❧ ❧ —

'Romanism is a Monster, with arms of Satanic power and strength, reaching to the very ends of the earth.'[43] This message was conveyed clearly in the image printed alongside this quote. The page showed an octopus crowned with a papal tiara stretching out tentacles of 'ignorance', 'superstition', 'tyranny' and 'subversion' to choke 'public money', 'public education', 'civil law' and the American flag. The picture illustrated a book with an equally damning title: *The Pope. Chief of White Slavers. High Priest of Intrigue*, by Jeremiah Crowley. The message was clear: Catholics in the USA were controlled by a pernicious internationalist power.[44] In the late nineteenth century, the polemic patent in this cartoon was rife in America, where many feared Catholic migrants were part of a papal plot to dominate the United States.[45] The situation of the pope certainly preoccupied the American Catholic population. During Pius IX's exile in Gaeta in 1850, the American Catholic press had painted the pope as a Christ-like figure, claiming that 'the hosannas of the day give way to the shout of the deluded multitude – "Crucify him! – Crucify him!"'[46] More papal sympathisers arrived in the diaspora of millions that poured out from Italy into the Americas between 1870 and 1910. American liberals, on the other hand, rejoiced as Rome was reborn at the heart of a liberal nation.[47] For them, Catholics in the US should be viewed with some suspicion as subjects of a pope asserting his divinely awarded temporal power. This attitude was hardly unique to America. The young Woodrow Wilson looked to Germany with admiration, where Chancellor Otto von Bismarck had worked strenuously to stem papal influence.[48] Closer to home, liberals in Mexico had banished 'foreign-born' Jesuits, while an ultramontane bishop, loyal to the pope, had been kicked out of Switzerland.[49]

The fears of men such as Crowley are surprising given the pope's actual situation: deprived of temporal power and confined to the palace at the Vatican. When Italy had taken Rome, the state of Ecuador provided a vociferous protest. The piercing gaze of its President Gabriel García Moreno viewed modern ideologies with just as much scorn as that of Pius IX. Moreno wrote supportive letters and aligned his laws with papal teachings, but these were rare acts of support from a small, remote state.[50] Even within Rome, the pope's presence was felt in fewer corners. When Pius' successor, Leo XIII, inaugurated a year of Holy Jubilee in 1900, the great liturgy of the Church was kept behind closed doors. Metaphorical walls were also built around the Church, as Pius and his successors shored it up against tides of change in the modern world. When some American Catholics appeared to interpret doctrine liberally in the hope of attracting Protestant converts, Leo sent Cardinal James Gibbons of Baltimore a clear reproof.[51] His successor Pius X (1903–14) would take more intensive measures to fight modernism in the Church. Shaped by roots in a peasant family in the Austrian-ruled Veneto, he defined himself as 'intransigent to the core'.[52] In his mission to stem change, he was flanked by his Secretary of State, Raphael Merry del Val, a deeply pious and impressive cardinal of Hispanic and Irish blood. With the 'spies' of under-secretary Monsignor Umberto Benigni, they sniffed out and expelled men with modern ideas, in the Vatican, universities, seminaries and pulpits of the Church.

By the time that Crowley published his book in 1913, the popes appeared to have put themselves in a position of defiance rather than influence in the modern world. However, the conservatism of the popes did not mean that they had given up on their global mission. With many European states rolling back their involvement in religion in the name of secularisation, the popes had much greater control over the workings of the Church.[53] In 1875, Pius IX had refused to host a jubilee in Rome because of the 'impiety, widespread scandals … corruption of morals, and the overturning of divine and human rights' caused by the Italian government.[54] He called for nothing less than the abandonment of the national regime and the restoration of the 'social kingdom of Christ'.[55] In the battle, Catholics around the world were ordered to wield spiritual arms: devotions to the Immaculate Conception and the universal protector of the Church, Saint Joseph. When Pius IX's successor, Leo XIII, announced a jubilee in 1900, 350,000 pilgrims travelled to Rome to support the ninety-year-old pontiff at a 'difficult and anxious' time.[56] Leo would continue his predecessor's call to spiritual warfare, writing a flurry of encyclicals that were published around the world. Casting his mind back to the Battle of Lepanto of 1571, he called the faithful to echo the triumphant Catholic navy by praying the Holy Rosary. Later, Pius X would continue to insist on the popes' role as universal father of the modern world, claiming that Christianity alone had 'everything that aids progress in true civilisation'.[57]

Even with an actual battle invoked, spiritual weapons might not seem particularly intimidating to world powers. Yet popular religion still represented a huge sphere of influence.[58] There were around 291 million Catholics in 1910, 65 per cent of whom lived in Europe.[59] The pope remained the ultimate authority in a creed by which huge swathes of the planet endeavoured to live their everyday lives. He could also win their affection by sanctioning popular devotions. When a nun in Paris revealed that the Virgin Mary had told her to have 'miraculous medals' made, only the pontiff could approve their manufacture and sale to millions of devotees.[60] Some officially endorsed devotions carried explicitly political messages, such as the visions of three peasant children in Fatima, Portugal. When Pope Pius XI approved the visions in 1930, he legitimised a narrative – believed by millions of pilgrims – in which the Communist revolution in Russia was damned by God himself.[61]

Moreover, even while the popes remained 'prisoners of the Vatican', they continued to involve themselves in public life. In the late nineteenth century, the effects of the industrial revolution sparked a striking intervention from Leo XIII. In 1891, he promulgated *Rerum Novarum*, an encyclical on the condition of the working classes. By that time, the machinery of mass production had spread from Britain to continental Europe and many Irish and Italian Catholics worked in factories in Britain and America. In Italy industrial development had been patchier, but by the 1890s artisanal production in many northern cities had developed into factory work.[62] In Rome, the pace of change was slower, but this did not mean that workers were content. At the archaeological excavations at the Palatine Hill and Forum labourers downed their tools when they faced a pay cut.[63] Across the Tiber at the state tobacco factory on Piazza Mastai, only fifty workers of around a thousand reached old age.[64] In the wake of unification, the women of the factory marched on the Capitoline and kidnapped the director when he introduced technology that threatened their jobs.[65] As profiteering and urbanisation burdened the lives of the poorest, the pope spoke out against both capitalist exploitation and radical new ideologies such as Marxism that predicted a class war, claiming that his 'apostolic office urge[d]' him to speak out.[66]

Gradually, Leo and his successors began to accept that the modern state was here to stay and shifted their focus on imbuing its structures with Christianity. Despite his staunch religious conservatism, Pius X was relatively accepting of the new political order. While Bishop of Venice, he had welcomed the Italian king and queen whom Pius IX had shunned. Pius IX had banned Catholics from voting in elections, ordering his flock not to engage with an Italian state that he refused to recognise. Pius X effectively revoked the measure in 1905. The previous year, the extreme wing of the Italian Socialist Party (PSI) had sparked a general strike that appeared to be a dress rehearsal for outright revolution.[67] Pius hoped that Catholics might vote for the 'forces of order' and marginalise 'subversive' candidates.[68] Some Catholics went further yet, seeking to enter the political fray themselves, but Pius was not about to sanction an alternative locus of Catholic power. Instead, he and many members of the faithful turned to Giovanni Giolitti, a pragmatic and authoritative centrist – instantly recognisable by his twirled moustache and bow tie – who would be elected Prime Minister five times. Giolitti maintained the separation of Church and state out of respect for nationalist principles, but he also shaped policies aimed at conservative Catholic voters: he allowed religious education in schools, opposed divorce and conducted a war on the Muslim country of Libya, which many saw as a Holy Crusade.[69]

For a while, the informal alliance worked. Giolitti won much of the Catholic vote and the interests of the Church were largely protected.[70] However, in 1914 both the pope and Giolitti found themselves powerless as Italy took its most significant decision yet. In July of that year, the world went to war, including Italy's ally Austria-Hungary. Giolitti swiftly declared that any stance but neutrality would be catastrophic for the young nation. In his view, Italy was an 'organism still weak, in formation'.[71] By late summer 1914 his voice was echoed by that of the new pope, Benedict XV. Known among Vatican staff as the 'little one', the diminutive Genoese nobleman began what would become a sustained cry for world peace.[72] The voices of the two men united with those of ordinary people across Italy who had no appetite for further unrest and bloodshed. But Giolitti had stepped down as Prime Minister in March and his successor, Antonio Salandra, was inching ever closer to war. As Austria had failed to consult Italy before provoking conflict with Serbia, Italy was not bound to defend its ally. In spring 1915, negotiations for the loyalty of Italy began. At one table, Salandra bartered with Austria over the price of Italian neutrality. At another, he discussed Italy's reward should she fight alongside Britain and France. In May 1915, the alliance with Austria-Hungary and Germany was declared null and void. Italy would fight in the First World War on the Allied side.

On the streets of Rome, a war cry sounded out as the poet, orator and journalist Gabriele D'Annunzio took to the Capitoline Hill.[73] Climbing the steps of the Palazzo Senatorio, overlooking the statue of Marcus Aurelius, D'Annunzio appeared like a prophet whose moment had finally arrived. In the past, his politics had shifted but they were always shaped by emotion and intensity. On that spring day he would pour out both, in a bombardment of rhetoric, on the captivated crowd. In an electrifying speech, d'Annunzio invoked the military pomp of the Caesars and the heroism of Giuseppe Garibaldi. For him, Italian engagement in the First World War would be the final dramatic act of the Risorgimento.

Soon thousands of Italian men would climb the blinding slopes of the Alps, facing barrages of Austrian bullets through thick white snow. Italy was at war, even if the Holy See maintained its neutrality. Still confined to the palace at Saint Peter's, Pope Benedict intervened doggedly for peace. Drafting numerous missives to both sides, he begged them to decrease armaments, exchange prisoners and find fair solutions to territorial claims. Some lauded the pope's efforts, deeming his 'Peace Note' of August 1917 'a diplomatic and international event of the first rank'.[74] In America, President Woodrow Wilson listened respectfully but ultimately viewed the pope as a purely spiritual leader.[75] In the end, Benedict's interventions were ignored by everybody involved. The great states of the world no longer acknowledged the popes' influence in the political realm. Worse still, in many quarters he had become a suspect figure. As persistent calls for the restoration of the Papal States lingered in the air, some feared that Benedict was merely seeking a seat at the negotiating table. Italy had gone to battle with a treaty that specifically excluded the pontiff from any peace talks.[76] The 'Central Powers' of Germany, Austria-Hungary, Bulgaria and the Ottoman Empire also harboured concerns about the pope's neutrality. Some believed that Benedict favoured traditionally Catholic France. As war tore across Europe, it seemed that, in the political sphere, fear of the papal octopus had taken away all of its power.

— ೮೪ ಜಿ ಜಿ —

Many Romans would rejoice when the Allies emerged victorious in November 1918. At the Piazza Venezia, an elderly man helped his grandchildren clamber happily onto seized Austrian cannons. Yet just a short walk away on the Corso Vittorio Emanuele a less celebratory mood filled the air. At the Palazzo Massimo alle Colonne the elderly prince, Vittorio Emanuele Massimo, was in a stand-off with his daughter-in-law. Despite the Allied victory, he refused to hang out the Italian flag. Desperate to celebrate the nation's triumph, his daughter-in-law Eleonora Brancaccio begged him to change his mind. As the resolute prince noted in his diary that evening, '...we objected, never having done so'.[77] The decision reflected the peculiar situation that persisted in Rome. For the Massimo prince and other members of the Black Aristocracy, the Roman Question was still unresolved. The pope was denied his rightful sovereignty and nothing the old prince had seen in the last half century had convinced him of the legitimacy of the national regime.

Before and after the First World War, dissatisfaction with the political powers in Rome was felt well beyond the old papal aristocracy. The seat of Italian power was also decried at the Milanese headquarters of the socialist paper *Avanti!*. For their bombastic editor-in-chief, Benito Mussolini, Rome was the source of 'the infection of national political life ... a vampiric city that sucks the best blood of the nation'.[78] Stating that 'fish begin to stink from their heads: Italy from Rome', a nationalist writer would offer an even blunter assessment.[79] Politics across the peninsula were starkly divided, but disappointment with the central government was a common theme. Anger became acute when the bloodshed of the First World War failed to baptise a bold new nation. In January 1919, the wartime Prime Minister Vittorio Orlando had entered the Paris Peace Conference styling himself the 'Premier of Victory' but he would not make it to the Hall of Mirrors at Versailles to sign the peace treaty that summer.[80] Unable to satisfy both the Allies and demands for the expansion of Italian territory into Dalmatia and Fiume, he had cracked, bursting into tears in the middle of negotiations.[81] A new Prime Minister, Francesco Nitti, was in place in time to go to Versailles. Back in Rome the agreement that he signed was dubbed a 'mutilated victory'. The clever mind behind that slur belonged to Gabriele D'Annunzio, who now seized the moment for triumph. Engaging disaffected soldiers and nationalists, D'Annunzio took what Orlando and Nitti had not dared, seizing Fiume for Italy for some fifteen months and ruling it with a constitution in which a 'cult of music' was a guiding organ of the state.[82] In an attempt to rein in D'Annunzio's influence, Nitti offered him a job, which D'Annunzio rejected. Nitti himself was forced to resign his office after a period of less than one year.

In Rome, one thing was stable: the pope remained in his Holy See. During the war, Benedict had refused to leave the city, even when Spain offered him sanctuary at the palace of El Escorial.[83] The pope remained devoted to the city, even as the war shone a stark light on his awkward situation in Rome. On the Vatican Hill, incoming post was delayed and frequently censored by Italian authorities.[84] Worse still, the pope's diplomatic relations became subject to national politics. When the Italian government sought to punish Austria for bombing Venice in 1916, they marched to the Austrian embassy at the Holy See at the Palazzo Venezia, requisitioning the Renaissance palace, built in large part by Pope Paul II.[85] There was also talk of the seizure of the pontifical German College, which stood on the periphery of the pope's enclave at the Vatican.[86]

For now, however, the question of the popes' temporal sovereignty was dwarfed by broader political concerns. In a climate of economic hardship, support for socialism had burgeoned in Italy. In 1919, the PSI openly declared their intention to enact 'the violent seizure of power on the part of the workers' and establish 'the dictatorship of the proletariat'.[87] Violent protests and strikes plagued the peninsula; men and women were urged to desecrate the flag. Even members of the socialist movement described the situation as 'a red nightmare' and 'civil war'.[88] This was a radical alternative to Giolitti's political pragmatism, with its conservative nods to Catholic creed. Even before the war, the socialists had boasted that they inspired many to secularism, sexual freedom and suicide.[89] Between 1901 and 1910, the number of Italians who claimed to have no religion soared from 36,000 to 874,000. While in power, Giolitti had tried stem the rise of the PSI with higher wages and Sunday rest. When the socialists dominated the general election of 1919, it was clear that he had failed.

In elections for local government the following year, socialists swept to power in seats across northern and central Italy. As the red flag was raised over the town hall in the Renaissance city of Ferrara, Pope Benedict XV became increasingly alarmed. Even his cautious predecessor, Pius X, had acted to stem the socialist threat, not only allowing Catholics to vote but also endorsing lay initiatives for the poor under the umbrella of 'Catholic Action'.[90] Breaking with Pius X's ban on Catholic political parties, Benedict now went even further. He sanctioned the Catholic Popular Party (PPI), led by the dynamic Sicilian priest and political activist, Father Luigi Sturzo.[91] The PPI would prove a swift success in the election of 1919. Sturzo led the PPI to become the second largest group in government, after the socialists.[92]

In the debating chamber of the Palazzo Montecitorio the PSI faced down Sturzo's Popular Party, but on the streets of Italy they had a much more menacing enemy. Repelled by the socialists' neutral stance on the First World War, the journalist Benito Mussolini had resigned his post at *Avanti!* and taken the first steps in forming the Italian fascist movement. Returning to his young baby and partner, Rachele, after quitting, Mussolini declared: 'I haven't a cent ... life will be hard for us ... I have decided to advocate Italy's entry into the war.'[93] By the end of 1914, he had started his own newspaper, *Il Popolo d'Italia*, precisely for that cause. The front pages of the paper cried out to the people: 'the hour to act is now!'[94] Called up to fight in 1915, Mussolini was back at his desk in 1917 after a bomb propelled forty metal shards into his flesh while he was at the front line. In the years that followed he would form a violent anti-socialist group: the *Fasci di combattimento*, or fascists. Meeting in a hall in Milan in 1919, the men were united by a commitment to 'Italy and to the fatherland alone', as well as a vitriolic hatred of socialism and the contemporary Italian regime.[95] Meanwhile, Mussolini capitalised shamelessly on the weaknesses of the government and D'Annunzio's romantic nationalist exploits in Fiume. The group expanded rapidly: the first meeting had gathered around a hundred men and by spring 1921 they had 187,588 members.[96] As an ideology of action and intensity, fascism could not be confined to rented halls for long. Across the north of Italy, young black-shirted *squadristi* burst into villages and cities. Attacking offices with grenades and gunfire and local politicians with clubs, daggers and even dried cod, they waged war on socialism in a campaign of unbridled terror.

Even Mussolini could not claim to be in full control of the movement, though this did not stop him from spurring them on from the headquarters of *Il Popolo d'Italia* in Milan. Looking northwards from Rome, we might imagine that the Italian government would be appalled. But, ever the pragmatist, Giolitti soon identified the fascists as a useful political tool. By the spring of 1921, there were thirty-five fascists sitting in government in Rome. They formed a core part of the National Bloc, a right-wing coalition organised by Giolitti to combat the expansion of socialism.

Before long fascist violence also arrived in the Italian capital. In November 1921, 30,000 fascists stalked the streets of Rome. They were in the city for their national congress, due to take place in the great circular tomb known as the Mausoleum of Augustus. One group had not even left the railway station at Termini before they had murdered their first civilian, a seventeen-year-old railway worker, Guglielmo Farinetti, who was killed on the job.[97] Skirmishes intensified as the *squadristi* reached the working-class region of San Lorenzo. For the fascists, this socialist quarter was 'a cancer that needed to be excised'.[98] Other attacks were driven by the fascists' desire for universal deference. One Roman veteran was beaten brutally when he failed to tip his hat to fascists passing by.[99] By the time the congress ended, five people had been murdered in Rome. To the horror of many, it seemed that the Italian government was now powerless to act. Giolitti had made a pact with Mussolini, and prospects for resistance did not improve when he was succeeded as Prime Minister by Ivanoe Bonomi in July. Mussolini had agreed to restrain the *squadristi* in August but at the congress in November this agreement was officially renounced.[100] Meanwhile, Bonomi claimed that any attempt to control the fascists would only lead to further bloodshed in Rome.

Mussolini had assured Bonomi of his modest ambitions: 'Fascism is still so provincial,' he claimed, 'that it has not been able to win over the ancient soul of Rome.'[101] Mussolini may have lacked admirers in the city, but it was central to his plans. When his group became a political party in 1921, their symbol would be the ancient Roman fasces, a tight bundle of rods surrounding an axe.[102] Meanwhile, Mussolini claimed that the fascists were the rightful successors of the men of the imperial city. In late October 1922, they came to take the capital. A few hundred Italian policemen could have stopped the fascists in their tracks: the force of around forty thousand poorly armed men had arrived in stolen cars and camped on the outskirts of the city, pounded by rain. Instead, the Italian troops who had been ordered to 'defend Rome to the last drop of your blood' ferried food to the would-be invaders as they lay in wait.[103] Convinced that the party would bring law and order, many state authorities openly supported the coup. Earlier that year, a priest in the Veneto had lamented the intimacy between the fascists and the police, who would 'travel around with them in their lorries, sing their hymns and eat and drink with [them]'.[104] Meanwhile, half a million Italian workers signed up to fascist trade unions.

There were brave forces of resistance. Many downed their tools to strike in protest in 1922. However, the fascists appeared to have already won battle for Italy when Mussolini seized the opportunity to swoop in and save the day. By the time that Giolitti and other liberals faced up to the threat, it was simply too late. On 28 October, yet another Prime Minister, Luigi Facta, made a last-ditch attempt to halt the fascists' rise. At 9am he waited for a telephone call from King Vittorio Emanuele III that would confirm that Rome was officially in a state of siege.[105] The call never came. By that time, even the king would not stand up to the fascists. Just a few weeks earlier, his own mother had broken bread with Mussolini's conspirators at the family's coastal villa at Bordighera in the north.[106] In a haze of disbelief, Facta resigned his position. Antonio Salandra declined the king's request to form a new government. Now the King of Italy turned to Benito Mussolini. Once again, the fascist leader was way ahead of the game. In a speech back in September, he had declared the fascists' intention 'to make Rome the city of our spirit ... the beating heart, the galvanising spirit of the imperial Italy that we dream of'.[107]

— ◌ ಏ ಏ —

As the triumphant *squadristi* marched into the capital, a new hymn echoed through the streets: *Giovinezza*, the official anthem of the Fascist Party, declared that fascism alone would be the salvation of the people. At the palace at Saint Peter's, a new pope, Pius XI, looked on as a new creed was enforced in Rome. Cardinal Pietro Gasparri, his Secretary of State, wrote to the Belgian ambassador to the Holy See, suggesting that they all keep an open mind: 'Let's give him a few months' credit, before making a judgement of the revolutionary coup d'état, which', the cardinal added, 'he has carried out in a masterly way.'[108] In a private conversation during Mussolini's first month as Prime Minister, Pius XI took a similarly pragmatic view. Outright praise of Mussolini was to be avoided, but so was open criticism. The small round glasses worn by the new pope reflected his background as a scholar, but Pius was also a man of stamina with a strong sense of realpolitik. Born – like Pius X – in the former Austrian area of Lombardy-Venetia, he climbed mountains as a hobby, claiming that 'once fear has been overcome' no other activity 'feeds both the soul and the body' in the same way.[109] The pope's courage had been plain when Benedict XV sent him on a mission to Poland where he was brave enough to stay in Warsaw as the Soviet Red Army advanced. As fascists streamed into Rome, he kept an equally cool head. It was essential because 'we have many interests to protect.'[110]

At first there did not seem to be much hope for the pope's interests in the rise of a man whose followers had forced priests to drink castor oil. Mussolini himself had compared the clergy to 'black microbes' that infected the minds of the young.[111] At one time, he had even called for the pope to pack up and leave Rome.[112] But just as Mussolini had adopted the city as a powerful symbol, he would use the Catholic religion as a potent political tool. During Mussolini's maiden speech as Prime Minister he startled the chamber by invoking divine aid.[113] Writing to D'Annunzio back in 1920 he had explained that 'Catholicism can be used as one of the greatest forces for the expansion of Italy in the World.'[114] Speaking to the people of Udine, he echoed Pope Leo the Great, painting the Church as the successor of 'that empire that the consular legions of Rome had driven to the ends of the earth.'[115] Moreover, once in power, Mussolini used the language of religion to reinforce the strength and legitimacy of his regime. At the Exhibition of the Fascist Revolution (1932–4) in Rome 'relics' included a blood-soaked handkerchief used to patch up Mussolini after an attempt on his life.[116] A shrine to the other fascist 'martyrs' was also erected, under a huge crucifix.[117]

Relations between the Church and fascist state began quickly in the early days of the regime. As the Holy See still refused to acknowledge the nation of Italy, a middle-aged Jesuit priest emerged as a secret agent to liaise between the two parties. Throughout the period of fascist rule, the figure of Father Pietro Tacchi-Venturi dashed between the office of Mussolini and the palace of the pope, arriving at the Prime Minister's desk with requests on a dizzying array of topics, from fashion magazines to Catholicism in Sweden, Roman brothels and women's swimwear.[118] In their discussions, Mussolini posed himself as an advocate of the Church, mandating religious instruction in schools and ordering that crucifixes be hung in public buildings even before the end of 1922.[119] In 1929, Mussolini achieved his greatest coup yet as defender of the Catholic faith: he resolved the Roman Question by granting the pope sovereignty over a new state. The Vatican City would be a patch of land of some 440,000 square metres, stretching from the square in front of Saint Peter's, beyond the basilica and up the Vatican Hill. The Papal States it was not, but the popes had long given up on them. Once again, the Bishop of Rome enjoyed 'the true and fitting sovereignty of the pope with a liberty and independence not only actual but visible to all.'[120] Across the city, the Vatican state would also have sovereignty over extra-territorial seats and full ownership of San Giovanni in Laterano, Santa Maria Maggiore, San Paolo fuori le Mura and other places of worship. Saint Peter's square was declared a hinterland: ruled by the Vatican but patrolled by Italian police.

Even beyond Bernini's colonnade, Mussolini's Lateran Treaty promised to enforce the will of the popes, declaring that the Italian state would 'take care to impede' anything that infringed on the 'sacred character' of Rome.[121] Soon, the pact between the pope and Mussolini would be written into the city streets. Throughout the thirties, Mussolini oversaw an orgy of destruction and construction that sought to transform key parts of Rome. Thousands of families were driven out to new developments on the periphery called the *borgate*, as their homes were razed to dust.[122] Meanwhile, particularly symbolic elements of ancient and papal Rome were reconfigured in bold new fascist designs. Striking a clear route to the Colosseum from the Piazza Venezia (where Mussolini had taken office), the via dell'Impero was a triumphal route for a modern imperial regime. Lined with figures of the great Caesars, the street hosted celebrations that equated Mussolini's brutal conquest of Ethiopia (1935–7) with the victories of ancient Rome.[123] A little further north, Mussolini would also write himself into the long history of the Roman Church. Erasing centuries of medieval, Renaissance and Baroque architecture, the via della Conciliazione laid a grand avenue between the Vatican City and the city of Rome. Punctuated with slim, modern obelisks, the new street presented the Basilica of Saint Peter in a position of renewed prestige. Yet rather than lauding the building as a religious symbol, it was presented as a prize won by the fascist regime. On the outskirts of the city, its distinctive outline would be borrowed for the church that dominated the skyline of EUR. This was a model fascist quarter that Mussolini intended to unveil to the world at the *Esposizione Universale Roma* of 1942, the exhibition – planned but never opened – that would give EUR its name.

By the spring of 1938, it was clear that fascism itself had violated the sacred character of the city. In May of that year, the pope retreated to his villa at Castel Gandolfo in disgust at events in Rome. Mussolini had tried to buy Pius XI's silence as even the tacit approval of the pope legitimised the regime. Even after Mussolini had made himself dictator, the pontiff could exert some influence by mentioning Catholics who called him to denounce the fascist regime.[124] On the Feast of the Holy Cross in 1938, Pius could not help but speak out, expressing his horror that Rome had been emblazoned with 'another cross that is not the cross of Christ'.[125] The Nazi dictator Adolf Hitler had arrived in Italy with a delegation so vast that it required three special trains. Across the peninsula, fascist authorities courted him lavishly. Now Rome was draped in swastika flags. Illuminating monuments along the via dell'Impero, Mussolini was eager to underline the unique prestige of the city as the first fascist capital. But nearby a less welcoming message appeared outside Mussolini's office on the Palazzo Venezia. Overnight a graffito was scrawled across the wall announcing, 'Rome receives from the Reich the scum with flagpoles, tripods and the cops.'[126]

In the months after Hitler's visit yet more alarmed voices emerged in Rome, as Mussolini imposed racist laws on Italian Jews. In an attempt to buy the pope's acquiescence, he assured Pius that Jews would 'not be subjected to treatment worse than that which was accorded to them for centuries and centuries by the popes.'[127] Emancipated from the ghetto in 1870, the assurance was little comfort to the Jewish community of Rome. In any case, the promise was soon exposed as a lie. Antisemitism was still rife in the Church and its institutions, but one age-old exemption also remained: if Jews converted to Catholicism they were not subject to antisemitic laws. Mussolini ignored this distinction. For him it was 'time that Italians proclaim themselves to be openly racist.'[128] Some of Mussolini's closest confidants would be horrified at this shift, including his former lover Margherita Grassini Sarfatti. In the aftermath of the announcement she wrote a letter in astonished tones, 'You know what happened to us! I am Catholic, & so are both my children, both married to Catholics, & fathers & mothers of Catholic children' yet 'I myself as well as my husband … both my children & myself are considered Jews'.[129] To Sarfatti, it seemed that they were guilty of 'the most heinous sin of today', erasing the family's long devotion to fascism as well as her 'son's glorious death, as a hero, at 17 years of age in the War'.[130]

By the end of January 1939, Pius XI had reached his limit. Sitting alone at his desk late into the night, he sketched out a denunciation of the fascist regime.[131] Mussolini had publicly acknowledged the pope's sovereignty, but he was hardly Charlemagne. Many earlier popes had made deals with rulers who wanted papal favour, but none since Napoleon had used them so cynically. More than this, none had asked them to anoint a political ideology that was a religion in itself, infringing on the Church's mission to educate and the pope's role as universal pastor. The Lateran Treaty had made Pius XI independent by law, but now fascist spies lingered in the corridors of papal power. In less than two weeks, the pope would read out a warning to every bishop in Italy.

When they received the summons to Saint Peter's, some bishops might have predicted the intentions of the pope. In public meetings, Pius had already expressed incredulity at Mussolini's increasing intimacy with the Führer of Germany.[132] But the bishops would never hear Pius XI's chilling warning in Rome. By the time that they were due to meet, the pope was dead. In the days before their meeting, he had admitted that his once robust health was declining and ordered that his remarks be printed instead. What happened after Pius' death proved that the pope had been from paranoid when he feared fascist spies: Mussolini knew all about the speech that he had planned to make. Telephoning the Secretary of State, now Cardinal Eugenio Pacelli, Mussolini ordered that every last copy be made to disappear. His master dead and his heart fearful of a fresh rupture between the Vatican and the Italian state, Pacelli conceded, sending out the order 'that the printer destroy all he possesses relative to that same discourse'.[133]

—— ☙ ❧ ❧ ——

Pius XI had been silenced by his own supposedly autonomous government. Cardinal Pacelli would be elected as Pius XII in the conclave that followed. In his first months as pope, he would tackle some of Mussolini's policies, speaking up for Jews who had converted to Catholicism. As persecution escalated, many Jews would be evacuated or hidden with the help of the Catholic Church; privately, Pius lamented their treatment by the fascists. He did not, however, officially condemn racist measures against Jews who remained in their faith.[134] Particularly acute criticism has surrounded his failure to make an intervention to help non-converted Jews when Nazis imprisoned thousands near the Vatican and then deported them from Rome.[135] Once again, the popes were compromised by their alliance with a political ruler. In the end, the fascist regime who had restored official recognition of papal sovereignty appeared to undermine the popes' role as universal pastor more than any power before. Meanwhile, the popes acted principally in the interests of the Church. It is also likely that Pius XII was driven by fear. In 1939 another world war broke out, sparked by the aggression of Italy's closest ally, Nazi Germany. Italy would enter the war on the side of Hitler in 1940 and, thanks to Mussolini, the Holy See now had much to lose.

And yet it would be Pius not Mussolini who emerged side-by-side with the Romans out of the wreckage of war. In the election campaign that followed the declaration of the Italian Republic in June 1946, even the Communists and Socialists proposed to negotiate with the Vatican.[136] In the end, they did not have to: the Christian Democrats began a long streak of electoral triumph in Italy. When the new assembly put together an Italian Constitution, the papal privileges of the Lateran Treaty were largely preserved. Some members of the government were appalled, decrying a system of dual sovereignty. The eminent Liberal intellectual Benedetto Croce labelled the decision 'an egregious logical error and juridical scandal.'[137] On the whole, however, the pope was accepted as a key figure in the public life of post-war Italy. By the time that the Pope John XXIII (1958–63) was elected, the Liberal party of the Risorgimento was happy to send the sovereign pontiff its warmest congratulations.[138] The pope even remained a major figure in Italian affairs during the radical political movements of the sixties and seventies. When the Communist Red Brigades kidnapped the former Prime Minister, Aldo Moro, in 1978, Pope Paul VI (1963–78) emerged at the centre of negotiations. Snatched outside of his home and bundled into a Fiat 132, Moro was held captive for fifty-four agonising days. The pope offered a ransom of billions of lire for his freedom.[139] Some even suggest that Pope Paul offered to take Moro's place as their hostage.[140] After Moro's body was discovered on via Caetani, dumped in an abandoned car, the anguished, frail pontiff presided over the state funeral at San Giovanni in Laterano.

Yet even if the alliance between Church and state endured in some form, the people of Rome appeared ever less heedful of the moral authority of the popes. Attitudes had begun changing much earlier, as we saw in the boasts of the socialists. In 1932, Rome's Cardinal-Vicar found entire *rioni* of the city where religious practice had become 'extremely low'.[141] Stories such as that of the Jewish prostitute, Porzia, in 1559 remind us that full churches were not necessarily evidence of broad obedience to the teachings of the Church. Still, lives and attitudes in Italy were entirely transformed in the wake of the Second World War. US aid flowed into the peninsula via the Marshall Plan, an attempt to curb the spread of communism and socialism through humanitarian support. Industry became more lucrative with new oil refineries and a major steel plant, expanding further through the demands of continued foreign wars.[142] In a matter of decades, Italy developed from a largely rural nation into a major world economy: it was dubbed the Economic Miracle. During this time, modern products were not only a new-found luxury but also a powerful agent of social and cultural change. Between 1954 and 1964, the number of cars on Italy's roads multiplied from 700,000 to more than 5 million.[143] As in so many places, young people defined themselves in radical contrast to the period before the war.[144] In Rome, the city filled with traffic; bells that had rung out over ages were frequently unheard. In 1964 the organisers of the annual procession for Saint Francis admitted permanent defeat.[145]

People had always deviated from Catholic morality in the city, but now previously taboo practices became widely accepted and even officially recognised. It was a gradual process, in which society and culture evolved together with criticism and resistance along the way. In 1958, Rugantino, a restaurant in Trastevere, was shut down after an event hosted there violated the sacred character of Rome. It had been the twenty-fifth birthday party of Countess Olghina di Robilant, but Aïché Nanà, a ballerina from Lebanon, stole the spotlight when she did an impromptu striptease to the music of the Roman New Orleans Jazz Band.[146] Nanà would end the evening in a police interrogation. Two years later, another member of the party, the Swedish film star Anita Ekberg, starred in Federico Fellini's *La Dolce Vita* (1960). Opening with a group of sunbathing women waving at a statue of Christ, the film was a glamorous if critical showcase of a Roman élite for whom Christian morals did not appear to apply.[147] Meanwhile, religious adherence in some quarters was painted as mere artifice. In Pier Paolo Pasolini's *La Ricotta* (1963), the bourgeoisie act out the Christian religion with crude superficiality while Rome's working classes are crucified, starving and poor.[148] The city's Catholic identity certainly appeared skin deep in 1975: as Paul VI welcomed pilgrims for a Holy Jubilee, the people of Rome voted in favour of divorce at a rate nearly ten per cent higher than the average across Italy.[149] This was a particular blow to Paul VI who, with his predecessor John XXIII, had sought to reform the Church through the Second Vatican Council (1962–5). In the wake of the council, a liturgy that was centuries old was updated in an effort to engage ordinary people: traditional Latin was widely abandoned, guitar-music was heard and priests turned away from the cross and towards the people as they celebrated Mass.

Popes such as John XXIII had hoped that they might update the language of the Church to speak more compellingly to the modern world. It seemed that many in Rome had already decided that they did not care what the popes had to say. By the end of the eighties, only fifteen per cent of people in the city went to Sunday Mass.[150] In 1981, nearly 70 per cent of the public voted to keep abortion legal, decidedly rejecting Vatican campaigns once again. Even during the Second Vatican Council, the Cardinal-Vicar of Rome, Angelo Dell'Acqua, surmised that the discussions of the delegates were 'an operation about which the Romans had not known a thing' – except those residents who hosted council fathers in their hotels or dodged the mini-buses and Mercedes that carried delegates to the Vatican.[151] Acknowledging the transformation of the life and character of the city, even the government gave up on preserving the sacred character of Rome. In 1983, the statement that had sought to preserve Rome as an innately holy city was diluted to an acknowledgment of the fact that Rome was special to Catholics: 'the Italian republic recognises the particular significance that Rome, the episcopal see, has for Catholicity'.[152] Looking out at the city that popes once ruled as the vicars of Christ, Pope John Paul II (1978–2005) detected an attitude towards Christian morality 'that comes close to indifference.'[153]

— ◌ ❧ ❧ —

On the afternoon of 13 May 1981, Rome and the world appeared far from indifferent to the pope. It was around half past five in the afternoon when John Paul II's limp body was sped from Saint Peter's Square. The pope's panicked security detail ran ahead of the white open-top Fiat Campagnola, known as the popemobile. They batted away journalists' cameras, clearing an escape route from the square. Just seconds before, John Paul II had been standing upright, ready to grasp the hands of the faithful who awaited his blessing as he passed. That day men and women had gathered at Saint Peter's in their tens of thousands, beaming, with flashing cameras, ready to meet their pope. As the basilica's bells had pealed to announce the arrival of the pontiff, the sound of gunshot had also rung out. The faces in the crowd contorted in horror: four bullets had been fired and two had struck the body of the pope.

The image of the twenty-three-year-old Turkish assailant, Ali Mehmet Ağca, flashed onto television screens around the world. Earlier in the afternoon, Ağca had taken the pleasant walk from his hotel in via Cicerone before sitting outside Saint Peter's, writing postcards from Rome.[154] In the minutes before the attack, he had been near invisible, clutching his gun behind a row of pilgrims waiting on the square. After opening fire on the Holy Father, Ağca tried to disappear again. Fleeing through the dense, alarmed crowd, his path was blocked by the formidable figure of the Franciscan nun, Letizia Giudici: 'I waited in vain that day for someone to block him' – 'it fell to me to catch Ali Ağca'.[155] With nowhere to run, the assassin turned his pistol on Giudici but another nun nearby grabbed his arm.[156] When the head of Vatican security, Camillo Cibin, leapt over a wooden barricade, even Ağca knew that the game was up.

By that time the pope was being sped northwards to Rome's Agostino Gemelli hospital where surgeons extracted fragments of bullet just millimetres from his heart. 'The World prays for the pope', a Catholic paper declared the next day.[157] For them, this was an attack that had not only hurt the pope but 'deeply wounded the heart of humanity.'[158] As John Paul II lay in hospital fighting for his life, the world's press and leaders also mourned the attack. In Canada, Prime Minister Pierre Elliott Trudeau lamented the 'barbaric' attempt to fell one of 'God's own messengers of peace'.[159] The Prime Minister of Israel, Menachem Begin, asked his people to pray for the pope and the resumption of 'his good works for all of mankind'.[160] Reflecting on the violent shooting, Begin added, 'if that could happen, anything could happen.'[161] Just as in centuries past, it seemed that Rome and its popes were symbolic protagonists in a drama that encompassed the whole world. Even Ağca, the assassin, eventually came to see the Roman pontiff as a potent actor in a great divine plan: 'I absolutely wanted to kill the pope and wanted to die in Saint Peter's square by suicide or lynching. After many years, I have understood ... that on the 13 May 1981 God realised a miracle in Saint Peter's square.'[162]

Ağca was far from the only individual to see the pope as a pivotal figure in the divine plan. Less than two weeks before his attack, an Aer Lingus Flight en route to London Heathrow had been hijacked by a fifty-four-year-old Australian man wielding demands for the pope.[163] An ex-monk from the Roman abbey built on the spot where Saint Paul had lost his head, Laurence James Downey had been expelled after punching his superior in the face. On the plane, he drenched himself in petrol before marching to the cockpit with his demands: the press must call the pope to reveal a mystery known as the Third Secret of Fatima. This was one of the messages that three Portuguese peasant children claimed to hear from the Virgin Mary in the summer of 1917.[164] Revealed to the public in 1941, the first two messages had offered a horrifying vision of hell and a warning of a second world war should offences against God continue and Communist Russia fail to convert.[165] In the third secret, Downey believed the pope held a message on which world history could turn. The millions who made pilgrimages to Fatima would have agreed. When John Paul II finally revealed the third secret in the year 2000, it only appeared to confirm his significance: it was a vision of a pope at whom men 'fired bullets and arrows'.[166]

Ağca's true motives for shooting the pope have never been established. Some have posited that he shot the pope as a symbol of the medieval Crusades. Later Ağca himself stated that he targeted John Paul II as 'the incarnation of all that is capitalism'.[167] Others have argued that the attack was ordered by the KGB, the security agents of the Communist Soviet Union where John Paul II defended the freedom of Catholics.[168] The sheer range of hypotheses suggests that the pope remains a meaningful figure, even if his precise significance in public life is up for debate.

Even within the Church, attitudes towards the popes are wildly mixed. For a great many, papal authority has been corroded by horrifying revelations that successive pontiffs covered up widespread sexual abuse. Under the sheer weight of the office, Pope Benedict XVI (2005–13) became the first pontiff to resign voluntarily since 1294. Many Romans were delighted when the Petrine authority passed to Francis I (2013–), who – even in the satirical portrayals of comedians such as Maurizio Crozza – is portrayed as a warm and merciful figure. Despite joy in some quarters, Francis' reforms to the liturgy and overtures to the modern world have exacerbated divisions among Catholics, with liberals delighted by change and conservatives predicting a schism in the Church. Beyond the Church, Francis is lauded by global leaders and Western media when he appears to conform to the norms of the day. However, when he pushes against accepted beliefs, he is not influential, but often derided or ignored. The pope's influence in the modern world is, therefore, contingent on an ever shifting political and moral landscape. Never in the history of the papacy have there been so many interpretations of the pope's role and influence.

And yet one tradition endures, unquestioned and, ostensibly, untouchable: the city of Rome and the papacy remain inextricably entwined. Of the more than one billion people who identify themselves as members of the Catholic Church, less than a quarter now live in Europe.[169] Despite this radical geographic shift, officially, all subscribe to the belief that the ultimate locus of authority remains in Rome, where the blood of Peter became a wellspring of authority still claimed by the pope today. Moreover, the city also remains a microcosm for broader conflicts in the Church. The pontiff's actions as head of the Church continue to reverberate in Rome, just as they did in the diplomatic dramas and spectacular ceremonies of the early modern age. When Pope Francis appeared to attack traditional Catholic groups in 2017, posters were pasted up in the city overnight. On walls all over Rome, the stony-faced pontiff looked out from above a statement that echoed those of Pasquino in centuries past, asking where the pope's trademark mercy had gone.

Rome also remains the platform from which the pope speaks to the world. In March 2020, its streets stood empty. But the pope still stood on the Vatican Hill. Coronavirus had hit in a global pandemic that would take a reported 179,000 Italian lives. The people of Rome were locked inside their houses as Francis walked alone, a solitary white figure, through Saint Peter's square. Reaching a specially erected platform, the pope faced a city that was eerily silent and lashed by heavy rain. That day Francis was accompanied by a single attendant and symbols that wrote him into a centuries-long narrative that unites the popes, people and city of Rome. On his left was the crucifix of San Marcello, carried through Roman streets ravaged by plague in 1522. On his right, stood the *Salus Populi Romani* – or the Salvation of the Roman People – an image of Mary that arrived in Rome in the late sixth century. At that time, Pope Gregory the Great had led a procession of beleaguered Romans towards Saint Peter's, imploring God for deliverance. In March 2020, Francis stood in Gregory's shadow, declaring that the colonnade outside the basilica still 'embraces Rome and the world'.

The pope cut a solitary figure that bleak day on Saint Peter's square. Despite appearances, however, the pontiff did not stand alone. Addressing Rome and the world, Francis took his place at the end of a line of more than 260 popes, and, like each and every one of them, on the grave of Peter himself. Speaking of the pandemic, the pope talked of 'a deafening silence and a distressing void'. At first glance, the quiet, empty square over which the pontiff presided might have seemed a damning metaphor for the gulf between the Church and the modern West. However, it was also a powerful testimony of the remarkable endurance of the papacy in a fluctuating and uncertain world, still rooted in the ground where those first devotees to Saint Peter had walked.

Notes

1. Henrietta Harrison, *The Missionary's Curse and Other Tales from a Chinese Catholic Village* (Berkeley: University of California Press, 2013), 10. In the last decade, the Chinese government has sought to exert greater control over Chinese Catholics by eroding the Roman character of the Church in China. See, for example, 'China wants to "sinicise" its Catholics', *Economist*, 22 November 2022.

CHAPTER 1: IN THE FOOTSTEPS OF PETER

1. Quoted in Eusebius of Caesarea, *Ecclesiastical History*, 2.25.5–7. The regnal dates of the first five popes, except Clement I, are uncertain and will not be included in the text.

2. Francesco Buranelli, *The Vatican Necropoles. Rome's City of the Dead* (Turnhout: Brepols, 2010), 55, fn.29.

3. Frederic Baumgartner, *Behind Locked Doors: A History of the Papal Elections* (London: Palgrave Macmillan, 2003), 4.

4. Peter Lampe, 'Roman Christians Under Nero (54–68 CE)' in Armand Puig I Tàrrech, John M. G. Barclay & Jörg Frey (eds), *The Last Years of Paul. Essays from the Tarragona Conference, June 2013* (Tübingen: Mohr Siebeck, 2015), 118.

5. Buranelli, ibid., 48.

6. Ibid., 52–4.

7. Rodolfo Lanciani, *Pagan and Christian Rome* (Boston & New York: Houghton Mifflin, 1892), 129–30 & H.P.V. Nunn, 'St. Peter's Presence in Rome: The Monumental Evidence', *Evangelical Quarterly*, vol. 22 (1950), 133.

8. John O'Malley, *A History of the Popes: From Peter to the Present* (Lanham: Rowman & Littlefield, 2009), 10.

9. Ludwig Kaas, *LIFE*, 27 March 1950, 82.

10. Orazio Marucchi, J. Armine Willis (trans.), *Christian Epigraphy. An Elementary Treatise with a collection of ancient Christian inscriptions mainly of Roman origin* (Cambridge: Cambridge University Press: 1912), 81.

11. Markus Vinzent, 'Rome' in Margaret M. Mitchell and Frances M. Young (eds), *Cambridge History of Christianity* (Cambridge: Cambridge University Press, 2006), vol.1, 402.

12. Roald Dijkstra, 'Peter, Popes, Politics and more: the Apostle as Anchor' in Dijkstra (ed.), *The Early Reception and Appropriation of the Apostle Peter (60–800 CE)* (Leiden: Brill, 2020), 4.

13. 1 Peter, 5:13.

14. George E. Demacopoulos, *The Invention of Peter: Apostolic Discourse and Papal Authority in Late Antiquity* (Philadelphia: University of Pennsylvania Press, 2013), 14.

15. Romans, 15:20.

16. Epistle of Ignatius to the Romans, Chapter 4.

17. Irenaeus of Lyon, *Against Heresies*, Book III, Chapter 3:3.

18. Mary Beard, John North & Simon Price, *Religions of Rome. Volume 1. A History* (Cambridge: Cambridge University Press, 1998), 295.

19. Peter Lampe, 'Roman Christians Under Nero (54–68 CE)', 122–123. See also, Lampe, Michael Steinhauser (trans.), *From Paul to Valentinus. Christians at Rome in the First Two Centuries* (London: Continuum, 2003).

20. Beard, North & Price, ibid., 177.

21. Ibid., 36.

22. Dionysius of Halicarnassus, *Roman Antiquities*, Book VII, 72:15–18.

23. Susanne William Rasmussen, 'Roman Religion' in Lisbeth Bredholt Christensen, Olav Hammer & David A. Warburton (eds.), *The Handbook of Religions of Ancient Europe* (London: Routledge, 2014), 203.

24. Suetonius, *Augustus*, 43:1.

25. Marietta Horster, 'Living on Religion: Professionals and Personnel' in Jörg Rüpke (ed.), *A Companion to Roman Religion* (Oxford: Wiley–Blackwell, 2011), 337.

26. Beard, North & Price, ibid., 298.

27. Mary Beard, 'The Cult of the "Great Mother" in Imperial Rome. The Roman and the "Foreign"' in J. Rasmus Brandt & Jon W. Iddeng (eds), *Greek and Roman Festivals. Content, Meaning and Practice* (Oxford: Oxford University Press, 2012), 340–1.

28. Beard, North & Price, ibid., 245.

29. Ibid., 226.

30. Michel Malaise, *Inventaire préliminaire des documents égyptiens découverts en Italie* (Leiden: Brill, 1972), 187–92.

31. Lampe, ibid., 118.

32. S.M. Savage, 'The Cults of Ancient Trastevere', *Memoirs of the American Academy in Rome*, vol. 17 (1940), 52–3.

33. Martijn Icks, *The Crimes of Elagabalus. The Life and Legacy of Rome's Decadent Boy Emperor* (London: I.B. Tauris, 2013), 30.

34. John Granger Cook, *Crucifixion in the Mediterranean World* (Tübingen: Mohr Siebeck, 2014), 182.

35. Gillian Clark, *Christianity and Roman Society* (Cambridge: Cambridge University Press, 2004), 6.

36. Erich Gruen, 'Jews of Rome Under Nero' in Puig I Tàrrech, Barclay & Frey (eds), *The Last Years of Paul*, 100.

37. Ibid., 93.

38. Bernard Green, *Christianity in Ancient Rome: The First Three Centuries* (London: Bloomsbury, 2010), 21–3.

39. Gruen, ibid., 93.

40. *Acts of the Apostles*, 18:1–3.

41. Lampe, *From Paul to Valentinus*, 359.

42. Kim Bowes, *Private Worship, Public Values and Religious Change in Late Antiquity* (Cambridge University Press, 2008), 49.

43. Minucius Felix, *Octavius*, 8:4.

44. Lampe, 'Roman Christians Under Nero (54–68 CE)', 118.

45. Lucius Apuleius, *The Golden Ass*, Book IX: 22–5.

46. Bowes, Ibid., 54.

47. Thomas H. Tobin, 'Paul's Letter to the Romans' in David E. Aune (ed.), *The Blackwell Companion to the New Testament* (Oxford: Wiley–Blackwell, 2010), 399.

48. Patricia Cox Miller, *Women in Early Christianity. Translations from Greek Texts* (Washington D.C.: The Catholic University of America Press, 2005), 62.

49. Puig i Tàrrech, 'Paul's Missionary Activity during his Roman Trial: The Case of Paul's Journey to Hispania' in Puig I Tàrrech, Barclay & Frey (eds), *The Last Years of Paul*, 473.

50. Brent D. Shaw, 'The Myth of the Neronian Persecution', *Journal of Roman Studies*, (2015), 4–5.

51. Ibid.

52. Suetonius, *The Lives of the Twelve Caesars*, 'Claudius', Chapter 25.

53. Tacitus, *Annals*, Book 15, Chapter 44.

54. These are the words of Lactantius, an author born around 250 AD, whose characterisation of Nero is typical of early Christian writers: Lactantius, *Of the Manner in which the Persecutors Died*, Chapter 2.

55. Tacitus, ibid.

56. Shaw, ibid.

57. Some have argued that Peter was crucified on the Janiculum Hill, but the scholarly consensus is that he died on the Vatican Hill. See Angelus A. de

Marco, *The Tomb of Saint Peter. A Representative and Annotated Bibliography of the Excavations* (Leiden: Brill, 1964), 44.

58. *The Acts of Peter*, Chapter 53.

59. Tertullian, *Prescription Against Heretics*, Chapter 36: 3.

60. Suetonius, *The Lives of the Twelve Caesars*, 'Nero', Chapter 16.

61. Pliny the Elder, *Natural History*, 17:5.

62. Pliny the Younger, *Letters* 10: 96–7.

63. Stephen Benko, *Pagan Rome and the Early Christians* (London: Batsford, 1985), 1.

64. Green, *Christianity in Ancient Rome*, 124–5.

65. Benko, ibid., 8.

66. Mary Beard & Keith Hopkins, *The Colosseum* (Harvard: Harvard University Press, 2005), 23.

67. Ibid., 2.

68. Green, ibid., 125.

69. Lampe, 'Roman Christians Under Nero', 127.

70. Manilio Simonetti, 'Le Origini di Roma Cristiana' in Angela Donati (ed.) *Pietro e Paolo. La Storia, il culto, la memoria nei primi secoli* (Milan: Electa, 2000), 24–5.

71. Ibid., 22–3.

CHAPTER 2: 'YOU HAVE WON, GALILEAN': THE RISE OF CHRISTIAN ROME

1. Jerome, Letters, 22:27 (to Eustochium).

2. Keith Hopkins & Christopher Kelly (eds), *Sociological Studies in Roman History* (Cambridge: Cambridge University Press, 2017), 439.

3. H.C. Teitler, *The Last Pagan Emperor. Julian the Apostate and the War Against Christianity* (Oxford: Oxford University Press, 2017).

4. Ibid., 3.

5. Christine Caldwell Ames, *Medieval Heresies: Christianity, Judaism and Islam* (Cambridge: Cambridge University Press, 2015), 45–7.

6. Jill Harries, *Imperial Rome AD 284 to 363. The New Empire* (Edinburgh: Edinburgh University Press, 2012), 42.

7. Ibid., 42–3.

8. Galerius (305–11) and Severus (306–7) would be Caesar Augusti of the East and West respectively, while Maximinius Daza (305–13) would be Constantine's counterpart, as Caesar in the East.

9. Adrastos Omissi, *Emperors and Usurpers in the Later Roman Empire. Civil War, Panegyric and the Construction of Legitimacy* (Oxford: Oxford University Press, 2018), 106.

10. Maxentius' father Maximian (286–305 / 306–8) had ruled with Diocletian before the latter retired.

11. Rebecca Usherwood, *Political Memory and the Constantinian Dynasty. Fashioning Disgrace* (Cham: Springer, 2022), 17.

12. Charles Matson Odahl, *Constantine and the Christian Empire* (London: Routledge, 2004), 81.

13. Hans A. Pohlsander, *The Emperor Constantine* (London: Routledge, 1996), 23–4.

14. Arnold Jones, *Constantine and the Conversion of Europe* (Toronto: University of Toronto Press, 1978), 49–50.

15. David Stone Potter, *Constantine the Emperor* (Oxford: Oxford University Press, 2015), 143.

16. Quoted in Potter, *Constantine the Emperor*, 143–4.

17. Lactantius, *On the Deaths of the Persecutors*, Chapter 44: 1–11.

18. Gregor Kalas, *The Restoration of the Roman Forum in Late Antiquity. Transforming Public Space* (Austin: Texas University Press, 2015), 51.

19. Eusebius, *Life of Constantine*, Chapter XL.

20. Mario Baghos, *From the Ancient Near East to Byzantium. Kings, Symbols and Cities* (Newcastle: Cambridge Scholars Publishing, 2021), 183.

21. Clark, *Christianity and Roman Society*, 95–105.

22. Alaric Watson, *Aurelian and the Third Century* (London Routledge, 2004), 200.

23. Eusebius, *Oration of Constantine*, Chapter 24

24. Eusebius, *Ecclesiastical History*, Book VII: Chapter 30: 21; Lactantius, *Of the Manner in which the Persecutors Died*, Chapter VI.

25. Green, *Christianity in Ancient Rome*, 210.

26. Clark, *Christianity and Roman Society*, 50–1.

27. Ibid., 50.

28. Elizabeth DePalma Digeser, *A Threat to Public Piety. Christians, Platonists and the Great Persecution* (Ithaca: Cornell University Press, 2012), 1–2.

29. Green, ibid., 211.

30. *P. Luther 4*: Decian Libellus, Theadelphia, 12 June–14 July 250 (Luther College, Iowa).

31. Beard, North & Price, *Religions of Rome. Volume 1*, 295.

32. Green, ibid.

33. Hopkins & Kelly (eds), *Sociological Studies in Roman History*, 452.

34. Lorne Bruce, 'A Note on Christian Libraries during the Great Persecution 303–305 AD', *The Journal of Library History*, (1980), 131–2.

35. Eusebius, *Ecclesiastical History*, Book VII, Chapter 13.

36. Lactantius, *Of the Manner in which the Persecutors Died*, Chapter XXXIV.

37. Green, *Christianity in Ancient Rome*, 212–13. By this point, there were numerous bishops who were defined as either the head of an individual

Christian community or, since the early third century, the leader of several Christian communities. Alistair C. Stewart, *The Original Bishops. Office and Order in the First Christian Communities* (Grand Rapids: Baker Academic, 2014), 1–2.

38. Ibid., 213.

39. Vinzent, 'Rome', 411.

40. Eusebius, *Ecclesiastical History*, Book X, Chapter 5.

41. Lactantius, *Of the Manner in which the Persecutors Died*, Chapter XLVIII.

42. Alan Cameron, *The Last Pagans of Rome* (Oxford: Oxford University Press, 2011), 3.

43. Sarah Iles Johnston (ed.), *Religions of the Ancient World* (London: Belknap Press, 2004), 278.

44. Kalas, *The Restoration of the Roman Forum in Late Antiquity*, 70–71.

45. Eric Thunø, *Image and Relic. Mediating the Sacred in Early Medieval Rome* (Rome: l'Erma di Bretschneider, 2002), 14.

46. Mark Humphries, *Early Christianity* (London: Routledge, 2006), 40.

47. 'Lançon, Nevill (trans.), *Rome in Late Antiquity*, 100.

48. Rosamond McKitterick, John Osborne, Carol M. Richardson & Joanna Story (eds), *Old Saint Peter's Rome* (Cambridge: Cambridge University Press, 2013), 2.

49. Ibid.

50. Lançon, Nevill (trans.), ibid.

51. Baumgartner, *Behind locked doors*, 5.

52. Lançon, Nevill (trans.), ibid; Michael Walsh, *The Conclave. A sometimes secret and occasionally bloody history of papal elections* (Norwich: Canterbury Press, 2003), 4–5.

53. Ignatius of Antioch, *Epistle of Ignatius to the Smyrnaeans*, Chapter 8.

54. Lançon, Nevill (trans.), ibid.

55. Lellia Cracco Ruggini, 'Rome in Late Antiquity: Clientship, Urban Topography and Prosopography', *Classical Philology*, vol. 98, no.4 (2003), 374.

56. Cynthia White, *The Emergence of Christianity* (Minneapolis: Fortress Press, 2007), 111.

57. Peter Norton, *Episcopal Elections 250–600. Hierarchy and Popular Will in Late Antiquity* (Oxford: Oxford University Press, 2007), 64.

58. Mark Humphries, *Cities and the Meanings of Late Antiquity* (Leiden: Brill, 2019), 58.

59. Ibid.

60. Dennis Trout, *Damasus of Rome. The Epigraphic Poetry* (Oxford: Oxford University Press, 2015), 7.

61. Lançon, Nevill (trans.), *Rome in Late Antiquity*, 101.

62. John R. Curran, *Pagan City and Christian Capital. Rome in the Fourth Century* (Oxford: Oxford University Press, 2002), 136.

63. Bill Leadbetter, 'From Constantine to Theodosius (and beyond)' in Philip F. Esler (ed.), *The Early Christian World. Volume I–II* (London: Routledge, 2000), 264.

64. Jonathan Bardill, *Constantine, Divine Emperor of the Christian Golden Age* (Cambridge: Cambridge University Press, 2012), 381.

65. Henry Chadwick, *The Church in Ancient Society. From Galilee to Gregory the Great* (Oxford: Oxford University Press, 2001), 198–9.

66. Eusebius, *Life of Constantine*, Book 3, Chapter 10.

67. Chadwick, ibid., 370.

68. Trout, ibid., 15.

69. Matthew Drever, *Image, Identity and the Forming of the Augustinian Soul* (Oxford: Oxford University Press, 2013), 89.

70. Clark, *Christianity and Roman Society*, 43.

71. Justin Martyr, *Dialogue with Trypho*, Chapter 110.

72. Marcus Aurelius, *Meditations*, Book 11, Chapter 3.

73. Tertullian, *Ad Scapulam*, Chapter V: 1.

74. Trout, ibid., 16.

75. Ibid.

CHAPTER 3: CROWNED ON THE GRAVE OF EMPIRE

1. Pelagius, *Letters*, 30 (to Demetrias) quoted in Peter Brown, *Augustine of Hippo. A Biography* (Berkeley: California University Press, 2000), 287.

2. Jerome, *Letters*, 127: 3 (to Principia).

3. Kim J. Hartswick, *The Gardens of Sallust. A Changing Landscape* (Austin: University of Texas Press, 2004), xii.

4. John Moorhead, *The Popes and the Church of Rome in Late Antiquity* (London: Routledge, 2015), 2–3.

5. David L. D'Avray, 'Stages of papal law', *Journal of the British Academy*, 5 (2017), 38.

6. Thomas Hobbes, *Leviathan; or, the matter, forme and power of a commonwealth, ecclesiasticall and civill* (London: Andrew Crooke, 1651), 386.

7. D'Avray, ibid., 37–56.

8. Jordanes, Charles Christopher Mierow (trans.), *The Gothic History of Jordanes* (Cambridge: Speculum Historiale, 1906), 98.

9. Jordanes, Mierow (trans.), *The Gothic History*, 98.

10. Andrew Merrills & Richard Miles, *The Vandals* (Oxford: Wiley, 2010), 117.

11. Ibid.

12. Michele Renee Salzman, *The Falls of Rome. Crises, Resilience and Resurgence in Late Antiquity* (Cambridge: Cambridge University Press, 2021).

13. Gerontius, 'The Life of Melania the Younger' in Carolinne Witte (trans.) (ed.), *Lives of Roman Christian Women* (London: Penguin, 2010).

14. Lynda L. Coon, *Sacred Fictions. Holy Women and Hagiography in Late Antiquity* (Philadelphia: University of Pennsylvania Press, 1997), 114.

15. Judith Herrin, *Unrivalled Influence. Women and Empire in Byzantium* (Princeton: Princeton University Press, 2013), 142.

16. Bowes, *Private Worship, Public Values and Religious Change in Late Antiquity*, 65.

17. I. M. Plant (ed.), *Women Writers of Ancient Greece and Rome. An Anthology* (Norman: University of Oklahoma Press, 2004), 170.

18. Augustine, *Letters*, 130:3 (to Anicia Faltonia Proba).

19. Geoffrey Dunn, 'The Christian Networks of the Aniciae: The example of the letter of Innocent I to Anicia Juliana', *Revue d'études augustiniennes et patristiques*, 55 (2009), 54–5.

20. Jerome, *Letters*, 130:1 (to Demetrias).

21. Penny MacGeorge, *Late Roman Warlords* (Oxford: Oxford University Press, 2002), 13.

22. Ibid.

23. Seth William Stevenson, C. Roach Smith & Frederic W. Madden, *A Dictionary of Roman Coins, Republican and Imperial* (London: George Bell, 1889), 482.

24. Judith Herrin, *Ravenna. Capital of Empire, Crucible of Europe* (Princeton: Princeton University Press, 2020), 11–12.

25. Lançon, *Rome in Late Antiquity*, 105.

26. Beard, North & Price, *Religions of Rome. Volume 1*, 262–3.

27. Richard Krautheimer, *Rome. Profile of a City, 312–1308* (Princeton: Princeton University Press, 2000), 35.

28. Joseph Mullooly, *Saint Clement, Pope and Martyr and His Basilica in Rome* (Rome: G. Barbera, 1873), 214.

29. Augustine, *Letters*, 138: 3 (to Marcellinus).

30. Ibid.

31. Beard, North & Price, ibid., 387.

32. Edward Gibbon, *The Decline and Fall of the Roman Empire* (London: W. Strahan, 1776–89).

33. Moorhead, *The Popes and the Church of Rome in Late Antiquity*, 8.

34. Prosper of Aquitaine, *Epitoma Chronicon* in Theodore Mommsen (ed.), *Monumenta Germaniae Historica. Inde ab anno Christi quingentesimo usque ad*

annum millesima et quingentesimum, vol. 9, part 2 (Berlin: Weidmannsche, 1891), 484.

35. Herwig Wolfram, Thomas Dunlap (trans.), *The Roman Empire and its Germanic Peoples* (Berkeley: University of California Press, 1990), 172.

36. Susan Wessel, *Leo the Great and the Spiritual Rebuilding of a Universal Rome* (Leiden: Brill, 2008), 37.

37. Hugh Elton, *The Roman Empire in Late Antiquity. A Political and Military History* (Cambridge: Cambridge University Press, 2018), 191.

38. Ibid.

39. Prosper of Aquitaine quoted in James Harvey Robinson, *Readings in European History. Volume 1* (Boston: The Athenaeum Press, 1904), 49–50.

40. Anonymous account quoted in Robinson, ibid., 50.

41. Ibid., 51.

42. McKitterick, Osborne, Richardson & Story (eds), *Old Saint Peter's Rome*, 3.

43. Klaus Schatz, *Papal Primacy. From Its Origins to the Present* (Collegeville: The Liturgical Press, 1996), 17.

44. Ibid., 17–18.

45. Turhan Kaçar, 'Constantinople and Asia Minor: Ecclesiastical Jurisdiction in the Fourth Century' in Stephen Mitchel & Philipp Pilhofer (eds), *Early Christianity in Asia Minor and Cyprus. From Margins to the Mainstream* (Leiden: Brill, 2019), 156.

46. J.E. Riddle, *The History of the Papacy, to the period of the Reformation* (London: Richard Bentley, 1856), 170.

47. See contemporary petitions against Dioscorus translated in Claude Fleury, *The Ecclesiastical History.* AD *429 to* AD *456* (Oxford: John Henry Parker, 1844), 355.

48. Pauline Allen & Bronwen Neil, *Crisis Management in Late Antiquity (410–590 CE)* (Leiden: Brill, 2013), 101.

49. Daniel Caner, *Wandering, Begging Monks. Spiritual Authority and the Promotion of Monasticism in Late Antiquity* (Berkeley: University of California Press, 2002), 227.

50. Schatz, ibid.

51. Ibid., 44.

52. Bronwen Neil, *Leo the Great* (Abingdon: Routledge, 2009), 43.

53. Schatz, ibid., 44.

54. Ibid., 44.

55. Neil, *Leo the Great*, 42.

56. Ibid., 43.

57. Moorhead, *The Popes and the Church of Rome in Late Antiquity*, 7.

58. Eamon Duffy, *Ten Popes Who Shook the World* (New Haven: Yale University Press, 2011), 42.

59. Nicola Denzey Lewis, *The Early Modern Invention of Late Antique Rome* (Cambridge: Cambridge University Press, 2020), 243.

60. Roger Dunkle, *Gladiators. Violence and Spectacle in Ancient Rome* (Abingdon: Routledge, 2008), 119.

61. Ibid., 79.

62. Tertullian, T. R. Glover (trans.), *Apology. De spectaculis. With an English translation by T. R. Glover* (London: William Heinemann Ltd., 1977), 231 & 249.

63. Ibid., 251–3.

64. Peter J. Leithart, *Defending Constantine. Twilight of an Empire and the Dawn of Christendom* Downers Grove: Intervarsity Press, 2010), 196.

65. Richard F. Devoe, *Christianity and the Roman Games. The Paganization of Christians by Gladiators, Charioteers, Actors and Actresses from the First through the Fifth Centuries* AD (Philadelphia: Xlibris, 2002), 140.

66. Theoderet, *Ecclesiastical History*, Chapter XXVI.

67. Ibid.

68. Ibid.

69. Constantine after victory over Maxentius in 312 and then briefly in 315 and 326; Constantius II four years after the overthrow of Magnentius in 357; Valentinian II in 388 as he fled the usurper Maximus; and Theodosius in 389 after his defeat of Maximus and again after his defeat of Eugenius.

70. Louise Ropes Loomis (ed.) (trans.), *The Book of the Popes (Liber Pontificalis)*, (New York: Nova, 2018), 146.

71. Veronica West-Harling, *Rome, Ravenna and Venice, 750–1000. Byzantine Heritage, Imperial Present and the Construction of City Identity* (Oxford: Oxford University, 2020), 112.

72. Ibid.

73. Paul the Deacon, *History of the Langobards*, Chapter XXIV.

74. Ibid.

75. Rosemary Horrox (trans.) (ed.), *The Black Death* (Manchester: Manchester University Press, 1994), 95.

76. Elizabeth Forbis, *Municipal Virtues in the Roman Empire. The Evidence of Italian Honorary Inscriptions* (Stuttgart: B.G. Teubner, 1996), 29–31.

77. Cicero, *On Duty*, 1:42.

78. Anneliese Parkin, '"You do him no service": an exploration of pagan almsgiving' in Margaret Atkins & Robin Osborne (eds), *Poverty in the Roman World* (Cambridge: Cambridge University Press, 2009), 64.

79. Alan Thacker, 'Popes, emperors and clergy at Old Saint Peter's from the fourth to the eighth century' in McKitterick, Osborne, Richardson & Story (eds), *Old Saint Peter's Rome*, 146.

80. Lançon, Nevill (trans.), *Rome in Late Antiquity*, 30.

81. Moorhead, *The Popes and the Church of Rome in Late Antiquity*, 6.

82. Thacker, ibid., 57.

83. Moorhead, ibid., 4.

84. Thacker, ibid., 144.

85. Ibid., 137–144.

86. Hagith Sivan, *Galla Placidia. The Last Roman Empress* (Oxford: Oxford University Press, 2011), 71.

87. François Dolbeau, 'Nouveaux sermons de saint Augustin pour la conversion des païens et des donatistes', *Revue des Études Augustiniennes*, 37 (1991), 76.

88. Ibid.

89. Paolo Liverani, 'Saint Peter's and the city of Rome between Late Antiquity and the early Middle Ages' in McKitterick, Osborne, Richardson & Story (eds), *Old Saint Peter's Rome*, 30.

90. Maijastina Kahlos, *Religious Dissent in Late Antiquity, 350–450* (Oxford: Oxford University Press, 2020), 155.

91. Ibid., 153.

92. Moorhead, ibid., 9.

93. Thunø, *Image and Relic*, 84.

94. Krautheimer, *Rome. Profile of a City, 312–1308*, 90.

95. Ibid.

CHAPTER 4: HOLY ROME: RELICS, INVADERS AND THE POLITICS OF POWER

1. Eleanor Shipley Duckett, *Death and Life in the Tenth Century* (Ann Arbor: University of Michigan Press, 1967), 88–9.

2. Gerd Tellenbach, Timothy Reuter (trans.), *The Church in Western Europe from the Tenth to the Early Twelfth Century* (Cambridge: Cambridge University Press, 1993), 71.

3. Peter Partner, *The Lands of St Peter. The Papal State in the Middle Ages and the Early Renaissance* (London: Eyre Methuen, 1972), 90.

4. Chris Wickham, *Medieval Rome. Stability & Crisis of a City* (Oxford: Oxford University Press, 2015), 336.

5. Walter Goffart, *Barbarian Tides. The Migration Age and the Later Roman Empire* (Philadelphia: University of Pennsylvania Press, 2006), 162.

6. Jonathan J. Arnold, *Theodoric and the Roman Imperial Restoration* (Cambridge: Cambridge University Press, 2014), 62.

7. Ibid.

8. Quoted in Peter Brown, *The World of Late Antiquity* (New York: W.W. Norton, 1989), 123.

9. Thomas S. Burns, 'Theodoric the Great and Concepts of Power in Late Antiquity', *Acta Classica*, vol. 25 (1982), 102.

10. Charles Freeman, *A New History of Early Christianity* (New Haven: Yale University Press, 2009), 308.

11. John W. Barker, *Justinian and the Later Roman Empire* (Madison: The University of Wisconsin Press, 1966), 102.

12. Samuel Cohen, 'Spelunca pravitatis hereticae: Gregory I and the Rededication of "Arian" Church Buildings in Late Antique Rome', *Journal of Early Christian Studies*, vol. 30, no. 1 (2002), 4–5.

13. M.J. Zeiller, 'Les Églises Ariennes de Rome a l'époque de la domination gothique', *Mélanges de l'école français de Rome*, vol. 24 (1904), 19.

14. Peter J. Heather, *Rome Resurgent. War and Empire in the Age of Justinian* (Oxford: Oxford University Press, 2018), 287–8.

15. Christian Hülsen, *S. Agata dei Goti* (Rome: Sansaini, 1924), 39.

16. Maya Maskarinec, *City of Saints. Rebuilding Rome in the Early Middle Ages* (Philadelphia: University of Pennsylvania Press, 2018), 81–2.

17. Andrew J. Ekonomou, *Byzantine Rome and the Greek Popes. Influences on Rome and the Papacy from Gregory the Great to Zacharias*, AD 590–752 (Lanham: Lexington Books: 2007), 4.

18. Kalas, *The Restoration of the Roman Forum in Late Antiquity*, 97.

19. Maskarinec, ibid., 80–1.

20. Cosmedin either refers to a monastery in Constantinople or the Greek word for ornament.

21. Baumgartner, *Behind locked doors*, 10.

22. Ekonomou, ibid., 199.

23. Peter Sarris, *Empires of Faith. The Fall of Rome to the Rise of Islam, 500–700* (Oxford: Oxford University Press, 2011), 283.

24. Ekonomou, ibid., 220.

25. Ibid., 270.

26. Herrin, *Ravenna*, 295.

27. Rosamond McKitterick, 'The papacy and Byzantium in the seventh- and early eighth-century sections of the Liber Pontificalis', *Papers of the British School at Rome*, vol. 84 (2016), 253.

28. The story appears for the first time in the sixteenth-century history of Cesare Baronio.

29. McKitterick, 'The papacy and Byzantium', 254.

30. Timothy E. Gregory, *History of Byzantium* (Oxford: Wiley–Blackwell, 2010), 209.

31. Andrew Louth, *Greek East and Latin West. The Church,* AD *681–1071* (Crestwood: St Vladimir's Seminary Press, 2007), 82.

32. Maskarinec, *City of Saints.*

33. Éamonn Ó Carragáin & Carol Neuman de Vegvar (eds), *Roma Felix – Formations and Reflections of Medieval Rome* (Aldershot: Ashgate, 2007), 2–3 & Maskarinec, City of Saints, 41.

34. Ó Carragáin & Neuman de Vegvar (eds), ibid.

35. Charles Freeman, *Holy Bones, Holy Dust. How Relics Shaped the History of Medieval Europe* (New Haven: Yale University Press, 2011), 57.

36. H.C.G. Matthew & Brian Harrison (eds), *Oxford Dictionary of National Biography. From the earliest times to the year 2000* (Oxford: Oxford University Press, 2004), 944–50.

37. Stephen of Ripon, *The Life of Bishop Wilfrid by Eddius Stephanus* (Cambridge: Cambridge University Press, 1985), 13.

38. Ibid., 67.

39. Ibid.

40. Freeman, ibid., 72.

41. Patrick J. Geary, 'Sacred Commodities: The Circulation of Medieval Relics' in *Living with the Dead in the Middle Ages* (Cornell University Press, 1994), 208.

42. The Venerable Bede, *Ecclesiastical History of England,* Book V, Chapter 7.

43. Paul the Deacon, William Dudley Foulke (trans.), Edward Peters (ed.), *History of the Lombards* (Philadelphia: University of Pennsylvania Press), 2–4.

44. Federico Marazzi, 'Byzantines and Lombards' in Salvatore Cosentino (ed.), *A Companion to Byzantine Italy* (Leiden: Brill, 2021), 169–70.

45. See, for example, the distractions of the late 740s: Herrin, ibid., 339.

46. Thomas F. X. Noble, *The Republic of St. Peter: The Birth of the Papal State, 680–825* (Philadelphia: University of Pennsylvania Press, 1984), 32.

47. Herrin, ibid., 342.

48. Noble, ibid., 78–9.

49. Mike Humphreys (ed.) *A Companion to Byzantine Iconoclasm* (Leiden: Brill, 2021), 35–6.

50. Noble, ibid., 80.

51. Mayke de Jong, 'Charlemagne's Church' in Joanna Story (ed.), *Charlemagne. Empire and Society* (Manchester: Manchester University Press, 2005), 116.

52. Ferdinand Lot, Philip Leon & Mariette Leon (trans.), *The End of the Ancient World* (Abingdon: Routledge, 2000), 301.

53. Katherine Fischer Drew, *Lombard Laws* (Philadelphia: University of Pennsylvania Press, 1996), 19–20.

54. Paul Balchin, *Rome: The Shaping of Three Capitals* (Abingdon: Routledge, 2020), 135.

55. Ekonomou, *Byzantine Rome and the Greek Popes*, 247.

56. Michael L. Nash, *The History and Politics of Exhumation. Royal Bodies and Lesser Mortals* (Cham: Springer International Publishing, 2019), 20–1.

57. Quoted in Liudprand of Cremona, Paolo Squatriti (trans.), *The Complete Works of Liudprand of Cremona*, 64.

58. Florin Curta, *Eastern Europe in the Middle Ages (500–1300)* (Leiden: Brill, 2019), vol.1, 205.

59. West-Harling, *Rome, Ravenna, & Venice, 750–1000*, 67.

60. Ibid.

61. Partner, *The Lands of St Peter*, 79–82.

62. Liudprand of Cremona, Squatriti (trans.), *The Complete Works*, 97.

63. Ibid., 96.

64. David S. Bachrach, *Warfare in Tenth-century Germany* (Woodbridge: Boydell Press, 2014), 62.

65. Liudprand of Cremona, Squatriti (trans.), ibid., 219.

66. West-Harling, ibid., 70.

67. Balchin, ibid., 135.

68. Ferdinand Gregorovius, *History of the City of Rome in the Middle Ages. Volume 3* (Cambridge University Press, 2010), 351–2.

69. Wickham, *Medieval Rome*, 22.

70. I.S. Robinson, *The Papal Reform of the Eleventh Century. Lives of Pope Leo IX and Pope Gregory VII* (Manchester: Manchester University Press, 2004), 2–4.

71. Uta-Renate Blumenthal, *The Investiture Controversy. Church and Monarchy from the Ninth to the Twelfth Century* (Philadelphia: University of Pennsylvania Press, 2010), 65.

72. H.E.J. Cowdrey, *Pope Gregory VII, 1073–85* (Oxford: Clarendon Press, 1998), 44.

73. Wickham, ibid., 181.

74. Beard & Hopkins, *The Colosseum*, 163.

75. Wickham, Medieval Rome, 181.

76. Krautheimer, *Rome. Profile of a City*, 157.

77. I.S. Robinson, *The Papacy 1073–1198. Continuity and innovation* (Cambridge: Cambridge University Press, 1990), 13.

78. Ibid., 14.

79. Kurt Stadtwald, *Roman Popes and German Patriots. Antipapalism in the politics of the German humanist movement from Gregor Heimburg to Martin Luther* (Geneva: Librairie Droz, 1996), 58.

80. Robinson, ibid., 16.

81. John of Salisbury, *Historia Pontificalis*, Chapter 27, n.13, 59 quoted in I.S. Robinson, *The Papacy 1073–1198. Continuity and innovation* (Cambridge: Cambridge University Press, 1990), 13.

CHAPTER 5: BETWEEN AVIGNON, BABYLON AND ROME

1. Louis Gayet, *Le Grand Schisme d'Occident. D'Après les documents contemporains déposés aux archives secrètes du Vatican* (Florence: Loescher & Seeber, 1889), 100–101.

2. Joëlle Rollo-Koster, 'Civil Violence and the Initiation of the Schism' in Rollo-Koster & Thomas M. Izbicki, *A Companion to the Great Western Schism* (Leiden: Brill, 2009), 24.

3. Joëlle Rollo-Koster, *Raiding Saint Peter. Empty Sees, Violence and the Initiation of the Great Western Schism* (Leiden: Brill, 2008), 17.

4. Ibid., 201.

5. Dante Alighieri, *Paradiso*, XXVII.

6. Unn Falkied, *The Avignon Papacy Contested. An Intellectual History from Dante to Catherine of Siena* (London: Harvard University Press, 2017), 2–3.

7. Thomas M. Izbicki, 'The Revival of Papalism at the Council of Basel' in Michiel Decaluwe, Thomas M. Izbicki & Gerald Christianson (eds), *A Companion to the Council of Basel* (Leiden: Brill, 2017), 137.

8. Marcus Bull, 'Origins' in Jonathan Riley-Smith (ed.), *The Oxford History of the Crusades* (Oxford: Oxford University Press, 1999), 27.

9. Paolo Prodi, *The Papal Prince. One body and two souls: the papal monarchy in early modern Europe* (Cambridge: Cambridge University Press: 1987), 46.

10. Dante Alighieri, *Inferno*, XIX: 115–17.

11. William of Ockham, Arthur Stephen McGrade (ed.), John Kilcullen (trans.), *A Short Discourse on the Tyrannical Government. Over Things Divine and Human, but Especially Over the Empire and Those Subject to the Empire, Usurped by Some Who Are Called Highest Pontiffs*, (Cambridge: Cambridge University Press, 1992), 18.

12. Joëlle Rollo-Koster, *Avignon and Its Papacy, 1309–1417. Popes, Institutions and Society* (Lanham: Rowman & Littlefield, 2015), 25.

13. Ronald G. Musto, *Apocalypse in Rome. Cola di Rienzo and the Politics of the New Age* (Berkeley: University of California, 2003), 60.

14. R. Ambrosi de Magistris, *Storia di Anagni* (Anagni: Vicenzo Apolloni, 1889), vol. I, 126.

15. Dario Internullo, *Ai margini dei giganti. La vita intellettuale dei romani nel Trecento (1305–1367 ca.)* (Rome: Viella, 2016), 23.

16. Debra Julie Birch, *Pilgrimage to Rome in the Middle Ages. Continuity and change* (Woodbridge: Boydell Press, 1998), 198.

17. Diana Webb, 'Pardons and Pilgrims' in R.N. Swanson, *Promissory Notes on the Treasury of Merits. Indulgences in Late Medieval Europe* (Leiden: Brill, 2006), 244.

18. Lucia Travaini, 'From the treasure chest to the pope's soup. Coins, mints and the Roman Curia (1150–1350)' in Werner Maleczek (ed.) *Die römische Kurie und das Geld. Von der Mitte des 12. Jahrhunderts bis zum frühen 14. Jahrhundert 20* (Ostfildern: Jan Thorbecke Verlag, 2018), 20.

19. Clifford William Maas, *The German Community in Renaissance Rome, 1378–1523* (Rome: Herder, 1981), 26.

20. Ibid., 26.

21. Travaini, ibid.

22. Internullo, ibid., 35.

23. Hastings Rashdall, *The Universities of Europe in the Middle Ages. Volume 2, Part 1: Italy, Spain, France, Germany, Scotland, etc.* (Cambridge: Cambridge University Press, 2010), 38.

24. Internullo, ibid., 36.

25. Falkied, *The Avignon Papacy Contested*, 3–4.

26. Joseph R. Strayer, *The Reign of Philip the Fair* (Princeton: Princeton University Press, 1980), 4.

27. William Chester Jordan, 'The Capetians from the death of Philip II to Philip IV' in David Abulafia (ed.), *The Cambridge Medieval History. Volume V c.1198-c.1300* (Cambridge: Cambridge University, 1999), 308.

28. Ibid.

29. John France, *The Crusades and the Expansion of Catholic Christendom 1000–1714* (London: Routledge, 2005), 220.

30. 'non tam ex infirmitate quam cordis angustia'.

31. Sophia Menache, *Clement V* (Cambridge: Cambridge University Press, 1998), 15.

32. Menache, *Clement V*, 17.

33. Barbara Bombi, *Anglo-Papal Relations in the Early Fourteenth Century* (Oxford: Oxford University Press, 2019), 135.

34. Menache, *Clement V*, 17–18.

35. Musto, *Apocalypse in Rome*, 60.

36. Joëlle Rollo-Koster, 'Mercator Florentinensis and others: Immigration in Papal Avignon' in J. Drendel & Kathryn Reyerson *Urban and Rural Communities in Medieval France* (Leiden: Brill, 1998), 73–4.

37. Internullo, *Ai margini dei giganti*, 41.

38. Ludwig von Pastor, *The History of the Popes, From the Close of the Middle Ages. Volume I* (London: Kegan Paul, Trench, Trübner, & co., 1906), 92.

39. Gur Zak, *Petrarch's Humanism and the Care of the Self* (Cambridge: Cambridge University Press, 2010), 7.

40. Francesco Petrarch in James Harvey Robinson (ed.), *Petrarch. The First Modern Scholar and Man of Letters* (New York: Haskell House, 1970), 65.

41. Petrarch, *Sine nomine* quoted in Falkied, *The Avignon Papacy Contested*, 98.

42. Petrarch, *Invectiva contra eum qui maledixit Italiae* quoted in Falkied, ibid., 105–6.

43. Ole J. Benedictow, *The Black Death 1346–1353. The Complete History* (Woodbridge: Boydell Press, 2004), 93.

44. Musto, ibid., 257.

45. Ibid.

46. Emilio Re, 'The English Colony in Rome during the Fourteenth Century', *Transactions of the Royal Historical Society*, (1923), vol. 66, 77–8.

47. Ibid.

48. James A. Palmer, *The Virtues of Economy. Governance, power and piety in late medieval Rome* (Ithaca: Cornell University Press, 2019), 14.

49. Musto, ibid., 23.

50. Robert Brentano, *Rome before Avignon. A Social History of Thirteenth-century Rome* (New York: Longman, 1974); Hendrik Dey, *The Making of Medieval Rome. A New Profile of the City, 400–1200* (Cambridge: Cambridge University Press, 2021), 170–5.

51. Internullo, ibid., 21.

52. Ibid., 26.

53. James A. Palmer, 'Medieval and Renaissance Rome: Mending the Divide', *History Compass*, (2017), 1–2.

54. Rollo-Koster, *Avignon and Its Papacy, 1309–1417*, 72.

55. F. Donald Logan, *A History of the Church in the Middle Ages* (London: Taylor and Francis, 2012), 303.

56. Emmanuel Ladurie, *Montaillou. Cathars and Catholics in a French Village 1294–1324* (London: Penguin, 2013).

57. Rollo-Koster, *Avignon and Its Papacy, 1309–1417*, 59.

58. Amanda Collins, *Greater than Emperor. Cola di Rienzo (ca. 1313–54) and the World of Fourteenth-century Rome* (Ann Arbor: The University of Michigan Press, 2002), 15.

59. Musto, *Apocalypse in Rome*, 71.

60. Ibid., 29–31.

61. Collins, ibid., 40.

62. Musto, ibid., 56.

63. James A. Palmer (ed.) (trans.), *The Chronicle of an Anonymous Roman. Rome, Italy and Latin Christendom, c.1325–1360* (New York: Italica Press, 2021), 183.

64. Ibid., 184.

65. Musto, ibid., 183.

66. Palmer (ed.) (trans.), ibid., 185.

67. Ibid.

68. Ibid., 186.

69. Collins, ibid., 38.

70. Musto, ibid., 180.

71. Palmer (ed.) (trans.), ibid., 193.

72. Palmer (ed.) (trans.), ibid., 193–4 & Amy Schwarz, 'Eternal Rome and Cola di Rienzo's Show of Power' in Laurie Postlewate & Wim Hüsken (eds), *Acts and Texts. Performance and Ritual in the Middle Ages and the Renaissance* (Amsterdam: Rodopi, 2007), 66.

73. Schwarz, ibid., 68.

74. Internullo, *Ai margini dei giganti*, 29.

75. Bridget Morris, *Birgitta of Sweden* (Woodbridge: Boydell Press, 1999), 2.

76. Ibid., 57.

77. Marta González Vázquez, 'Women and Pilgrimage in Medieval Galicia' in Carlos Andrés González-Paz (ed.), *Women and Pilgrimage in Medieval Galicia* (London: Routledge, 2016), 38.

78. Falkied, *The Avignon Papacy Contested*, 27.

79. Re, 'The English Colony in Rome during the Fourteenth Century', 76.

80. Claire L. Sahlin, *Birgitta of Sweden and the Voice of Prophecy* (Woodbridge: Boydell Press, 2001), 55.

81. Re, ibid., 82–3.

82. Ibid., 80–1.

83. Judith F. Champ, *The English Pilgrimage to Rome. A Dwelling for the Soul* (Leominster: Gracewing, 2000), 45–6.

84. Re, 'The English Colony in Rome during the Fourteenth Century', 83. See also, Champ, *The English Pilgrimage to Rome*, 45–6.

85. Anna Esposito, 'National Confraternities in Rome and Italy in the Late Middle Ages and Early Modern Period: Identity, Representation, Charity' in Konrad Eisenbichler (ed.), *A Companion to Medieval and Early Modern Confraternities* (Leiden: Brill, 2019), 246.

86. Ibid., 240.

87. Internullo, *Ai margini dei giganti*, 30.

88. Schwarz, 'Eternal Rome and Cola di Rienzo's Show of Power', 69.

89. Partner, *The Lands of St Peter*, 333–4.

90. Collins, *Greater than Emperor*, 236–7.

91. Falkied, *The Avignon Papacy Contested*, 118.

92. Musto, *Apocalypse in Rome*, 172.

93. Ibid.

94. Palmer (ed.) (trans.), *The Chronicle of an Anonymous Roman*, 273.

95. Musto, ibid., 344.

96. Falkied, ibid., 103.

97. Rollo-Koster, *Avignon and Its Papacy, 1309–1417*, 89.

98. Palmer, *The Virtues of Economy*, 15.

99. Irene Fosi, Thomas V. Cohen (trans.), *Papal Justice. Subjects and Courts in the Papal State, 1500–1700* (Washington D.C.: The Catholic University of America Press, 2011), 41.

100. Bridget of Sweden, Denis Searby (trans.), Bridget Morris (ed.), *The Revelations of St. Birgitta of Sweden. Volume 2* (Oxford: Oxford University Press, 2008), 249.

101. Carol M. Richardson, *Reclaiming Rome. Cardinals in the Fifteenth Century* (Leiden: Brill, 2009), 15.

CHAPTER 6: ECHOES OF THE ANCIENTS: THE RENAISSANCE OF PAPAL ROME

1. Partner, *The Lands of St Peter*, 398.

2. Katherine Rinne, 'Renovatio Aquae: Aqueducts, Fountains and the Tiber River in Early Modern Rome' in Pamela M. Jones, Barbara Wisch & Simon Ditchfield (eds), *A Companion to Early Modern Rome, 1492–1692* (Leiden: Brill, 2019), 327.

3. There is some debate over the precise date of Finicella's trial. See Franco Mormando, *Bernardino of Siena and the Social Underworld of Early Renaissance Italy* (Chicago: University of Chicago, 1999), 236.

4. Gary K. Waite, *Heresy, Magic and Witchcraft in Early Modern Europe* (Basingstoke: Palgrave Macmillan, 2003), 38.

5. Jeffrey Burton Russell, *Witchcraft in the Middle Ages* (Ithaca: Cornell University Press, 1972), 216.

6. Fosi, Cohen (trans.), *Papal Justice*, 1–6.

7. Thomas V. Cohen & Elizabeth S. Cohen, 'Justice and Crime' in Jones, Wisch & Ditchfield (eds), *A Companion to Early Modern Rome*, 122; Fosi, Cohen (trans.), *Papal Justice*, 53.

8. Cohen & Cohen, 'Justice and Crime', 115–16.

9. Ibid.,122.

10. Ferdinand Gregorovius, Annie Hamilton (trans.), *History of the City of Rome in the Middle Ages. Volume 6. Part 2* (Cambridge: Cambridge University Press, 2010), 668.

11. Ibid., 669.

12. Elizabeth McCahill, *Reviving the Eternal City. Rome and the Papal Court 1420–47* (Cambridge Mass.: Harvard University Press, 2013), 4.

13. Gregorovius, Hamilton (trans.), ibid., 493.

14. John M. Hunt, *The Vacant See in Early Modern Rome. A Social History of the Papal Interregnum* (Leiden: Brill, 2016), 73.

15. Ibid., 26.

16. Ibid, 43–4.

17. John M. Hunt, 'Rome and the Vacant See' in Jones, Wisch & Ditchfield (eds), *A Companion to Early Modern Rome*, 112.

18. Hunt, *The Vacant See in Early Modern Rome*, 44.

19. Rollo-Koster, 'Civil Violence and The Initiation of the Schism', 11.

20. Logan, *A History of the Church in the Middle Ages*, 289.

21. Partner, *The Lands of St Peter*, 368.

22. Joëlle Rollo-Koster, *The Great Western Schism, 1378–1417. Performing Legitimacy, Performing Unity* (Cambridge: Cambridge University Press, 2022), 248.

23. Ibid, 2.

24. Logan, *A History of the Church in the Middle Ages*, 307.

25. McCahill, ibid., 12.

26. Eleonora Canepari & Laurie Nussdorfer, 'A Civic Identity' in Jones, Wisch & Ditchfield (eds), *A Companion to Early Modern Rome*, 35.

27. Ibid., 35.

28. Ibid., 30.

29. Miles Pattenden, *Electing the Pope in Early Modern Italy, 1450–1700* (Oxford: Oxford University Press, 2017), 34.

30. Ibid., 34.

31. Pattenden, 'The Roman Curia' in Jones, Wisch & Ditchfield (eds), *A Companion to Early Modern Rome*, 46.

32. McCahill, *Reviving the Eternal City*, 12.

33. Jennifer Mara DeSilva, 'Articulating Work and Family: Lay Relatives in the Papal States, 1420–1549', *Renaissance Quarterly*, vol.69, no.1 (2016), 2.

34. *Dizionario Biografico degli Italiani* (Rome: Istituto della Enciclopedia Italiana, 1982), vol. 27, 320–21.

35. Partner, *The Lands of St Peter*, 397.

36. Birgit Emich, 'The Cardinal Nephew' in Mary Hollingsworth, Miles Pattenden & Arnold Witte (eds), *A Companion to the Early Modern Cardinal* (Leiden: Brill, 2020), 85.

37. Ferdinand Gregorovius, Annie Hamilton (trans.), *History of the City of Rome in the Middle Ages. Volume 7. Part 1* (Cambridge: Cambridge University Press, 2010), 10.

38. Rinaldo degli Albizzi, *Comissioni di Rinaldo degli Albizzi per il Comune di Firenze dal MCCCXCIX AL MCCCCXXXIII. Volume secondo [1424–1426]* (Florence: M. Cellini, 1869), 160.

39. Ibid.

40. Richardson, *Reclaiming Rome*, 6.

41. Pattenden, 'The Roman Curia', 50–1.

42. Mario Rosa, 'Curia Romana e pensioni ecclesiastiche: fiscalità pontificia nel mezzogiorno (secoli xvi–xviii), *Quaderni* storici, vol. 14, no. 42 (1979), 1030.

43. Paul F. Grendler, *Universities of the Italian Renaissance* (Baltimore: The Johns Hopkins University Press, 2002), 497.

44. Richardson, ibid., 7.

45. Cowdrey, *Pope Gregory VII, 1073–1085*, 44.

46. Norman Zacour, 'The Cardinals' View of the Papacy, 1150–1300' in Christopher Ryan (ed.), *The Religious Roles of the Papacy: Ideals and Realities 1150–1300* (Toronto: Pontifical Institute of Medieval Studies, 1989), 416.

47. Katherina M. Wilson, *Medieval Women Writers* (Manchester: Manchester University Press, 1984), 257.

48. Ibid.

49. Catherine Fletcher, *Diplomacy in Renaissance Rome. The Rise of the Resident Ambassador* (Cambridge: Cambridge University Press, 2015), 17.

50. Ludwig von Pastor, *The History of the Popes, From the Close of the Middle Ages. Volume I* (London: Kegan Paul, Trench, Trübner, & co., 1906), 263.

51. McCahill, *Reviving the Eternal City*, 3.

52. *Dizionario Biografico degli Italiani* (Rome: Istituto della Enciclopedia Italiana, 2004), vol. 63, 40.

53. Maas, *The German Community in Renaissance Rome*, 2.

54. Gregorovius, Hamilton (trans.), *History of the City of Rome in the Middle Ages. Volume 6. Part 2*, 655.

55. Marina Belozerskaya, *To Wake the Dead. A Renaissance Merchant and the Birth of Archaeology* (New York: W.W. Norton & Company, 2009), 130.

56. Peter Partner, *Renaissance Rome, 1500–1559. A Portrait of a Society* (Berkeley: University of California Press,1979), 5.

57. Flavio Biondo, *Roma Instaurata* (Verona: Bonino de Boninis, 1482), ff.a1or-v.

58. Ibid.

59. John Doran & Damian J. Smith (eds), *Pope Innocent II (1130–43). The world vs the city* (London: Routledge, 2016), 7.

60. Horace, *Odes*, 3. 29. 5–12.

61. Anthony Grafton, *Leon Battista Alberti: Master Builder of the Italian Renaissance* (Cambridge, Mass.: Harvard University Press, 2000), 240.

62. Renata Ago, 'Rome's Economic Life, 1492–1692' in Jones, Wisch, & Ditchfield, *A Companion to Early Modern Rome*, 188

63. Jill Burke, *Rethinking the High Renaissance. The Culture of the Visual Arts in Early Sixteenth-century Rome* (London: Taylor and Francis, 2017), 41–2.

64. Ibid., 42.

65. Belozerskaya, ibid.

66. Ibid., 150.

67. Kathryn Blair Moor, *The Architecture of the Christian Holy Land. Reception from Late Antiquity through the Renaissance* (Cambridge: Cambridge University Press, 2017), 54.

68. Alison Brown, *The Return of Lucretius to Renaissance Florence* (Cambridge, Mass.: Harvard University Press, 2010).

69. Christopher C. Celenza, *The Intellectual World of the Italian Renaissance* (Cambridge: Cambridge University Press, 2018), 237.

70. Giuseppe Antonio Guazzelli, 'Roman Antiquities and Christian Archaeology' in Pamela M. Jones, Barbara Wisch & Simon Ditchfield (eds), *A Companion to Early Modern Rome, 1492–1692*, 531–2.

71. David Coffin, *Gardens and Gardening in Papal Rome* (Princeton: Princeton University Press, 1991), 17.

72. Celenza, *The Intellectual World of the Italian Renaissance*, 237.

73. Kenneth Gouwens, 'Institutions and Dynamics of Learned Exchange' in Jones, Wisch & Ditchfield (eds), *A Companion to Early Modern Rome*, 502.

74. Paolo Sachet, *Publishing for the Popes. The Roman Curia and the Use of Printing (1527–1555)* (Leiden: Brill, 2020), 7–8.

75. Margaret Meserve, *Papal Bull. Print, politics and propaganda in Renaissance Rome* (Baltimore: Johns Hopkins University Press, 2021), 66.

76. Shulamit Furstenburg-Levi, *The Academia Pontaniana. A Model of a Humanist Network* (Leiden: Brill, 2016), 92.

77. Lorenzo Valla, G. W. Bowersock (trans.), *On the Donation of Constantine* (Cambridge, Mass.: Harvard University Press, 2008).

78. Ibid., 45.

79. Carlos M. N. Eire, *Reformations. The Early Modern World, 1450–1650* (New Haven: Yale University Press, 2016), 74.

80. Lisa Beaven, 'Elite Patronage and Collecting' in Jones, Wisch & Ditchfield (eds), *A Companion to Early Modern Rome*, 390–1

81. Poggio Bracciolini, Davide Canfrona (ed.), *De vera nobilitate* (Rome: Edizioni di Storia e Letteratura, 2002), 6–7.

82. Ibid.

83. Partner, *Renaissance Rome, 1500–1559*, 5.

84. Ibid., 82–3.

85. Pattenden, 'The Roman Curia', 54–5.

86. Laurie Nussdorfer, 'Men at Home in Baroque Rome', *I Tatti Studies in the Italian Renaissance*, vol. 17, number 1 (2014), 103.

87. John Capgrave, C.A. Mills (ed.), *Ye Solace of Pilgrimes: a description of Rome, circa A.D. 1450* (Oxford: Oxford University Press, 1911) 161.

88. Champ, *The English Pilgrimage to Rome*, 50.

89. Capgrave, Mills (ed.), ibid., 162.

90. Daniele Filippi, 'Roma Sonora: An Atlas of Roman Sounds and Musics' in Jones, Wisch & Ditchfield (eds), *A Companion to Early Modern Rome*, 267.

91. Nadja Horsch, 'The New Passion Relics at the Lateran, Fifteenth to Sixteenth Centuries: A Translocated Sacred Topography' in L. Bosman, I. P. Haynes & P. Liverani, *The Basilica of Saint John Lateran to 1600* (Cambridge: Cambridge University Press, 2020), 447.

92. Jonathan Sumption, *The Age of Pilgrimage. The Medieval Journey to God* (Mahwah: HiddenSpring, 2003), 368.

93. Jerry L. Walls, *Purgatory. The Logic of Total Transformation* (Oxford: Oxford University Press, 2012), 16.

94. Stuart Jenks (ed.), *Documents on the Papal Plenary Indulgences 1300–1517 Preached in the Regnum Teutonicum* (Leiden: Brill, 2018), 112. My translation.

95. Capgrave & Mills (ed.), *Ye Solace of Pilgrimes*, 80.

96. Ibid., 112 & 138.

97. Ibid.

98. Eire, *Reformations*, 131.

99. McKitterick, Osborne, Richardson & Story (eds), *Old Saint Peter's Rome*, 10.

100. Martin Luther quoted in Ferdinand Gregorovius, *History of the City of Rome in the Middle Ages. Volume 8. Part 1* (Cambridge: Cambridge University Press, 2010), 250.

101. Martin Luther, *Table Talk* (London: Fount, 1995), 248.

102. Ibid., 248.

103. Archivum Romanum Societatis Iesu, *Med. Hist.* 79, ff.7v–8v.

104. Christopher J. Gilbert, 'If this Statue Could Talk: Statuary Satire in the Pasquinade Tradition', *Rhetoric and Public Affairs*, vol. 18, (2015), 81.

105. Jennifer Mara DeSilva, *The Sacralization of Space and Behavior in the Early Modern World. Studies and Sources* (London: Routledge, 2016), 179–80.

106. Gilbert, ibid.

107. Anthony Grafton, Glenn W. Most & Salvatore Settis (eds), *The Classical Tradition* (Cambridge, Mass.: The Belknap Press of Harvard University Press, 2010), 694.

108. John Hunt, 'The Pope's Two Souls and the Space of Ritual Protest during Rome's Sede Vacanta, 1559–1644' in DeSilva (ed.), *The Sacralization of Space and Behavior in the Early Modern World*, 177–96.

109. Anthony D'Elia, *A Sudden Terror: The Plot to Murder the Pope in Renaissance Rome* (Cambridge, Mass.: Harvard University Press, 2009), 40–48.

110. Anthony D'Elia, 'Stefano Porcari's Conspiracy against Pope Nicholas V in 1453 and Republican Culture in Papal Rome', *Journal of the History of Ideas*, vol. 68, no. 2 (2007), 207–31.

111. Ludwig von Pastor, *The History of the Popes, from the Close of the Middle Ages. Volume II* (London: Kegan Paul, Trench, Trübner & Co., 1889), 310.

112. Ludwig von Pastor, *The History of the Popes ... Volume I*, 170–71.

113. Eire, ibid., 1–2.

114. Carla Keyvanian, *Hospitals and Urbanism in Rome, 1200–1500* (Leiden: Brill, 2015), 382.

115. Hans Gross, *Rome in the Age of Enlightenment* (Cambridge: Cambridge University Press, 1990), 17.

116. Nussdorfer, 'Men at Home in Baroque Rome', 118.

117. Carla Keyvanian, 'Papal Urban Planning and Renewal: Real and Ideal', c.1471–1667 in Jones, Wisch & Ditchfield (eds), *A Companion to Early Modern Rome*, 309.

118. Nicholas Temple, *Renovatio Urbis. Architecture, Urbanism and Ceremony in the Rome of Julius II* (London: Taylor and Francis, 2011), 27.

119. Paolo Prodi, *The Papal Prince. One body and two souls: the papal monarchy in early modern Europe* (Cambridge: Cambridge University Press: 1987).

120. Desiderius Erasmus, Paul Pascal (trans.), J. Kelley Edwards (ed.), *The Julius Exclusus of Erasmus* (Bloomington: Indiana University Press, 1968), 48.

CHAPTER 7: THEATRE OF THE WORLD

1. Matteo Salvadore, *The African Prester John and the Birth of Ethiopian-European Relations, 1402–1555* (London: Routledge, 2019), 54.

2. Kate Lowe, '"Representing" Africa: Ambassadors and Princes from Christian Africa to Renaissance Italy and Portugal, 1402–1608', *Transactions of the Royal Historical Society*, vol. 17 (2007), 102.

3. Verena Krebs, *Medieval Ethiopian Kingship, Craft and Diplomacy with Latin Europe* (London: Palgrave Macmillan, 2021), 207.

4. Salvadore, ibid.

5. Krebs, ibid.

6. Olivia Adankpo-Labadie, 'A Faith between Two Worlds. Expressing Ethiopian Devotion and Crossing Cultural Boundaries at Santo Stefano dei Mori in Early Modern Rome' in Matthew Coneys-Wainwright & Emily Michelson (eds), *A Companion to Religious Minorities in Early Modern Rome* (Leiden: Brill, 2022), 170.

7. Salvadore, ibid., 7.

8. A. Edward Siecienski, *The Papacy and the Orthodox. Sources and History of a Debate* (Oxford: Oxford University Press, 2017), 241–2.

9. Mary Stroll, *Popes and Antipopes. The Politics of Eleventh Century Church Reform* (Leiden: Brill, 2012), 44–5.

10. Sam Kennerley, 'Ethiopian Christians in Rome, c.1400–c.1700' in Coneys-Wainwright & Michelson (eds), *A Companion to Religious Minorities in Early Modern Rome*, 145.

11. Ibid., 146.

12. Lowe, ibid., 122–3.

13. Simon Ditchfield, 'Papal Prince or Pastor? Beyond the Prodi Paradigm', *Archivum Historiae Pontificiae*, vol. 51 (2013) 130; Luca Riccardi, 'An outline of Vatican diplomacy in the early modern age' in Daniela Frigo (ed.), Adrian Belton (trans.), *Politics and Diplomacy in Early Modern Italy. The Structure of Diplomatic Practice, 1450–1800* (Cambridge: Cambridge University Press, 2000), 95–108.

14. Lapo da Castiglionchio, *De curiae commodis*, 139–41 quoted in Fletcher, *Diplomacy in Renaissance Rome*, 15.

15. Lyndal Roper, *Martin Luther. Renegade and Prophet* (London: The Bodley Head, 2016), 17.

16. Andrew Pettegree, *Brand Luther. 1517, Printing and the Making of the Reformation* (London: Penguin, 2015), 32.

17. Roper, ibid., 47.

18. Ibid.

19. Ibid., 65.

20. Richard Marius, *Martin Luther. The Christian Between God and Death* (Cambridge, Mass.: The Belknap Press, 1999), 135.

21. Martin Luther, Theses 27–28 quoted in Robert A. Yelle, *Sovereignty and the Sacred. Secularism and the Political Economy of Religion* (Chicago: University of Chicago Press, 2019), 156.

22. Ibid.

23. Martin Luther, Thesis 86 quoted in Larry D. Mansch & Curtis H. Peters, *Martin Luther. The Life and Lessons* (Jefferson: McFarland & Company, 2016), 57.

24. Pettegree, *Brand Luther.*

25. Henry VIII, King of England, Louis O'Donovan (ed.), *Assertio Septem Sacramentorum or Defence of the Seven Sacraments* (New York: Benziger Brothers, 1908), 20.

26. Ibid., 154.

27. Geoffrey Parker, *Emperor. A New Life of Charles V* (New Haven: Yale University Press, 2019), xii.

28. Ludwig von Pastor, *The History of the Popes, From the Close of the Middle Ages. Volume IX* (London: Routledge & Kegan Paul Ltd, 1950), 271.

29. Fletcher, *Diplomacy in Renaissance Rome*, 16.

30. Eugenio Albèri (ed.), *Le relazioni degli ambasciatori veneti al Senato* (Florence: Tipografia all'insegna di Clio, 1857), vol. 10, 359.

31. Christopher Columbus, *The Letter of Columbus on the Discovery of America* (New York: Lenox Library, 1892), 1–2.

32. Ibid.

33. Andrea Moudarres, 'The Geography of the Enemy: Old and New Empires between Humanist Debates and Tasso's Gerusalemme liberata' in Andrea Moudarres & Christiana Purdy Moudarres (eds), *New Worlds and the Renaissance. Contributions to the History of European Intellectual Culture* (Leiden: Brill, 2012), 313–14.

34. Simon Ditchfield, 'Translating Christianity in an Age of Reformations', *Studies in Church History*, vol. 53 (2017), 165.

35. Elizabeth Jeffreys & Cyril Mango, 'Towards a Franco-Greek Culture' in Cyril Mango (ed.), *The Oxford History of Byzantium* (Oxford: Oxford University Press, 2002), 294.

36. Kenneth M. Setton, *The Papacy and the Levant (1204–1571). Volume II. The Fifteenth Century (Philadelphia: The American Philosophical Society*, 1978), 232–3.

37. Charles A. Frazee, *Catholics and Sultans: the church and the Ottoman Empire 1453–1923* (Cambridge: Cambridge University Press, 1983),13.

38. Setton, ibid., 238.

39. Christine Ison-Verhaaren & Kent F. Schull, *Living in the Ottoman Realm. Empire and Identity, 13th to 20th Centuries* (Bloomington: Indiana University Press, 2016), 18.

40. Frazee, *Catholics and Sultans*, 18–20.

41. Rhoads Murphey, *Exploring Ottoman Sovereignty. Tradition, Image and Practice in the Ottoman Imperial Household, 1400–1800* (London: Continuum, 2008), 62.

42. Frazee, ibid., 20.

43. Maya Maskarinec, 'Mobilizing sanctity: Pius II and the head of Andrew in Rome' in Yuen-Gen Liang & Jarbel Rodriguez, *Authority and Spectacle in Medieval and Early Modern Europe. Essays in Honor of Teofilo F. Ruiz* (London: Routledge, 2017), 186–202.

44. Han Lamers, *Greece Reinvented. Transformations of Byzantine Hellenism in Renaissance Italy* (Leiden: Brill, 2015), 112.

45. Ludwig von Pastor, *The History of the Popes, from the Close of the Middle Ages. Volume III* (London: Kegan Paul, Trench, Trübner & Co, 1894), 259.

46. Lamers, ibid.; von Pastor, ibid.

47. Jones, Wisch & Ditchfield (eds), *A Companion to Early Modern Rome*, 4.

48. Ditchfield, 'Romanus and Catholicus: Counter-Reformation Rome as Caput Mundi' in Jones, Wisch & Ditchfield (eds), *A Companion to Early Modern Rome, 1492–1692*, 139.

49. Lowe, '"Representing" Africa', 120.

50. Ibid.

51. Paul H.D. Kaplan, 'Italy, 1490–1700' in Daniel Bindman & Henry Louis Gates, Jr. (eds), *The Image of the Black in Western Art. Vol. III: From the "Age of Discovery" to the Age of Abolition: Artists of the Renaissance and Baroque* (Cambridge, Mass.: Belknap Press of the Harvard University Press, 2010), 167.

52. Partner, *Renaissance Rome, 1500–1559*, 32.

53. Ibid.

54. Judith Hook, *The Sack of Rome 1527* (London: Palgrave Macmillan, 2004), 177.

55. Idan Sherer, *Warriors for a Living. The Experience of the Spanish Infantry During the Italian Wars, 1494–1559* (Leiden: Brill, 2017), 172.

56. Marin Sanudo, Paulo Margaroli (ed.), *I diarii (1496–1533). Pagine scelte* (Vicenza: Neri Pozza Editore, 1997), 517.

57. Michael Mallett & Christine Shaw, *The Italian Wars, 1494–1559. War, State and Society in Early Modern Europe* (London: Routledge, 2014), 10–14.

58. Christine Shaw, 'The Papacy and the European Powers' in Shaw (ed.), *Italy and the European Powers. The Impact of War, 1500–1530* (Leiden: Brill, 2006), 108.

59. Pattenden, *Electing the Popes in Early Modern Italy*, 46.

60. Hook, *The Sack of Rome 1527*, 38–9.

61. Mallett & Shaw, *The Italian Wars, 1494–1559*, 155.

62. Pastor, *The History of the Popes ... Volume IX*, 271.

63. Ibid.

64. Hook, ibid., 29.

65. Iain Fenlon, 'Music and Crisis in Florence and Rome, 1527–30' in Christine Shaw (ed.), *Italy and the European Powers. The Impact of War, 1500–1530* (Leiden: Brill, 2006), 279.

66. Barbara McClung Hallman, 'The "Disastrous" Pontificate of Clement VII: Disastrous for Giulio de' Medici?' in Kenneth Gouwens & Sheryl E. Reiss (eds), *The Pontificate of Clement VII. History, Politics, Culture* (Abingdon: Routledge, 2005), 36.

67. Ibid.

68. Ferdinand Gregorovius, Annie Hamilton (trans.), *History of the City of Rome in the Middle Ages. Volume 8. Part 2* (Cambridge: Cambridge University Press, 2010), 633.

69. Helge Gamrath, *Farnese. Pomp, Power and Politics in Renaissance Italy* (Rome: <<L'Erma>> di Bretschneider, 2007), 75–6.

70. Mayu Fujikawa, 'Papal Ceremonies for the Embassies of Non-Catholic Rulers' in Coneys-Wainwright & Michelson, *A Companion to Religious Minorities in Early Modern Rome*, 17.

71. Osborne, 'Diplomatic Culture in Early Modern Rome' in Jones, Wisch & Ditchfield (eds), *A Companion to Early Modern Rome*, 64.

72. Thomas James Dandelet, *Spanish Rome, 1500–1700* (Yale: Yale University Press, 2001), 205.

73. Jones, Wisch & Ditchfield (eds), *A Companion to Early Modern Rome*, 20.

74. Partner, *Renaissance Rome*, 76.

75. Ibid., 87.

76. Esposito, 'National Confraternities in Rome and Italy', 238.

77. Thomas V. Cohen & Elizabeth Storr Cohen, *Words and Deeds in Renaissance Rome. Trials Before the Papal Magistrates* (Toronto: University of Toronto Press, 1993), 58.

78. Partner, *Renaissance Rome*, 75.

79. Maas, *The German Community in Renaissance Rome*, 3.

80. Krautheimer, *Rome: Profile of a City*, 156.

81. Maas, ibid., 1–3.

82. Ibid., 3.

83. Irene Fosi, 'The Plural City: Urban Spaces and Foreign Communities' in Jones, Wisch & Ditchfield (eds), *A Companion to Early Modern Rome*, 181.

84. Maas, *The German Community in Renaissance Rome*, 11.

85. Meredith J. Gill, 'The Fourteenth and Fifteenth Centuries' in Marcia B. Hall (ed.), *Artistic Centers of the Italian Renaissance*. Rome (Cambridge: Cambridge University Press, 2005), 62.

86. Anna Esposito, 'Il cardinale Guglielmo d'Estouteville, Ambrogio di Cori e l'area di Colli Albani' in Carla Frova, Raimondo Michetti & Domenico Palombi (eds), *La carriera di un uomo di curia nella Roma del Quattrocento. Ambrogio Massari da Cori, agostiniano: cultura umanistica e committenza artistica* (Rome: Viella, 2008), 161.

87. Minou Schraven, '*Roma theatrum mundi*: Festivals and Processions in the Ritual City', in Jones, Wisch & Ditchfield (eds), *A Companion to Early Modern Rome*, 263–4

88. Laurie Nussdorfer, 'The Politics of Space in Early Modern Rome', *Memoirs of the American Academy in Rome*, vol. 42 (1997), 170.

89. Ibid.

90. Ibid.

91. John M. Hunt, 'The Ceremonial Possession of a City: Ambassadors and their Carriages in Early Modern Rome', *Royal Studies Journal*, vol. 3 (2016), 72.

92. John M. Hunt, 'Carriages, Violence and Masculinity in Early Modern Rome', *I Tatti Studies in the Italian Renaissance*, vol. 17 (2014), 183, fn.29.

93. Joana Fraga, 'Representing the King: The Images of João IV of Portugal (1640–1652)' in David de Boer, Malte Griesse & Monika Barget (eds), *Revolts and Political Violence in Early Modern Imagery* (Leiden: Brill, 2021), 210.

94. Hunt, 'The Ceremonial Possession of a City', 82.

95. Ibid.

96. Bibliothèque Nationale de France, *La Rencontre et combat des ambassadeurs d'Espagne et de Portugal, arrive à Romme, l'an 1642* (Paris, 1642) reproduced in Hunt, 'The Ceremonial Possession of a City'.

97. Fraga, ibid., 210.

98. Terry Kirk, 'The Political Topography of Early Modern Rome, 1870–1936: Via XX Settembre to Via dell'Impero' in Dorigen Caldwell & Lesley Caldwell (eds), *Rome Continuing Encounters between Past and Present* (London: Routledge, 2011), 112.

CHAPTER 8: INQUISITORS, THE GHETTO AND ECSTATIC SAINTS

1. Samuel D. Gruber, 'Mapping Jews: Cartography and Topography in Rome's Ghetto' in Ian Verstegen & Allan Ceen (eds), *Giambattista Nolli and*

Rome. Mapping the City before and after the Pianta Grande (Rome: Studium Urbis, 2013), 121.

2. Katherine Aron–Beller, 'Ghettoization: The Papal Enclosure and its Jews' in Jones, Wisch & Ditchfield (eds), *A Companion to Early Modern Rome*, 232.

3. Francisco Gaude (ed.), *Bullarum Diplomatum et Privilegiorum. Tomus VI* (Turin: Seb. Franco et Henrico Dalmazzo, 1860), 498–500.

4. Aron-Beller, ibid., 236.

5. Gaude (ed.), *Bullarum Diplomatum et Privilegiorum. Tomus VI*, 498.

6. Ibid, 499.

7. Emily Michelson, *Catholic Spectacle and Rome's Jews. Early Modern Conversion and Resistance* (Princeton: Princeton University Press, 2022), 8. The ghetto was enlarged in 1589 by Sixtus V, increasing the space to three hectares. See Anna Foa, Andrea Grover (trans.), *The Jews of Europe after the Black Death* (Berkeley: University of California Press, 2000), 145.

8. Aron-Beller, ibid., 237.

9. Ibid.

10. Dana E. Katz, *The Jewish Ghetto and the Visual Imagination of Early Modern Venice* (Cambridge: Cambridge University Press, 2017), 41–2.

11. Ibid., 8.

12. Girolamo Priuli quoted in Robert Finlay, 'The Foundation of the Ghetto: Venice, the Jews, and the War of the League of Cambrai', *Proceedings of the American Philosophical Society*, vol. 126, no. 2 (1982), 140.

13. Ibid.

14. Serena di Nepi, *Surviving the Ghetto. Toward a Social History of the Jewish Community in 16th-century Rome* (Leiden: Brill, 2020), 27.

15. Schraven, 'Roma Theatrum Mundi', 255–6.

16. di Nepi, ibid., 30–2.

17. Foa & Grover (eds), *The Jews of Europe after the Black Death*, 124–5.

18. Michael J. Levin, *Agents of Empire. Spanish Ambassadors in Sixteenth-century Italy* (Ithaca: Cornell University Press, 2005), 64.

19. Miles Pattenden, *Pius IV and the Fall of the Carafa: Nepotism and Papal Authority in Counter-Reformation Rome* (Oxford: Oxford University Press, 2013), 9.

20. Ibid., 8.

21. The quote was given by Venetian ambassador Bernardo Navagero on 23 Oct 1557. See Daniele Santarelli (ed.), *La corrispondenza di Bernardo Navagero, ambasciatore veneziano a Roma (1555– 1558)* (Rome: Aracne, 2011), 587–90.

22. Pattenden, *Electing the Pope in Early Modern Italy*, 166.

23. Ibid.

24. Piet Van Boxel, 'Jews in 16th-century Italy and the Vicissitudes of the Hebrew Book' in Coneys-Wainwright & Michelson, *A Companion to Religious Minorities in Early Modern Rome*, 330.

25. Christopher F. Black, *The Italian Inquisition* (London: Yale University Press, 2016); Adriano Prosperi, *Tribunali della Coscienza : Inquisitori, Confessori, Missionari* (Turin: Einaudi, 1996).

26. Delio Cantimori & Adriano Prosperi (ed.), *Eretici italiani del Cinquecento e altri scritti* (Turin: Einaudi, 1992); Frederic Church, *The Italian reformers, 1534– 1564* (New York: Columbia University Press, 1932).

27. Harro Höpfl, *Jesuit Political Thought: The Society of Jesus and the State, c. 1540–1630* (Cambridge: Cambridge University Press, 2008), 67.

28. Henry Kamen, *The Spanish Inquisition a Historical Revision* (London: Yale University Press, 2014).

29. Archivio di Stato di Modena, *Inquisizione*, busta 270, fasc. 3

30. Daniele Santarelli, 'Morte di un eretico impenitente. Alcune note e documenti su Pomponio Algieri di Nola', *Medioevo Adriatico*, vol. 1, (2007), 117– 34.

31. Cohen & Cohen, 'Justice and Crime', 123.

32. Girolamo Giganti, *Tractatus de crimine laesae maiestatis insignis* (Lyon: Jacopo Giunta, 1552), 445.

33. Massimo Firpo, *La presa di potere dell'Inquisizione Romana (1550–1553)* (Rome: Laterza, 2014); Gigliola Fragnito, *La Bibbia al Rogo: la censura ecclesiastica e i volgarizzamenti della Scrittura 1471–1605* (Bologna: Il Mulino, 1997).

34. Ditchfield, 'Papal Prince or Pastor?', 122.

35. Ingrid D. Rowland, *Giordano Bruno. Philosopher/Heretic* (New York: Farrar, Straus and Giroux, 2008) 270.

36. Frances Yates, *Giordano Bruno and the Hermetic tradition* (London: Routledge, 2002).

37. Rowland, ibid., 273–4.

38. di Nepi, *Surviving the Ghetto*, 14.

39. Irene Fosi, 'Court and city in the ceremony of the *possesso* in the sixteenth century' in Gianvittorio Signorotto & Maria Antonietta Visceglia (eds), *Court and Politics in Papal Rome, 1492–1700* (Cambridge: Cambridge University Press, 2002), 31–52.

40. Simon Ditchfield, 'Reading Rome as a sacred landscape, c.1586–1635' in *W. Coster and A. Spicer (eds), Sacred Space in Early Modern Europe* (Cambridge: Cambridge University Press, 2005), 167.

41. Ibid.

42. Ibid., 171–5.

43. Ditchfield, 'Romanus and Catholicus', 137.

44. Christopher F. Black, *Italian Confraternities in the Sixteenth Century* (Cambridge: Cambridge University Press, 1989), 111.

45. John R. Cihak (ed.), Ansgar Santogrossi (trans.), *Charles Borromeo. Selected Orations, Homilies and Writings* (London: Bloomsbury T&T Clark, 2017), 12–13.

46. John O'Malley, *The Jesuits and the Popes. A Historical Sketch of Their Relationship* (Philadelphia: Saint Joseph's University Press, 2016), 13–14.

47. Ignatius Loyola, Michael Ivens (trans.), *The Spiritual Exercises of Saint Ignatius of Loyola* (Leominster: Gracewing, 2004), 21.

48. Luke Clossey, *Salvation and Globalization in the Early Jesuit Missions* (Cambridge: Cambridge University Press, 2008), 142.

49. Mary Laven, *Mission to China: Matteo Ricci and the Jesuit Encounter with the East* (London: Faber and Faber, 2011).

50. Michela Fontana, *Matteo Ricci. A Jesuit in the Ming Court* (London: Rowman & Littlefield, 2011), 61.

51. Silvia Mostaccio, 'A Conscious Ambiguity: The Jesuits Viewed in Comparative Perspective in Light of Some Recent Italian Literature', *Journal of Early Modern History*, 12 (2008), 410– 41.

52. Pamela M. Jones, 'Celebrating New Saints in Rome and across the Globe' in Jones, Wisch & Ditchfield (eds), *A Companion to Early Modern Rome*, 151.

53. Ditchfield, 'Romanus and Catholicus', 131.

54. Alexandre Coello de la Rosa, *Jesuits at the Margins. Missions and Missionaries in the Marianas (1668–1769)* (London: Routledge, 2016), 22–3. See also, Adriano Prosperi, *La vocazione. Storie di gesuiti tra Cinquecento e Seicento* (Turin: Einaudi, 2016).

55. Paul Gwynne, *Francesco Benci's Quinque martyres. Introduction, Translation and Commentary* (Leiden: Brill, 2018).

56. Simon Ditchfield, *Liturgy, Sanctity and History in Tridentine Italy. Pietro Maria Campi and the Preservation of the Particular* (Cambridge: Cambridge University Press, 1995), 90.

57. Paul F. Grendler, *The Jesuits & Italian Universities 1548–1773* (Washington, D.C.: The Catholic University Press, 2017), 320.

58. Cheryl Petreman, 'Host Desecration Narratives: Confirming Christ's Physical Presence' in Torrance Kirby & Matthew Milner (eds), *Mediating Religious Cultures in Early Modern Europe* (Newcastle: Cambridge Scholars Publishing, 2013), 67.

59. Barbara R. Walters, 'The Feast and its Founder' in Walters, Vincent Corrigan & Peter T. Ricketts (eds), *The Feast of Corpus Christi* (Philadelphia: Penn State University Press, 2006), 9–10.

NOTES

60. Thomas Turke & John Milton quoted by Allison P. Coudert, 'The Ultimate Crime: Cannibalism in Early Modern Minds and Imaginations' in Albrecht Classen & Connie Scarborough (eds), *Crime and Punishment in the Middle Ages and Early Modern Age* (Berlin: De Gruyter, 2012), 528.

61. Markus Friedrich, *The Jesuits. A History* (Princeton: Princeton University Press, 2022), 217.

62. Schraven, 'Roma theatrum mundi', 259.

63. Peter Burke, 'Varieties of Performance in Seventeenth-century Italy' in Peter Gillgren & Mårten Snickare (eds), *Performativity and Performance in Baroque Rome* (London: Routledge, 2016), 17.

64. Andrea Lepage, 'Art and the Counter-Reformation' in Alexandra Bamji, Geert H. Janssen & Mary Laven (eds), *The Ashgate Research Companion to the Counter-Reformation* (London: Routledge, 2013), 378–9.

65. Teresa of Avila, *The Life of St. Teresa of Avila* (New York: Cosimo, 2011), 226.

66. Franco Mormando, *Bernini. His Life and his Rome* (Chicago: University of Chicago Press, 2011), 240.

67. Fujikawa, 'Papal Ceremonies for Embassies of Non-Catholic Rulers', 19.

68. Giorgio Cosmacini, *Storia della medicina e della sanità in Italia* (Rome: Laterza, 1988), 132.

69. Bernadette Andrea, 'The Global Travels of Teresa Sampsonia Sherley's Carmelite Relic' in Patricia Akhimie & Bernadette Andrea (eds), *Travel and Travail. Early Modern Women, English Drama and the Wider World* (Lincoln, University of Nebraska Press, 2019), 106.

70. Irene Fosi, 'Conversion and Autobiography: Telling Tales before the Roman Inquisition', *Journal of Early Modern History*, vol. 17 (2013), 449.

71. Irene Fosi, 'Between Conversion and Reconquest. The Venerable English College between the Late 16th and 17th Centuries' in Matthew Coneys-Wainwright & Emily Michelson, *A Companion to Religious Minorities in Early Modern Rome*, 118 & 136.

72. Fosi, 'Conversion and Autobiography', 448–9.

73. Oskar Garstein, *Rome and the Counter-Reformation in Scandinavia. The Age of Gustavus Adolphus and Queen Christina of Sweden 1622–1656* (Leiden: Brill, 1992), 749.

74. Garstein, *Rome and the Counter-Reformation in Scandinavia*, 742–3.

75. 'Felice fausto q. ingressui. Anno dom. MDCLV.'

76. Susanna Åkerman, *Queen Christina of Sweden and Her Circle. The Transformation of a Seventeenth-century Philosophical Libertine* (Leiden: Brill, 1991), 225.

77. Salvatore Rotta, 'L'accademia fisico-matematica Ciampiniana: un'iniziativa di Cristina?' in W. di Palma, T. Bovi, B. Lindberg, F. Abbri, M.L.

[359]

Rodén, S. Rotta, G., Iacovelli, S. Åkermann & F. Craaford (eds), *Cristina di Svezia. Scienza ed Alchimia nella Roma Barocca* (Bari: Edizioni Dedalo, 1990), 107.

78. Mary Hollingsworth, 'Cardinals in Conclave' in Hollingsworth, Miles Pattenden & Arnold Witte (eds), *A Companion to the Early Modern Cardinal* (Leiden: Brill, 2020), 70.

79. Garstein, *Rome and the Counter-Reformation in Scandinavia*, 767.

80. Ibid.

81. Theresa A. Kutasz Christensen, 'Allegory, Antiquities and a Gothic Apollo: Queen Christina of Sweden and the Manufacture of Cultural Identity' in Jennifer Cochran Anderson & Douglas N. Dow (eds), *Visualising the Past in Renaissance Art* (Leiden: Brill, 2021), 53.

82. Archivio della Congregatione per la Dottrina di Fede (ACDF), *Decreta 1548–58*, 118v.

83. James Nelson Nuova, 'Being a New Christian in Early Modern Rome' in Matthew Coneys-Wainwright & Emily Michelson, *A Companion to Religious Minorities in Early Modern Rome*, 197.

84. Ibid., 205.

85. Emily Michelson, 'Resist, Refute, Redirect. Roman Jews Attend Conversionary Sermons' in Coneys-Wainwright & Michelson, *A Companion to Religious Minorities in Early Modern Rome*, 349–50.

86. Eric R. Dursteler, *Renegade Women. Gender, Identity and Boundaries in the Early Modern Mediterranean* (Baltimore: Johns Hopkins University Press, 2011), 5.

87. Ibid., 93.

88. Ioanna Iordanou, *Venice's Secret Service. Organizing Intelligence in the Renaissance* (Oxford: Oxford University Press, 2019), 178

89. Michelson, *Catholic Spectacle and Rome's Jews*, 29.

90. Michelson, 'Resist, Refute, Redirect', 351.

91. Barbara Wisch, 'Promoting Piety, Coercing Conversion: The Roman Archconfraternity of the Santissima Trinità dei Pellegrini e Convalescenti and its Oratory', *Predella. Journal of Visual Arts*, vol. 47, (2020), 267.

92. Michelson, 'Resist, Refute, Redirect', 353–4.

93. ACDF, *Decreta 1548–58*, f.125r.

94. Aron–Beller, 'Ghettoization', 239.

95. Anna Esposito, '"Charitable" Assistance between Lay Foundations and Pontifical Initiatives' in Jones, Wisch & Ditchfield (eds), *A Companion to Early Modern Rome*, 199–200.

96. Brenda Bolton, 'Received in His Name: Rome's Busy Baby Box', *Studies in Church History*, vol. 31 (1994), 153–67.

97. Christian Laes, *Disabilities and the Disabled in the Roman World* (Cambridge: Cambridge University Press, 2018), 23.

98. Elisabeth Cohen, 'Honour and Gender in the Streets of Early Modern Rome', *The Journal of Interdisciplinary History*, vol. 22, no. 4 (Spring 1922), 600–603

99. Esposito, '"Charitable" Assistance', 210.

100. Ibid.

101. Eire, *Reformations*, 432–3.

102. Ibid.

103. Peter Burke, *Play in Renaissance Italy* (Cambridge: Polity Press, 2021), 129.

104. Pietro Bacci, Frederick Ignatius Antrobus (ed.), *The Life of Saint Philip Neri. Apostle of Rome and Founder of the Congregation of the Oratory* (London: Kegan Paul, Trench, Trübner & Co., 1902), 113.

105. Eire, ibid., 433.

106. Esposito, ibid., 205.

107. Matthew Coneys-Wainright, 'Non-Catholic Pilgrims and the Hospital of SS. Trinita dei Pellegrini e Convalescenti (1575–1650)' in Matthew Coneys-Wainwright & Emily Michelson, *A Companion to Religious Minorities in Early Modern Rome*, 96.

108. Simon Ditchfield, '"One World is Not Enough": The "Myth" of Roman Catholicism as a "World Religion"' in Simone Maghenzani & Stefano Villani (eds), *British Protestant Missions and the Conversion of Europe, 1600–1900* (London: Routledge, 2021), 25–6.

109. Tessa Storey, *Carnal Commerce in Counter-Reformation Rome* (Cambridge: Cambridge University Press, 2008), 1.

110. Ibid.

CHAPTER 9: FROM THE SUBLIME TO THE PATHETIC:

EIGHTEENTH-CENTURY ROME

1. Johann Wolfgang Goethe, W.H. Auden & Elizabeth Mayer (trans.), *Johann Wolfgang von Goethe, Italian Journey 1786–8* (San Francisco: North Point Press, 1962), 477.

2. Nicholas Boyle, *Goethe. The Poet and the Age. Volume 1. The Poetry of Desire (1749–1790)* (Oxford: Oxford University Press, 1992), 353.

3. Jonathan I. Israel, *Radical Enlightenment. Philosophy and the Making of Modernity 1650–1750* (Oxford: Oxford University Press, 2001), 273–4.

4. Goethe, Auden & Mayer (trans.), *Italian Journey 1786–8*, 115.

5. Samuel Taylor Coleridge, 'The Principles of Genial Criticism' in Coleridge, H.J. Jackson & J.R. de J. Jackson (eds), *Shorter Works and Fragments* (Princeton: Princeton University Press, 1995), vol. 1, 364.

6. Goethe, Auden & Mayer (trans.), *Italian Journey 1786–8*, 115.

7. Ibid., 116.

8. Ibid., 115.

9. Ibid., 116.

10. Ibid., 477.

11. Ibid..

12. Ibid.

13. John Evelyn, Austin Dobson (ed.), *The Diary of John Evelyn. With an Introduction and Notes. Volume 1* (Cambridge: Cambridge University Press, 2015), 203.

14. William Makepeace Thackeray, Arthur Pendennis (ed.), *The Newcomes. Memoirs of a Most Respectable Family* (New York: Harper & Brothers, 1856), vol.2, 7.

15. Ibid.

16. Ibid.

17. Evelyn, Dobson (ed.), *The Diary of John Evelyn*, 204.

18. Rosemary Sweet, *Cities and the Grand Tour. The British in Italy, c.1690–1820* (Cambridge: Cambridge University Press, 2012), 99–163.

19. Charlotte A. Eaton, *Rome in the Nineteenth Century* (London: George Bell, 1892), vol.1, 59.

20. Ibid., 62.

21. Philip Ayres, *Classical Culture and the Idea of Rome in Eighteenth-century England* (Cambridge: Cambridge University Press, 1997).

22. Philip Dormer Stanhope, *The Letters of Philip Dormer Stanhope, Earl of Chesterfield* (Philadelphia: J.B. Lipincott Company, 1892), vol. 1, 307.

23. Ayres, ibid., 74.

24. William Godwin, *The Enquirer* (London, 1797), vi quoted in Jonathan Sachs, *Romantic Antiquity. Rome in the British Imagination, 1789–1832* (Oxford: Oxford University Press, 2010), 7.

25. Paul F. Grendler, *Jesuit Schools and Universities in Europe, 1548–1773* (Leiden: Brill, 2019), 13; Robert Maryks, *Saint Cicero and the Jesuits. The Influence of the Liberal Arts on the Adoption of Moral Probabilism* (Aldershot: Ashgate, 2008).

26. Ronnie Po-Chia Hsia, *The World of Catholic Renewal, 1540–1770*. 2nd edition (Cambridge: Cambridge University Press, 2005), 32.

27. Marisa Linton, *Choosing Terror. Virtue, Friendship and Authenticity in the French Revolution* (Oxford: Oxford University Press, 2013), 34.

28. Harold T. Parker, *The Cult of Antiquity and the French Revolutionaries: A Study in the Development of the Revolutionary Spirit* (New York: Octagon, 1965), 39.

29. Johann Joachim Winckelmann, Alex Potts (ed.), Harry Francis (trans.), *Johann Joachim Winckelmann. History of the Art of Antiquity* (Los Angeles: Getty Research Institute, 2006), 8.

30. Goethe, Auden & Mayer (trans.), *Italian Journey 1786–8*, 125.

31. Ibid., 127.

32. *The Present State of the Republick of Letters. For January, 1734. Vol. XIII* (London: W. Innys & R. Manby, 1734), 153.

33. Melissa Dabakis, 'Angelika Kauffmann, Goethe and the Arcadian Academy in Rome' in Evelyn K. Moore & Patricia Anne Simpson (eds), *The Enlightened Eye. Goethe and Visual Culture* (Amsterdam: Rodopi, 2007), 33.

34. Ibid.

35. Jacques Casanova de Seingalt, *The Memoires of Casanova. Volume IV* (Frankfurt: Outlook, 2018), 113.

36. Dabakis, ibid., 33.

37. Germaine de Staël, Sylvia Raphael (trans.), *Corinne, or Italy* (Oxford: Oxford University Press, 2008), 22–3.

38. *Dizionario Biografico degli Italiani* (Rome: Istituto della Enciclopedia Italiana, 2012), vol. 76, 640.

39. Gross, *Rome in the Age of Enlightenment*, 2.

40. Valter Curzi, 'Moral Subjects and Exempla Virtutis at the Start of the Eighteenth Century: Art and Politics in England, Rome and Venice' in Paolo Coen (ed.), *The Art Market in Rome in the Eighteenth Century. A Study in the Social History of Art* (Leiden: Brill, 2019), 122.

41. Ghislain de Diesbach, *Madame de Staël* (Paris: Librairie Académique Perrin, 1983), 347.

42. Ibid.

43. Ibid.

44. Angelica Goodden, *Madame de Staël. The Dangerous Exile* (Oxford: Oxford University Press, 2008), 167.

45. Goethe, Auden & Mayer (trans.), ibid., 120.

46. Richard Lassels, *The voyage of Italy, or, A compleat journey through Italy in two parts* (Paris: 1670).

47. Irene Fosi, *Convertire lo straniero. Forestieri e Inquisizione a Roma in età moderna* (Rome: Viella, 2011), 235–8.

48. Gerrit Verhoeven, 'Calvinist Pilgrimages and Popish Encounters: Religious Identity and Sacred Space on the Dutch Grand Tour (1598–1685)', *Journal of Social History*, Spring (2010), 615.

49. *Goethe, Auden & Mayer (trans.), Italian Journey 1786–8*, 120.

50. Eaton, *Rome in the Nineteenth Century*, vol.1, 66.

51. Ibid.

52. Andrew Hadfield, 'The English and Other Peoples' in Thomas N. Corns (ed.), *A Companion to Milton* (Oxford: Blackwell, 2003), 182–3; Franck Lessay, 'Hobbes, Rome's Enemy' in Marcus P. Adams (ed.), *A Companion to Hobbes* (Oxford: Wiley Blackwell, 2021), 332–48.

53. Verhoeven, 'Calvinist Pilgrimages', 618.

54. Ibid., 615.

55. Edward Chaney, *The Evolution of the Grand Tour. Anglo-Italian Cultural Relations since the Renaissance* (London: Routledge, 1998), 83.

56. Fosi, *Convertire lo straniero*, 235–6.

57. Gross, *Rome in the Age of Enlightenment*, 3.

58. W.J. Conybeare & J.S. Howson, *The Life and Epistles of St. Paul* (London: Longman, Brown, Green, Longmans & Roberts, 1856), vol. 2, 597.

59. Ibid.

60. Ibid.

61. Fosi, Cohen (trans.), *Papal Justice*, 23–4.

62. Edward Corp, *The Stuarts in Italy, 1719–1766* (Cambridge: Cambridge University Press, 2011), 330.

63. Pietro Palazzini, 'Le Congregazioni Romane da Sisto V a Giovani Paolo ii' in Marcello Fagiolo & Maria Luisa Madonna (eds), *Sisto V. I. Roma e il Lazio* (Rome: Libreria dello Stato, 1992), 23–5.

64. Maria Antoinetta Visceglia, *Morte e elezione del papa. Norme, riti e conflitti. L'Età moderna* (Rome: Viella, 2013), 362.

65. Gross, ibid., 45–7.

66. Gianvittorio Signorotto & Maria Antonietta Visceglia (eds), *Court and Politics in Papal Rome, 1492–1700* (Cambridge: Cambridge University Press, 2004), 152.

67. Gross, ibid., 51.

68. Ibid., 53–4.

69. A.D. Wright, *The Early Modern Papacy. From the Council of Trent to the French Revolution, 1564–1789* (London: Longman, 2000), 247.

70. Gross, ibid., 45–7.

71. Maurice Andrieux, Mary Fitton (trans.), *Daily Life in Papal Rome* (London: Allen & Unwin, 1968), 70.

72. Ibid., 70–1.

73. Eaton, *Rome in the Nineteenth Century*, vol.1, 181.

74. Ibid.

75. Donatella Strangio, 'Public Debt in the Papal States, Sixteenth to Eighteenth Century', The Journal of Interdisciplinary History, vol. 43, no. 4 (Spring 2013), 511.

76. Gross, ibid., 36 & 112.

77. Ibid., 37.

78. Vittorio E. Giuntella, *Roma nel settecento* (Bologna: Licinio Capelli, 1971), 56.

79. Gross, *Rome in the Age of Enlightenment*, 175.

80. Andrieux, Fitton (trans.), *Daily Life in Papal Rome*, 69–70.

81. Martin Papenheim, 'The Pope, the Beggar, the Sick and the Brotherhoods: Health Care and Poor Relief in 18th and 19th Century Rome' in Ole Peter Grell, Andrew Cunningham & Bernd Roeck (eds), *Health Care and Poor Relief in 18th and 19th Century Southern Europe* (London: Routledge, 2017), 166–7.

82. Susan Vandiver Nicassio, *Imperial City. Rome Under Napoleon* (Chicago: University of Chicago Press, 2009), 94.

83. Andrieux, Fitton (trans.), ibid., 73.

84. Barbara Wisch, 'Violent Passions: Plays, Pawnbrokers and the Jews of Rome, 1539' in Allie Terry-Fritsch & Erin Felicia Labbie, *Beholding Violence in Medieval and Early Modern Europe* (London: Routledge, 2016), 202.

85. Andrieux, Fitton (trans.), ibid., 70–71.

86. Michelson, *Catholic Spectacle and Rome's Jews*, 47.

87. Andrieux, Fitton (trans.), ibid., 84.

88. Ibid., 86.

89. Ludwig von Pastor, Ernst Graf (ed.), *History of the Popes. From the Close of the Middle Ages. Volume XXXIV* (St Louis: B. Herder Book Co., 1941), 353.

90. Gross, ibid., 126–9.

91. Pattenden, *Electing the Pope in Early Modern Italy, 1450–1700*, 242.

92. von Pastor, Graf (ed.), ibid., 354.

93. von Pastor, E.F. Peeler (ed.), *History of the Popes. From the Close of the Middle Ages. Volume XXXV* (London: Routledge & Kegan Paul Ltd., 1961), 143.

94. Gaetano Moroni, *Dizionario di Erudizione Storico-Ecclesiastica da S. Pietro sino ai nostri giorni. Vol. LXXIII* (Venice: Tipografia Emiliana, 1855), 309.

95. Ditchfield, 'Papal Prince or Pastor?',129.

96. John O'Malley, *Trent: What Happened at the Council* (Cambridge, Mass.: The Belknap Press of the Harvard University Press, 2013), 250.

97. O'Malley, *Trent*.

98. Daniel J. Weeks, *Gateways to Empire. Quebec and New Amsterdam to 1664* (Bethlehem: Lehigh University Press, 2019), 143.

99. J. Lynch, 'Philip II and the Papacy', *Transactions of the Royal Historical Society*, vol. 11 (1961), 23.

100. Ronald G. Asch, '1618–1629' in Olaf Asbach & Peter Schröder (eds), *The Ashgate Research Companion to the Thirty Years War* (Farnham: Ashgate, 2014), 127–9.

101. *Bullarum diplomatum et privilegorium sanctorum romanorum pontificum. Tomus XV. Ab Urbano VIII (an. MDCXXXIX ad Innocentium X (an. MDCLIV)* (Turin: A. Vecco et Sociis, 1868), 604.

102. Christian Schneider, '"Types" of Peacemakers: Exploring the Authority and Self-Perception of the Early Modern Papacy' in Stephen Cummins & Laura Kounine (eds), *Cultures of Conflict Resolution in Early Modern Europe* (London: Routledge, 2016), 96.

103. Gross, *Rome in the Age of Enlightenment*, 43.

104. Guido Braun, 'The Papacy' in Olaf Asbach & Peter Schröder (eds), *The Ashgate Research Companion to the Thirty Years War* (Farnham: Ashgate, 2014), 111.

105. Maria Teresa Fattori, 'Lambertini's Treatises and the Cultural Project of Benedict XIV' in Rebecca Messbarger, Christopher M.S. Johns, & Philip Gavitt (eds), *Benedict XIV and the Enlightenment. Art, Science and Spirituality* (Toronto: University of Toronto Press, 2016), 259–66.

106. Dale K. Van Kley, *Reform Catholicism and the International Suppression of the Jesuits in Enlightenment Europe* (New Haven: Yale University Press), 244.

107. Jeffrey D. Burson & Jonathan Wright (eds), *The Jesuit Suppression in Global Context. Causes, events and consequences* (Cambridge: Cambridge University Press, 2015), 1–2.

108. Dale K. Van Kley 'Plots and Rumors of Plots. The Role of Conspiracy in the International Campaign against the Society of Jesus, 1758–1768' in Jeffrey D. Burson & Jonathan Wright (eds), *The Jesuit Suppression in Global Context. Causes, events and consequences* (Cambridge: Cambridge University Press, 2015), 31.

109. Dale K. Van Kley, *Reform Catholicism and the International Suppression of the Jesuits in Enlightenment Europe*, 5.

110. Clement XIV, *Dominus ac Redemptor noster* (Rome: Camera Apostolica, 1773).

111. Richard Krautheimer, *The Rome of Alexander VII, 1655–1667* (Princeton: Princeton University Press, 1985), 25.

112. Gross, ibid., 10.

113. Ana Gutierrez-Folch, 'The Neo-Classical *Klismos* Chair: Early Sources and Avenues of Diffusion' in Elizabeth Simpson (ed.), *The Adventure of the Illustrious Scholar. Papers Presented to Oscar White Muscarella* (Leiden: Brill, 2018), 574.

114. Jeffrey Collins, *Papacy and Politics in Eighteenth-century Rome. Pius VI and the Arts* (Cambridge: Cambridge University Press, 2004), 172.

115. Richard Wittman, 'A Partly Vacated Historicism: Artifacts, Architecture and Time in Nineteenth-century Papal Rome', *Grey Room*, vol. 84, (2021), 11–12.

116. Ibid., 48.

117. Elisa Andretta & Federica Favino, 'Scientific and Medical Knowledge in Early Modern Rome' in Jones, Wisch & Ditchfield (eds), *A Companion to Early Modern Rome*, 523–4.

118. Maurice A. Finocchiaro, *The Galileo Affair. A Documentary History* (Berkeley: University of California Press, 1989), 303.

119. Ibid., 32–3.

120. Frederick Hammond, 'The Artistic Patronage of the Barberini and the Galileo Affair' in Victor Coelho (ed.), *Music and Science in the Age of Galileo* (Dordrecht: Kluwer Academic Publishers, 1992), 73.

121. Paula Findlen, 'Women on the Verge of Science: Aristocratic Women and Knowledge in Early Eighteenth-Century Italy' in Sarah Knott & Barbara Taylor (eds), *Women, Gender and Enlightenment* (London: Palgrave Macmillan, 2005), 265.

122. Gilles Montègre, *La Rome des Français au temps des lumières, 1769–1791* (Rome: École Francaise de Rome, 2011), 9.

123. W.E. Knowles Middleton, 'Science in Rome, 1675–1700, and the Accademia Fisciomatematica of Giovanni Giustino Ciampini' in *The British Journal for the History of Science*, Vol. 8, no. 2 (July, 1975), 141.

124. Ibid., 142.

125. Nancy K. Leverne, *Spinoza's Revelation. Religion, Democracy and Reason* (Cambridge: Cambridge University Press, 2004), 79–80.

126. Steven Nadler, *A Book Forged in Hell: Spinoza's Scandalous Treatise and the Birth of the Secular Age* (Princeton: Princeton University Press, 2011), 7.

127. Finocchiaro, ibid., 38.

128. Rivka Feldhay, *Galileo and the Church. Political Inquisition or Critical Dialogue* (Cambridge: Cambridge University Press, 1995), 27.

129. Finocchiaro, ibid., 32–3.

130. Gross, *Rome in the Age of Enlightenment*, 248.

131. Frank Coppa, *The Modern Papacy since 1789* (London: Longman, 1998), 27.

132. Paolo Alvazzi Del Frate, 'Rivoluzione e giornalismo politico nello Stato pontificio', *Mélanges de l'École française de Rome. Italie et Méditerranée*, vol. 102, no.2 (1990), 412.

133. Vandiver Nicassio, *Imperial City*, 18–19.

134. Jean-François, Baron de Bourgoing, *Historical and philosophical memoirs of Pius the Sixth and of his Pontificate, down to the period of his retirement into Tuscany* (Dublin: H. Colbert, W. Porter, J. Boyce, J. Rice & R.E. Mercier & co., 1800), 150.

135. Gross, *Rome in the Age of Enlightenment*, 150.

136. Coppa, *The Modern Papacy*, 30.

137. Gross, ibid., 150.

138. Vandiver Nicassio, *Imperial City*, 20.

139. Ibid.

140. Diana Rowell, *Paris: The 'New Rome' of Napoleon I* (London: Bloomsbury, 2012), 140–41.

141. Andrea Giardina & André Vauchez, *Il Mito di Roma. Da Carlo Magnio a Mussolini* (Bari: Laterza, 2000), 117–18.

142. Vandiver Nicassio, ibid., 21.

CHAPTER 10: *NON POSSUMUS*: POPES OF ROME IN THE AGE OF REVOLUTIONS

1. Sheridan Gilley, 'The Papacy' in Sheridan Gilley & Brian Stanley (eds), *The Cambridge History of Christianity. World Christianities c.1815-c.1914. Volume 8* (Cambridge: Cambridge University Press, 2006), 13.

2. Harry Hearder, *Italy in the Age of the Risorgimento* (London: Routledge, 2013).

3. Manuel Borutta, 'Anti-Catholicism and the Culture War in Risorgimento Italy' in Silvana Patriarca & Lucy Riall (eds), *The Risorgimento Revisited: Nationalism and Culture in Nineteenth-century Italy* (Basingstoke: Palgrave Macmillan, 2011), 201–3.

4. Lucy Riall, *Garibaldi. Invention of a Hero* (New Haven: Yale University Press, 2008), 38.

5. Owen Chadwick, *A History of the Popes, 1830–1914* (Oxford: Oxford University Press, 1998), 266.

6. David Kertzer, *Prisoner of the Vatican* (Boston: Houghton Mifflin Company, 2004), 60–1.

7. Tommaso di Carpegna Falconieri, 'Ritratto in bianco e nero di un'aristocrazia' in Marina Formica (ed.), *Roma capitale. La città laica, la città religiosa (1870–1915)* (Rome: Viella, 2021), 267.

8. Kertzer, ibid., 79.

9. Edmondo de Amicis, *Ricordi del 1870–71* (Florence: G. Barbèra, 1873), 101.

10. Charles A. Coulombe, *The Pope's Legion. The Multinational Fighting Force that Defended the Vatican* (Basingstoke: Palgrave Macmillan, 2008), 51–8.

11. Ignazio Veca, 'Oggetti animati. Materialità, circolazione e usi della figura di Pio IX (1846–1849)', *Il Risorgimento*, vol. 64, no. 1 (2017), 75.

12. Ibid., 75.

13. See, for example, the impact of events in Rome among Catholic communities in America discussed by Peter D' Agostino, *Rome in America. Transnational Catholic Ideology from the Risorgimento to Fascism* (Chapel Hill: University of North Carolina Press, 2005).

14. Ambrogio A. Caiani, *To Kidnap a Pope. Napoleon and Pius VII* (New Haven: Yale University Press, 2021), 39.

15. Chevalier Artaud de Montor, William Hayes Neligan (ed.), *The Lives and Times of the Roman Pontiffs. From St Peter to Pius IX* (New York: D. & J. Sadler & co., 1866), vol. 2, 494.

16. Nigel Aston, *Christianity and revolutionary Europe, 1750–1830* (Cambridge: Cambridge University Press, 2002), 253.

17. James Kolla, *Sovereignty, International Law and the French Revolution* (Cambridge: Cambridge University Press, 2017), 267.

18. Napoleon Bonaparte, D.A. Bingham (ed.), *A Selection from the Letters and Despatches of the First Napoleon* (London: Chapman & Hall Ltd., 1884) vol. 1, 282–3.

19. Giancarlo Rostirolla, *La Capella Giulia, 1513–2013. Cinque secoli di musica sacra in San Pietro* (Kassell: Bärenreiter-Verlag, 2018), 744.

20. G.A. Sala, *Diario Romano degli anni 1798–99. Parte II. dal I. Luglio al 31. Decembre 1798* (Rome: Società Romana di Storia Patria, 1882), 4.

21. Ibid., 3.

22. Luca Topi, 'Un elenco di 'giacobini romani' dalle carte del console Pierelli (1798–9)', *Eurostudium*, (October-December 2013), 24.

23. Ibid.

24. Vandiver Nicassio, *Imperial City*, 16.

25. 'Napoleon Bonaparte' in Peter McPhee & Philip Dwyer (eds), *The French Revolution and Napoleon: A Sourcebook* (London: Routledge, 2002), 142–3.

26. Ibid.

27. Caiani, *To Kidnap a Pope*, 56.

28. Coppa, *The Modern Papacy*, 36–7.

29. Caiani, ibid.

30. Christopher M. S. Johns, *Antonio Canova and the Politics of Patronage in Revolutionary and Napoleonic Europe* (Berkeley: University of California Press, 1998), 65.

31. Coppa, ibid., 40.

32. Hearder, *Italy in the Age of the Risorgimento*, 100.

33. Aston, *Christianity and revolutionary Europe,* 267.

34. Philip Dwyer, *Citizen Emperor* (New Haven: Yale University Press, 2013), 317.

35. Julia Hell, *The Conquest of Ruins. The Third Reich and the Fall of Rome* (Chicago: University of Chicago Press, 2019), 160.

36. Pius VII, *Quum memoranda*, 10 June 1809 quoted in Mary H. Allies, *The Life of Pope Pius the Seventh* (London: Burns and Oates, 1875), 161–3.

37. Dwyer, *Citizen Emperor*.

38. Napoleon Bonaparte, R.M. Johnston (ed.), *The Corsican: A Diary of Napoleon's Life in His Own Words* (Boston: Houghton Mifflin Company, 1910), 328.

39. Ibid.

40. Vandiver Nicassio, *Imperial City*, 16.

41. Stephen L. Dyson, *In Pursuit of Ancient Pasts. A History of Classical Archaeology in the Nineteenth and Twentieth Centuries* (New Haven: Yale University Press, 2006), 226.

42. Johns, *Antonio Canova and the Politics of Patronage*, 65.

43. Raffaele de Cesare, *I Romani e la nascita del Re di Roma* (Rome: Storia e Letterature, 1996), 198.

44. Ibid.

45. Vandiver Nicassio, ibid., 188.

46. Michael Broers, *Politics and Religion in Napoleonic Italy. The War Against God, 1801–1814* (London: Taylor Francis, 2003), 25.

47. Bruce Ware Allen, *Tiber. Eternal River of Rome* (Lebanon, New Hampshire: Foredge, 2019), 232.

48. Vandiver Nicassio, ibid.

49. Italo Insolera & Lucia Bozzola, Roberto Einaudi, & Marco Zumaglini (eds), *Modern Rome. From Napoleon to the Twenty-First Century* (Newcastle: Cambridge Scholars Publishing, 2018), 11–18.

50. Sala, *Diario Romano ...Parte II*, 159–60.

51. Alexander Kaberidze, *The Napoleonic Wars. A Global History* (Oxford: Oxford University Press, 2020), 528–9.

52. Frederick C. Schneid, *Napoleon's Italian Campaigns* (Westport: Praeger, 2002), 139–40.

53. Francisco Javier Ramón Salons, 'A Renewed Global Power: The Restoration of the Holy See and the Triumph of Ultramontanism, 1814–48' in Michael Broers, Ambrogio A. Caiani & Stephen Bann (eds), *A History of the European Restorations. Volume Two. Culture, Society and Religion* (London: Bloomsbury Academic, 2020), 73.

54. Ibid.

55. Matthijs Lok, 'The Congress of Vienna as a Missed Opportunity: Conservative Visions of a New European Order after Napoleon' in Beatrice de Graaf, Ido de Haan & Brian Vick (eds), *Securing Europe after Napoleon. 1815 and the New European Security Culture* (Cambridge: Cambridge University Press, 2019), 69.

56. Salons, 'A Renewed Global Power', 74.

57. Adriano Prosperi, Jeremy Carden (trans.), *Crime and Forgiveness. Christianising Execution in Medieval Europe* (Cambridge, Mass.: Harvard University Press, 2020), 459.

58. Ibid., 460.

59. Fabio Cavedagna & Marcello Donativi (eds), *Memorie di un boia* (Edizioni Trabant: 2009), 14–15.

60. Ibid., 6–7.

61. *The Reformer*, Philadelphia, January, 1826. Vol. VII, no. 73, 30.

62. Ibid.

63. Ibid.

64. Gilley, 'The Papacy', 14.

65. Brian E. Vick, *The Congress of Vienna. Power and Politics after Napoleon* (Cambridge, Mass.: Harvard University Press, 2014), 156.

66. Robin Anderson, *Papa Pio VII (Barnaba Chiaramonti). La vita, il regno e il conflitto con Napoleone nel periodo seguente alla rivoluzione francese (1742–1823)* (Rome: Benedictina Editrice, 2000), 159–60.

67. Johns, *Antonio Canova and the Politics of Patronage*, 179–84.

68. Coppa, *The Modern Papacy*, 51.

69. Michelson, *Catholic Spectacle and Rome's Jews*, 79.

70. Frank Coppa, *The Papacy, the Jews and the Holocaust* (Washington D.C.: The Catholic University of America Press, 2006), 63.

71. Ibid.

72. Gilley, 'The Papacy', 15.

73. *Diario di Roma*, no.10, 5 February 1831.

74. John Gooch, *The Unification of Italy* (London: Routledge, 1986), 5.

75. Chadwick, *A History of the Popes, 1830–1914*, .

76. A. Ademollo, *Le Giustizie a Roma. Dal 1674 al 1739. E dal 1796 a 1840* (Rome: Forzani e C., 1881), 112.

77. Ibid.

78. Ibid.

79. Christopher Duggan, *The Force of Destiny. A History of Italy Since 1796* (Boston: Houghton Mifflin, 2008), 58–9.

80. Ibid., 58.

81. Massimo Cattaneo 'L'opposizione popolare al <<giacobinismo>> a Roma e nello Stato Pontifico', *Studi Storici*, vol. 39, no. 2 (Le insorgenze popolari nell'Italia rivoluzionaria e napoleonica) (1998), 544.

82. Ibid.

83. Cattaneo 'L'opposizione popolare', 544.

84. Stefano Recchia & Nadia Urbinati (eds), *A Cosmopolitanism of Nations: Giuseppe Mazzini's Writings on Democracy, Nation Building and International Relations* (Princeton: Princeton University Press, 2009), 4–5.

85. Pius VII, *Litterae Apostolicae, quibus Societas vulgo – Carbonariorum nuncupata condemnatur* (Rome: Typographia Rev. Camerae Apostolicae, 1821).

86. R. John Rath, 'The Carbonari: Their Origins, Initiation Rites and Aims, *The American Historical Review*, vol. 69, no.2 (1964), 353-70.

87. Fosi, Cohen (trans.), *Papal Justice*, 237–8.

88. Hearder, *Italy in the Age of the Risorgimento*, 78–80.

89. Denis Mack Smith, 'The Revolutions of 1848–1849 in Italy' in R.J.W. Evans & Hartmut Pogge von Strandmann (eds), *The Revolutions in Europe 1848–1849* (Oxford: Oxford University Press, 2000), 64–66.

90. The cartoon is reproduced in Borutta, 'Anti-Catholicism and the Culture War in Risorgimento Italy', 204–5.

91. Chadwick, *A History of the Popes, 1830–1914*, 50.

92. Schatz, *Papal Primacy*, 190.

93. Eamon Duffy, *Faith of our Fathers. Reflections on Catholic Tradition* (London: Continuum, 2004), 172.

94. Roberto de Mattei, John Laughland (ed.), *Pius IX* (Leominster: Gracewing, 2004), 14.

95. *Ragguaglio storico di quanto è avvenuto in Roma e in tutte le province dello Stato pontificio in seguito del perdono accordato dalla santità di N.S. papa Pio IX come dal suo editto del 16 luglio* (Rome: A. Ajani,1846), 48.

96. Ibid.

97. Veca, 'Oggetti animati', 69–70.

98. de Mattei, Laughland (ed.), ibid., 20.

99. Ibid., 26.

100. Borutta, ibid., 191.

101. Giacomo Martina, *Pio IX (1846–1850)* (Rome: Università Gregoriana, 1974), 204.

102. de Mattei, Laughland (ed.), ibid., 26, fn. 83.

103. Pius IX, *Qui pluribus. On Faith and Religion*, (1846).

104. Friedrich Engel-Janosi, 'The Return of Pius IX in 1850', *The Catholic Historical Review*, vol. 36, no. 2 (July 1950), 130.

105. Coppa, *The Modern Papacy*, 88.

106. Martina, ibid., 205.

107. Ibid., 118.

108. Frank Coppa, 'Cardinal Antonelli, the Papal States and the Counter-Risorgimento', *Journal of Church and State*, vol. 16, no. 3 (Autumn 1974), 460.

109. Coppa, 'Cardinal Antonelli', 461.

110. Martina, *Pio IX (1846–1850)*, 287.

111. Ibid., 287–8.

112. Priscilla Smith Robertson, *Revolutions of 1848. A Social History* (Princeton: Princeton University Press, 2020), 362.

113. Engel-Janosi, 'The Return of Pius IX', 130.

114. Kertzer, *Prisoner of the Vatican*, 9.

115. Nicola Roncalli, Raffaele Ambrosi de Magistris (ed.), *Diario di Nicola Roncalli dall'Anno 1849 al 1870* (Rome: Fratelli Bocca Librai, 1884), 55.

116. Ibid.

117. Smith Robertson, ibid., 367.

118. Marchese Luigi Lancellotti, *Diario della rivoluzione di Roma. Dal 1 Novembre 1848 al 31 luglio 1849* (Naples: Tipografia Guerrera, 1862), 128.

119. Smith Robertson, ibid., 370.

120. Lancellotti, ibid., 128.

121. Martina, ibid., 328 & de Mattei, Laughland (ed.), *Pius IX*, 34.

122. Lancellotti, ibid.,109.

123. de Mattei, Laughland (ed.), ibid., 38.

124. George Macaulay Trevelyan, *Garibaldi's Defence of the Roman Republic* (London: Longmans, Green, & Co, 1912), 111.

125. Ibid.

126. Lancellotti, ibid.,128.

127. Temistocle Mariotti quoting Pietro Sterbini, *La Difesa di Roma nel 1849* (Rome: Casa Editrice Italiana, 1892), 180.

128. Smith Robertson, ibid., 372.

129. Lancellotti, ibid.,129.

130. Donato Tamblé, 'Documents in the State Archive of Rome' in Charles Capper & Cristina Giorcelli (eds), *Margaret Fuller. Transatlantic Crossings in a Revolutionary Age* (Madison: University of Wisconsin Press, 2007), 242.

131. Tamblé, 'Documents in the State Archive of Rome', 242.

132. Smith Robertson, ibid., 375.

133. Trevelyan, ibid., 227.

134. de Mattei, Laughland (ed.), ibid., 45.

135. Engel-Janosi, ibid., 136.

136. Ibid., 159.

137. Chadwick, *A History of the Popes, 1830–1914*, 65.

138. Engel-Janosi, ibid., 136.

139. Coppa, *The Modern Papacy*, 96.

140. Ibid., 100.

141. Roncalli, de Magistris (ed.), *Diario di Nicola Roncalli*, 287–8.

142. Engel-Janosi, 'The Return of Pius IX in 1850', 136.

143. Ciarán O'Carroll, 'Pius IX: pastor and prince' in James Corkery & Thomas Worcester, *The Papacy Since 1500. From Italian Prince to Universal Pastor* (Cambridge: Cambridge University Press, 2010), 137.

144. Agostino Chigi, *Diario del principe Agostino Chigi Albani. Parte prima* (Tolentino: F. Filelfo, 1906), 132.

145. O'Carroll, ibid., 131–2.

146. Wittman, 'A Partly Vacated Historicism', 22–3.

147. David Kertzer, *The Kidnapping of Edgardo Mortara* (New York: Picador, 1997). 171.

148. For a detailed account of the incident described here and its consequences see David Kertzer, *The Kidnapping of Edgardo Mortara*.

149. Kertzer, ibid., 5.

150. Ibid., 6–7.

151. *The Spectator*, 13 November 1858, 1197.

152. Kertzer, ibid., 123.

153. C.S. Monaco, *The Rise of Modern Jewish Politics. Extraordinary Movement* (London: Routledge, 2013), 114.

154. Kertzer, ibid., 128.

155. Ibid., 120.

156. Vittorio Messori, *Kidnapped by the Vatican? The Unpublished Memoirs of Edgardo Mortara* (San Francisco: Ignatius Press, 2017), 91.

157. Silvio Negro, *Seconda Roma. 1850–1870* (Vicenza: Neri Pozzi, 2015), 18.

158. Karim Schelkens, John A. Dick, & Jürgen Mettepenningen, *Aggiornamento? Catholicism from Gregory XVI to Benedict XVI* (Leiden: Brill, 2013), 44.

159. Chadwick, *A History of the Popes, 1830–1914*, 215.

160. Raffaele de Cesare, *The Last Days of Papal Rome, 1850–1870* (Boston: Houghton Mifflin, 1909), 444.

161. Ibid.

162. Ibid., 454.

163. Kertzer, *Prisoner of the Vatican*, 56.

CHAPTER 11: A TALE OF TWO CITIES: ROME AND THE VATICAN

1. Insolera, *Modern Rome*, 193.

2. Carol Rittner & John K. Roth, *Pope Pius XII and the Holocaust* (London: Bloomsbury Academic, 2016), 28.

3. William Bruce Johnson, *Miracles and Sacrilege. Roberto Rossellini, the Church and Film Censorship* (Toronto: University of Toronto Press, 2008), 192.

4. Jenö Levai, 'Interventions by the Pope and the Nuncio' in Patrick J. Gallo (ed.), *Pius XII, the Holocaust and the Revisionists: Essays* (Jefferson: McFarland & Company, 2006), 111.

5. Philip Morgan, *The Fall of Mussolini. Italy, the Italians and the Second World War* (Oxford: Oxford University Press, 2008), 26–8.

6. Ibid., 29.

7. H. James Burgwyn & Amedeo Osti Guerrazzi, *Mussolini and the Salò Republic, 1943–1945. The Failure of a Puppet Regime* (London: Palgrave Macmillan, 2018), 8.

8. Robert Katz, *The Battle for Rome. The Germans, the Allies, the Partisans and the Pope, September 1943–June 1944* (London: Simon & Schuster, 2003), 39.

9. Ibid.

10. Paolo Monelli, *Roma 1943* (Rome: Migliaresi, 1945), 403.

11. Ibid.

12. Katz, ibid., 193.

13. Leonidas Hill, *Die Weizsäcker Papiere*, 347 quoted in Michael R. Marrus (ed.), *The Nazi Holocaust. Historical Articles on the Destruction of European Jews* (London: Meckler, 1989), 1267.

14. Ibid.

15. Francesco Margiotta Broglio, 'Dalla Conciliazione al giubileo 2000' in Luigi Fiorani & Adriano Prosperi, *Roma, la città del papa. Vita civile e religiosa dal giubileo di Bonifacio VIII al giubileo di papa Wojtyla* (Turin: Giulio Einaudi, 2000), 1178.

16. Ibid., 1177.

17. Giardina & Vauchez, *Il Mito di Roma*, 187.

18. Ibid.

19. Dora Dumont, 'The nation as seen from below: Rome in 1870', *European Review of History – Revue européenne d'histoire*, vol. 15, no. 5 (October, 2008), 481.

20. Gene Burns, *The Frontiers of Catholicism. The Politics of Ideology in a Liberal World* (Berkeley: University of California Press, 1994), 29.

21. Kertzer, *The Prisoner in the Vatican*, 79.

22. Ibid., 78.

23. Broglio, ibid., 1157.

24. Dumont, ibid., 482.

25. Ibid.

26. Falconieri, 'Ritratto in bianco e nero di un'aristocrazia', 265.

27. Frank Coppa, *The Origins of the Italian Wars of Independence* (London: Taylor and Francis, 2014), 143.

28. Dumont, ibid., 484.

29. Coppa, *The Origins of the Italian Wars of Independence*, 143.

30. A. William Salomone & Gaetano Salvemini, *Italy in the Giolittian Era. Italian Democracy in the Making* (Philadelphia: University of Pennsylvania Press, 2016), 8.

31. Insolera, *Modern Rome*, 371.

32. Dumont, 'The nation as seen from below', 484.

33. Gabriele D'Annunzio, Agatha Huges (trans.), *The Virgins of the Rocks* (London: William Heinemann, 1899), 55–6.

34. Insolera, ibid., 31.

35. Aristotle Kallis, *The Third Rome, 1922–1943. The Making of the Fascist Capital* (London: Palgrave Macmillan, 2014), 4; 26.

36. Terry Kirk, 'The Political Topography of Modern Rome, 1870–1936: Via XX Settembre to Via dell'Impero' in Caldwell & Caldwell (eds), *Rome Continuing Encounters*, 105.

37. Ibid.

38. Terry Kirk, *The Architecture of Modern Italy. Volume 1: The Challenge of Tradition, 1750–1900* (New York: Princeton Architectural Press, 2005), 231.

39. Kirk, 'The Political Topography of Modern Rome', 113.

40. Ibid.

41. Ibid.

42. Riall, *Garibaldi*, 379.

43. Jeremiah J. Crowley, *The Pope. Chief of white slavers. High priest of intrigue* (Aurora: The Menace Publishing Company, 1913), 430.

44. Ibid., 9.

45. Maura Jane Farrelly, *Anti-Catholicism in America, 1620–1860* (Cambridge: Cambridge University Press, 2018), 162–89.

46. D'Agostino, *Rome in America*, 29.

47. Ibid., 30–1

48. John T. McGreevy, *Catholicism. A Global History from the French Revolution to Pope Francis* (W. W. Norton & Company, 2022), Chapter 5: Milieu. Why Nationalists Attacked Catholics and How Catholics Responded, I, para. 6.

49. Ibid.

50. John Lynch, *New Worlds. A Religious History of Latin America* (New Haven: Yale University Press, 2012), 208–10.

51. Leo XIII, *Testem benevolentiae nostrae*, 22 January 1899.

52. Coppa, *The Papacy, the Jews and the Holocaust*, 126.

53. Burns, *The Frontiers of Catholicism*, 4–5.

54. Pius IX, *Gravibus ecclesiae*, 24 December 1874.

55. Daniele Menozzi, 'Un nuovo rapporto tra Chiesa e società' in Formica (ed.), *Roma capitale*, 91.

56. Russell Hittinger, 'Pope Leo XIII (1810–1903)' in Joseph Witte & Frank S. Alexander (eds), *The Teachings of Modern Roman Catholicism* (New York: Columbia University Press, 2007), 39.

57. Pius X, *Iucunda sane*, 12 March 1904.

58. Mariano P. Barbato, 'The Holy See, Public Spheres and Postsecular Transformations of International Relations: An Introduction' in Mariano P. Barbato (ed.), *The Pope, the Public and International Relations* (Cham: Palgrave Macmillan, 2020), 9–11.

59. Pew Research Center, *The Global Catholic Population*, 13 February 2013.

60. Barbato, ibid., 10.

61. Chris Maunder, *Our Lady of the Nations. Apparitions of Mary in Twentieth-century Catholic Europe* (Oxford: Oxford University Press, 2016), 29–40.

62. Lucy Riall, *The Italian Risorgimento. State, Society and National Unification* (London: Routledge, 1994), 48–53.

63. Dumont, 'The nation as seen from below', 489.

64. Vincenzo Palmesi, *Del tabacco, specialmente del tobacco da fumo. Studii* (Reggio-Emilia: Luigi Bondavalli, 1876), 58.

65. Dumont, ibid., 488.

66. Leo XIII, *Rerum novarum*, 15 May 1891; John F. Pollard, *Money and the Rise of the Modern Papacy. Financing the Vatican, 1850–1950* (Cambridge: Cambridge University Press, 2005), 76.

67. A. James Gregor, *Italian Fascism and Developmental Dictatorship* (Princeton: Princeton University Press, 2014), 22.

68. Franklin Hugh Adler, *Italian Industrialists from Liberalism to Fascism. The Political Development of the Industrial Bourgeoisie, 1906–34* (Cambridge: Cambridge University Press, 2002), 15.

69. Frank Coppa, *Politics and the Papacy in the Modern World* (Westport: Praeger, 2008), 72–4.

70. Coppa, *The Modern Papacy*, 149–51.

71. Alexander De Grand, *The Hunchback's Tailor. Giovanni Giolitti and Liberal Italy from the Challenge of Mass Politics to the Rise of Fascism, 1882–1922* (Westport: Praeger, 2001), 200.

72. David Kertzer, *The Pope and Mussolini. The Secret History of Pius XI and the Rise of Fascism in Europe* (Oxford: Oxford University Press, 2014), 3–4.

73. Andrea Carteny, 'The Intervention of Volunteers for the French Front (1914): D'Annunzio and the Italian Legion' in Antonello Biagini and Giovanni Motta (eds), *The First World War. Analysis and Interpretation. Volume 1* (Newcastle: Cambridge Scholars Publishing, 2015), 395.

74. Coppa, *Politics and the Papacy in the Modern World*, 87.

75. D'Agostino, *Rome in America*, 104.

76. Coppa, *The Modern Papacy*, 159.

77. Falconieri, 'Ritratto in bianco e nero di un'aristocrazia', 271.

78. Giardina & Vauchez, *Il Mito di Roma*, 213.

79. Duggan, *The Force of Destiny*, 378.

80. Michael S. Neiberg, *The Treaty of Versailles. A Concise History* (Oxford: Oxford University Press: 2017), 28.

81. Ibid., 29–30.

82. John Woodhouse, *Gabriele D'Annunzio. Defiant Archangel* (Oxford: Oxford University Press, 2001), 345.

83. John F. Pollard, *The Papacy in the Age of Totalitarianism, 1914–58* (Oxford: Oxford University Press, 2014), 49.

84. Ibid., 48.

85. John F. Pollard, *Benedict XV. The Unknown Pope and the Pursuit of Peace* (London: Bloomsbury Academic, 2005), 99.

86. Ibid.

87. Emilio Gentile, 'Paramilitary Violence in Italy: The Rationale of Fascism and the Origins of Totalitarianism' in Robert Gerwarth & John Horne (eds), *War in Peace. Paramilitary Violence in Europe after the Great War* (Oxford: Oxford University Press, 2012), 88.

88. Ibid.

89. Duggan, ibid., 367.

90. Pius X, *In Fermo Proposito*, 11 June 1905.

91. John F. Pollard, *The Vatican and Italian Fascism, 1929–32* (Cambridge: Cambridge University Press, 2005), 21.

92. Eric O. Hanson, *The Catholic Church in World Politics* (Princeton: Princeton University Press, 1987), 50.

93. A. James Gregor, *Young Mussolini and the Intellectual Origins of Fascism* (Berkeley: University of California Press, 1979), 178.

94. *Popolo d'Italia*, vol. 1, no. 36, 20 December, 1914.

95. Duggan, ibid., 416–17.

96. Ibid., 424.

97. Giulia Albanese, *The March on Rome. Violence and the Rise of Italian Fascism* (London: Taylor and Francis, 2019), Chapter 2: Political Violence, para. 38.

98. Paul Baxa, *Roads and Ruins. The Symbolic Landscapes of Fascist Rome* (Toronto: University of Toronto Press, 2010), 44.

99. Albanese, *The March on Rome*, Chapter 2, para. 40.

100. Emilio Gentile, 'Fascism in Power. The totalitarian experiment' in Matthew Feldman & Roger Griffin (eds), *Fascism. Critical Concepts in Political Science* (London: Routledge, 2004), 22.

101. Albanese, ibid., para. 42.

102. Giardina & Vauchez, *Il Mito di Roma*, 224.

103. Donald Sassoon, *Mussolini and the Rise of Fascism* (London: Harper Press, 2012), 13.

104. Christopher Duggan, *Fascist Voices: An Intimate History of Mussolini's Italy* (Oxford: Oxford University Press, 2013), 55.

105. Denis Mack Smith, *Italy and its Monarchy* (New Haven: Yale University Press, 1989) 249.

106. Claudio G. Segre, *Italo Balbo. A Fascist Life* (Berkeley: University of California Press, 1990), 100.

107. Walter L. Adamson, 'Modernism and Fascism: The Politics of Culture in Italy, 1903–1922', *The American Historical Review*, vol. 95, no.2 (April, 1990), 359.

108. Lucia Ceci, *The Vatican and Mussolini's Italy* (Leiden: Brill, 2016), 81.

109. Emma Fattorini, *Hitler, Mussolini and the Vatican. Pope Pius XI and the Speech that was Never Made* (Cambridge: Polity Press, 2011), 23.

110. Kertzer, *The Pope and Mussolini*, 48.

111. Duggan, ibid., 81.

112. Ibid.

113. Kertzer, ibid., 49.

114. Pollard, *The Vatican and Italian Fascism, 1929–32*, 22.

115. Adamson, 'Modernism and Fascism', 359.

116. Duggan, ibid., 205.

117. Ibid.

118. Robert Maryks, *Pouring Jewish Water into Fascist Wine. Untold Stories of (Catholic) Jews from the Archive of Mussolini's Jesuit Pietro Tacchi Venturi* (Leiden: Brill, 2017), 9.

119. Martin Blinkhorn, *Fascists and Conservatives. The Radical Right and the Establishment in Twentieth-century Europe* (London: Taylor and Francis, 2012), 41.

120. Broglio, 'Dalla Conciliazione al giubileo 2000', 1154.

121. *Lateran Pacts* (1929), Section 3: The Concordat, Article 1.

122. Borden W. Painter, *Mussolini's Rome. Rebuilding the Eternal City* (Basingstoke: Palgrave Macmillan, 2005), 93–4.

123. Mabel Berezin, 'Festival State: Celebration and Commemoration in Fascist Italy', *Journal of Modern European History*, vol. 4, no.1 (2006), 70.

124. Albert C. O'Brien, 'Benito Mussolini, Catholic Youth and the Origins of the Lateran Treaties', *Journal of Church and State*, vol. 23, no. 1 (1981), 124–6.

125. Fattorini, *Hitler, Mussolini and the Vatican*, 131.

126. Christian Goeschel, *Mussolini and Hitler. The Forging of a Fascist Alliance* (New Haven: Yale University Press, 2020), 131.

127. David Kertzer, 'Pietro Tacchi Venturi, Mussolini, Pius XI and the Jews' in James Bernauer & Robert Aleksander Maryks (eds), *"The Tragic Couple". Encounters Between Jews and Jesuits* (Leiden: Brill, 2013), 271.

128. Michael A. Livingstone, *The Fascists and the Jews of Italy. Mussolini's Race Laws, 1938–1943* (Cambridge: Cambridge University Press, 2014), 17.

129. Maryks, *Pouring Jewish Water into Fascist Wine*, 10–13.

130. Ibid.

131. Fattorini, *Hitler, Mussolini and the Vatican*, 188–9.

132. Kertzer, *The Pope and Mussolini*, xxx-i.

133. Fattorini, ibid., 189.

134. David Kertzer, *The Pope at War. The Secret History of Pius XII, Mussolini and Hitler* (New York: Random House, 2022), 37–40.

135. Ibid., 363–9.

136. Broglio, 'Dalla Conciliazione al giubileo 2000', 1179.

137. Giuliana Chamedes, *A Twentieth-century Crusade. The Vatican's Battle to Remake Christian Europe* (Cambridge, Mass.: Harvard University Press, 2019), 255.

138. Broglio, ibid., 1186.

139. Richard Drake, *The Aldo Moro Murder Case* (Cambridge, Mass.: Harvard University Press, 1995), 53.

140. Dennis Castillo, *Papal Diplomacy from 1914 to 1989* (Lanham: Lexington Books, 2019), 191.

141. Broglio, ibid., 1186.

142. Marcello de Cecco, 'The Italian Economy Seen from Abroad' in Gianni Toniolo (ed.), *The Oxford Handbook of the Italian Economy since Unification* (Oxford: Oxford University Press, 2013), 146.

143. Guido Crainz, *Storia del Miracolo Italiano. Culture, identità, trasformazioni fra anni cinquanta e sessanta* (Rome: Donzelli Editore 1996), 136.

144. Ibid.

145. Broglio, ibid., 1188.

146. Roy Domenico, *The Devil and the Dolce Vita. Catholic Attempts to Save Italy's Soul, 1948–1974* (Washington: Catholic University of America Press, 2021), 233.

147. Ibid., 254–8.

148. Virgilio Fantuzzi, 'La Ricotta' in Mary Lea Bandy & Antonio Monda (eds), *The Hidden God. Film and Faith* (New York: Museum of Modern Art, 2003), 104. On Pasolini and Rome see Jacopo Benci, '"An Extraordinary Proliferation of Layers" Pasolini's Rome(s)' in Caldwell & Caldwell (eds), *Rome: Continuing Encounters*, 153–88.

149. Broglio, 'Dalla Conciliazione al giubileo 2000', 1196–7.

150. Ibid., 1193.

151. Ibid., 1188.

152. Ibid., 1198.

153. Ibid., 1203.

154. George Weigel, *Witness to Hope. The Biography of Pope John Paul II* (New York: Harper Collins, 2001), 398.

155. Quoted in *L'eco di Bergamo*, 10 January 2006.

156. Antonio Socci has identified this nun as Cristina Montella. See Socci, *Il Segreto di Padre Pio* (Milan: Rizzoli, 2007), 40.

157. 'Il Mondo prega per il Papa– – Il crudele attentato profonda ferita al cuore dell'umanità', *Avvenire*, 14 May 1981.

158. Ibid.

159. Quoted in George J. Church, Lance Morrow, Mayo Mohs, John Leo & Richard N. Ostling, 'Hand of Terrorism', *Time*, 25 May 1981.

160. Frank J. Prial, 'Leaders around the world voice shock and anger', *New York Times*, 14 May 1981, 5.

161. Ibid.

162. 'Ali Ağca non si pente: "Volevo Uccidere Wojtyla, sua sopravvivenza un miracolo"', *La Repubblica*, 24 April 2014.

163. 'Obsessions of ex-monk hijacker', *Sydney Morning Herald*, 5 May 1981.

164. C.C. Martindale, *The Meaning of Fatima* (New York: P.J. Kennedy and Sons, 1950).

165. Chris Maunder, *Our Lady of the Nations. Apparitions of Mary in Twentieth-century Catholic Europe* (Oxford: Oxford University Press, 2016), 29–40.

166. Manuel A. Vásquez & Marie Friedmann Marquardt, *Globalizing the Sacred. Religion across the Americas* (New Brunswick: Rutgers University Press, 2003), 173.

167. 'Ağca recalls prison visit by pope', *New York Times*, 5 February 1985.

168. Jeffrey Tranzillo, *John Paul II on the Vulnerable* (Washington D.C.: The Catholic University of America Press, 2013), 49.

169. Pew Research Center, *The Global Catholic Population*, 13 February 2013.

Selected Bibliography

Secondary Sources

Adams, Marcus P. (ed.), *A Companion to Hobbes* (Oxford: Wiley Blackwell, 2021).

Adamson, Walter L., 'Modernism and Fascism: The Politics of Culture in Italy, 1903–1922', *The American Historical Review*, vol. 95, no. 2 (April, 1990), 359–390.

Adankpo-Labadie, Olivia, 'A Faith between Two Worlds. Expressing Ethiopian Devotion and Crossing Cultural Boundaries at Santo Stefano dei Mori in Early Modern Rome' in Matthew Coneys-Wainwright & Emily Michelson (eds), *A Companion to Religious Minorities in Early Modern Rome* (Leiden: Brill, 2022), 169–191.

Ademollo, Alessandro, *Le Giustizie a Roma. Dal 1674 al 1739. E dal 1796 a 1840* (Rome: Forzani e C., 1881).

Adler, Franklin Hugh, *Italian Industrialists from Liberalism to Fascism. The Political Development of the Industrial Bourgeoisie, 1906–34* (Cambridge: Cambridge University Press, 2002).

D'Agostino, Peter, *Rome in America. Transnational Catholic Ideology from the Risorgimento to Fascism* (Chapel Hill: University of North Carolina Press, 2005).

Åkerman, Susanna, *Queen Christina of Sweden and Her Circle. The Transformation of a Seventeenth-Century Philosophical Libertine* (Leiden: Brill, 1991).

Albanese, Giulia, *The March on Rome. Violence and the Rise of Italian Fascism* (London: Taylor and Francis, 2019).

Allen, Pauline & Bronwen Neil, *Crisis Management in Late Antiquity (410–590 CE)* (Leiden: Brill, 2013).

Allies, Mary H., *The Life of Pope Pius the Seventh* (London: Burns and Oates, 1875).

Alvazzi del Frate, Paolo, 'Rivoluzione e giornalismo politico nello Stato pontificio', *Mélanges de l'École française de Rome. Italie et Méditerranée*, vol. 102, no. 2 (1990), 411–422.

Anderson, Robin, *Papa Pio VII (Barnaba Chiaramonti). La vita, il regno e il conflitto con Napoleone nel periodo seguente alla rivoluzione francese (1742–1823)* (Rome: Benedictina Editrice, 2000).

Andrea, Bernadette, 'The Global Travels of Teresa Sampsonia Sherley's Carmelite Relic' in Patricia Akhimie & Bernadette Andrea (eds), *Travel and Travail. Early Modern Women, English Drama and the Wider World* (Lincoln, University of Nebraska Press, 2019), 102–120.

Andretta, Elisa & Federica Favino, 'Scientific and Medical Knowledge in Early Modern Rome' in Pamela M. Jones, Barbara Wisch & Simon Ditchfield (eds), *A Companion to Early Modern Rome, 1492–1692* (Leiden: Brill, 2019), 515–529.

Andrieux, Maurice, Mary Fitton (trans.), *Daily Life in Papal Rome* (London: Allen & Unwin, 1968).

Arnold, Jonathan J., *Theodoric and the Roman Imperial Restoration* (Cambridge: Cambridge University Press, 2014).

Aron-Beller, Katherine, 'Ghettoization: The Papal Enclosure and Its Jews' in Jones, Wisch & Ditchfield (eds), *A Companion to Early Modern Rome, 1492–1692* (Leiden: Brill, 2019), 232–246.

Asbach, Olaf & Peter Schröder (eds), *The Ashgate Research Companion to the Thirty Years War* (Farnham: Ashgate, 2014).

Asch, Ronald G., '1618–1629' in Olaf Asbach & Peter Schröder (eds), *The Ashgate Research Companion to the Thirty Years War* (Farnham: Ashgate, 2014), 127–138.

Aston, Nigel, *Christianity and revolutionary Europe, 1750–1830* (Cambridge: Cambridge University Press, 2002).

D'Avray, David L., 'Stages of papal law', *Journal of the British Academy*, 5 (2017), 37–59.

Ayres, Philip, *Classical Culture and the Idea of Rome in Eighteenth-Century England* (Cambridge: Cambridge University Press, 1997).

Bacci, Pietro, Frederick Ignatius Antrobus (ed.), *The Life of Saint Philip Neri. Apostle of Rome and Founder of the Congregation of the Oratory* (London: Kegan Paul, Trench, Trübner & Co., 1902).

Bachrach, David S., *Warfare in Tenth-Century Germany* (Woodbridge: Boydell Press, 2014).

Baghos, Mario, *From the Ancient Near East to Byzantium. Kings, Symbols and Cities* (Newcastle: Cambridge Scholars Publishing, 2021).

Balchin, Paul, *Rome: The Shaping of Three Capitals* (Abingdon: Routledge, 2020).

Bamji, Alexandra, Geert H. Janssen & Mary Laven (eds), *The Ashgate Research Companion to the Counter-Reformation* (London: Routledge, 2013).

Barbato, Mariano P., 'The Holy See, Public Spheres and Postsecular Transformations of International Relations: An Introduction' in Mariano P. Barbato (ed.), *The Pope, the Public, and International Relations* (Cham: Palgrave Macmillan, 2020), 1–24.

Barbato, Mariano P. (ed.), *The Pope, the Public, and International Relations* (Cham: Palgrave Macmillan, 2020).

Bardill, Jonathan, *Constantine, Divine Emperor of the Christian Golden Age* (Cambridge: Cambridge University Press, 2012).

Barker, John W., *Justinian and the Later Roman Empire* (Madison: The

University of Wisconsin Press, 1966).

Baumgartner, Frederic, *Behind locked doors: A History of the Papal Elections* (London: Palgrave Macmillan, 2003).

Baxa, Paul, *Roads and Ruins. The Symbolic Landscapes of Fascist Rome* (Toronto: University of Toronto Press, 2010).

Beard, Mary, 'The Cult of the "Great Mother" in Imperial Rome. The Roman and the "Foreign"' in J. Rasmus Brandt & Jon W. Iddeng (eds), *Greek and Roman Festivals. Content, Meaning and Practice* (Oxford: Oxford University Press, 2012), 323–362.

Beard, Mary & Keith Hopkins, *The Colosseum* (Harvard: Harvard University Press, 2005).

Beard, Mary, John North & Simon Price, *Religions of Rome. Volume 1. A History* (Cambridge: Cambridge University Press, 1998).

Beaven, Lisa, 'Elite Patronage and Collecting' in Jones, Wisch & Ditchfield (eds), *A Companion to Early Modern Rome, 1492–1692* (Leiden: Brill, 2019), 387–411.

Belozerskaya, Marina, *To Wake the Dead. A Renaissance Merchant and the Birth of Archaeology* (New York: W.W. Norton & Company, 2009).

Benedictow, Ole J., *The Black Death 1346–1353. The Complete History* (Woodbridge: Boydell Press, 2004).

Benko, Stephen, *Pagan Rome and the Early Christians* (London: Batsford, 1985).

Berezin, Mabel, 'Festival State: Celebration and Commemoration in Fascist Italy', *Journal of Modern European History*, vol. 4, no. 1 (2006), 60—74.

Bernauer, James & Robert Aleksander Maryks (eds), *"The Tragic Couple". Encounters Between Jews and Jesuits* (Leiden: Brill, 2013).

Birch, Debra Julie, *Pilgrimage to Rome in the Middle Ages. Continuity and Change* (Woodbridge: Boydell Press, 1998).

Black, Christopher F., *Italian Confraternities in the Sixteenth Century* (Cambridge: Cambridge University Press, 1989).

Black, Christopher F., *The Italian Inquisition* (London: Yale University Press, 2016).

Blinkhorn, Martin, *Fascists and Conservatives. The Radical Right and the Establishment in Twentieth-century Europe* (London: Taylor and Francis, 2012).

Blumenthal, Uta-Renate, *The Investiture Controversy. Church and Monarchy from the Ninth to the Twelfth Century* (Philadelphia: University of Pennsylvania Press, 2010).

Boer, David de, Malte Griesse & Monika Barget (eds), *Revolts and Political Violence in Early Modern Imagery* (Leiden: Brill, 2021).

Bolton, Brenda, 'Received in His Name: Rome's Busy Baby Box', *Studies in Church History*, vol. 31 (1994), 153–167.

Bombi, Barbara, *Anglo-Papal Relations in the Early Fourteenth Century* (Oxford: Oxford University Press, 2019).

Borutta, Manuel, 'Anti-Catholicism and the Culture War in Risorgimento Italy' in Silvana Patriarca & Lucy Riall (eds), *The Risorgimento Revisited: Nationalism and Culture in Nineteenth-Century Italy* (Basingstoke: Palgrave Macmillan, 2011), 191–213.

Bosman, L., I. P. Haynes & P. Liverani, *The Basilica of Saint John Lateran to 1600* (Cambridge: Cambridge University Press, 2020).

Bourgoing, Jean-François de, *Historical and philosophical memoirs of Pius the Sixth and of his Pontificate, down to the period of his retirement into Tuscany* (Dublin: H. Colbert, W. Porter, J. Boyce, J. Rice & R.E. Mercier & co., 1800), 2 vols.

Bowersock, Glen W., 'Peter and Constantine' in William Tronzo (ed.), *St. Peter's in the Vatican* (Cambridge: Cambridge University Press, 2005), 3–15.

Bowes, Kim, *Private Worship, Public Values and Religious Change in Late Antiquity* (Cambridge University Press, 2008).

Boyle, Nicholas, *Goethe. The Poet and the Age. Volume 1. The Poetry of Desire (1749–1790)* (Oxford: Oxford University Press, 1992).

Brandt, J. Rasmus & Jon W. Iddeng (eds), *Greek and Roman Festivals. Content, Meaning and Practice* (Oxford: Oxford University Press, 2012).

Braun, Guido, 'The Papacy' in Asbach & Schröder (eds), *The Ashgate Research Companion to the Thirty Years War* (Farnham: Ashgate, 2014), 101–114.

Bredholt Christensen, Lisbeth, Olav Hammer & David A. Warburton (eds.), *The Handbook of Religions of Ancient Europe* (London: Routledge, 2014).

Brentano, Robert, *Rome before Avignon. A Social History of Thirteenth-century Rome* (New York: Longman, 1974).

Bridget of Sweden, Denis Searby (trans.) & Bridget Morris (ed.), *The Revelations of St. Birgitta of Sweden. Volume 2* (Oxford: Oxford University Press, 2008).

Broers, Michael, *Politics and Religion in Napoleonic Italy. The War Against God, 1801–1814* (London: Taylor and Francis, 2003).

Brown, Alison, *The Return of Lucretius to Renaissance Florence* (Cambridge, Mass.: Harvard University Press, 2010).

Brown, Peter, *The World of Late Antiquity* (New York: W.W. Norton, 1989).

Bruce, Lorne, 'A Note on Christian Libraries during the Great Persecution 303–305 AD', *The Journal of Library History*, (1980), 127–137.

Buranelli, Francesco, *The Vatican Necropoles. Rome's City of the Dead* (Turnhout: Brepols, 2010).

Burgwyn, H. James & Amedeo Osti Guerrazzi, *Mussolini and the Salò Republic, 1943–1945. The Failure of a Puppet Regime* (London: Palgrave Macmillan, 2018).

Burke, Jill, *Rethinking the High Renaissance. The Culture of the Visual Arts in Early Sixteenth-Century Rome* (London: Taylor and Francis, 2017).

Burke, Peter, *Play in Renaissance Italy* (Cambridge: Polity Press, 2021).

Burke, Peter, 'Varieties of Performance in Seventeenth-Century Italy' in Peter Gillgren & Mårten Snickare (eds), *Performativity and Performance in Baroque Rome* (London: Routledge, 2016), 15–23.

Burns, Gene, *The Frontiers of Catholicism. The Politics of Ideology in a Liberal World* (Berkeley: University of California Press, 1994).

Burns, Thomas S., 'Theodoric the Great and Concepts of Power in Late Antiquity', *Acta Classica*, vol. 25 (1982), 99–118.

Burson, Jeffrey D. & Jonathan Wright (eds), *The Jesuit Suppression in Global Context. Causes, Events and Consequences* (Cambridge: Cambridge University Press, 2015).

Caiani, Ambrogio A., *To Kidnap a Pope. Napoleon and Pius VII* (New Haven: Yale University Press, 2021).

Caldwell, Dorigen & Lesley Caldwell (eds), *Rome Continuing Encounters between Past and Present* (London: Routledge, 2011).

Caldwell Ames, Christine, *Medieval Heresies: Christianity, Judaism and Islam* (Cambridge: Cambridge University Press, 2015).

Cameron, Alan, *The Last Pagans of Rome* (Oxford: Oxford University Press, 2011).

Canepari, Eleonora & Laurie Nussdorfer, 'A Civic Identity' in Jones, Wisch & Ditchfield (eds), *A Companion to Early Modern Rome, 1492–1692* (Leiden: Brill, 2019), 29–43.

Cantimori, Delio, Adriano Prosperi (ed.), *Eretici italiani del Cinquecento e altre scritti* (Turin: Einaudi, 1992).

Capgrave, John, C.A. Mills (ed.), *Ye Solace of Pilgrimes: a description of Rome, circa A.D. 1450* (Oxford: Oxford University Press, 1911).

Carpegna Falconieri, Tommaso di, 'Ritratto in bianco e nero di un'aristocrazia' in Marina Formica (ed.), *Roma capitale. La città laica, la città religiosa (1870–1915)* (Rome: Viella, 2021), 265–273.

Carteny, Andrea, 'The Intervention of Volunteers for the French Front (1914): D'Annunzio and the Italian Legion' in Antonello Biagini and Giovanni Motta (eds), *The First World War. Analysis and Interpretation. Volume 1* (Newcastle: Cambridge Scholars Publishing, 2015), 389-397.

Castillo, Dennis, *Papal Diplomacy from 1914 to 1989* (Lanham: Lexington Books, 2019).

Cattaneo, Massimo, 'L'opposizione popolare al <<giacobinismo>> a Roma e nello Stato Pontifico', *Studi Storici*, Anno 39, no. 2 (1998), 533–568.

Cavedagna, Fabio & Marcello Donativi (eds), *Memorie di un boia* (Edizioni Trabant: 2009).

Ceci, Lucia, *The Vatican and Mussolini's Italy* (Leiden: Brill, 2016).

Celenza, Christopher C., *The Intellectual World of the Italian Renaissance* (Cambridge: Cambridge University Press, 2018).

Cecco, Marcello de, 'The Italian Economy Seen from Abroad' in Gianni Toniolo (ed.), *The Oxford Handbook of the Italian Economy since Unification* (Oxford: Oxford University Press, 2013).

Cesare, Raffaele de, *I Romani e la nascita del Re di Roma* (Rome: Storia e Letterature, 1996).

Cesare, Raffaele de, *The Last Days of Papal Rome, 1850–1870* (Boston: Houghton Mifflin, 1909).

Chadwick, Henry, *The Church in Ancient Society. From Galilee to Gregory the Great* (Oxford: Oxford University Press, 2001).

Chadwick, Owen, *A History of the Popes, 1830–1914* (Oxford: Oxford University Press, 1998).

Chamedes, Giuliana, *A Twentieth-Century Crusade. The Vatican's Battle to Remake Christian Europe* (Cambridge, Mass.: Harvard University Press, 2019).

Champ, Judith F., *The English Pilgrimage to Rome. A Dwelling for the Soul* (Leominster: Gracewing, 2000).

Chaney, Edward, *The Evolution of the Grand Tour. Anglo-Italian Cultural Relations since the Renaissance* (London: Routledge, 1998).

Christensen, Theresa A. Kutasz, 'Allegory, Antiquities, and a Gothic Apollo: Queen Christina of Sweden and the Manufacture of Cultural Identity' in Jennifer Cochran Anderson & Douglas N. Dow (eds), *Visualising the Past in Renaissance Art* (Leiden: Brill, 2021), 53–79.

Church, Frederic, *The Italian reformers, 1534–1564* (New York: Columbia University Press, 1932).

Cihak, John R. (ed.), Ansgar Santogrossi (trans.), *Charles Borromeo. Selected Orations, Homilies and Writings* (London: Bloomsbury T&T Clark, 2017).

Clark, Gillian, *Christianity and Roman Society* (Cambridge: Cambridge University Press, 2004),

Clossey, Luke, *Salvation and Globalization in the Early Jesuit Missions* (Cambridge: Cambridge University Press, 2008).

Coelho, Victor (ed.), *Music and Science in the Age of Galileo* (Dordrecht: Kluwer Academic Publishers, 1992).

Coello de la Rosa, Alexandre, *Jesuits at the Margins. Missions and Missionaries in the Marianas (1668-1769)* (London: Routledge, 2016).

Coen, Paolo (ed.), *The Art Market in Rome in the Eighteenth Century. A Study in the Social History of Art* (Leiden: Brill, 2019).

Coffin, David, *Gardens and Gardening in Papal Rome* (Princeton: Princeton University Press, 1991).

Cohen, Elisabeth, 'Honour and Gender in the Streets of Early Modern Rome', *The Journal of Interdisciplinary History*, vol. 22, no. 4 (Spring 1922), 597–625.

Cohen, Samuel, 'Spelunca pravitatis hereticae': Gregory I and the

Rededication of "Arian" Church Buildings in Late Antique Rome', *Journal of Early Christian Studies*, vol. 30, no. 1 (2022), 119–148.

Cohen, Thomas V. & Elizabeth S. Cohen, 'Justice and Crime' in Jones, Wisch & Ditchfield (eds), *A Companion to Early Modern Rome, 1492–1692* (Leiden: Brill, 2019), 115–130.

Cohen, Thomas V. & Elizabeth S. Cohen, *Words and Deeds in Renaissance Rome. Trials Before the Papal Magistrates* (Toronto: University of Toronto Press, 1993).

Collins, Amanda, *Greater than Emperor. Cola di Rienzo (ca. 1313–54) and the World of Fourteenth-Century Rome* (Ann Arbor: The University of Michigan Press, 2002).

Collins, Jeffrey, *Papacy and Politics in Eighteenth-Century Rome. Pius VI and the Arts* (Cambridge: Cambridge University Press, 2004).

Coneys-Wainwright, Matthew & Emily Michelson (eds), *A Companion to Religious Minorities in Early Modern Rome* (Leiden: Brill, 2022).

Coneys-Wainwright, Matthew, 'Non-Catholic Pilgrims and the Hospital of SS. Trinita dei Pellegrini e Convalescenti (1575–1650)' in Coneys-Wainwright & Michelson, *A Companion to Religious Minorities in Early Modern Rome* (Leiden: Brill, 2022), 89–114.

Cook, John Granger, *Crucifixion in the Mediterranean World* (Tübingen: Mohr Siebeck, 2014).

Coon, Lynda L., *Sacred Fictions. Holy Women and Hagiography in Late Antiquity* (Philadelphia: University of Pennsylvania Press, 1997).

Columbus, Christopher, *The Letter of Columbus on the Discovery of America* (New York: Lenox Library, 1892).

Coppa, Frank, 'Cardinal Antonelli, the Papal States, and the Counter-Risorgimento', *Journal of Church and State*, vol. 16, no. 3 (Autumn 1974), 453–471.

Coppa, Frank, *Politics and the Papacy in the Modern World* (Westport: Praeger, 2008).

Coppa, Frank, *The Modern Papacy since 1789* (London: Longman, 1998).

Coppa, Frank, *The Origins of the Italian Wars of Independence* (London: Taylor and Francis, 2014).

Coppa, Frank, *The Papacy, the Jews, and the Holocaust* (Washington D.C.: The Catholic University of America Press, 2006).

Corkery, James & Thomas Worcester, *The Papacy Since 1500. From Italian Prince to Universal Pastor* (Cambridge: Cambridge University Press, 2010).

Corp, Edward, *The Stuarts in Italy, 1719–1766* (Cambridge: Cambridge University Press, 2011).

Cosentino, Salvatore (ed.), *A Companion to Byzantine Italy* (Leiden: Brill, 2021).

Cosmacini, Giorgio, *Storia della medicina e della sanità in Italia* (Rome: Laterza, 1988).

Coster, W. & A. Spicer (eds), *Sacred Space in Early Modern Europe*

(Cambridge: Cambridge University Press, 2005).

Coulombe, Charles A., *The Pope's Legion. The Multinational Fighting Force that Defended the Vatican* (Basingstoke: Palgrave Macmillan, 2008).

Cowdrey, H.E.J., *Pope Gregory VII, 1073–1085* (Oxford: Clarendon Press, 1998).

Cracco Ruggini, Lellia, 'Rome in Late Antiquity: Clientship, Urban Topography, and Prosopography', *Classical Philology*, vol. 98, no. 4 (2003), 366–382.

Crainz, Guido, *Storia del Miracolo Italiano. Culture, identità, trasformazioni fra anni cinquanta e sessanta* (Rome: Donzelli Editore 1996).

Curran, John R., *Pagan City and Christian Capital. Rome in the Fourth Century* (Oxford: Oxford University Press, 2002).

Curta, Florin, *Eastern Europe in the Middle Ages (500–1300)* (Leiden: Brill, 2019).

Curzi, Valter, 'Moral Subjects and Exempla Virtutis at the Start of the Eighteenth Century: Art and Politics in England, Rome and Venice' in Paolo Coen (ed.), *The Art Market in Rome in the Eighteenth Century. A Study in the Social History of Art* (Leiden: Brill, 2019), 115–130.

Dabakis, Melissa, 'Angelika Kauffmann, Goethe, and the Arcadian Academy in Rome' in Evelyn K. Moore & Patricia Anne Simpson (eds), *The Enlightened*

Eye. Goethe and Visual Culture (Amsterdam: Rodopi, 2007), 25–40.

Dandelet, Thomas James, *Spanish Rome, 1500–1700* (Yale: Yale University Press, 2001).

Demacopoulos, George E., *The Invention of Peter: Apostolic Discourse and Papal Authority in Late Antiquity* (Philadelphia: University of Pennsylvania Press, 2013).

Denzey Lewis, Nicola, *The Early Modern Invention of Late Antique Rome* (Cambridge: Cambridge University Press, 2020).

DePalma Digeser, Elizabeth, *A Threat to Public Piety. Christians, Platonists and the Great Persecution* (Ithaca: Cornell University Press, 2012).

DeSilva, Jennifer Mara, 'Articulating Work and Family: Lay Relatives in the Papal States, 1420–1549', *Renaissance Quarterly*, vol. 69, no. 1 (2016), 1–39.

DeSilva Jennifer Mara, *The Sacralization of Space and Behavior in the Early Modern World. Studies and Sources* (London: Routledge, 2016).

Devoe, Richard F., *Christianity and the Roman Games. The Paganization of Christians by Gladiators, Charioteers, Actors and Actresses from the First through the Fifth Centuries, A.D.* (Philadelphia: Xlibris, 2002).

Dey, Hendrik, *The Making of Medieval Rome. A New Profile of the City, 400–1200* (Cambridge: Cambridge University Press, 2021).

Diesbach, Ghislain de, *Madame de Staël* (Paris: Librairie Académique Perrin, 1983).

Dijkstra, Roald, 'Peter, Popes, Politics and More: the Apostle as Anchor' in Dijkstra (ed.), *The Early Reception and Appropriation of the Apostle Peter (60–800 CE)* (Leiden: Brill, 2020), 3–25.

Dijkstra, Roald (ed.), *The Early Reception and Appropriation of the Apostle Peter (60–800 CE)* (Leiden: Brill, 2020).

Ditchfield, Simon, *Liturgy, Sanctity and History in Tridentine Italy. Pietro Maria Campi and the Preservation of the Particular* (Cambridge: Cambridge University Press, 1995).

Ditchfield, Simon, '"One World is Not Enough": The "Myth" of Roman Catholicism as a "World Religion"' in Simone Maghenzani & Stefano Villani (eds), *British Protestant Missions and the Conversion of Europe, 1600–1900* (London: Routledge, 2021).

Ditchfield, Simon, 'Papal Prince or Pastor? Beyond the Prodi Paradigm', *Archivum Historiae Pontificiae*, vol. 51 (2013), 117–132.

Ditchfield, Simon, 'Reading Rome as a sacred landscape, c. 1586–1635' in W. Coster and A. Spicer *(eds), Sacred Space in Early Modern Europe* (Cambridge: Cambridge University Press, 2005), 167–192.

Ditchfield, Simon, 'Romanus and Catholicus: Counter-Reformation Rome as Caput Mundi' in Jones, Wisch & Ditchfield (eds), *A Companion to Early Modern Rome, 1492–1692* (Leiden: Brill, 2019), 131–147.

Ditchfield, Simon, 'Translating Christianity in an Age of Reformations', *Studies in Church History*, vol. 53 (2017), 164–195.

Dizionario Biografico degli Italiani (Rome: Istituto della Enciclopedia Italiana, 1960–2019), 95 vols.

Dolbeau, François, 'Nouveaux sermons de saint Augustin pour la conversion des païens et des donatistes', *Revue des Études Augustiniennes*, 37 (1991), 69–141.

Domenico, Roy, *The Devil and the Dolce Vita. Catholic Attempts to Save Italy's Soul, 1948–1974* (Washington: Catholic University of America Press, 2021).

Donati, Angela (ed.) *Pietro e Paolo. La Storia, il culto, la memoria nei primi secoli* (Milan: Electa, 2000).

Doran, John & Damian J. Smith (eds), *Pope Innocent II (1130–43). The world vs the city* (London: Routledge, 2016).

Drake, Richard, *The Aldo Moro Murder Case* (Cambridge, Mass.: Harvard University Press, 1995).

Drever, Matthew, *Image, Identity and the Forming of the Augustinian Soul* (Oxford: Oxford University Press, 2013).

Duckett, Eleanor Shipley, *Death and Life in the Tenth Century* (Ann Arbor: University of Michigan Press, 1967).

Duffy, Eamon, *Faith of our Fathers. Reflections on Catholic Tradition* (London: Continuum, 2004).

Duffy, Eamon, *Ten Popes Who Shook the World* (New Haven: Yale University Press, 2011).

Duggan, Christopher, *Fascist Voices: An Intimate History of Mussolini's Italy* (Oxford: Oxford University Press, 2013).

Duggan, Christopher, *The Force of Destiny. A History of Italy Since 1796* (Boston: Houghton Mifflin, 2008).

Dumont, Dora, 'The nation as seen from below: Rome in 1870', *European Review of History - Revue européenne d'histoire*, vol. 15, no. 5 (October, 2008), 479-496.

Dunkle, Roger, *Gladiators. Violence and Spectacle in Ancient Rome* (Abingdon: Routledge, 2008).

Dunn, Geoffrey, 'The Christian Networks of the Aniciae: The example of the letter of Innocent I to Anicia Juliana', *Revue d'études augustiniennes et patristiques*, vol. 55 (2009), 53–72.

Dursteler, Eric R., *Renegade Women. Gender, Identity, and Boundaries in the Early Modern Mediterranean* (Baltimore: Johns Hopkins University Press, 2011).

Dwyer, Philip, *Citizen Emperor* (New Haven: Yale University Press, 2013).

Dyson, Stephen L., *In Pursuit of Ancient Pasts. A History of Classical Archaeology in the Nineteenth and Twentieth Centuries* (New Haven: Yale University Press, 2006).

Eire, Carlos M. N., *Reformations. The Early Modern World, 1450–1650* (New Haven: Yale University Press, 2016).

Eisenbichler, Konrad (ed.), *A Companion to Medieval and Early Modern Confraternities* (Leiden: Brill, 2019).

Ekonomou, Andrew J., *Byzantine Rome and the Greek Popes. Influences on Rome and the Papacy from Gregory the Great to Zacharias, A.D. 590–752* (Lanham: Lexington Books: 2007).

D'Elia, Anthony, *A Sudden Terror: The Plot to Murder the Pope in Renaissance Rome* (Cambridge, Mass.: Harvard University Press, 2009).

D'Elia, Anthony, 'Stefano Porcari's Conspiracy against Pope Nicholas V in 1453 and Republican Culture in Papal Rome', *Journal of the History of Ideas*, vol. 68, no. 2 (2007), 207-231.

Elton, Hugh, *The Roman Empire in Late Antiquity. A Political and Military History* (Cambridge: Cambridge University Press, 2018).

Emich, Birgit, 'The Cardinal Nephew' in Mary Hollingsworth, Miles Pattenden & Arnold Witte (eds), *A Companion to the Early Modern Cardinal* (Leiden: Brill, 2020), 71–87.

Engel-Janosi, Friedrich, 'The Return of Pius IX in 1850', *The Catholic Historical Review*, vol. 36, no. 2 (July 1950), 129–162.

Esposito, Anna, '"Charitable" Assistance between Lay Foundations and Pontifical Initiatives' in Jones, Wisch & Ditchfield (eds), *A Companion to Early Modern Rome, 1492–1692* (Leiden: Brill, 2019), 199-213.

Esposito, Anna, 'Il cardinale Guglielmo d'Estouteville, Ambrogio di Cori e l'area di Colli Albani' in Carla Frova, Raimondo Michetti & Domenico Palombi (eds), *La carriera di un uomo di curia nella Roma del Quattrocento. Ambrogio Massari da Cori, agostiniano: cultura umanistica e committenza artistica* (Rome: Viella, 2008), 161–172.

Esposito, Anna, 'National Confraternities in Rome and Italy in the Late Middle Ages and Early Modern Period: Identity, Representation, Charity' in Konrad Eisenbichler (ed.), *A Companion to Medieval and Early Modern Confraternities* (Leiden: Brill, 2019), 235–256.

Evans, R.J.W. & Hartmut Pogge von Strandmann (eds), *The Revolutions in Europe 1848–1849* (Oxford: Oxford University Press, 2000).

Fagiolo, Marcello & Maria Luisa Madonna (eds), *Sisto V. I. Roma e il Lazio* (Rome: Libreria dello Stato, 1992).

Falkied, Unn, *The Avignon Papacy Contested. An Intellectual History from Dante to Catherine of Siena* (London: Harvard University Press, 2017).

Farrelly, Maura Jane, *Anti-Catholicism in America, 1620–1860* (Cambridge: Cambridge University Press, 2018).

Fattori, Maria Teresa, 'Lambertini's Treatises and the Cultural Project of Benedict XIV' in Rebecca Messbarger, Christopher M.S. Johns, & Philip Gavitt (eds), *Benedict XIV and the Enlightenment. Art, Science, and Spirituality* (Toronto: University of Toronto Press, 2016), 255–276.

Fattorini, Emma, *Hitler, Mussolini and the Vatican. Pope Pius XI and the Speech that was Never Made* (Cambridge: Polity Press, 2011).

Feldhay, Rivka, *Galileo and the Church. Political Inquisition or Critical Dialogue* (Cambridge: Cambridge University Press, 1995).

Fenlon, Iain, 'Music and Crisis in Florence and Rome, 1527-30' in Christine Shaw (ed.), *Italy and the European Powers. The Impact of War, 1500–1530* (Leiden: Brill, 2006).

Filippi, Daniele, 'Roma Sonora: An Atlas of Roman Sounds and Musics' in Jones, Wisch & Ditchfield (eds), *A Companion to Early Modern Rome, 1492–1692* (Leiden: Brill, 2019), 266–284.

Findlen, Paula, 'Women on the Verge of Science: Aristocratic Women and Knowledge in Early Eighteenth-Century Italy' in Sarah Knott & Barbara Taylor (eds), *Women, Gender and Enlightenment* (London: Palgrave Macmillan, 2005), 265–287.

Finocchiaro, Maurice A., *The Galileo Affair. A Documentary History* (Berkeley: University of California Press, 1989).

Fiorani, Luigi & Adriano Prosperi, *Roma, la città del papa. Vita civile e religiosa dal giubileo di Bonifacio VIII al giubileo di papa Wojtyla* (Turin: Giulio Einaudi, 2000).

Firpo, Massimo, *La presa di potere dell'Inquisizione Romana (1550–1553)* (Rome: Laterza, 2014).

Fischer Drew, Katherine, *Lombard Laws* (Philadelphia: University of Pennsylvania Press, 1996).

Fletcher, Catherine, *Diplomacy in Renaissance Rome. The Rise of the Resident Ambassador* (Cambridge: Cambridge University Press, 2015).

Foa, Anna, Andrea Grover (trans.), *The Jews of Europe after the Black Death* (Berkeley: University of California Press, 2000).

Fontana, Michela, *Matteo Ricci. A Jesuit in the Ming Court* (London: Rowman & Littlefield, 2011).

Forbis, Elizabeth, *Municipal Virtues in the Roman Empire. The Evidence of Italian Honorary Inscriptions* (Stuttgart: B.G. Teubner, 1996).

Formica, Marina (ed.), *Roma capitale. La città laica, la città religiosa (1870–1915)* (Rome: Viella, 2021).

Fosi, Irene, 'Between Conversion and Reconquest. The Venerable English College between the Late 16th and 17th Centuries' in Matthew Coneys-Wainwright & Emily Michelson, *A Companion to Religious Minorities in Early Modern Rome* (Leiden: Brill, 2021), 115–141.

Fosi, Irene, 'Conversion and Autobiography: Telling Tales before the Roman Inquisition', *Journal of Early Modern History*, vol. 17 (2013), 437–456.

Fosi, Irene, *Convertire lo straniero. Forestieri e Inquisizione a Roma in età moderna* (Rome: Viella, 2011).

Fosi, Irene, 'Court and city in the ceremony of the *possesso* in the sixteenth century' in Gianvittorio Signorotto & Maria Antonietta Visceglia (eds), *Court and Politics in Papal Rome, 1492–1700* (Cambridge:

Cambridge University Press, 2002), 31–52.

Fosi, Irene, Thomas V. Cohen (trans.), *Papal Justice. Subjects and Courts in the Papal State, 1500–1700* (Washington D.C.: The Catholic University of America Press, 2011).

Fosi, Irene, 'The Plural City: Urban Spaces and Foreign Communities' in Jones, Wisch & Ditchfield (eds), *A Companion to Early Modern Rome, 1492–1692* (Leiden: Brill, 2019), 169–183.

Fraga, Joana, 'Representing the King: The Images of João IV of Portugal (1640–1652)' in David de Boer, Malte Griesse & Monika Barget (eds), *Revolts and Political Violence in Early Modern Imagery* (Leiden: Brill, 2021), 198–218.

Fragnito, Gigliola, *La Bibbia al Rogo: la censura ecclesiastica e i volgarizzamenti della Scrittura 1471-1605* (Bologna: Il Mulino, 1997).

France, John, *The Crusades and the Expansion of Catholic Christendom 1000–1714* (London: Routledge, 2005).

Frazee, Charles A., *Catholics and Sultans: the church and the Ottoman Empire 1453–1923* (Cambridge: Cambridge University Press, 1983).

Freeman, Charles, *A New History of Early Christianity* (New Haven: Yale University Press, 2009).

Freeman, Charles, *Holy Bones, Holy Dust. How Relics Shaped the History of Medieval Europe* (New Haven: Yale University Press, 2011).

Friedrich, Markus, *The Jesuits. A History* (Princeton: Princeton University Press, 2022).

Frova, Carla, Raimondo Michetti & Domenico Palombi (eds), *La carriera di un uomo di curia nella Roma del Quattrocento. Ambrogio Massari da Cori, agostiniano: cultura umanistica e committenza artistica* (Rome: Viella, 2008).

Fujikawa, Mayu, 'Papal Ceremonies for the Embassies of Non-Catholic Rulers' in Coneys-Wainwright & Michelson, *A Companion to Religious Minorities in Early Modern Rome* (Leiden: Brill, 2021), 13–54.

Furstenburg-Levi, Shulamit, *The Academia Pontaniana. A Model of a Humanist Network* (Leiden: Brill, 2016).

Gallo, Patrick J. (ed.), *Pius XII, the Holocaust and the Revisionists: Essays* (Jefferson: McFarland & Company, 2006).

Gamrath, Helge, *Farnese. Pomp, Power and Politics in Renaissance Italy* (Rome: <<L'Erma>> di Bretschneider, 2007).

Garstein, Oskar, *Rome and the Counter-Reformation in Scandinavia. The Age of Gustavus Adolphus and Queen Christina of Sweden 1622–1656* (Leiden: Brill, 1992).

Gayet, Louis, *Le Grand Schisme d'Occident. D'Après les documents contemporains déposés aux archives secrètes du Vatican* (Florence: Loescher & Seeber, 1889), 2 vols.

Geary, Patrick J., *Living with the Dead in the Middle Ages* (Cornell University Press, 1994).

Gentile, Emilio, 'Paramilitary Violence in Italy: The Rationale of Fascism and the Origins of Totalitarianism' in Robert Gerwarth & John Horne (eds), *War in Peace. Paramilitary Violence in Europe after the Great War* (Oxford: Oxford University Press, 2012), 85–106.

Gentile, Emilio, 'Fascism in Power. The totalitarian experiment' in Matthew Feldman & Roger Griffin (eds), *Fascism. Critical Concepts in Political Science* (London: Routledge, 2004), 17–46.

Giardina, Andrea & André Vauchez, *Il Mito di Roma. Da Carlo Magno a Mussolini* (Bari: Laterza, 2000).

Gilbert, Christopher J., 'If this Statue Could Talk: Statuary Satire in the Pasquinade Tradition', *Rhetoric and Public Affairs*, vol. 18 (2015), 79–112.

Gill, Meredith J., 'The Fourteenth and Fifteenth Centuries' in Marcia B. Hall (ed.), *Artistic Centers of the Italian Renaissance. Rome* (Cambridge: Cambridge University Press, 2005), 27–108.

Gilley, Sheridan, 'The Papacy' in Sheridan Gilley & Brian Stanley (eds), *The Cambridge History of Christianity. World Christianities c. 1815–c. 1914. Volume 8* (Cambridge: Cambridge University Press, 2006), 13–29.

Gilley, Sheridan & Brian Stanley (eds), *The Cambridge History of Christianity. World Christianities c. 1815–c. 1914. Volume 8* (Cambridge: Cambridge University Press, 2006).

Gillgren, Peter & Mårten Snickare (eds), *Performativity and Performance in Baroque Rome* (London: Routledge, 2016).

Giuntella, Vittorio E., *Roma nel settecento* (Bologna: Licinio Capelli, 1971).

Goeschel, Christian, *Mussolini and Hitler. The Forging of a Fascist Alliance* (New Haven: Yale University Press, 2020).

Goffart, Walter, *Barbarian Tides. The Migration Age and the Later Roman Empire* (Philadelphia: University of Pennsylvania Press, 2006).

González Vázquez , Marta, 'Women and Pilgrimage in Medieval Galicia' in Carlos Andrés González-Paz (ed.), *Women and Pilgrimage in Medieval Galicia* (London: Routledge, 2016), 27–50.

Gooch, John, *The Unification of Italy* (London: Routledge, 1986).

Goodden, Angelica, *Madame de Staël. The Dangerous Exile* (Oxford: Oxford University Press, 2008).

Gouwens, Kenneth, 'Institutions and Dynamics of Learned Exchange' in Jones, Wisch & Ditchfield (eds), *A Companion to Early Modern Rome, 1492–1692* (Leiden: Brill, 2019), 500–514.

Graaf, Beatrice de, Ido de Haan & Brian Vick (eds), *Securing Europe after Napoleon. 1815 and the New European Security Culture* (Cambridge: Cambridge University Press, 2019).

Grafton, Anthony, *Leon Battista Alberti: Master Builder of the Italian Renaissance* (Cambridge, Mass.: Harvard University Press, 2000).

Grafton, Anthony, Glenn W. Most & Salvatore Settis (eds), *The Classical Tradition* (Cambridge, Mass.: The Belknap Press of Harvard University Press, 2010).

Grand Alexander de, *The Hunchback's Tailor. Giovanni Giolitti and Liberal Italy from the Challenge of Mass Politics to the Rise of Fascism, 1882–1922* (Westport: Praeger, 2001).

Green, Bernard, *Christianity in Ancient Rome: The First Three Centuries* (London: Bloomsbury, 2010).

Gregor, A. James, *Italian Fascism and Developmental Dictatorship* (Princeton: Princeton University Press, 2014).

Gregor, A. James, *Young Mussolini and the Intellectual Origins of Fascism* (Berkeley: University of California Press, 1979).

Gregorovius, Ferdinand, Annie Hamilton (trans.), *History of the City of Rome in the Middle Ages* (Cambridge University Press, 2010), 8 vols.

Gregory, Timothy E., *History of Byzantium* (Oxford: Wiley-Blackwell, 2010).

Grell, Ole Peter, Andrew Cunningham & Bernd Roeck (eds), *Health Care and Poor Relief in 18th and 19th Century Southern Europe* (London: Routledge, 2017).

Grendler, Paul F., *Jesuit Schools and Universities in Europe, 1548–1773* (Leiden: Brill, 2019).

Grendler, Paul F., *The Jesuits & Italian Universities 1548–1773* (Washington,

D.C.: The Catholic University Press, 2017).

Grendler, Paul F., *Universities of the Italian Renaissance* (Baltimore: The Johns Hopkins University Press, 2002).

Grig, Lucy, 'Throwing parties for the poor: poverty and splendour in the late antique church' in Robin Osbourne and Margaret Atkins (eds), *Poverty in the Roman World* (Cambridge: Cambridge University Press, 2006), 145–161.

Gross, Hans, *Rome in the Age of Enlightenment* (Cambridge: Cambridge University Press, 1990).

Gruber, Samuel D., 'Mapping Jews: Cartography and Topography in Rome's Ghetto' in Ian Verstegen & Allan Ceen (eds), *Giambattista Nolli and Rome. Mapping the City before and after the Pianta Grande* (Rome: Studium Urbis, 2013), 121–132.

Gruen, Erich, 'Jews of Rome Under Nero' in Armand Puig I Tàrrech, John M. G. Barclay & Jörg Frey (eds), *The Last Years of Paul. Essays rom the Tarragona Conference, June 2013* (Tübingen: Mohr Siebeck, 2015), 91–109.

Guazzelli, Giuseppe Antonio, 'Roman Antiquities and Christian Archaeology' in Jones, Wisch & Ditchfield (eds), *A Companion to Early Modern Rome, 1492–1692* (Leiden: Brill, 2019), 530–545.

Gutierrez-Folch, Ana, 'The Neo-Classical *Klismos* Chair: Early Sources and Avenues of Diffusion' in Elizabeth Simpson (ed.), *The Adventure of the Illustrious Scholar. Papers Presented to Oscar White Muscarella* (Leiden: Brill, 2018), 564–598.

Gwynne, Paul, *Francesco Benci's Quinque martyres. Introduction, Translation, and Commentary* (Leiden: Brill, 2018).

Hadfield, Andrew, 'The English and Other Peoples' in Thomas N. Corns (ed.), *A Companion to Milton* (Oxford: Blackwell, 2003), 174–190.

Hammond, Frederick, 'The Artistic Patronage of the Barberini and the Galileo Affair' in Victor Coelho (ed.), *Music and Science in the Age of Galileo* (Dordrecht: Kluwer Academic Publishers, 1992), 67–89.

Hanson, Eric O., *The Catholic Church in World Politics* (Princeton: Princeton University Press, 1987).

Harries, Jill, *Imperial Rome AD 284 to 363. The New Empire* (Edinburgh: Edinburgh University Press, 2012).

Hartswick, Kim J., *The Gardens of Sallust. A Changing Landscape* (Austin: University of Texas Press, 2004).

Hearder, Harry, *Italy in the Age of the Risorgimento* (London: Routledge, 2013).

Heather, Peter J., *Rome Resurgent. War and Empire in the Age of Justinian* (Oxford: Oxford University Press, 2018).

Hell, Julia, *The Conquest of Ruins. The Third Reich and the Fall of Rome* (Chicago: University of Chicago Press, 2019).

Herrin, Judith, *Ravenna. Capital of Empire, Crucible of Europe* (Princeton: Princeton University Press, 2020).

Herrin, Judith, *Unrivalled Influence. Women and Empire in Byzantium* (Princeton: Princeton University Press, 2013).

Hittinger, Russell, 'Pope Leo XIII (1810–1903)' in Joseph Witte & Frank S. Alexander (eds), *The Teachings of Modern Roman Catholicism* (New York: Columbia University Press, 2007), 39–105.

Hollingsworth, Mary, 'Cardinals in Conclave' in Hollingsworth, Pattenden & Witte (eds), *A Companion to the Early Modern Cardinal* (Leiden: Brill, 2020), 58–70.

Hollingsworth, Mary, Miles Pattenden & Arnold Witte (eds), *A Companion to the Early Modern Cardinal* (Leiden: Brill, 2020).

Hook, Judith, *The Sack of Rome 1527* (London: Palgrave Macmillan, 2004).

Höpfl, Harro, *Jesuit Political Thought: The Society of Jesus and the State, c. 1540–1630* (Cambridge: Cambridge University Press, 2008).

Hopkins, Keith & Christopher Kelly (eds), *Sociological Studies in Roman History* (Cambridge: Cambridge University Press, 2017).

Horrox, Rosemary (trans.) & (ed.), *The Black Death* (Manchester: Manchester University Press, 1994).

Horsch, Nadja, 'The New Passion Relics at the Lateran, Fifteenth to Sixteenth Centuries: A Translocated Sacred Topography'

in Bosman, Haynes & Liverani, *The Basilica of Saint John Lateran to 1600* (Cambridge: Cambridge University Press, 2020), 428–465.

Horster, Marietta, 'Living on Religion: Professionals and Personnel' in Jörg Rüpke (ed.), *A Companion to Roman Religion* (Oxford: Wiley-Blackwell, 2011).

Hülsen, Christian, *S. Agata dei Goti* (Rome: Sansaini, 1924).

Humphreys, Mike (ed.), *A Companion to Byzantine Iconoclasm* (Leiden: Brill, 2021).

Humphries, Mark, *Early Christianity* (London: Routledge, 2006).

Humphries, Mark, *Cities and the Meanings of Late Antiquity* (Leiden: Brill, 2019).

Hunt, John M., 'Carriages, Violence, and Masculinity in Early Modern Rome', *I Tatti Studies in the Italian Renaissance*, vol. 17 (2014), 175–196.

Hunt, John M., 'The Ceremonial Possession of a City: Ambassadors and their Carriages in Early Modern Rome', *Royal Studies Journal*, vol. 3 (2016), 69–89.

Hunt, John, 'The Pope's Two Souls and the Space of Ritual Protest during Rome's Sede Vacanta, 1559–1644' in DeSilva (ed.), *The Sacralization of Space and Behavior in the Early Modern World*, 177–196.

Hunt, John M., 'Rome and the Vacant See' in Jones, Wisch & Ditchfield (eds), *A Companion to Early Modern Rome, 1492–1692* (Leiden: Brill, 2019), 99–114.

Hunt, John M., *The Vacant See in Early Modern Rome. A Social History of the Papal Interregnum* (Leiden: Brill, 2016).

Icks, Martijn, *The Crimes of Elagabalus. The Life and Legacy of Rome's Decadent Boy Emperor* (London: I.B. Tauris, 2013).

Insolera, Italo, Lucia Bozzola, Roberto Einaudi, & Marco Zumaglini (eds), *Modern Rome. From Napoleon to the Twenty-First Century* (Newcastle: Cambridge Scholars Publishing, 2018).

Internullo, Dario, *Ai margini dei giganti. La vita intellettuale dei romani nel Trecento (1305–1367 ca.)* (Rome: Viella, 2016).

Iordanou, Ioanna, *Venice's Secret Service. Organizing Intelligence in the Renaissance* (Oxford: Oxford University Press, 2019).

Ison-Verhaaren, Christine & Kent F. Schull, *Living in the Ottoman Realm. Empire and Identity, 13th to 20th Centuries* (Bloomington: Indiana University Press, 2016).

Israel, Jonathan I., *Radical Enlightenment. Philosophy and the Making of Modernity 1650–1750* (Oxford: Oxford University Press, 2001).

Izbicki, Thomas M. & Rollo-Koster &, *A Companion to the Great Western Schism* (Leiden: Brill, 2009).

Izbicki, Thomas M., 'The Revival of Papalism at the Council of Basel' in Michiel Decaluwe, Thomas M. Izbicki & Gerald Christianson (eds), *A Companion to the Council of Basel* (Leiden: Brill, 2017), 137-163.

Jeffrey, Elizabeth & Cyril Mango, 'Towards a Franco-Greek Culture' in Cyril Mango (ed.), *The Oxford History of Byzantium* (Oxford: Oxford University Press, 2002), 294–307.

Jenks, Stuart (ed.), *Documents on the Papal Plenary Indulgences 1300–1517 Preached in the Regnum Teutonicum* (Leiden: Brill, 2018).

Johns, Christopher M. S., *Antonio Canova and the Politics of Patronage in Revolutionary and Napoleonic Europe* (Berkeley: University of California Press, 1998).

Johnson, William Bruce, *Miracles and Sacrilege. Roberto Rossellini, the Church and Film Censorship* (Toronto: University of Toronto Press, 2008).

Johnston, Sarah Iles (ed.), *Religions of the Ancient World* (London: Belknap Press, 2004).

Jones, Arnold, *Constantine and the Conversion of Europe* (Toronto: University of Toronto Press, 1978).

Jones, Pamela M., 'Celebrating New Saints in Rome and across the Globe' in Jones, Wisch & Ditchfield (eds), *A Companion to Early Modern Rome, 1492–1692* (Leiden: Brill, 2019), 148–168.

Jones, Pamela M., Barbara Wisch & Simon Ditchfield (eds), *A Companion to Early Modern Rome, 1492–1692* (Leiden: Brill, 2019).

Jong, Mayke de, 'Charlemagne's Church' in Joanna Story (ed.), *Charlemagne. Empire and Society*

(Manchester: Manchester University Press, 2005), 103–135.

Jordan, William Chester, 'The Capetains from the death of Philip II to Philip IV' in David Abulafia (ed.), *The Cambridge Medieval History. Volume V c.1198–c.1300* (Cambridge: Cambridge University, 1999), 279–313.

Kaberidze, Alexander, *The Napoleonic Wars. A Global History* (Oxford: Oxford University Press, 2020).

Kaçar, Turhan, 'Constantinople and Asia Minor: Ecclesiastical Jurisdiction in the Fourth Century' in Stephen Mitchel & Philipp Pilhofer (eds), *Early Christianity in Asia Minor and Cyprus. From Margins to the Mainstream* (Leiden: Brill, 2019), 148–164.

Kahlos, Maijastina, *Religious Dissent in Late Antiquity, 350–450* (Oxford: Oxford University Press, 2020).

Kalas, Gregor, *The Restoration of the Roman Forum in Late Antiquity. Transforming Public Space* (Austin: Texas University Press, 2015).

Kallis, Aristotle, *The Third Rome, 1922–1943. The Making of the Fascist Capital* (London: Palgrave Macmillan, 2014).

Kamen, Henry, *The Spanish Inquisition a Historical Revision* (London: Yale University Press, 2014).

Kaplan, Paul H.D., 'Italy, 1490–1700' in Daniel Bindman & Henry Louis Gates, Jr. (eds), *The Image of the Black in Western Art. vol. III: From the "Age of Discovery" to the Age of Abolition: Artists of the Renaissance and Baroque*

(Cambridge, Mass.: Belknap Press of the Harvard University Press, 2010), 93–101.

Katz, Dana E, *The Jewish Ghetto and the Visual Imagination of Early Modern Venice* (Cambridge: Cambridge University Press, 2017).

Katz, Robert, *The Battle for Rome. The Germans, the Allies, the Partisans, and the Pope, September 1943–June 1944* (London: Simon & Schuster, 2003).

Kennerley, Sam, 'Ethiopian Christians in Rome, c.1400–c.1700' in Coneys-Wainwright & Michelson (eds), *A Companion to Religious Minorities in Early Modern Rome* (Leiden: Brill, 2021), 142–168.

Kertzer, David, *The Kidnapping of Edgardo Mortara* (New York: Picador, 1997).

Kertzer, David, 'Pietro Tacchi Venturi, Mussolini, Pius XI, and the Jews' in Bernauer & Maryks (eds), *"The Tragic Couple". Encounters Between Jews and Jesuits* (Leiden: Brill, 2013), 265–274.

Kertzer, David, *The Pope and Mussolini. The Secret History of Pius XI and the Rise of Fascism in Europe* (Oxford: Oxford University Press, 2014).

Kertzer, David, *The Pope at War. The Secret History of Pius XII, Mussolini, and Hitler* (New York: Random House, 2022).

Kertzer, David, *Prisoner of the Vatican* (Boston: Houghton Mifflin Company, 2004).

Keyvanian, Carla, 'Papal Urban Planning and Renewal: Real and Ideal', c.1471–1667 in Jones, Wisch

& Ditchfield (eds), *A Companion to Early Modern Rome, 1492–1692* (Leiden: Brill, 2019), 305–323.

Kirby, Torrance & Matthew Milner (eds), *Mediating Religious Cultures in Early Modern Europe* (Newcastle: Cambridge Scholars Publishing, 2013).

Kirk, Terry, 'The Political Topography of Modern Rome, 1870–1936: Via XX Settembre to Via dell'Impero' in Caldwell & Caldwell (eds), *Rome Continuing Encounters*, 101–128.

Kirk, Terry, *The Architecture of Modern Italy. Volume 1: The Challenge of Tradition, 1750–1900* (New York: Princeton Architectural Press, 2005).

Knowles Middleton, W.E., 'Science in Rome, 1675–1700, and the Accademia Fisciomatematica of Giovanni Giustino Ciampini', *The British Journal for the History of Science*, vol. 8, no. 2 (July, 1975), 138–154.

Kolla, James, *Sovereignty, International Law, and the French Revolution* (Cambridge: Cambridge University Press, 2017).

Krautheimer, Richard, *Rome. Profile of a City, 312–1308* (Princeton: Princeton University Press, 2000).

Krautheimer, Richard, *The Rome of Alexander VII, 1655–1667* (Princeton: Princeton University Press, 1985).

Krebs, Verena, *Medieval Ethiopian Kingship, Craft, and Diplomacy with Latin Europe* (London: Palgrave Macmillan, 2021).

Ladurie, Emmanuel, *Montaillou. Cathars and Catholics in a French Village 1294–1324* (London: Penguin, 2013).

Laes, Christian, *Disabilities and the Disabled in the Roman World* (Cambridge: Cambridge University Press, 2018).

Lamers, Han, *Greece Reinvented. Transformations of Byzantine Hellenism in Renaissance Italy* (Leiden: Brill, 2015).

Lampe, Peter, Michael Steinhauser (trans.), *From Paul to Valentinus. Christians at Rome in the First Two Centuries* (London: Continuum, 2003).

Lampe, Peter, 'Roman Christians Under Nero (54–68 CE)' in Armand Puig I Tàrrech, John M. G. Barclay & Jörg Frey (eds), *The Last Years of Paul. Essays rom the Tarragona Conference, June 2013* (Tübingen: Mohr Siebeck, 2015), 111–129.

Lanciani, Rodolfo, *Pagan and Christian Rome* (Boston & New York: Houghton Mifflin, 1892).

Lançon, Bertrand, Antonia Nevill (trans.), *Rome in Late Antiquity. Everyday Life and Urban Change, AD 312–609* (Edinburgh: Edinburgh University Press).

Lassels, Richard, *The voyage of Italy, or, A compleat journey through Italy in two parts* (Paris: 1670).

Laven, Mary, *Mission to China: Matteo Ricci and the Jesuit Encounter with the East* (London: Faber and Faber, 2011).

Leadbetter, Bill, 'From Constantine to Theodosius (and beyond)' in Philip F. Esler (ed.), *The Early Christian World. Volume I–II* (London: Routledge, 2000), 258–294.

Leithart, Peter J., *Defending Constantine. Twilight of an Empire and the Dawn of Christendom* (Downers Grove: Intervarsity Press, 2010).

Lepage, Andrea, 'Art and the Counter-Reformation' in Alexandra Bamji, Geert H. Janssen & Mary Laven (eds), *The Ashgate Research Companion to the Counter-Reformation* (London: Routledge, 2013), 373–394.

Lessay, Franck, 'Hobbes, Rome's Enemy' in Marcus P. Adams (ed.), *A Companion to Hobbes* (Oxford: Wiley Blackwell, 2021), 332–347.

Levai, Jenő, 'Interventions by the Pope and the Nuncio' in Patrick J. Gallo (ed.), *Pius XII, the Holocaust and the Revisionists: Essays* (Jefferson: McFarland & Company, 2006), 104–109.

Leverne, Nancy K., *Spinoza's Revelation. Religion, Democracy, and Reason* (Cambridge: Cambridge University Press, 2004).

Levin, Michael J., *Agents of Empire. Spanish Ambassadors in Sixteenth-Century Italy* (Ithaca: Cornell University Press, 2005).

Liverani, Paolo, 'Saint Peter's and the city of Rome between Late Antiquity and the early Middle Ages' in Rosamond McKitterick, John Osborne, Carol M. Richardson & Joanna Story (eds), *Old Saint Peter's Rome* (Cambridge: Cambridge University Press, 2013), 21–34.

Livingstone, Michael A., *The Fascists and the Jews of Italy. Mussolini's Race Laws, 1938–1943* (Cambridge: Cambridge University Press, 2014).

Logan, F. Donald, *A History of the Church in the Middle Ages* (London: Taylor and Francis, 2012).

Lok, Matthijs, 'The Congress of Vienna as a Missed Opportunity: Conservative Visions of a New European Order after Napoleon' in Beatrice de Graaf, Ido de Haan & Brian Vick (eds), *Securing Europe after Napoleon. 1815 and the New European Security Culture* (Cambridge: Cambridge University Press, 2019), 56–72.

Lot, Ferdinand, Philip Leon & Mariette Leon (trans.), *The End of the Ancient World* (Abingdon: Routledge, 2000).

Louth, Andrew, *Greek East and Latin West. The Church, AD 681–1071* (Crestwood: St Vladimir's Seminary Press, 2007).

Lowe, Kate, '"Representing" Africa: Ambassadors and Princes from Christian Africa to Renaissance Italy and Portugal, 1402–1608', *Transactions of the Royal Historical Society*, vol. 17 (2007), 101–128.

Lynch, John, *New Worlds. A Religious History of Latin America* (New Haven: Yale University Press, 2012).

Lynch, J., 'Philip II and the Papacy', *Transactions of the Royal Historical Society*, vol. 11 (1961), 23–42.

Maas, Clifford William, *The German Community in Renaissance Rome, 1378–1523* (Rome: Herder, 1981).

MacGeorge, Penny, *Late Roman Warlords* (Oxford: Oxford University Press, 2002).

Magistris, R. Ambrosi de, *Storia di Anagni* (Anagni: Vicenzo Apolloni, 1889).

Malaise, Michel, *Inventaire préliminaire des documents égyptiens découverts en Italie* (Leiden: Brill, 1972).

Mallett, Michael & Christine Shaw, *The Italian Wars, 1494–1559. War, State and Society in Early Modern Europe* (London: Routledge, 2014).

Mango, Cyril (ed.), *The Oxford History of Byzantium* (Oxford: Oxford University Press, 2002).

Mansch, Larry D. & Curtis H. Peters, *Martin Luther. The Life and Lessons* (Jefferson: McFarland & Company, 2016).

Marazzi, Federico, 'Byzantines and Lombards' in Salvatore Cosentino (ed.), *A Companion to Byzantine Italy* (Leiden: Brill, 2021), 169–199.

Marco, Angelus A. de, *The Tomb of Saint Peter. A Representative and Annotated Bibliography of the Excavations* (Leiden: Brill, 1964).

Marius, Richard, *Martin Luther. The Christian Between God and Death* (Cambridge, Mass.: The Belknap Press, 1999).

Marrus, Michael R. (ed.), *The Nazi Holocaust. Historical Articles on the Destruction of European Jews* (London: Meckler, 1989).

Martina, Giacomo Martina, *Pio IX (1846–1850)* (Rome: Università Gregoriana, 1974).

Martindale, C.C., *The Meaning of Fatima* (New York: P.J. Kennedy and Sons, 1950).

Marucchi, Orazio & J. Armine Willis (trans.), *Christian Epigraphy. An Elementary Treatise with a collection of ancient Christian inscriptions mainly of Roman origin* (Cambridge: Cambridge University Press: 1912).

Maryks, Robert, *Pouring Jewish Water into Fascist Wine. Untold Stories of (Catholic) Jews from the Archive of Mussolini's Jesuit Pietro Tacchi Venturi.* (Leiden: Brill, 2017).

Maryks, Robert, *Saint Cicero and the Jesuits. The Influence of the Liberal Arts on the Adoption of Moral Probabilism* (Aldershot: Ashgate, 2008).

Maskarinec, Maya, *City of Saints. Rebuilding Rome in the Early Middle Ages* (Philadelphia: University of Pennsylvania Press, 2018).

Maskarinec, Maya, 'Mobilizing sanctity: Pius II and the head of Andrew in Rome' in Yuen-Gen Liang & Jarbel Rodriguez, *Authority and Spectacle in Medieval and Early Modern Europe. Essays in Honor of Teofilo F. Ruiz* (London: Routledge, 2017), 186–202.

Mattei, Roberto de, John Laughland (ed.), *Pius IX* (Leominster: Gracewing, 2004).

Maunder, Chris, *Our Lady of the Nations. Apparitions of Mary in Twentieth-Century Catholic Europe*

(Oxford: Oxford University Press, 2016).

McCahill, Elizabeth, *Reviving the Eternal City. Rome and the Papal Court 1420–1447* (Cambridge Mass.: Harvard University Press, 2013).

McClung Hallman, Barbara McClung, 'The "Disastrous" Pontificate of Clement VII: Disastrous for Giulio de' Medici?' in Kenneth Gouwens & Sheryl E. Reiss (eds), *The Pontificate of Clement VII. History, Politics, Culture* (Abingdon: Routledge, 2005), 29–40.

McGreevy, John T., *Catholicism. A Global History from the French Revolution to Pope Francis* (W. W. Norton & Company, 2022).

McKitterick, Rosamond, John Osborne, Carol M. Richardson & Joanna Story (eds), *Old Saint Peter's Rome* (Cambridge: Cambridge University Press, 2013).

McKitterick, Rosamond, 'The papacy and Byzantium in the seventh- and early eighth-century sections of the Liber Pontificalis', *Papers of the British School at Rome*, vol. 84 (2016), 241–273.

McPhee, Peter & Philip Dwyer (eds), *The French Revolution and Napoleon: A Sourcebook* (London: Routledge, 2002).

Menache, Sophia, *Clement V* (Cambridge: Cambridge University Press, 1998).

Menozzi, Daniele, 'Un nuovo rapporto tra Chiesa e società' in Formica (ed.), *Roma capitale. La*

città laica, la città religiosa (1870–1915) (Rome: Viella, 2021), 89–100.

Merrills, Andrew & Richard Miles, *The Vandals* (Oxford: Wiley, 2010).

Meserve, Margaret, *Papal Bull. Print, politics and propaganda in Renaissance Rome* (Baltimore: Johns Hopkins University Press, 2021).

Messbarger, Rebecca, Christopher M.S. Johns, & Philip Gavitt (eds), *Benedict XIV and the Enlightenment. Art, Science, and Spirituality* (Toronto: University of Toronto Press, 2016).

Messori, Vittorio, *Kidnapped by the Vatican? The Unpublished Memoirs of Edgardo Mortara* (San Francisco: Ignatius Press, 2017).

Michelson, Emily, *Catholic Spectacle and Rome's Jews. Early Modern Conversion and Resistance* (Princeton: Princeton University Press, 2022).

Michelson, Emily, 'Resist, Refute, Redirect. Roman Jews Attend Conversionary Sermons' in Coneys-Wainwright & Michelson, *A Companion to Religious Minorities in Early Modern Rome* (Leiden: Brill, 2021), 349–374.

Miller, Patricia Cox, *Women in Early Christianity. Translations from Greek Texts* (Washington D.C.: The Catholic University of America Press, 2005).

Monaco, C.S., *The Rise of Modern Jewish Politics. Extraordinary Movement* (London: Routledge, 2013).

Montègre, Gilles, *La Rome des Français au temps des lumières, 1769–1791* (Rome: École Francaise de Rome, 2011).

Moor, Kathryn Blair, *The Architecture of the Christian Holy Land. Reception from Late Antiquity through the Renaissance* (Cambridge: Cambridge University Press, 2017).

Moore, Evelyn K. & Patricia Anne Simpson (eds), *The Enlightened Eye. Goethe and Visual Culture* (Amsterdam: Rodopi, 2007).

Morgan, Philip, *The Fall of Mussolini. Italy, the Italians, and the Second World War* (Oxford: Oxford University Press, 2008).

Moorhead, John, *The Popes and the Church of Rome in Late Antiquity* (London: Routledge, 2015).

Mormando, Franco, *Bernardino of Siena and the Social Underworld of Early Renaissance Italy* (Chicago: University of Chicago, 1999).

Mormando, Franco, *Bernini. His Life and his Rome* (Chicago: University of Chicago Press, 2011).

Moroni, Gaetano, *Dizionario di Erudizione Storico-Ecclesiastica da S. Pietro sino ai nostri giorni. Vol. LXXIII* (Venice: Tipografia Emiliana, 1855).

Morris, Bridget, *Birgitta of Sweden* (Woodbridge: Boydell Press, 1999).

Mostaccio, Silvia, 'A Conscious Ambiguity: The Jesuits Viewed in Comparative Perspective in Light of Some Recent Italian Literature', *Journal of Early Modern History*, 12 (2008), 410–41.

Moudarres, Andrea, 'The Geography of the Enemy: Old and New Empires between Humanist Debates and Tasso's Gerusalemme liberata' in Andrea Moudarres &

Christiana Purdy Moudarres (eds), *New Worlds and the Renaissance. Contributions to the History of European Intellectual Culture* (Leiden: Brill, 2012), 291–332.

Mullooly, Joseph, *Saint Clement, Pope and Martyr, and His Basilica in Rome* (Rome: G. Barbera, 1873).

Murphey, Rhoads, *Exploring Ottoman Sovereignty. Tradition, Image and Practice in the Ottoman Imperial Household, 1400–1800* (London: Continuum, 2008).

Musto, Ronald G., *Apocalypse in Rome. Cola di Rienzo and the Politics of the New Age* (Berkeley: University of California, 2003).

Nadler, Steven, *A Book Forged in Hell: Spinoza's Scandalous Treatise and the Birth of the Secular Age* (Princeton: Princeton University Press, 2011).

Nash, Michael L., *The History and Politics of Exhumation. Royal Bodies and Lesser Mortals* (Cham: Springer International Publishing, 2019).

Negro, Silvio, *Seconda Roma. 1850–1870* (Vicenza: Neri Pozzi, 2015).

Neiberg, Michael S., *The Treaty of Versailles. A Concise History* (Oxford: Oxford University Press: 2017).

Neil, Bronwen, *Leo the Great* (Abingdon: Routledge, 2009).

Nepi, Serena di, *Surviving the Ghetto. Toward a Social History of the Jewish Community in 16th-Century Rome* (Leiden: Brill, 2020).

Noble, Thomas F. X., *The Republic of St. Peter: The Birth of the Papal State, 680–825* (Philadelphia: University of Pennsylvania Press, 1984).

Norton, Peter, *Episcopal Elections 250–600. Hierarchy and Popular Will in Late Antiquity* (Oxford: Oxford University Press, 2007).

Nunn, H.P.V., 'St. Peter's Presence in Rome: The Monumental Evidence', *Evangelical Quarterly*, vol. 22 (1950), 126–144.

Nuova, James Nelson, 'Being a New Christian in Early Modern Rome' in Coneys-Wainwright & Michelson, *A Companion to Religious Minorities in Early Modern Rome*, (Leiden: Brill, 2021), 192–236.

Nussdorfer, Laurie, 'Men at Home in Baroque Rome', *I Tatti Studies in the Italian Renaissance*, vol. 17, number 1 (2014), 103–129.

Nussdorfer, Laurie, 'The Politics of Space in Early Modern Rome', *Memoirs of the American Academy in Rome*, vol. 42 (1997), 161–186.

O'Brien, Albert C., 'Benito Mussolini, Catholic Youth, and the Origins of the Lateran Treaties', *Journal of Church and State*, vol. 23, no. 1 (1981), 117–129.

Ó Carragáin, Éamonn & Carol Neuman de Vegvar (eds), *Roma Felix – Formations and Reflections of Medieval Rome* (Aldershot: Ashgate, 2007).

O'Carroll, Ciarán, 'Pius IX: pastor and prince' in James Corkery & Thomas Worcester, *The Papacy Since 1500. From Italian Prince to Universal Pastor* (Cambridge: Cambridge University Press, 2010), 125–142.

O'Malley, John, *A History of the Popes: From Peter to the Present* (Lanham: Rowman & Littlefield, 2009).

O'Malley, John, *The Jesuits and the Popes. A Historical Sketch of Their Relationship* (Philadelphia: Saint Joseph's University Press, 2016).

O'Malley, John, *Trent: What Happened at the Council* (Cambridge, Mass.: The Belknap Press of the Harvard University Press, 2013).

Odahl, Charles Matson, *Constantine and the Christian Empire* (London: Routledge, 2004).

Omissi, Adrastos, *Emperors and Usurpers in the Later Roman Empire. Civil War, Panegyric and the Construction of Legitimacy* (Oxford: Oxford University Press, 2018).

Osborne, Toby, 'Diplomatic Culture in Early Modern Rome' in Jones, Wisch & Ditchfield (eds), *A Companion to Early Modern Rome, 1492–1692* (Leiden: Brill, 2019), 60–74.

Painter, Borden W., *Mussolini's Rome. Rebuilding the Eternal City* (Basingstoke: Palgrave Macmillan, 2005).

Palazzini, Pietro, 'Le Congregazioni Romane da Sisto V a Giovani Paolo ii' in Fagiolo & Madonna (eds), *Sisto V. I. Roma e il Lazio* (Rome: Libreria dello Stato, 1992), 19–38.

Palma, W. di, T. Bovi, B. Lindberg, F. Abbri, M.L. Rodén, S. Rotta, G., Iacovelli, S. Åkermann & F. Craaford (eds), *Cristina di Svezia. Scienza ed Alchimia nella Roma Barocca* (Bari: Edizioni Dedalo, 1990).

Palmer, James A. (ed.) & (trans.), *The Chronicle of an Anonymous Roman. Rome, Italy, and Latin Christendom, c.1325–1360* (New York: Italica Press, 2021).

Palmer, James A., 'Medieval and Renaissance Rome: Mending the Divide', *History Compass*, (2017), 1–10.

Palmer, James A., *The Virtues of Economy. Governance, power, and piety in late medieval Rome* (Ithaca: Cornell University Press, 2019).

Papenheim, Martin, 'The Pope, the Beggar, the Sick, and the Brotherhoods: Health Care and Poor Relief in 18th and 19th Century Rome' in Cunningham, Grell & Roeck (eds), *Health Care and Poor Relief in 18th and 19th Century Southern Europe* (London: Routledge, 2017), 164–186.

Parker, Geoffrey, *Emperor. A New Life of Charles V* (New Haven: Yale University Press, 2019).

Parker, Harold T., *The Cult of Antiquity and the French Revolutionaries: A Study in the Development of the Revolutionary Spirit* (New York: Octagon, 1965).

Parkin, Anneliese, '"You do him no service": an exploration of pagan almsgiving' in Margaret Atkins & Robin Osborne (eds), *Poverty in the Roman World* (Cambridge: Cambridge University Press, 2009), 60–82.

Partner, Peter, *The Lands of St Peter. The Papal State in the Middle Ages and the Early Renaissance* (London: Eyre Methuen, 1972).

Partner, Peter, *Renaissance Rome, 1500–1559. A Portrait of a Society* (Berkeley: University of California Press, 1979).

Pastor, Ludwig von, *History of the Popes: From the Close of the Middle Ages, Drawn from the Secret Archives of the Vatican and Other Original Sources* (London: 1891–1953), 40 vols.

Patriarca, Silvana & Lucy Riall (eds), *The Risorgimento Revisited: Nationalism and Culture in Nineteenth-Century Italy* (Basingstoke: Palgrave Macmillan, 2011).

Pattenden, Miles, *Electing the Pope in Early Modern Italy, 1450–1700* (Oxford: Oxford University Press, 2017).

Pattenden, Miles, *Pius IV and the Fall of the Carafa: Nepotism and Papal Authority in Counter-Reformation Rome* (Oxford: Oxford University Press, 2013).

Pattenden, Miles, 'The Roman Curia' in Jones, Wisch & Ditchfield (eds), *A Companion to Early Modern Rome, 1492–1692* (Leiden: Brill, 2019), 44–59.

Peters, Edward (ed.), Paul the Deacon and William Dudley Foulke (trans.), *History of the Lombards* (Philadelphia: University of Pennsylvania Press).

Petreman, Cheryl, 'Host Desecration Narratives: Confirming Christ's Physical Presence' in Torrance Kirby & Matthew Milner (eds), *Mediating Religious Cultures in Early Modern Europe* (Newcastle: Cambridge Scholars Publishing, 2013), 65–84.

Pettegree, Andrew, *Brand Luther. 1517, Printing, and the Making of the Reformation* (London: Penguin, 2015).

Puig I Tàrrech, Armand, John M. G. Barclay & Jörg Frey (eds), *The Last Years of Paul. Essays from the Tarragona Conference, June 2013* (Tübingen: Mohr Siebeck, 2015).

Plant, I. M. (ed.), *Women Writers of Ancient Greece and Rome. An Anthology* (Norman: University of Oklahoma Press, 2004).

Po-Chia Hsia, Ronnie, *The World of Catholic Renewal, 1540–1770.* 2nd edition (Cambridge: Cambridge University Press, 2005).

Pohlsander, Hans A., *The Emperor Constantine* (London: Routledge, 1996).

Pollard, John F., *Benedict XV. The Unknown Pope and the Pursuit of Peace* (London: Bloomsbury Academic, 2005).

Pollard, John F., *Money and the Rise of the Modern Papacy. Financing the Vatican, 1850–1950* (Cambridge: Cambridge University Press, 2005).

Pollard, John F., *The Papacy in the Age of Totalitarianism, 1914–1958* (Oxford: Oxford University Press, 2014).

Pollard, John F., *The Vatican and Italian Fascism, 1929–32* (Cambridge: Cambridge University Press, 2005.

Postlewate, Laurie & Wim Hüsken (eds), *Acts and Texts. Performance and Ritual in the Middle Ages and the Renaissance* (Amsterdam: Rodopi, 2007).

Potter, David Stone, *Constantine the Emperor* (Oxford: Oxford University Press, 2015).

Prodi, Paolo, *The Papal Prince. One body and two souls: the papal monarchy in early modern Europe* (Cambridge: Cambridge University Press: 1987).

Prosperi, Adriano, Jeremy Carden (trans.), *Crime and Forgiveness. Christianising Execution in Medieval Europe* (Cambridge, Mass.: Harvard University Press, 2020).

Prosperi, Adriano, *Tribunali della Coscienza : Inquisitori, Confessori, Missionari* (Turin: Einaudi, 1996).

Prosperi, Adriano, *La vocazione. Storie di gesuiti tra Cinquecento e Seicento* (Turin: Einaudi, 2016)

Rashdall, Hastings, *The Universities of Europe in the Middle Ages. Volume 2, Part 1: Italy, Spain, France, Germany, Scotland, etc.* (Cambridge: Cambridge University Press, 2010).

Rasmussen, Susanne William, 'Roman Religion' in Lisbeth Bredholt Christensen, Olav Hammer & David A. Warburton (eds.), *The Handbook of Religions of Ancient Europe* (London: Routledge, 2014), 192–207.

Rath, R. John, 'The Carbonari: Their Origins, Initiation Rites, and Aims, *The American Historical Review,* vol. 69, no. 2 (1964), 353–370.

Re, Emilio, 'The English Colony in Rome during the Fourteenth Century', *Transactions of the Royal Historical* Society, vol. 66, (1923), 73–92.

Recchia, Stefano & Nadia Urbinati (eds), *A Cosmopolitanism of Nations: Giuseppe Mazzini's Writings on Democracy, Nation Building, and International Relations* (Princeton: Princeton University Press, 2009).

Riccardi, Luca, 'An outline of Vatican diplomacy in the early modern age' in Daniela Frigo (ed.), Adrian Belton (trans.), *Politics and Diplomacy in Early Modern Italy. The Structure of Diplomatic Practice, 1450–1800* (Cambridge: Cambridge University Press, 2000), 95–108.

Riall, Lucy, *Garibaldi. Invention of a Hero* (New Haven: Yale University Press, 2008).

Riall, Lucy, *The Italian Risorgimento. State, Society and National Unification* (London: Routledge, 1994).

Richardson, Carol M., *Reclaiming Rome. Cardinals in the Fifteenth Century* (Leiden: Brill, 2009).

Riddle, J.E., *The History of the Papacy, to the period of the Reformation* (London: Richard Bentley, 1856).

Rinne, Katherine, 'Renovatio Aquae: Aqueducts, Fountains, and the Tiber River in Early Modern Rome' in Jones, Wisch & Ditchfield (eds), *A Companion to Early Modern Rome, 1492–1692* (Leiden: Brill, 2019), 324–341.

Rittner, Carol Rittner & John K. Roth, *Pope Pius XII and the Holocaust* (London: Bloomsbury Academic, 2016).

Robinson, James Harvey (ed.), *Petrarch. The First Modern Scholar and Man of Letters* (New York: Haskell House, 1970).

Robinson, James Harvey, *Readings in European History. Volume 1* (Boston: The Athenaeum Press, 1904).

Robinson, I.S., *The Papacy 1073–1198. Continuity and innovation* (Cambridge: Cambridge University Press, 1990).

Robinson, I.S., *The Papal Reform of the Eleventh Century. Lives of Pope Leo IX and Pope Gregory VII* (Manchester: Manchester University Press, 2004).

Rocca, Samuele, *In the Shadow of the Caesars: Jewish Life in Roman Italy* (Leiden: Brill, 2022).

Rollo-Koster, Joëlle, *Avignon and Its Papacy, 1309–1417. Popes, Institutions, and Society* (Lanham: Rowman & Littlefield, 2015).

Rollo-Koster, Joëlle, 'Civil Violence and the Initiation of the Schism' in Rollo-Koster & Thomas M. Izbicki, *A Companion to the Great Western Schism* (Leiden: Brill, 2009), 9–66.

Rollo-Koster, Joëlle & Thomas M. Izbicki, *A Companion to the Great Western Schism* (Leiden: Brill, 2009).

Rollo-Koster, Joëlle, 'Mercator Florentinensis and others: Immigration in Papal Avignon' in J. Drendel & Kathryn Reyerson *Urban and Rural Communities in Medieval France* (Leiden: Brill, 1998), 73–100.

Rollo-Koster, Joëlle, *Raiding Saint Peter. Empty Sees, Violence, and the Initiation of the Great Western Schism* (Leiden: Brill, 2008).

Roper, Lyndal, *Martin Luther. Renegade and Prophet* (London: The Bodley Head, 2016).

Ropes Loomis, Louise (ed. & trans.), *The Book of the Popes (Liber Pontificalis)*, (New York: Nova, 2018).

Rosa, Mario, 'Curia Romana e pensioni ecclesiastiche: fiscalità pontificia nel mezzogiorno (secoli xvi–xviii), *Quaderni storici*, vol. 14, no. 42 (1979), 1015–1055.

Rostirolla, Giancarlo, *La Capella Giulia, 1513–2013. Cinque secoli di musica sacra in San Pietro* (Kassell: Bärenreiter-Verlag, 2018).

Rotta, Salvatore, 'L'accademia fisico-matematica Ciampiniana: un'iniziativa di Cristina?' in W. di Palma, T. Bovi, B. Lindberg, F. Abbri, M.L. Rodén, S. Rotta, G., Iacovelli, S. Åkermann & F. Craaford (eds), *Cristina di Svezia. Scienza ed Alchimia nella Roma Barocca* (Bari: Edizioni Dedalo, 1990), 99–186.

Rowell, Diana, *Paris: The 'New Rome' of Napoleon I* (London: Bloomsbury, 2012).

Rowland, Ingrid D., *Giordano Bruno. Philosopher / Heretic* (New York: Farrar, Straus and Giroux, 2008).

Russell, Jeffrey Burton, *Witchcraft in the Middle Ages* (Ithaca: Cornell University Press, 1972).

Sachet, Paolo, *Publishing for the Popes. The Roman Curia and the Use of Printing (1527–1555)* (Leiden: Brill, 2020).

Sachs, Jonathan, *Romantic Antiquity. Rome in the British Imagination, 1789–1832* (Oxford: Oxford University Press, 2010).

Sahlin, Claire L., *Birgitta of Sweden and the Voice of Prophecy* (Woodbridge: Boydell Press, 2001).

Salomone, A. William & Gaetano Salvemini, *Italy in the Giolittian Era. Italian Democracy in the Making* (Philadelphia: University of Pennsylvania Press, 2016).

Salons, Francisco Javier Ramón, 'A Renewed Global Power: The Restoration of the Holy See and the Triumph of Ultramontanism, 1814–48' in Michael Broers, Ambrogio A. Caiani & Stephen Bann (eds), *A History of the European Restorations. Volume Two. Culture, Society and Religion* (London: Bloomsbury Academic, 2020), 72–84.

Savadore, Matteo, *The African Prester John and the Birth of Ethiopian-European Relations, 1402–1555* (London: Routledge, 2019).

Salzman, Michele Renee, *The Falls of Rome. Crises, Resilience, and Resurgence in Late Antiquity* (Cambridge: Cambridge University Press, 2021).

Santarelli, Daniele (ed.), *La corrispondenza di Bernardo Navagero, ambasciatore veneziano a Roma (1555–1558)* (Rome: Aracne, 2011).

Santarelli, Daniele, 'Morte di un eretico impenitente. Alcune note e documenti su Pomponio Algieri di Nola', *Medioevo Adriatico*, vol. 1 (2007), 117–34.

Sarris, Peter, *Empires of Faith. The Fall of Rome to the Rise of Islam, 500–700* (Oxford: Oxford University Press, 2011).

Sassoon, Donald, *Mussolini and the Rise of Fascism* (London: Harper Press, 2012).

Savage, S.M., 'The Cults of Ancient Trastevere', *Memoirs of the American Academy in Rome*, vol. 17 (1940), 26–56.

Schatz, Klaus, *Papal Primacy. From Its Origins to the Present* (Collegeville: The Liturgical Press, 1996).

Schelkens, Karim, John A. Dick, & Jürgen Mettepenningen, *Aggiornamento? Catholicism from Gregory XVI to Benedict XVI* (Leiden: Brill, 2013).

Schneid, Frederick C., *Napoleon's Italian Campaigns* (Westport: Praeger, 2002).

Schneider, Christian, '"Types" of Peacemakers: Exploring the Authority and Self-Perception of the Early Modern Papacy' in Stephen Cummins & Laura Kounine (eds), *Cultures of Conflict Resolution in Early Modern Europe* (London: Routledge, 2016), 77–104.

Schraven, Minou, '*Roma theatrum mundi*: Festivals and Processions in the Ritual City', in Jones, Wisch & Ditchfield (eds), *A Companion to Early Modern Rome, 1492–1692* (Leiden: Brill, 2019), 247–265.

Schwartz, Amy, 'Eternal Rome and Cola di Rienzo's Show of Power' in Laurie Postlewate & Wim Hüsken (eds), *Acts and Texts. Performance and Ritual in the Middle Ages and the Renaissance* (Amsterdam: Rodopi, 2007), 63–76.

Segre, Claudio G., *Italo Balbo. A Fascist Life* (Berkeley: University of California Press, 1990).

Setton, Kenneth M., *The Papacy and the Levant (1204–1571). Volume II. The Fifteenth Century* (Philadelphia: The American Philosophical Society, 1978).

Shaw, Christine (ed.), *Italy and the European Powers. The Impact of War, 1500–1530* (Leiden: Brill, 2006).

Shaw, Brent D., 'The Myth of the Neronian Persecution', *Journal of Roman Studies*, (2015), 73–100.

Shaw, Christine, 'The Papacy and the European Powers' in Shaw (ed.), *Italy and the European Powers. The Impact of War, 1500–1530* (Leiden: Brill, 2006), 107–128.

Shere, Idan Sherer, *Warriors for a Living. The Experience of the Spanish Infantry During the Italian Wars, 1494–1559* (Leiden: Brill, 2017).

Siecienski, A. Edward, *The Papacy and the Orthodox. Sources and History of a Debate* (Oxford: Oxford University Press, 2017).

Signorotto, Gianvittorio & Maria Antonietta Visceglia (eds), *Court and Politics in Papal Rome, 1492–1700* (Cambridge: Cambridge University Press, 2002).

Simonetti, Manlio, 'Le Origini di Roma Cristiana' in Angela Donati (ed.) *Pietro e Paolo. La Storia, il culto, la memoria nei primi secoli* (Milan: Electa, 2000), 10–26.

Siva, Hagith, *Galla Placidia. The Last Roman Empress* (Oxford: Oxford University Press, 2011).

Smith, Denis Mack, *Italy and its Monarchy* (New Haven: Yale University Press, 1989).

Smith, Denis Mack, 'The Revolutions of 1848–1849 in Italy' in R.J.W. Evans & Hartmut Pogge von Strandmann (eds), *The Revolutions in Europe 1848–1849* (Oxford: Oxford University Press, 2000), 55-82.

Smith Robertson, Priscilla, *Revolutions of 1848. A Social History* (Princeton: Princeton University Press, 2020).

Stadtwald, Kurt, *Roman Popes and German Patriots. Antipapalism in the politics of the German humanist movement from Gregor Heimburg to Martin Luther* (Geneva: Librairie Droz, 1996).

Stevenson, Seth William, C. Roach Smith & Frederic W. Madden, *A Dictionary of Roman Coins, Republican and Imperial* (London: George Bell, 1889).

Storey, Tessa, *Carnal Commerce in Counter-Reformation Rome* (Cambridge: Cambridge University Press, 2008).

Strayer, Joseph R., *The Reign of Philip the Fair* (Princeton: Princeton University Press, 1980).

Stroll, Mary, *Popes and Antipopes. The Politics of Eleventh Century Church Reform* (Leiden: Brill, 2012).

Sumption, Jonathan, *The Age of Pilgrimage. The Medieval Journey to God* (Mahwah: HiddenSpring, 2003).

Sweet, Rosemary, *Cities and the Grand Tour. The British in Italy, c. 1690–1820* (Cambridge: Cambridge University Press, 2012).

Tamilia, Donato, *Il Sacro Monte di Pietà di Roma: ricerche storiche e documenti inediti: contributo alla storia della beneficenza e alla storia economica di Rome* (Rome: Forzani E.C., 1900).

Teitler, H.C., *The Last Pagan Emperor. Julian the Apostate and the War Against Christianity* (Oxford: Oxford University Press, 2017).

Tellenbach, Gerd, Timothy Reuter (trans.), *The Church in Western Europe from the Tenth to the Early Twelfth Century* (Cambridge: Cambridge University Press, 1993).

Temple, Nicholas, *Renovatio Urbis. Architecture, Urbanism and Ceremony in the Rome of Julius II* (London: Taylor and Francis, 2011).

Terry-Fritsch, Allie & Erin Felicia Labbie, *Beholding Violence in Medieval and Early Modern Europe* (London: Routledge, 2016).

Thacker, Alan, 'Popes, emperors and clergy at Old Saint Peter's from the fourth to the eighth century' in Rosamond McKitterick, John Osborne, Carol M. Richardson & Joanna Story (eds), *Old Saint Peter's Rome* (Cambridge: Cambridge University Press, 2013), 137–156.

Thackeray, William Makepeace, Arthur Pendennis (ed.), *The Newcomes. Memoirs of a Most Respectable Family* (New York: Harper & Brothers, 1856), vols.

Thunø, Eric, *Image and Relic. Mediating the Sacred in Early Medieval Rome* (Rome: l'Erma di Bretschneider, 2002).

Tobin, Thomas H., 'Paul's Letter to the Romans' in David E. Aune (ed.), *The Blackwell Companion to the New Testament* (Oxford: Wiley-Blackwell, 2010), 388–412.

Topi, Luca, 'Un elenco di 'giacobini romani' dalle carte del console Pierelli (1798–9)', *Eurostudium*, (October–December 2013), 20–43.

Tranzillo, Jeffrey, *John Paul II on the Vulnerable* (Washington D.C.: The Catholic University of America Press, 2013).

Travaini, Lucia, 'From the treasure chest to the pope's soup. Coins, mints and the Roman Curia (1150–1350)' in Werner Maleczek (ed.) *Die römische Kurie und das Geld. Von der Mitte des 12. Jahrhunderts bis zum frühen 14. Jahrhundert 20* (Ostfildern: Jan Thorbecke Verlag, 2018), 27–64.

Trevelyan, George Macaulay, *Garibaldi's Defence of the Roman Republic* (London: Longmans, Green, & Co, 1912).

Tronzo, William (ed.), *St. Peter's in the Vatican* (Cambridge: Cambridge University Press, 2005).

Trout, Dennis, *Damasus of Rome. The Epigraphic Poetry* (Oxford: Oxford University Press, 2015).

Usherwood, Rebecca, *Political Memory and the Constantinian Dynasty. Fashioning Disgrace* (Cham: Springer, 2022).

Van Boxel, Piet, 'Jews in 16th-century Italy and the Vicissitudes of the Hebrew Book' in Coneys-Wainwright & Michelson (eds), *A Companion to Religious Minorities in Early Modern Rome* (Leiden: Brill, 2022), 324–348.

Van Kley, Dale K., 'Plots and Rumors of Plots. The Role of Conspiracy in the International Campaign against the Society of Jesus, 1758–1768' in Jeffrey D. Burson & Jonathan Wright (eds), *The Jesuit Suppression in Global Context. Causes, events and consequences* (Cambridge: Cambridge University Press, 2015), 13–39.

Van Kley, Dale K., *Reform Catholicism and the International Suppression of the Jesuits in Enlightenment Europe* (New Haven: Yale University Press).

Vandiver Nicassio, Susan, *Imperial City. Rome Under Napoleon* (Chicago: University of Chicago Press, 2009).

Vásquez, Manuel A. & Marie Friedmann Marquardt, *Globalizing the Sacred. Religion across the Americas* (New Brunswick: Rutgers University Press, 2003).

Vázquez, Marta González, 'Women and Pilgrimage in Medieval Galicia' in Carlos Andrés González-Paz (ed.), *Women and Pilgrimage in Medieval Galicia* (London: Routledge, 2016), 27–50.

Veca, Ignazio, 'Oggetti animati. Materialità, circolazione e usi della figura di Pio IX (1846–1849)', *Il Risorgimento*, vol. 64, no. 1 (2017), 63–98.

Verhoeven, Gerrit, 'Calvinist Pilgrimages and Popish Encounters: Religious Identity and Sacred Space on the Dutch Grand Tour (1598–1685)', *Journal of Social History*, (Spring 2010), 615–634.

Vick, Brian E., *The Congress of Vienna. Power and Politics after Napoleon* (Cambridge, Mass.: Harvard University Press, 2014).

Vinzent, Markus, 'Rome' in Margaret M. Mitchell and Frances M. Young (eds), *Cambridge History of Christianity* (Cambridge: Cambridge University Press, 2006).

Visceglia, Maria Antoinetta, *Morte e elezione del papa. Norme, riti e conflitti. L'Età moderna* (Rome: Viella, 2013).

Waite, Gary K., *Heresy, Magic and Witchcraft in Early Modern Europe* (Basingstoke: Palgrave Macmillan, 2003).

Walls, Jerry L., *Purgatory. The Logic of Total Transformation* (Oxford: Oxford University Press, 2012).

Walsh, Michael, *The Conclave. A sometimes secret and occasionally bloody history of papal elections* (Norwich: Canterbury Press, 2003).

Walters, Barbara R., 'The Feast and its Founder' in Walters, Vincent Corrigan & Peter T. Ricketts (eds), *The Feast of Corpus Christi* (Philadelphia: Penn State University Press, 2006), 3–56.

Watson, Alaric, *Aurelian and the Third Century* (London Routledge, 2004).

Webb, Diana, 'Pardons and Pilgrims' in R.N. Swanson, *Promissory Notes on the Treasury of Merits. Indulgences in Late Medieval Europe* (Leiden: Brill, 2006).

Weeks, Daniel J., *Gateways to Empire. Quebec and New Amsterdam to 1664* (Bethlehem: Lehigh University Press, 2019).

Weigel, George, *Witness to Hope. The Biography of Pope John Paul II* (New York: Harper Collins, 2001).

Wessel, Susan, *Leo the Great and the Spiritual Rebuilding of a Universal Rome* (Leiden: Brill, 2008).

West-Harling, Veronica, *Rome, Ravenna, and Venice, 750–1000. Byzantine Heritage, Imperial Present, and the Construction of City Identity* (Oxford: Oxford University, 2020).

White, Cynthia, *The Emergence of Christianity* (Minneapolis: Fortress Press, 2007).

Wickham, Chris, *Medieval Rome. Stability & Crisis of a City* (Oxford: Oxford University Press, 2015).

Wilson, Katherina M., *Medieval Women Writers* (Manchester: Manchester University Press, 1984).

Winckelmann, Johann Joachim, Alex Potts (ed.) & Harry Francis (trans.), *Johann Joachim Winckelmann. History of the Art of Antiquity* (Los Angeles: Getty Research Institute, 2006).

Wisch, Barbara, 'Promoting Piety, Coercing Conversion: The Roman Archconfraternity of the Santissima Trinità dei Pellegrini e Convalescenti and its Oratory', *Predella. Journal of Visual Arts*, vol. 47, (2020), 255–277.

Wisch, Barbara, 'Violent Passions: Plays, Pawnbrokers, and the Jews of

Rome, 1539' in Allie Terry-Fritsch & Erin Felicia Labbie (eds), *Beholding Violence in Medieval and Early Modern Europe* (London: Routledge, 2016), 197–214.

Witte, Carolinne (trans. & ed.), *Lives of Roman Christian Women* (London: Penguin, 2010).

Witte, Joseph & Frank S. Alexander (eds), *The Teachings of Modern Roman Catholicism* (New York: Columbia University Press, 2007).

Wittman, Richard, 'A Partly Vacated Historicism: Artifacts, Architecture, and Time in Nineteenth-Century Papal Rome', *Grey Room*, vol. 84, (2021), 11–2.

Wolfram, Herwig, Thomas Dunlap (trans.), *The Roman Empire and its Germanic Peoples* (Berkeley: University of California Press, 1990).

Woodhouse, John, *Gabriele d'Annunzio. Defiant Archangel* (Oxford: Oxford University Press, 2001).

Wright, A.D., *The Early Modern Papacy. From the Council of Trent to the French Revolution, 1564–1789* (London: Longman, 2000).

Yates, Frances, *Giordano Bruno and the Hermetic tradition* (London: Routledge, 2002).

Yelle, Robert A., *Sovereignty and the Sacred. Secularism and the Political Economy of Religion* (Chicago: University of Chicago Press, 2019).

Zacour, Norman, 'The Cardinals' View of the Papacy, 1150–1300' in Christopher Ryan (ed.), *The Religious Roles of the Papacy: Ideals and Realities 1150–1300* (Toronto: Pontifical Institute of Medieval Studies, 1989), 413–438.

Zak, Gur, *Petrarch's Humanism and the Care of the Self* (Cambridge: Cambridge University Press, 2010).

Zeiller, M.J., 'Les Églises Ariennes de Rome a l'époque de la domination gothique', *Mélanges de l'école français de Rome*, vol. 24 (1904), 17–33.

Selected Primary Sources

Acts of Peter in Alexander Roberts & James Donaldson (trans.) (eds), *The Ante-Nicene Fathers. Translations of the writings of the fathers down to A.D. 325* (Edinburgh: T. & T. Clark, 1873), vol. 16.

Albèri, Eugenio (ed.), *Le relazioni degli ambasciatori veneti al Senato* (Florence: Tipografia all'insegna di Clio, 1839–63), 15 vols.

Albizzi, Rinaldo degli, *Comissioni di Rinaldo degli Albizzi per il Comune di Firenze dal MCCCXCIX AL MCCCCXXXIII. Volume secondo [1424–1426]* (Florence: M. Cellini, 1869).

Amicis, Edmondo de, *Ricordi del 1870–71* (Florence: G. Barbèra, 1873).

D'Annunzio, Gabriele, Agatha Hughes (trans.), *The Virgins of the Rocks* (London: William Heinemann, 1899).

Augustine of Hippo, *Letters* in J.G. Cunningham (trans.), Philip Schaff & Henry Wace (eds), *A Select Library of Nicene and Post-Nicene Fathers* of the Christian Church. First Series (Buffalo, N.Y.: Christian Literature Publishing Co., 1887), vol. 1.

Biondo, Flavio, Roma Instaurata (Verona: Bonino de Boninis, 1482).

Bonaparte, Napoleon, D.A. Bingham (ed.), A Selection from the Letters and Despatches of the First Napoleon (London: Chapman & Hall Ltd., 1884).

Bonaparte, Napoleon, R.M. Johnston (ed.), The Corsican: A Diary of Napoleon's Life in His Own Words (Boston: Houghton Mifflin Company, 1910).

Bracciolini, Poggio, Davide Canfrona (ed.), De vera nobilitate (Rome: Edizioni di Storia e Letteratura, 2002).

Casanova de Seingalt, Jacques, The Memoires of Casanova. Volume IV (Frankfurt: Outlook, 2018).

Chigi, Agostino, Diario del principe Agostino Chigi Albani. Parte prima (Tolentino: F. Filelfo, 1906).

Cicero, Walter Miller (trans.), De officiis [On Duty] (Cambridge, Mass.: Harvard University Press, 1913).

Coleridge, Samuel Taylor, 'The Principles of Genial Criticism' in Coleridge, H.J. Jackson & J.R. de J. Jackson (eds), Shorter Works and Fragments (Princeton: Princeton University Press, 1995), vol. 1.

Coleridge, Samuel, H.J. Jackson & J.R. de J. Jackson (eds), Shorter Works and Fragments (Princeton: Princeton University Press, 1995).

Conybeare, W.J. & J.S. Howson, The Life and Epistles of St. Paul (London: Longman, Brown, Green, Longmans & Roberts, 1856), 2 vols.

Crowley, Jeremiah J., The Pope. Chief of white slavers. High priest of intrigue (Aurora: The Menace Publishing Company, 1913).

Dante Alighieri, Courtney Langdon (trans.), The Divine Comedy of Dante Alighieri (Cambridge, Mass., Harvard University Press, 1918–21), 3 vols.

Dionysius of Halicarnassus, Earnest Cary (trans.), The Roman Antiquities of Dionysius (Cambridge, Mass.: Harvard University Press, 1937–1950), 7 vols.

Eaton, Charlotte A., Rome in the Nineteenth Century. (London: George Bell, 1892), 3 vols.

Erasmus, Desiderius, Paul Pascal (trans.), J. Kelley Edwards (ed.), The Julius Exclusus of Erasmus (Bloomington: Indiana University Press, 1968).

Eusebius of Caesarea, Ecclesiastical History in Arthur Cushman McGiffert (trans.), Philip Schaff & Henry Wace (eds), A Select Library of Nicene and Post-Nicene Fathers of the Christian Church. Second Series. Volume 1. Eusebius (Buffalo, N.Y.: Christian Literature Publishing Co., 1890).

Eusebius of Caesarea, Oration of Constantine in Ernest Cushing Richardson (trans.), Schaff & Wace (eds), A Select Library of Nicene and Post-Nicene Fathers of the Christian Church...Eusebius (Buffalo, N.Y.: Christian Literature Publishing Co., 1890).

Eusebius of Caesarea, *Life of Constantine* in Cushing Richardson (trans.), Schaff & Wace (eds), *A Select Library of Nicene and Post-Nicene Fathers of the Christian Church... Eusebius* (Buffalo, N.Y.: Christian Literature Publishing Co., 1890).

Evelyn, John , Austin Dobson (ed.), *The Diary of John Evelyn. With an Introduction and Notes. Volume 1* (Cambridge: Cambridge University Press, 2015).

Gibbon, Edward, *The Decline and Fall of the Roman Empire* (London: W. Strahan, 1776–89).

Giganti, Girolamo, *Tractatus de crimine laesae maiestatis insignis* (Lyon: Jacopo Giunta, 1552).

Goethe, Johann Wolfgang, W.H. Auden & Elizabeth Mayer (trans.), *Johann Wolfgang von Goethe, Italian Journey 1786–8* (San Francisco: North Point Press, 1962).

Ignatius of Antioch, *Letters* in Alexander Roberts & James Donaldson (trans.), Robertson, Donaldson & A. Cleveland Cox (eds), *The Ante-Nicene Fathers. Translations of the writings of the fathers down to A.D. 325* (Buffalo, N.Y.: Christian Literature Publishing Co., 1885), vol. 1.

Irenaeus of Lyon, *Against Heresies* in Roberts & Donaldson (trans.), Robertson, Donaldson & Cleveland Cox (eds), *The Ante-Nicene Fathers. Translations of the writings of the fathers down to A.D. 325* (Buffalo, N.Y.: Christian Literature Publishing Co., 1885), vol. 1.

Jerome, *Letters* in W.H. Fremantle, G. Lewis & W.G. Martley (trans.), Philip Schaff & Henry Wace (eds), *A Select Library of Nicene and Post-Nicene Fathers of the Christian Church. Second Series. Volume 6* (Buffalo, N.Y.: Christian Literature Publishing Co., 1893).

Jordanes, Charles Christopher Mierow (trans.), *The Gothic History of Jordanes* (Cambridge: Speculum Historiale, 1906).

Justin Martyr, *Dialogue with Trypho* in Marcus Dods & George Reith (trans.), Roberts, Donaldson & Cox (eds), *The Ante-Nicene Fathers. Translations of the writings of the fathers down to A.D. 325* (Buffalo, N.Y.: Christian Literature Publishing Co., 1885), vol.1.

Kaas, Ludwig, *LIFE* (27 March, 1950).

Lactantius, *Of the Manner in Which the Persecutors Died* in William Fletcher (trans.), Alexander Roberts & James Donaldson (trans.), Robertson, Donaldson & Cleveland Cox (eds), *The Ante-Nicene Fathers. Translations of the writings of the fathers down to A.D. 325* (Buffalo, N.Y.: Christian Literature Publishing Co., 1886), vol. 7.

Loyola, Ignatius, Michael Ivens (trans.), *The Spiritual Exercises of Saint Ignatius of Loyola* (Leominster: Gracewing, 2004).

Liudprand of Cremona, Paolo Squatriti (trans.), *The Complete Works of Liudprand of Cremona* (Washington D.C.: The Catholic University of America Press, 2007).

Monelli, Paolo, *Roma 1943* (Rome: Migliaresi, 1945).

Paul the Deacon, William Dudley Foulke (trans.), *The History of the Langobards* (New York: Longman, Green & Co., 1906).

Priuli, Girolamo, Arturo Segre (ed.), *I Diarii di Girolamo Priuli* (Bologna: Rerum Italicarum Scriptores, 1912–38).

Roncalli, Nicola, Raffaele Ambrosi de Magistris (ed.), *Diario di Nicola Roncalli dall'Anno 1849 al 1870* (Rome: Fratelli Bocca Librai, 1884).

Sala, G.A., *Diario Romano degli anni 1798–99. Parte II. dal I. Luglio al 31. Decembre 1798* (Rome: Società Romana di Storia Patria, 1882).

Sanudo, Marin, Paulo Margaroli (ed.), *I diarii (1496–1533). Pagine scelte* (Vicenza: Neri Pozza Editore, 1997).

Staël, Germaine de, Sylvia Raphael (trans.), *Corinne, or Italy* (Oxford: Oxford University Press, 2008).

Stanhope, Philip Dormer, *The Letters of Philip Dormer Stanhope, Earl of Chesterfield* (Philadelphia: J.B. Lipincott Company, 1892).

Suetonius, J.C. Rolfe (trans.), *The Lives of the Twelve Caesars* (Cambridge, Mass.: Harvard University Press, 1913-1914), 2 vols.

Tertullian, T. R. Glover (trans.), *Apology. De spectaculis. With an English translation by T. R. Glover* (London: William Heinemann Ltd., 1977).

Tomassetti, A. (ed.), *Bullarum diplomatum et privilegiorum sanctorum Romanorum pontificum Taurinensis editiolocupletior facta* (Turin: Seb. Franco, H. Fory and H. Dalmazzo, 1857–88), 25 vols.

Valla, Lorenzo, G. W. Bowersock (trans.), *On the Donation of Constantine* (Cambridge, Mass.: Harvard University Press, 2008).

Selected Archival Sources

Archivio della Congregazione per la Dottrina della Fede, *Decreta 1548–58.*

Archivio di Stato di Modena, *Inquisizione*, busta 270.

Archivum Romanum Societatis Iesu, *Med. Hist. 79.*

A Note on Translations

Where a quotation in the text is from an original source in Latin or a foreign language and is referenced to an English-language work, the reader can assume that the translator is the author of that work or another translator cited in their reference.

Quotations from biblical texts draw on the New Revised Standard Version Catholic Edition, except in the case of the Acts of Peter.

In a very few cases where translations, particularly of ancient texts, are somewhat old-fashioned, I have made extremely limited adaptations for clarity e.g. swapping 'trophies' for 'monuments'.

Timeline

Due to the length of this history and the number of protagonists involved, this timeline is selective. Therefore, it does not provide an exhaustive list of rulers and events, but rather those figures and events that are most significant for our narrative.

41 – Reign of Claudius begins

54 – Reign of Claudius ends

54 – Reign of Nero begins

c. 61 – Arrival of Saint Paul in Rome

64 – Great Fire of Rome

c. 64 – Earliest date, according to tradition, of the deaths of Saints Peter and Paul in Rome

68 – Reign of Nero ends

98 – Reign of Trajan begins

117 – Reign of Trajan ends

177 – Reign of Commodus begins (as co-ruler with his father, Marcus Aurelius)

192 – Reign of Commodus ends

249 – Reign of Decius begins

251 – Reign of Decius ends

253 – Reign of Gallienus begins (as co–ruler with his father, Valerian)

268 – Reign of Gallienus ends

270 – Reign of Aurelian begins

275 – Reign of Aurelian ends

284 – Reign of Diocletian begins

293 – Diocletian establishes the tetrarchy, dividing rule of the Roman Empire between two senior Caesar *Augusti* and two junior Caesars

293 – Reign of Galerius as Caesar of the Eastern Empire begins

303 – Persecution of Christians at the court of Diocletian

305 – Reign of Diocletian ends; Galerius becomes Caesar Augustus of the East

306 – Constantine becomes Caesar of the West

306 – Maxentius assumes rule over Rome as a usurper

308 – Reign of Licinius as Caesar Augustus of the West begins

311 – Reign of Galerius as Caesar Augustus of the East ends

312 – Constantine defeats Maxentius in the Battle of the Milvian Bridge

313 – Constantine and Licinius rule as Caesar Augusti; they grant liberty to Christians in the 'Edict of Milan'

c. 324 – The Lateran Basilica (later San Giovanni in Laterano) is founded; work on Saint Peter's Basilica underway

324 – Licinius is executed

324 – Foundation of Constantinople

325 – The first ever council of the Church meets at Nicaea

337 – Reign of Constantine I ends

361 – Reign of Julian I (the Apostate) begins

363 – Reign of Julian I ends

393 – Reign of Honorius begins (as co-ruler with his father Theodosius)

395 – Rule of Alaric I King of the Visigoths begins

410 – Visigoths sack Rome

410 – Death of Alaric I King of the Visigoths in Italy

423 – Reign of Honorius ends

425 – Reign of Valentinian III begins

428 – Rule of Gaiseric King of the Vandals begins

449 – The Second Council of Ephesus, the so-called 'Gangster Synod'

451 – The Council of Chalcedon

452 – Pope Leo the Great meets Attila the Hun

455 – Murder of Valentinian III in Rome

455 – Vandals sack Rome

475 – Reign of Romulus Augustulus, the last Emperor of the West, begins

476 – Deposition of Romulus Augustulus

476 – Odoacer becomes King of Italy

493 – Theodoric the Great of the Goths murders Odoacer and becomes King of Italy

477 – End of Gaiseric's reign over the Vandals

526 – Death of Theodoric; reign of Athalaric as King of Italy begins

527 – Reign of Justinian I as Emperor of the East (Byzantine Emperor) begins

565 – Reign of Justinian I ends

590 – Plague arrives in Rome

609 – The Pantheon becomes the church of Santa Maria ad Martyres

685 – First reign of Justinian II as Byzantine Emperor begins

692 – Quinisext Council condemns Roman religious practices

695 – First reign of Justinian II ends

717 – Reign of Leo III (the Isaurian) as Byzantine Emperor begins

729 – Pope Gregory II meets Liutprand, the Lombard King, at Sutri

741 – Reign of Leo III ends

751 – Official reign of Pepin III (the Short), King of the Franks, begins

753 – Pope Stephen II sets out to meet with Pepin, King of the Franks

754 – Pepin is anointed as king by Pope Stephen II near Paris

768 – Reign of Charlemagne as King of Franks begins

800 – Coronation of Charlemagne as Emperor of the Romans (later Holy Roman Emperor) by Pope Leo III in Rome

814 – Reign of Charlemagne ends

897 – The corpse of Pope Formosus is tried at the 'Cadaver Synod'

950 – Berengar II, Marchese d'Ivrea, becomes King of Italy

959 – Berengar II sets out to invade Rome

962 – Otto I, King of the Germans, defeats Berengar II and is crowned Holy Roman Emperor by Pope John XII

963 – Berengar II imprisoned by Otto I

973 – Reign of Otto I ends

1054 – Beginning of Great Schism between the Roman and Eastern Churches

1143 – Revolution and founding of commune in Rome

1155 – Frederick Barbarossa is crowned Holy Roman Emperor in Rome

1188 – The Concord Pact reunites Pope Clement III and the people

1285 – Reign of Philip IV (the Fair) as King of France begins

1300 – First year of Holy Jubilee inaugurated by Boniface VIII in Rome

1303 – Pope Boniface VIII attacked at Anagni; death of Boniface VIII

1309 – Avignon Papacy begins

1314 – Reign of Philip IV ends

1342 – The Thirteen Good Men elected to rule Rome

1342 – A Roman embassy, including Cola di Rienzo, travels to Avignon

1347 – Cola declares himself Tribune of Rome

1348 – Plague arrives in Rome

1349 – Earthquake damages many monuments in Rome

1354 – Cola murdered in Rome

1377 – Papacy returns to Rome from Avignon

1378 – Western Schism begins after the conclave rejects Urban VI

1413 – Ladislaus of Naples sacks Rome

1417 – Braccio da Montone invades Rome

1417 – The Council of Constance ends the Western Schism by electing Pope Martin V

1434 – Uprising against Pope Eugenius IV

1450 – Holy Jubilee proclaimed by Pope Nicholas V

1453 – Stefano Porcari unsuccessfully attempts an uprising in Rome

1478 – The foundation of the Spanish Inquisition

1489 – Discovery of the Apollo Belvedere near Rome

1492 – Jews expelled from Spain

1494 – Italian Wars begin after Charles VIII invades Naples

1506 – Rebuilding of Saint Peter's Basilica begun by Pope Julius II

1512 – Michelangelo completes his ceiling fresco in the Sistine Chapel

1517 – Luther proposes his 95 Theses for disputation in Wittenberg

1519 – Charles V begins reign as Holy Roman Emperor

1527 – Sack of Rome by the troops of Charles V

1542 – The foundation of the Roman Inquisition

1545 – Council of Trent begins

1553 – Copies of the Talmud are burned on the Campo de' Fiori

1555 – The Roman Ghetto is established

1555 – The Peace of Augsburg divides Europe into Lutheran and Catholic states

1556 – Retirement of Charles V as Holy Roman Emperor

1559 – Italian Wars end with Treaty of Cateau–Cambrésis

1618 – Beginning of the Thirty Years' War

1648 – The Treaty of Westphalia ends the Thirty Years' War

1667 – Bernini completes his colonnade in Saint Peter's square

1716 – First known burial at the non–Catholic cemetery in Rome

1771 – Vatican collections of art and antiquities open as a museum

1773 – Formal suppression of the Jesuits by Pope Clement XIV

1789 – The French Revolution begins

1793 – Murder of French diplomat Nicolas de Basseville in Rome

1797 – The Treaty of Tolentino between France and the Papal States

1797 – Death of French general Mathurin-Léonard Duphot in Rome

1798 – French occupation of Rome; attempted liberation by Ferdinand, King of Naples

1799 – Abduction of Pius VI by the French

1800 – Pius VII returns papacy to Rome

1804 – Pius VII attends the coronation of Napoleon Bonaparte in Paris

1808 – French troops occupy Rome

1809 – Abduction of Pius VII by the French

1811 – Napoleon Bonaparte has his son crowned King of Rome

1814 – Return of Pius VII to Rome

1815 – End of the Napoleonic Wars

1830 – Revolts begin in the Papal States

1831 – Foundation of Young Italy by Giuseppe Mazzini

1848 – The First Italian War of Independence begins

1848 – Assassination of Pius IX's Minister of the Interior Pellegrino Rossi

1848 – Pius IX flees Rome

1849 – Rome is briefly declared a republic

1850 – Pius IX is restored to Rome

1858 – Kidnapping of Edgardo Mortara

1861 – The Kingdom of Italy is established

1869 – The First Vatican Council begins

1870 – French troops leave Rome; Rome is captured

1870 – Pius IX declares himself Prisoner in the Vatican

1878 – King Vittorio Emanuele and Pius IX die

1878 – Reign of Umberto I as King of Italy begins

1900 – Leo XIII proclaims a Holy Jubilee

1914 – World War One begins

1915 – Italy enters the First World War on the side of the Allies

1918 – First World War ends with the victory of the Allies

1919 – Paris Peace Conference begins

1921 – The National Fascist Party is founded at the Third Fascist Congress in Rome

1922 – General strike in Italy;
Mussolini's 'March on Rome'

1929 – The Lateran Treaty; foundation
of the Vatican City state

1933 – Concordat secured between
the Nazis and the Holy See

1938 – Hitler visits Rome

1940 – Italy enters the Second World
War on the side of the Nazis

1943 – Rome is bombed; Rome is
declared an 'open city'

1945 – The Second World War ends
in victory for the Allies

1946 – Italy becomes a republic

1962 – Second Vatican Council opens

1975 – Year of Holy Jubilee

1978 – Kidnapping and murder of
former prime minister Aldo Moro

1981 – Attempted assassination of
Pope John Paul II in Rome

2013 – Resignation of Pope Benedict
XVI

Papal Timeline

As even approximate dates for the first five popes, except Clement I, are not established, they are not given here. Antipopes – men who declared themselves pope in opposition to a pope with a more legitimate claim – are included in square brackets. Where antipopes assumed a number that was later used by a legitimate pope, the number is framed in round brackets. Most ancient lists exclude Saint Peter; our list follows this convention. Due to an error in transcription in the medieval period, there has never been a Pope John XX. This list is based on the list published by Eamon Duffy in *Saints and Sinners. A History of the Popes* (London: Yale University Press, 2006).

	Linus	254–257	Stephen I
	Anacletus	257–258	Sixtus II
c. 96–?	Clement I	260–268	Dionysius
	Evaristus	269–274	Felix I
	Alexander I	275–283	Eutychian
c. 116–c. 125	Sixtus I	283–296	Gaius
c. 125–c. 136	Telesphorus	296–? (d. 304)	Marcellinus
c. 138–c. 142	Hyginus	c. 308–309	Marcellus
c. 142–c. 155	Pius I	310	Eusebius
c. 155–c. 166	Anicetus	311–314	Miltiades
c. 166–c. 174	Soter	314–335	Sylvester I
c. 175–c. 189	Eleutherius	336	Mark
c. 189–c. 199	Victor	337–352	Julius I
c. 199–c. 217	Zephyrinus	352–366	Liberius
c. 217–222	Callistus I	[355–365	Felix II]
[217–c. 235	Hippolytus]	366–384	Damasus I
c. 222–230	Urban I	[366–367	Ursinus]
230–235	Pontian	384–399	Siricius
235–236	Anterus	399–401	Anastasius I
236–250	Fabian	401–417	Innocent I
251–253	Cornelius	417–418	Zosimus
[251–258	Novatian]	[418	Eulalius]
253–254	Lucius I	418–422	Boniface

422–432	Celestine I	684–685	Benedict II
432–440	Sixtus III	685–686	John V
440–461	Leo I	686–687	Conon
461–468	Hilarus	[687	Theodore]
468–483	Simplicius	[687	Paschal]
483–492	Felix III	687–701	Sergius I
492–496	Gelasius I	701–705	John VI
496–498	Anastasius II	705–707	John VII
498–514	Symmachus	708	Sissinius
[498–499, 501–506	Laurence]	708–715	Constantine I
514–523	Hormisdas	715–731	Gregory II
523–526	John I	731–741	Gregory III
526–530	Felix IV	741–752	Zacharias
[530	Dioscorus]	752–757	Stephen II
530–532	Boniface II	757–767	Paul I
533–535	John II	[767–768	Constantine]
535–536	Agapitus I	[768	Philip]
536–537	Silverius	768–772	Stephen III
537–555	Vigilius	772–795	Hadrian I
556–561	Pelagius I	795–816	Leo III
561–574	John III	816–817	Stephen IV
575–579	Benedict I	817–824	Paschal I
579–590	Pelagius II	824–827	Eugenius II
590–604	Gregory I	827	Valentine
604–606	Sabinian	827–844	Gregory IV
607	Boniface III	[844	John]
608–615	Boniface IV	844–847	Sergius II
615–618	Adeodatus I	847–855	Leo IV
619–625	Boniface V	855–858	Benedict III
625–638	Honorius I	[855	Anastasius
640	Severinus	Bibliothecarius]	
640–642	John IV	858–867	Nicholas I
642–649	Theodore I	867–872	Hadrian II
649–653	Martin I	872–882	John VIII
654–657	Eugenius I	882–884	Marinus I
657–672	Vitalian	884–885	Hadrian III
672–676	Adeodatus II	885–891	Stephen V
676–678	Donus	891–896	Formosus
678–681	Agatho	896	Boniface VI
682–683	Leo II	896–897	Stephen VI

897	Romanus	1046–1047	Clement II
897	Theodore II	1047–1048	Benedict IX
898–900	John IX	(returned again)	
900–903	Benedict IV	1048	Damasus II
903	Leo V	1049–1054	Leo IX
[903–904	Christopher]	1055–1057	Victor II
904–911	Sergius III	1057–1058	Stephen IX
911–913	Anastasius III	[1058–1059	Benedict X]
913–914	Lando	1058–1061	Nicholas II
914–928	John X	1061–1073	Alexander II
928	Leo VI	[1061–1064	Honorius (II)]
928–931	Stephen VII	1073–1085	Gregory VII
931–935/6	John XI	[1080, 1084–1100	Clement III]
936–939	Leo VII	1086–1087	Victor III
939–942	Stephen VIII	1088–1099	Urban II
942–946	Marinus II	1099–1118	Paschal II
946–955	Agapitus II	[1100–1101	Theodoric]
955–964	John XII	[1101/2	Albert]
963–965	Leo VIII	[1105–1111	Sylvester IV]
964	Benedict V	1118–1119	Gelasius II
965–972	John XIII	[1118–1121	Gregory (VIII)]
973–974	Benedict VI	1119–1124	Callistus II
[974, 984–985	Boniface VII]	1124–1130	Honorius II
974–983	Benedict VII	[1124	Celestine II]
983–984	John XIV	1130–1143	Innocent II
985–996	John XV	[1130–1138	Anacletus]
996–999	Gregory V	[1138	Victor IV]
[997–998	John XVI]	1143–1144	Celestine II
999–1003	Sylvester II	1144–1145	Lucius II
1003	John XVII	1145–1153	Eugenius III
1003–1009	John XVIII	1153–1154	Anastasius IV
1009–1012	Sergius IV	1154–1159	Hadrian IV
[1012	Gregory VI]	1159–1181	Alexander III
1012–1024	Benedict VIII	[1159–1164	Victor IV]
1024–1032	John XIX	[1164–1168	Paschal III]
1032–1044	Benedict IX	[1168–1178	Callistus III]
1045	Sylvester III	[1179–1180	Innocent III]
1045	Benedict IX	1181–1185	Lucius III
	(returned)	1185–1187	Urban III
1045–1046	Gregory VI	1187	Gregory VIII

1187–1191	Clement III	1431–1447	Eugenius IV
1191–1198	Celestine III	[1439–1449	Felix V]
1198–1216	Innocent III	1447–1455	Nicholas V
1216–1227	Honorius III	1455–1458	Callistus III
1227–1241	Gregory IX	1458–1464	Pius II
1241	Celestine IV	1464–1471	Paul II
1243–1254	Innocent IV	1471–1484	Sixtus IV
1254–1261	Alexander IV	1484–1492	Innocent VIII
1261–1264	Urban IV	1492–1503	Alexander VI
1265–1268	Clement IV	1503	Pius III
1271–1276	Gregory X	1503–1513	Julius II
1276	Innocent V	1513–1521	Leo X
1276	Hadrian V	1522–1523	Hadrian VI
1276–1277	John XXI	1523–1534	Clement VII
1277–1280	Nicholas III	1534–1549	Paul III
1281–1285	Martin IV	1550–1555	Julius III
1285–1287	Honorius IV	1555	Marcellus II
1288–1292	Nicholas IV	1555–1559	Paul IV
1294	Celestine V	1559–1565	Pius IV
1294–1303	Boniface VIII	1566–1572	Pius V
1303–1304	Benedict XI	1572–1585	Gregory XIII
1305–1314	Clement V	1585–1590	Sixtus V
1316–1334	John XXII	1590	Urban VII
[1328–1330	Nicholas (V)]	1590–1591	Gregory XIV
1334–1342	Benedict XII	1591	Innocent IX
1342–1352	Clement VI	1592–1605	Clement VIII
1352–1362	Innocent VI	1605	Leo XI
1362–1370	Urban V	1605–1621	Paul V
1370–1378	Gregory XI	1621–1623	Gregory XV
1378–1389	Urban VI	1623–1644	Urban VIII
[1378–1394	Clement VII]	1644–1655	Innocent X
1389–1404	Boniface IX	1655–1667	Alexander VII
[1394–1417	Benedict XIII]	1667–1669	Clement IX
1404–1406	Innocent VII	1670–1676	Clement X
1406–1415	Gregory XII	1676–1689	Innocent XI
[1409–1410	Alexander V]	1689–1691	Alexander VIII
[1410–1415	John XXIII]	1691–1700	Innocent XII
1417–1431	Martin V	1700–1721	Clement XI
[1423–1429	Clement VIII]	1721–1724	Innocent XIII
[1425	Benedict (XIV)]	1724–1730	Benedict XIII

1730–1740	Clement XII	1903–1914	Pius X
1740–1758	Benedict XIV	1914–1922	Benedict XV
1758–1769	Clement XIII	1922–1939	Pius XI
1769–1774	Clement XIV	1939–1958	Pius XII
1775–1799	Pius VI	1958–1963	John XXIII
1800–1823	Pius VII	1963–1978	Paul VI
1823–1829	Leo XII	1978	John Paul I
1829–1830	Pius VIII	1978–2005	John Paul II
1831–1846	Gregory XVI	2005–2013	Benedict XVI
1846–1878	Pius IX	2013–	Francis I
1878–1903	Leo XIII		

Acknowledgements

Compiling a history of a city like Rome over nearly two millennia could never be the work of a lone individual. In the course of writing this book, in several countries and over a several years, I have relied on invaluable help from colleagues, friends and institutions, as well as the rich scholarship of the numerous historians referenced in this work.

My knowledge of Rome's history, particularly that of the early modern period, is grounded in my years of research in the city. For their assistance and support during that time, I thank the British School at Rome, the University of Saint Andrews and the Society for Renaissance Studies, as well as the staff of the Archivio Apostolico Vaticano, Archivio del Dicastero per la Dottrina della Fede, Archivio di Stato di Roma, Archivum Romanum Societatis Iesu, Archivio storico della Penitenzieria Apostolica, Biblioteca Apostolica Vaticana, Biblioteca Nazionale Centrale di Roma and Biblioteca di Storia Moderna e Contemporanea. While in Rome, my understanding of the city and its history was enriched by conversations with some of the historians whom I admire most. I remain particularly indebted to Professor Irene Fosi, Professor Vincenzo Lavenia, Dr Emily Michelson, Dr Camilla Russell and many others for the kindness and generosity with which they fielded my many questions and ideas. For taking me to some of the remoter sites of the city and illuminating their history, I thank Father Anthony Robbie.

Compiling this contribution to the history of Rome from further afield, I have relied on the work of many great scholars as well as the custodians of their books at the British Library, Institute of Classical Studies, Warburg Institute and Kungliga biblioteket in Stockholm. Outside of the reading room, friends back in Rome have helped me to navigate attitudes and ideas that are often not recorded on the printed page. I thank Jacopo Benci and Manuela Gazzano especially for helping me to gather insights on the more recent history of Rome and its people. For generously allowing me to access to the private quarters of some of the protagonists in this history, I am grateful to the nuns of the Casa di Santa Brigida and church of San Girolamo della Carità in Rome.

Both the research for this book and the final text have benefitted greatly from the interventions and ideas of scholars, editors and experts whom I am blessed to know personally. I am particularly grateful to James Cross, Christopher Mason, Tom Perrin and Dr Arthur der Weduwen who took the time to read the text, in part or in full, from the proposal stage to the final drafts. My heartfelt thanks go to Professor Simon Ditchfield, who not only read the full text but, with characteristic generosity of spirit, helped to clarify and shape my ideas through hours of conversation. I am also indebted to Professor Andrew Pettegree for his discerning comments on parts of the early drafts, as well as his encouragement and practical help as I took the leap from the academic world into trade publishing.

Needless to say, any errors in the final text are my own.

Throughout the process of writing this book, I could not have wished for a more supportive and skilled literary agent than Catherine Clarke. I am thankful to her and to Duncan Heath, formerly of Icon Books, for recognising the potential of the idea immediately and having faith in my ability to execute the project. My potential to do so benefitted immensely from Duncan's patient guidance and sage interventions as I wrote the text. It has been a pleasure to work with him and my other editors at Icon and Pegasus, particularly Connor Stait, whose energy, care and hard work were so vital in the final stages before publication.

Finally, this book would not have been completed without the support of friends and family, particularly my unfailingly encouraging parents, brother and parents-in-law, my dear friend James Cossey and the ever-sage and supportive Les Clarke and Tom Perrin. The inspiration, insights and editorial assistance of my husband, Karl Gustel Wärnberg, have enriched this project, from its genesis to completion. For this reason, and countless others, this book is dedicated to him.

Jessica Wärnberg, London

Index

Abbas I, Shah of Persia
216–17
Accademia dei Lincei 251
Accademia Fisico-
Matematica 251–2
Achaea 185
Acqua Vergine 141
Addison, Joseph 234
Aetius (Roman general)
65–6, 70
Ağca, Ali Mehmet 323–4
Agostino Gemelli
(hospital) 323
Ahenobarbus, Lucius
Domitius 76
Aistulf, King of Lombardy
100–1
Alaric, King of the Visigoths
(395–410) 61, 64, 66, 68,
77, 82, 294
Albani, Cardinal Alessandro
251, 252
Alberico I, Duke of
Spoleto 105
Albizzi, Cardinal Francesco
degli 151
Albizzi, Rinaldo degli 150
Albornoz, Cardinal Gil
Álvarez Carillo de 137
Alexander, Tsar of
Russia 267
Alexandria 72, 174, 176
Algieri, Pomponio 206, 208
Ambrose of Milan 35
Ameyden, Dirk 195
Anagni 118, 119–20, 127, 144,
146, 149
Ancona, Ciriaco d' 157, 162
Andronicus 9
Annabaldi family 134

Annunzio, Gabriele D' 299,
307, 309, 311, 314
Antioch 72, 174
Antonelli, Cardinal
Giacomo 285, 288, 290
Antoninus Pius 102
Antoninus, Emperor
(Heliogabalus) 18
Anubis 17
Anzio 157
Apollo Belvedere 157
Appian Way 12, 13, 14, 21,
24, 250
Apuleius 22
Aquila (husband for
Priscilla) 9, 20–3
Arc du Triomphe, Paris 256
Arcangeli, Francesco 236
Arch of Titus 267
Archinto, Cardinal
Alberico 235
Arnold of Brescia 110–11,
125, 300
Arnulf of Carinthia 104
Atargatis 18
Athalaric, King of the
Ostrogoths 92
Attalus, Priscus 66
Attila the Hun 70–1
Attis 16
Augusta 49
Augustine, Bishop of Hippo
35, 54, 64, 65, 68, 74,
81, 130
Augustus III of Poland 235
Augustus, Emperor (27–14
bc) 16, 49, 131, 137, 240
Aurelian Walls 39, 125, 290
Aurelian, Emperor (270–75)
41–2

Aurelius Sarapammon
43, 45
Aurelius, Emperor Marcus
(161–80) 56, 85, 282, 293
Aventine Hill 21, 35, 83, 91
Avignon 116, 122–126, 131,
138, 146, 147, 151, 161
Azeglio, Massimo d' 299
Azzolino, Cardinal
Decio 219

Babylon 12–13
Badoglio, Pietro 294
Barber, Bernardino 192
Baronio, Cesare 209
Basseville, Nicholas Hugou
de 254, 255
Bassi Veratti, Laura 251
Bassus, Junius (prefect)
81, 82
Batoni, Pompeo 238
Battle of Lepanto 304
Bayezid II, Ottoman
Emperor 184
Beaufort, Cardinal
Hugo de 132
Beg, Ali-Qoli 216–17
Begin, Menachem 323
Beijing 211
Belgiojoso, Princess
Trivulzio 284
Bellarmino, Cardinal
Roberto 207, 253
Benigni, Monsignor
Umberto 303–4
Benso, Camillo, Count of
Cavour see Cavour
Berengar II, King of
Italy 106
Bernardino of Siena 142

Bernini, Gian Lorenzo 11, 13, 197, 209, 215, 216, 217, 219, 315
Bessarion, Cardinal 185
Bilotti, Father Carlo 274
Biondo, Flavio 154, 155, 156, 157, 158, 233
Birgersdotter, Bridget and Ulf *see* Saint Bridget of Sweden
Bismarck, Chancellor Otto von 303
Bithynia 26
Black Death 124
Blanche of Namur 131
Bocca della Verità 285
Boccaccio, Giovanni 167
Bologna 272–4, 287
Bonaparte, Joseph 255, 261
Bonaparte, Lucien 261
Bonaparte, Napoleon *see* Napoleon I
Bonaparte, President Louis-Napoleon *see* Napoleon III
Bondone, Giotto di 1, 4
Bonomi, Ivanoe 312
Booth, Barton 234
Borgo 193–4, 258, 300
Boris I, King of Bulgaria 104
Borromeo, Carlo 210
Bosco Parrasio 236
Boyle, Robert 250
Bracciolini, Poggio 158, 161
Bramante, Donato 216
Brancaccio, Eleonora 308
Brunetti, Angelo (*Ciceruacchio*) 284
Bruno, Giordano 207
Byzantium *see* Constantinople

Caedwalla, King of Wessex 97, 100
Caelian Hill 21, 35, 48, 97
Caesar, Emperor Julius 94, 234, 262; Temple of 15
Caetani family 118–20, 134, 146

Caetani, Onorato, Count of Campagna 146
Caffè dei Crociferi 281, 282
Campo de' Fiori 170, 205, 207, 274
Campo Marzio 17, 18, 65, 156, 223, 274
Camponeschi, Vittoria 203
Camposanto Teutonico 86
Canova, Antonio 250, 271
Capella Paolina 290
Capgrave, John 163, 165
Capitoline Hill 15, 67, 68, 85, 109, 111, 125, 128–9, 136, 142, 144, 169, 170, 237, 245–6, 250, 259, 266, 278, 282, 300, 301, 305
Caracalla, Emperor (198–217) 118
Carafa, Gian Pietro *see* Paul IV
Caravaggio, Michelangelo Merisi da 209
Carbonari 273–5, 284
Carlo Alberto of Sardinia-Piedmont 275–6
Casa dei Catecumeni 222
Casa di Crescenzio 111
Casanova, Giacomo 237
Castel Gandolfo 316
Castel Sant'Angelo 79, 87, 142, 160, 184, 206, 264–5, 266, 286, 291
Catacombs of San Callisto 75
Catacombs of Santa Priscilla 209
Catherine of Aragon 180, 181, 190
Cato 234
Cavour, Count of (Camillo Benso) 288, 289, 296–7, 300
Cawdor, Lord (John Campbell) 271
Cem, son of Mehmed II 184
Cemetery of Priscilla 12
Ceres 118
Cestius, Caius 241

Charlemagne, Holy Roman Emperor (768–814) 86, 100–2, 103, 265, 318
Charles I of England 243
Charles IV, Holy Roman Emperor 136–8
Charles V, Holy Roman Emperor 180, 188–9, 191
Charles VIII of France 188
Chesterfield, Lord (Philip Dormer Stanhope) 234
Chijiwa, Miguel 191
Christina, Queen of Sweden 218–20
Chrysoloras, Manuel 153–4, 156
Ciampini, Monsignor Giovanni Giustino 251–2
Cibin, Camillo 323
Cicero 79, 234–5
Circus Maximus 16, 28, 67
Città Alta 300
Clarke-Jervoise, H. 298
Claudius II, Emperor 38–9
Claudius, Emperor (41–54) 24
Coke, Thomas (Earl of Leicester) 238
Cola di Rienzo 127–8, 129–31, 135–7, 300
Coleridge, Samuel Taylor 231
Colonna family 132, 134, 149–50, 168
Colonna the Younger, Stefano 127–8
Colonna, Cardinal Prospero 155–6, 161, 168
Colonna, Giordano 149–50
Colosseum 29, 67, 75, 238, 316
Columbus, Christopher 182
Commodus, Emperor (180–192) 30
Concord Pact of 1188 111, 114
Concord, Temple of 15
Confucius 5, 211
Congo 176

Congress of Vienna 270
Consalvi, Cardinal Ercole
263, 270, 271
Constantia 46
Constantine I (the Great)
(306–37) 3, 4, 36–7,
38–40, 45–7, 49, 53–4, 61,
66, 72, 76, 80, 82, 87, 93,
129, 160, 165
Constantine V, Emperor
(741–75) 100
Constantini, Sante 285
Constantinople (Byzantium)
54, 72–3, 88, 89, 93, 157,
174, 175, 176, 183, 221, 265;
University of 93
Constantius 37
Contarini, Cardinal
Gasparo 211
Conybear, William 241
Copernicus, Nicolaus
231, 253
Corilla Olimpica (Maria
Maddalena Morelli) 237
Corinth 13, 20, 22, 27, 29
Coscia, Cardinal
Niccolò 246
Council of Chalcedon 74
Council of Florence 175
Council of Nicaea 54
Council of Trent 247, 277
Coyer, Gabriel-Francois 244
Crescenti family 109
Crescentius the Elder 87
Crescenzi family 104
Crispi, Francesco 297, 301
Crispolti, Filippo 298
Croce, Benedetto 319
Cromwell, Thomas 180, 220
Crowley, Jeremiah 302,
303, 304
Crozza, Maurizio 325
Cuba 182
Curia Savelli 146, 206, 224, 226

Damascus 23
D'Annunzio, Gabriele see
Annunzio, Gabriele D'
Dante Alighieri 114–16

Dati, Agostino 164
Decius, Emperor (249–51)
43, 45
Delicado, Francis 192
Dell'Acqua, Angelo 322
Demetrias (Anicia) 65
Diet of Worms 189
Dio, Cassius 25, 26
Diocletian, Emperor
(284–305) 37, 42–4, 91
Dionysius, Bishop of
Corinth 13
Dioscorus, Bishop of
Alexandria 73–4, 174
Downey, Laurence
James 324
Duphot, Léonard 255
Dürer, Albrecht 232

Eaton, Charlotte Anne
233–4, 239–40
Ecuador 303
Edict of Milan 46
Edict of Serdica 44
Edward I, King of
England 121
El Gabal 18
Epicureanism 158
Erasmus, Desiderius 171,
187, 188
Erfurt, University of 177
Esquiline Hill 52, 53, 85–6, 155
Este, Cardinal Alessandro
d' 186
Esterházy, Count Moritz
284–5
Estouteville, Cardinal
Guillaume d' 194
Ethiopia 173–6, 316
Eusebius 26, 40, 41, 46, 54
Eutychius 95
Evelyn, John 232

Facta, Luigi 313
Farinetti, Guglielmo 312
Farmacia dei Peretti 273
Farnese family 191
Fatima (miracle) 305, 324
Feletti, Pier Gaetano 288

Fellini, Federico 321
Ferdinand and Isabella of
Spain 182, 202, 205
Ferdinand, King of Naples
(1759–1806; 1815–1816)
262–3
Ferrara 310
Ficoroni, Francesco 236,
238–9
Finicella 141–2
First Vatican Council 277
Flavian, Bishop of
Constantinople 73
Florence 117, 168, 189, 223,
250, 282, 300
Fontana, Domenico 240
Forum (Roman) 67, 91,
256, 267
Frangipani, Cencio 108–9
Frangipani, Leone 108–9
Frangipani family 108–9
Frascati 150
Fratelli d'Alessandri 291
Frederick Barbarossa, Holy
Roman Emperor 110–11
Fulda Abbey, Hesse 158
Fuller, Margaret 284

Gaeta 281, 282, 283,
285, 302
Gaiseric, King of the
Vandals (428–77) 63, 65,
69, 71
Gaius 9–10, 13–14, 31
Galerius, Emperor (305–11)
42–3, 44
Galilei, Galileo 251,
252–3, 300
Galliani, Celestino 252
Gallienus, Emperor
(253–68) 44
Garibaldi, Giuseppe 258,
283–4, 289, 300, 307
Gasparri, Cardinal
Pietro 314
Gattilusio, Niccolò 183
George IV of England 271
German College 310
Gibbon, Edward 68, 79, 233

Gibbons of Baltimore,
Cardinal James 303
Gioberti, Vincenzo 279
Giolitti, Giovanni 306–7,
310, 311–12
Giudici, Letizia 323
Gizzi, Cardinal
Tomasso 280
Godwin, William 234
Goethe, Johann Wolfgang
von 229–32, 236, 239
Gordon, Colonel
William 238
Gregory, Bishop of
Tours 96
Gros, Pierre 256
Guerrini, Agostino 274
Gustavus Adolphus of
Sweden 248

Hadad 18
Hadrian, Emperor 1, 48, 81
Haiti 182
Haller (French
Commissioner) 256
Hara, Martinho 191
Hawkwood, John (Giovanni
Acuto) 132
Heemskerck, Martin van
154–5
Hein, Simon 218
Helena, Empress 48, 95,
163, 186
Henry II, Holy Roman
Emperor 175
Henry V, Holy Roman
Emperor 108
Henry VII, Holy Roman
Emperor 127
Henry VIII of England 180,
181, 190, 270
Herculaneum 236
Herculanus, Bassus 70
Hermes Trismegistus 207
Hitler, Adolf 294, 317
Hobbes, Thomas 62, 240
Honoria (sister of Emperor
Valentinian III) 70

Honorius, Western Emperor
(395–423) 66, 77, 81
Hope, Samuel 217
Hopkins, Harry 294
Horace 155, 234
Howson, John 241

Ignatius, Bishop of
Antioch 13
Il Caffè degli Milanesi 274
Il Caffè Nuovo 274
Il Gesù (church) 256
Illyria 73
Ine, King of Wessex 97–8
Ireland 96
Irenaeus of Lyon 13
Isis 17, 18

James II of England 234, 239
Janiculum Hill 236, 283, 300
Jean II, Duke of Brittany 121
Jerome 33–4, 35, 52–3, 61,
65, 82
Jerusalem 3, 5, 9, 13, 19, 48
João II of Portugal 182
João of Braganza 195
Jordanes 63
Judea 19
Julian I (the Apostate),
Emperor (361–3) 34, 36
Juliana of Liège 214
Juliana (Anicia) 65
Jupiter Optimus Maximus,
Temple of 15, 17, 301
Justin I, Eastern Emperor
(518–527) 89
Justin Martyr 34, 56
Justinian I, Eastern Emperor
(527–65) 90
Justinian II, Eastern
Emperor (685–95) 93

Kaas, Monsignor Ludwig 11
Kait Bey, Mamluk Sultan of
Cairo 184
Karl August, Duke of
Saxe-Weimar-Eisenach 230
Keats, John 241
Kyiv 271

Lactantius 40, 42, 46
Ladislaus of Naples
(1386–1414) 154
Lambert, Prince of
Spoleto 104
Lamego, Archbishop of
195–6
Lamennais, Felicité de
268–9
Lancelotti family 259
Lante, Villa 283
Lanza, Giovanni 298, 299
Laocoön 157
Lapo da Castiglionchio the
Younger 176
Lassels, Father Richard 239
Lateran Basilica (San
Giovanni in Laterano) 48,
49, 50, 80, 85, 124, 163,
164, 315, 320
Lateran Palace 84, 93, 103,
126, 150, 297
Lateran Treaty 315, 318–19
Leo I, Eastern Emperor
(457–74) 88
Leo the Isaurian, Eastern
Emperor (717–41)
94–5, 101
Lesbos 183, 184
Leto, Giulio Pomponio
159–60, 168
Levi, Primo 301
Liberian Basilica 52
Libya 306
Licinius, Emperor (308–24)
46, 53
Lilliecrona, Gustav 218
Liutprand of Cremona
105–6, 107
Liutprand, King of
Lombardy (712–44)
98–9, 100
Livy 238
Lombardy 70, 98–100, 257,
264, 276, 280, 289, 314
Longfellow, Henry
Wadsworth 290
Los Velez, Marquis de 196

Louis XII of France 181
Louis XIV of France 194,
  197, 244
Louis XV of France 249
Louis XVI of France 243
Louis XVIII of France 271
Lucan 65
Lucretius 158
Luder, Heine 166
Lumley, Lord 239
Lupercalia 15
Luther, Martin 165–6,
  177–80, 181, 189, 205–6
Lyon 121

Macarius 52–3
Macron, Emmanuel 5
Maderno, Carlo 209, 217
Maecenas 155–6
Magna Mater 16
Maistre, Joseph de 268
Mälzer, General Kurt 295
Mancio, Itō 191
Manicheans 42
Manuel I of Portugal 220
Marcellinus, Ammianus 52,
  68, 158
Marcian, Eastern Emperor
  (450–57) 69, 74
Margaret of Parma 247
Marino 150
Marotti, Father Joseph 260
Marozia (daughter of
  Teofilatto) 105, 107, 111
Marshall Plan 320
Massimo family 159,
  194, 259
Massimo, Vittorio Emanuele
  298–9, 308
Mastro Titta (Giovanni
  Battista Bugatti) 269–70
Mattei family 194
Maxentius, Emperor
  (306–12) 37–40, 47, 48
Maximian, Emperor
  (286–305; 306–8) 37,
  38, 44
Maximilian, Holy Roman
  Emperor (1508–19) 189

Maximinius Daza, Emperor
  (305–13) 38
Mazzini, Giuseppe 274, 276,
  278–9, 281–4
Mehmed II, Ottoman
  Emperor 183, 184
Melania the Elder 64
Melania the Younger 64
Menotti, Ciro 275
Mercier, Louis-Sébastien 235
Merry del Val, Cardinal
  Raphael 303–4
Metternich, Klemens von 270
Mexico 303
Michelangelo (Buonarotti)
  26, 157, 169, 170, 216, 291
Michiel, Beatrice (Fatima) 221
Milan (Mediolanum) 39, 46,
  66, 77, 189, 191, 263, 276,
  308, 311
Milton, John 240
Milvian Bridge 39, 40
Misson,
  François-Maximilien 240
Mithras 17
Modena 275–6
Monaldeschi, Gian
  Rinaldo 220
Monelli, Paolo 295
Montaigne, Michel de
  222, 232
Montanari, Leonida 269,
  271, 273, 275
Monte di Pietà 244, 255
Montefiore, Sir Moses 288
Montesquieu 235
Monti 272–3
Montone, Braccio da 154
Moratín, Leandro
  Fernández de 250
More, Thomas 180
Moreno, President Gabriel
  García 303
Moro, Aldo 320
Morrison, Fynes 240–1
Mortara, Edgardo 286–9
Moscow 176
Mullooly, Father Joseph 67
Muro Torto 241

Museum Pium Clementinum
  (Museum Clementinum) 250
Mussolini, Benito (1922–43)
  5, 101, 293–5, 308, 311–119

Nakaura, Julião 191
Nanà, Aïché 321
Naples 93, 117, 124, 135, 188,
  191, 203, 208, 240, 257,
  262–3, 274, 275, 281, 283
Napoleon I 255, 261, 263–8,
  273–4, 297
Napoleon III, President
  and Emperor of France
  (1848–70) 283, 288–9
Ne Vunda, Emanuel 176,
  186, 191
Nelson, Horatio 262
Nenni, Pietro 296
Nero, Emperor (54–68)
  4, 25–6
Newton, Isaac 250, 251
Nitti, Francesco 309
Nogaret, Guillaume de 120
Notre Dame, Paris 264

O'Clery, Patrick 298
Odoacer, King of Italy
  (476–93) 81–2, 87–8
Oppenheim, Daniel
  Moritz 287
Orlando, Vittorio 309
Orsini family 134, 168
Orsini, Bertoldo 128
Orvieto 117, 190
Ospizio dei Convertendi
  217–18
Otto, Holy Roman Emperor
  I (961–73) 87, 106–7

Pachamama 2
Palatine Hill 15, 16, 19
Palazzo Caetani 173, 175
Palazzo Corsini 255, 283
Palazzo dei Conservatori
  167–8, 170
Palazzo dei Convertendi
  217

Palazzo della Cancellaria 281, 282
Palazzo di Giustizia 300
Palazzo Farnese 192, 219
Palazzo Massimo alle Colonne 308
Palazzo Mondaleschi 192
Palazzo Montecitorio 310
Palazzo Senatorio 307
Palazzo Venezia 309, 317
Palencia, Alfonso de 154, 161–2
Pannartz, Arnold 159
Pantheon 17, 94, 130, 301, 302
Paris Peace Conference 309
Paruta, Paulo 181
Pasolini, Pier Paolo 321
Pasquino 167, 259, 266, 325
Paul the Deacon 98
Peace of Augsburg 208, 247
Peace of Cateau-Cambrésis 191
Pelagius 35, 61, 65
Pepin the Short, King of the Franks (751–68) 100–2
Persia 42
Peter the Deacon 78
Peter the Prefect 85–7, 105
Petrarch, Francesco 114, 116, 123, 124, 127, 135, 157, 203, 237
Petri, Johannes and Catherine 133
Philip II of Spain (1556–1598) 247
Philip IV 'the Fair' of France (1285–1314) 116, 120–2
Phocas I, Eastern Emperor (602–10) 91, 94
Phoebe (deaconess) 22–3
Piazza del Popolo 267, 270, 273, 282
Piazza Giudia 199, 201
Piazza Venezia 316
Pierleoni, Giordano 109, 110, 111, 125
Pietro, Dario di 193
Pilate, Pontius 24, 163

Pinian (husband of Melania the Younger) 64
Pisa 147
Pizzi, Gioacchino 237
Plannck, Stephan 182
Plato 207
Pliny the Elder 26
Pliny the Younger 26
Plutarch 235
Pomerium 14–15, 17–18
Pompadour, Madame de 249
Pompeii 236
Ponte Sant'Angelo 1
Ponthion 100–1
Pontus 20
Popes:
   Agatho (678–81) 92
   Alexander V (1409–1410) 147
   Alexander VI (1492–1503) 167, 181, 182, 192, 202–3, 205
   Alexander VII (1655–67) 218, 219–20, 250
   Anacletus 10, 30
   Anterus (236–250) 75
   Benedict VI (973–4) 87
   Benedict VIII (1012–24) 175
   Benedict XI (1303–4) 121
   Benedict XII (1334–42) 122–3, 125, 207
   Benedict XIII (antipope) (1394–1417) 147
   Benedict XIII (1724–30) 246
   Benedict XIV (1740–58) 246, 248, 251, 275
   Benedict XV (1914–1922) 306–10, 314
   Benedict XVI (2005–13) 325
   Boniface III (607) 94
   Boniface IV (608–15) 94
   Boniface VII (Cardinal Franco Ferrucci) (974 and 984–5) 87

Boniface VIII (1294–1303) 114, 118–21, 128, 144
Boniface IX (1389–1404) 149, 154
Callistus III (1455–8) 192
Celestine I (422–32) 77
Clement I (c. 96–?) 10, 30
Clement III (1187–91) 111
Clement V (1305–14) 121–2
Clement VI (1342–52) 122–3, 126–8, 132, 135–6, 151–2
Clement VII (1523–34) 146–7, 170, 170, 180–1, 188–9, 197
Clement VIII (1592–1605) 181, 215
Clement XI (1700–21) 250
Clement XII (1730–40) 242, 245, 248, 273, 275
Clement XIV (1769–74) 244, 249, 250
Constantine I (708–15) 93
Cornelius (251–3) 45, 75
Damasus I (366–84) 51–2, 55, 57–8, 75
Dionysius (260–8) 44, 75
Eugenius I (654–7) 93
Eugenius III (1145–53) 110, 152
Eugenius IV (1431–47) 168, 170
Evaristus 30
Fabian (236–50) 45
Felix (269–274) 75
Formosus I (891–6) 104
Francis I (2013–) 5, 325
Gelasius II (1118–1119) 108
Gregory I (the Great) (590–604) 78–9, 97, 99, 190, 326
Gregory II (715–31) 95, 98–9, 101
Gregory III (731–41) 95
Gregory VII (1073–85) 107–8, 114–15
Gregory VIII (1187) 108

INDEX

Gregory XI (1370–78)
138, 144

Gregory XII
(1406–1415) 147

Gregory XIII (1572–85)
212, 221, 224

Gregory XV (1621–3) 212

Gregory XVI (1831–46)
272–3, 276–7, 278

Hadrian I (772–95)
92, 102

Hadrian IV (1154–9) 110

Hadrian VI (1522–3) 167

Hilarius (461–8) 73, 80

Honorius I (625–38) 94

Innocent I (401–17) 65

Innocent II (1130–43) 109

Innocent III (1198–1216)
115–16

Innocent VI
(1352–62) 136

Innocent VIII (1484–92)
184, 188

Innocent X (1644–55)
247–8

Innocent XII
(1691–1700) 150

John I (523–6) 89

John V (685–6) 103–4

John XI (931–5/6) 105

John XII (955–64) 106–7

John XIII (965–72) 87,
95, 105

John XXII (1316–34)
122, 126

John XXIII (antipope)
(1410–1415) 147, 149

John XXIII (1958–63)
319, 321

John Paul II (1978–2005)
322–4

Julius I (337–52) 54–5

Julius II 'Warrior Pope'
(1503–13) 157, 166, 171,
188, 214, 216, 314

Leo I (the Great) (440–61)
69–72, 73–5, 183, 190

Leo III (795–816) 86, 101

Leo VIII (963–5) 107

Leo X (1513–21) 159, 167,
170, 179–80, 189, 207

Leo XII (1823–9) 271,
273, 275

Leo XIII (1878–1903) 301,
303, 305

Liberius (352–66) 53, 54

Linus 10, 13

Lucius II (1144–5) 110

Marcellinus (296–c.304) 45

Marcellus II (1555) 204

Martin I (649–53) 93

Martin V (1417–31)
(Oddone Colonna)
143–4, 147–53, 155, 162,
175, 193, 202

Nicholas I (858–67) 104

Nicholas V (1447–55)
(Thomas of Sarzana)
158, 159, 161, 163, 164,
166, 168–9

Paschal (817–24) 102–3

Paul II (1464–71) 160, 309

Paul III (1534–1549) 170,
191, 204, 205, 210, 211,
247, 300

Paul IV (1555–9) (Gian
Pietro Carafa) 168, 200,
202–7, 221

Paul V (1605–21) 186,
216–17

Paul VI 321

Pelagius II (579–90) 78

Pius II (1458–64) 158, 183,
184–5

Pius IV (1559–65) 247

Pius V (1566–72) 223

Pius VI (1775–99) 231–2,
250, 252–6, 257, 260–

Pius VII (1800–23) 257,
262–8, 270–2, 275, 284

Pius VIII (1829–30)
272, 296

Pius IX (1846–78) 257–60,
277–83, 284–91, 296,
297–8, 302, 303, 304, 305

Pius X (1903–14) 303–5,
310, 314

Pius XI (1922–39) 5, 78,
313–18

Pius XII (1939–58)
(Cardinal Eugenio
Pacelli) 227, 293–6,
318–19

Sergius III (904–11) 105

Sixtus II (257–8) 45

Sixtus III (432–40) 73,
75, 83

Sixtus IV (1471–84) 159,
169–70, 216

Sixtus V (1585–90) 201,
223, 240

Stephen II (752–7) 100–2

Stephen VI (896–7)
104, 107

Theodore I (642–9) 92–3

Urban IV (1261–4) 214

Urban V (1362–70) 137–8

Urban VI (1378–89)
145–6, 152

Urban VIII (1623–44)
196–7, 251, 252–3, 300

Victor (c. 189–c. 199)
30, 31

Porcari, Stefano 168–9

Porta San Paolo 295

Porticus of Octavia (*Porticus
Octaviae*) 67

Portugal 182

Pozzo, Andrea 210, 213,
225, 249

Pozzuoli 9, 25

Praetextatus, Vettius
Agorius 51

Prati 300

Priscilla (wife of Aquila)
9, 20–3

Priscillian, Bishop of Ávila
35

Priuli, Girolamo 201

Proba, (Anicia) Faltonia
64–5

Prosper of Aquitaine 69–71

Pudens (senator) 102

Quinisext Council 93

Quirinal Hill 15, 159, 231, 262, 278, 300
Quirinal Palace 251, 264, 278, 280, 281, 285, 297

Raphael 169, 214
Ravenna 65–6, 77, 78, 81, 88, 89, 91, 95, 98, 100, 101
Regina Coeli (prison) 295
Ricci, Father Matteo 5, 211
Ricimer, Flavius 90
Rienzo, Nicola 'Cola' di see Cola di Rienzo
Ripa 109, 125, 132, 147
Rizokopos, John 93
Robilant, Countess Olghina di 321
Roman Inquisition 141, 205–8, 217–18
Romano, Giuliano 283
Romulus and Remus 14–15, 256
Romulus Augustulus, Western Emperor (475–6) 81, 87
Roosevelt, President Franklin D. 294
Rossi, Count Pellegrino 280–1, 285
Rousseau, Jean-Jacques 230
Ruspi, Carlo 273
Russell, Odo 288

Sacchetti family 259
Saint Agnes 68, 83
Saint Andrew 54, 184–5
Saint Anne 178
Saint Bridget of Sweden 130–1, 133, 138
Saint Catherine of Siena 138, 152
Saint Conon 90
Saint Dominic 207
Saint Eutychius 57, 58
Saint Filippo Neri 223–5
Saint Francis of Assisi 131, 134, 320
Saint Francis Xavier 212
Saint George 90, 129

Saint Iñigo de Loyola 210–11, 212, 213, 222, 223, 224, 256
Saint Isidore the Labourer 212
Saint John the Baptist 1, 89
Saint Joseph 304
Saint Laurence 56, 68, 79, 294; Basilica of 80, 134, 165, 294
Saint Luke 54
Saint Mark the Evangelist 174
Saint Michael the Archangel 79, 99
Saint Nicholas of Myra 134
Saint Paul 9–10, 12, 13, 19, 22–5, 26–8, 31, 68, 71, 83, 99, 103, 129, 241, 295; Basilica of 12, 80–2, 88, 95, 111, 118, 119, 124, 164, 315
Saint Peter 3–6, 9–12, 25–6, 28, 31, 49–50, 51, 52, 55, 57, 68, 71, 74–5, 80–3, 95, 99, 103, 111, 129, 145, 147, 151, 163, 164, 171, 174, 181, 277, 278, 301, 326; Basilica of 33–4, 35, 36, 49–50, 71, 80–2, 86, 88, 97, 102, 118, 126, 129, 137, 143, 145, 154, 164, 165–6, 169, 178–9, 185, 187, 212, 216, 240, 249, 255, 258, 262, 266, 283, 290–1, 295, 297, 301–2, 315, 316, 323, 326
Saint Philip the Apostle 151
Saints Prassede (Praxedes) and Pudenziana (Pudentiana) 102
Saint Sebastian 91
Saint Teresa of Ávila 216, 225
Saint Wilfrid 96–7, 100
Sala, Giuseppe 262
Salandra, Antonio 306–7, 313
Sallust 235
Salò 294

Salus Populi Romani (icon) 326
San Carlo al Corso (church) 210
San Ciriaco (church) 165
San Clemente (basilica) 67
San Domenico e Sisto (monastery) 262
San Giacomo degli Spagnoli (church) 195
San Giacomo in Augusta (church) 210
San Giorgio in Velabro (church) 91
San Giorgio Maggiore (church), Venice 263
San Giovanni dei Fiorentini (church) 187
San Giovanni in Laterano (basilica) see Lateran Basilica
San Girolamo della Carità (church) 224
San Lorenzo (district) 294, 312
San Lorenzo fuori le Mura see Saint Laurence, Basilica of
San Luigi dei Francesi (church) 192
San Niccolò degli Arcione (church) 134
San Paolo fuori le Mura see Saint Paul, Basilica of
San Pietro in Vincoli (basilica) 278, 286
San Sebastiano fuori le Mura (basilica) 12
San Severino (church) 89–90
San Silvestro in Capite (church) 156
San Vitale (church) 165
Sangallo, Antonio da 187
Sangallo, Giuliano 157
Sant'Adriano al Foro (church) 94
Sant'Agata dei Goti (basilica) 89–90
Sant'Agnese (basilica) 52

Sant'Agnese in Agone 251
Sant'Agostino (basilica) 194
Sant'Andrea al Quirinale
  (church) 215
Sant'Angelo in Pescheria
  (church) 129, 271
Sant'Eusebio (church) 252
Sant'Ignazio (church) 213,
  225, 249
Santa Croce in
  Gerusalemme (basilica)
  49, 186
Santa Elisabetta
  (church) 194
Santa Maria ad Martyres
  (basilica) 94
Santa Maria dei Miracoli
  (church) 210
Santa Maria del Popolo
  (basilica) 130, 143,
  185, 239
Santa Maria dell'Anima
  (church) 194
Santa Maria della Vittoria
  (church) 216
Santa Maria in Ara Coeli
  (basilica) 134–5, 137, 301
Santa Maria in Cosmedin
  (basilica) 91–2
Santa Maria in Montesanto
  (basilica) 210
Santa Maria in Palmis
  (church) 163
Santa Maria in Vallicella
  (church) 225
Santa Maria Maggiore
  (basilica) 53, 83, 89, 125,
  164, 169, 186, 315
Santa Maria Novella
  (monastery), Florence 168
Santa Maria sopra Minerva
  (basilica) 130, 282, 300
Santa Maria in Traspontina
  (church) 1
Santa Maria in Trastevere
  (basilica) 78
Santa Prassede (basilica)
  102–3

Santa Pudenziana (basilica)
  57–8
Santiago de Compostela,
  Spain 131
Santissima Trinità dei
  Pellegrini (church)
  221, 225
Santo Domingo 182
Santo Spirito in Sassia
  (church) 216, 223, 251
Santo Stefano Maggiore
  (Santo Stefano degli
  Abissini) (basilica) 176
Santo Stefano Rotondo
  (basilica) 213
Sanudo, Marin 187
Sapienza (La Sapienza or
  University of Rome)
  187, 251
Sarapis 17
Sarfatti, Margherita
  Grassini 317
Saturnalia 15–16
Savelli family 155
Scala Sancta 164, 166, 178
Scialoja, Vittorio 298
Second Council of Ephesus
  ('Gangster Synod')
  73–4, 174
Second Vatican Council
  321–2
Sella, Quintino 300
Senate House (ancient) 94
Seneca 79
Septimus Severus, Emperor
  (193–211) 118
Serapis 17
Sessorian Palace 48
Seti I (Egyptian pharaoh)
  239–40
Shelley, Percy Bysshe 241
Shepherd, John and
  Alice 133
Shirley, Robert 191
Sicinini family 53
Sigismund of Luxembourg,
  Holy Roman Emperor
  (1433–7) 157
Simios 18

Sistine Chapel 169, 229,
  232, 233
Soderini, Edoardo 302
Sol 18
Sol Invictus 41
Spezieria della Regina 274
Spina, Giuseppe Maria 260
Spinoza, Baruch 252
Staël, Germaine de 237,
  238–9
Stefaneschi, Giacomo 119
Stelluti, Francesco 251
Story, William Wetmore 284
Sturzo, Father Luigi 310
Suetonius 24–5, 26
Sulla, Lucius Cornelius 75
Sutri 98–9
Sweynheym, Conrad 159
Switzerland 240, 274, 303
Symmachus, Quintus
  Aurelius 82
Syria 18, 19

Tacchi-Venturi, Father
  Pietro 315
Tacitus 24, 25, 26–7, 158
Taparelli d'Azeglio,
  Luigi 279
Targhini, Angelo 269, 271,
  273, 275
Tasso, Tarquato 237
Teatro d'Alimbert 278
Teatro degli Arcadi 236
Telemachus 77, 81
Teofilatti family 104, 106
Teofilatto, Count of
  Tusculum 105, 111
Tertullian 26, 76
Testaccio 125
Tetzel, Johann 178–9
Thackeray, William
  Makepeace 232–3
Theatre of Marcellus
  67, 155
Theatre of Pompey 17
Theodora, wife of
  Teofilatto 105
Theodoret 77

Theodoric the Great, King of the Ostrogoths 82, 88–9
Thirteen Good Men 127–8
Tiber (river) 1, 10, 17–18, 21, 39–40, 78, 111, 141, 167, 187, 223, 267, 297
Tiberius, Emperor (14–37) 18, 24
Titulus Crucis (relic) 186
Titus, Emperor (79–81) 63
Tivoli 109, 111
Tor di Nona 142, 219
Torre delle Milizie 124
Tosti, Girolama 194
Tournon, Camille de 267
Trajan, Emperor (98–117) 26
Trastevere 10, 18, 21, 22, 25, 78, 109, 148, 255, 282, 283
Treaty of Lodi 188
Treaty of Tolentino 255
Treaty of Tordesillas 182
Treaty of Westphalia 248
Trinità dei Monti (church) 194
Trudeau, Pierre Elliott 323
Trullan Decrees 93, 174

Umberto I of Italy 300, 301

Ursinus 52

Vadstena, Sweden 130–1
Valentinian III, Western Emperor (425–55) 65–6, 70, 73, 74
Valerian, Emperor (253–60) 44, 45
Valla, Lorenzo 158, 159–61
Vandals 63–4
Vasari, Giorgio 165
Vasi, Giuseppe 199
Vatican City 315–16
Vatican Hill 10, 13, 21, 25, 29, 80, 81, 144, 300, 315, 326
Vatican Palace 144, 181, 190, 214, 257, 285, 297
Veillot, Louis 286–7
Vélez de Guevara, Íñigo 192
Venerable English College 133, 240
Venice 168, 189, 201, 221, 263, 306, 309
Ventura, Guglielmo 119
Venus, Temple of 15
Verri, Alessandro 244
Vesta, Temple of 67
Vestal Virgins 19
Vico, Francesco di 127

Vigna Moroni 236
Virgil 234, 237
Visigoths 62–3, 77
Vittoriano (Monument to Vittorio Emanuele II) 301–2
Vittorio Emanuele II of Italy (1861–78) 258, 289–90, 296–301, 302
Vittorio Emanuele III of Italy (1900–46) 293, 285, 313

Weizsächer, Ernst von 296
William of Ockham 115, 116
William of Orange 234, 239
Wilson, President Woodrow 303, 307
Wilton, Joseph 234
Winckelmann, Johann 235–6

Zeno, Eastern Emperor (474–91) 88
Zingarelli, Niccolò Antonio 266
Zoroastrianism 42
Zouaves 4, 259, 290, 291, 298